Does God Love *All* or Some?

"From the pen of a seasoned pastor and thoughtful former Calvinist—this book peels back the layers of obfuscation that often encrust the hard realities of what is entailed in Calvinistic theology. This is probably the most penetrating summary critique of the biblical, theological, logical, and practical incongruences inherent in Calvinistic theology I have read. Rogers goes beyond the surface level of criticism to the deeper layers of contradictions, exposing the soft underbelly of much of Reformed theology. Irenic, respectful, yet thoroughly probing, this is a must read for all who want to understand the issues more deeply."

—**David L. Allen**, Dean, School of Preaching, Southwestern Baptist Theological Seminary

"*Does God Love All or Some?* should be required reading for all students preparing for ministry. Ronnie Rogers covers an array of topics that, unfortunately, are all-too-often neglected in theological education and personal conversations. From persuasively correcting the mythical narrative that one must be either an Arminian or a Calvinist to tackling the illogical fallacy of compatibilism, the author, with wit and balance, shares his personal theological journey and works through the maze of biblical complexities. I wish such a volume was available when I attended seminary years ago."

—**Emir Caner**, President, Truett McConnell University, Professor of History and Christian Studies

"I highly recommend this latest work by Ronnie Rogers to you. The ministry the Lord has worked through this man (his church, his other writings, and most obvious to me in my work at Criswell College, the people he has influenced) is truly remarkable and itself merits paying attention to his writings. But his treatment of the extensive nature of the atonement also deserves attention because he has written it as a person formerly ensconced in the doctrines of grace. His familiarity with the issues relevant to those who really are trying to work their way through Scripture, theology, and ministry is apparent in individual chapters dealing with so many of the nuances involved in addressing the question. I am grateful he has shared the gleanings of his own journey with the Christian community."

—**Barry Creamer**, President, Criswell College

Does God Love *All* or Some?

Comparing Biblical Extensivism and Calvinism's Exclusivism

Ronnie W. Rogers

FOREWORD BY
Adam Harwood

WIPF & STOCK · Eugene, Oregon

DOES GOD LOVE ALL OR SOME?
Comparing Biblical Extensivism and Calvinism's Exclusivism

Copyright © 2019 Ronnie W. Rogers. All rights reserved. Except for brief quotations in critical publications or reviews, no part of this book may be reproduced in any manner without prior written permission from the publisher. Write: Permissions, Wipf and Stock Publishers, 199 W. 8th Ave., Suite 3, Eugene, OR 97401.

Wipf & Stock
An Imprint of Wipf and Stock Publishers
199 W. 8th Ave., Suite 3
Eugene, OR 97401

www.wipfandstock.com

PAPERBACK ISBN: 978-1-5326-8177-6
HARDCOVER ISBN: 978-1-5326-8178-3
EBOOK ISBN: 978-1-5326-8179-0

Cover photograph of Hillsborough Parish Church Copyright © 2010 David Cleland, FlixelPix.com Northern Ireland

Scripture quotations taken from the New American Standard Bible® (NASB), Copyright © 1960, 1962, 1963, 1968, 1971, 1972, 1973, 1975, 1977, 1995 by The Lockman Foundation

Used by permission. www.Lockman.org

Manufactured in the U.S.A.

I lovingly dedicate this book to my grandson, Charles Bancroft Crosby. I pray this book will, one day, help you to understand and live in the full depth and breadth of God's love for you. For that is where true riches are found. You are immeasurably special to me, and I love you Charles Bancroft.

Contents

Foreword by Adam Harwood | ix
Acknowledgements | xi
Abbreviations | xii
Introduction Extensivism: A Biblical Alternative to Calvinism's Exclusivism | xiii

1. My Journey from Calvinism to Extensivism | 1
2. In Consideration of Calvinism | 7
3. Why I Chose the Term Extensivism | 13
4. Why Some Extensivists Identify as Calvinists | 19
5. One Man's Suggestions for Calvinists and Extensivists | 24
6. The TULIP: The Petals and the Leaves | 30
7. Compatibilism or Libertarianism? | 38
8. Can Human Acts like Prayers and Childrearing Really Affect Someone's Salvation? | 50
9. Calvinism: Origin of Sin and Offer of Salvation | 54
10. Extensivism: Origin of Sin and Offer of Salvation | 61
11. Does Physical Birth Demonstrate That Spiritual Birth Precedes Faith? | 67
12. Does Faith Precede or Result from the New Birth? | 70
13. God, Creation, and Sin: Calvinism's Dilemma | 81
14. Is Reprobation Necessary for God to Demonstrate His Holiness? | 89
15. Is Man Totally Passive Prior to Monergistic Regeneration? | 97
16. Does It Please God to Damn Most to Eternal Torment? | 102
17. Are We to Hope for the Hopeless and Blame and Reward the Determined? | 105
18. Does Unconditional Election Include a Forced Change, a Freely Chosen Change, or Both? | 113

19 Does God Have Two Wills? | 121
20 A Better Gospel! | 132
21 Do the Doctrines of Grace Affect Evangelism? | 139
22 Is Libertarian Free Will Eternal? | 144
23 Equally Lost and Equally Savable: No Distinctions! | 148
24 The Exalted God of Scripture | 151
25 Good Faith Offer or Bad Deception? | 153
26 Rejecting Calvinism Does Not Require a Weak View of Depravity | 160
27 Faith Is the Condition of Salvation and Grace Is the Work of Salvation | 166
28 God Can Know the Free Acts of Man without Determinism | 181
29 The Dynamic of the Gospel Encounter | 192
30 What about Those Who Never Hear the Gospel: Analyzing the Argument | 200
31 What about Those Who Never Hear the Gospel: The Old Testament | 209
32 What about Those Who Never Hear the Gospel: The New Testament | 218
33 What about Those Who Never Hear the Gospel: Foreordination versus Foreknowledge | 235
34 The Place of Creation in Witnessing to Pagan Gentiles | 245

Appendix 1   The Order of Elective Decrees | 253
Appendix 2   Leigh Vicens on Theological Determinism | 257
Appendix 3   A Guide for Determining a Pastoral Candidate's Level of Commitment to Calvinism | 258
Appendix 4   A Response to Calvinists' Attempt to Moderate the Sequential Order of Regeneration and Faith | 262

Authorial Glossary | 267
Bibliography | 275
Author Index | 281
Subject Index | 283
Scripture Index | 289

Foreword

THE TITLE OF THIS book asks a question which deserves consideration, Does God love all or some? One's answer to that single question reveals much about one's views of God, humanity, sin, the cross, the gospel, missions, evangelism, and salvation. In the last decade, a wave of resources has been published by Calvinists to advocate for their views. This wave has created an imbalance in the literature on the doctrine of salvation. General agreement exists across the spectrum of conservative evangelicalism on the basic contours of the Christian faith, such as affirming God as Trinity, Christ as truly divine and truly human, and salvation by grace through faith in Jesus Christ. When specific issues of soteriology arise, however, on which conservative evangelicals differ, the perspective most frequently heard is distinctly Calvinistic. Historically, Calvinists have had an inordinate desire to communicate to others their distinct views of God and his ways.

Ronnie Rogers notes this imbalance of Christian scholarship which favors a distinctly Calvinistic perspective and offers this volume to articulate a comprehensive doctrine of salvation not encumbered by the commitments particular to Calvinism. He refers to this view as Extensivism, which he regards as broadly embracing Arminianism, Molinism, and "Traditional" Southern Baptist theology. In my estimation, Rogers is correct and what he labels as Extensivism can be understood simply as evangelical Christianity minus the Calvinistic presuppositions. Extensivism views God as the loving and holy triune creator who desires a relationship with the people he created and who has provided a way for every person to be restored to relationship with him through faith in his Son by his work on the cross, his Spirit in the world, and his grace which enables every person to accept or reject the message of the gospel.

Rogers' work reflects careful thought, precise language, and a gentle tone. He appeals to those who affirm Calvinistic theology to consider whether their presuppositions and definitions provide clarity to their reading of Scripture or reinforce their theological framework into which they place and through which they interpret Scripture. From this position of theological inquiry, Rogers deftly probes key issues such as the nature of God, providence, the human condition, compatibilism, God's desire for lost humanity, the order of salvation, grace, the gospel, and the dilemmas faced by Calvinists and Extensivists. Readers who desire to examine the distinctions between Christianity with Calvinism and Christianity without Calvinism will find this book to be a storehouse of perceptive theological inquiry and faithful exegetical analysis.

Adam Harwood, Ph.D.
Associate Professor of Theology
McFarland Chair of Theology
Director of the Baptist Center for Theology & Ministry
Editor of the *Journal for Baptist Theology & Ministry*
New Orleans Baptist Theological Seminary

Acknowledgements

Most of all, I thank Jesus for the work he has done in my life. I thank Gina my wife, confidant, friend, and co-laborer in life and ministry who has made the greatest impact upon my life other than Jesus.

I would also like to thank Norm Miller, who invited me to start writing articles in 2012 for SBC Today. This experience helped me to develop my thinking and writing about the ideas encapsulated in this book. I'm also thankful to Larry Toothaker and Billy Wolfe for their gracious willingness to proof my manuscript and provide invaluable insights; Anita Charlson for tirelessly and professionally editing this manuscript; David Allen and Adam Harwood for providing invaluable theological and practical insights; JR Crosby for his invaluable cover design insights; Trinity's elders for their unwavering support of my commitment to study and their untiring encouragement to equip the saints and to write; as well as my brothers and sisters at Trinity Baptist Church whom I have been blessed beyond measure to serve for twenty years. You have loved me without measure and provided me the greatest opportunity for spiritual growth. My longevity as your pastor is a testimony of your Christ-like gracious and generous forbearing love towards me. No man could deserve such a life of being loved, but none so little as me.

I will live and die indebted to all of you for your love and support.

Abbreviations

SBC   Southern Baptist Convention

TD   Total Depravity

TULIP   An acronym for the five points of Calvinism. 1. Total depravity 2. Unconditional election 3. Limited atonement 4. Irresistible grace 5. Perseverance of the saints.

Introduction

Extensivism: A Biblical Alternative to Calvinism's Exclusivism

It seems certain that the debate between Calvinism and those who reject Calvinism will never end. I am under no illusion that my meager contribution will end the discussion. I do pray my thoughts will contribute to the discussion by possibly clarifying some of the issues and further exposing the incongruence between Calvinism and Scripture. Even more so, I want not only to offer a critique of many of the claims and interpretations of Calvinism, but also an alternative understanding that I believe is more reflective of Scripture and consistent logic. I call my position Extensivism, which I more precisely define and explain in chapter 3 and the Authorial Glossary. In its broadest application, it encompasses all who believe God's salvific love is for every person in contrast to Calvinism's exclusivism, which limits God's salvific love to only some.

I have five primary objectives in this book. First, my considerations would result in a deeper and clearer understanding of our God and his greatness. Second, to demonstrate that God truly does salvationally love every single person. He says he loves all humanity (John 3:16), desires everyone to be saved (1 Tim 2:4), and he demonstrates this love by providing everything needed, including opportunity, for every person to know him and be saved. This is the position of Extensivism, which is rejected by Calvinism. Third, to offer a precise and respectful critique of some of Calvinism's internal and biblical incongruences. This inconsistency is due in large measure to its commitment to compatibilism, which is often gauzily masked but left unresolved by such concepts as the good faith offer or claims such as "God loves everyone."

Fourth, to demonstrate that God being sovereign over his creation and having freely chosen to endow man with libertarian freedom is a more biblical perspective. Calvinism seeks to maintain God's foreknowledge and sovereignty but distorts man's freedom as created in God's image. At the other end of the spectrum, Open Theism distorts God's foreknowledge and sovereignty in an attempt to maintain man's freedom to choose otherwise. Extensivism attempts to provide a perspective that recognizes God's sovereignty and his foreknowledge of every event, and man's libertarian freedom. Such freedom harmonizes with the simplest reading of the scriptural depiction of the ever-present interactions of God and man.

Fifth, I desire for people to understand what Calvinism actually believes so they can make an informed choice of whether they truly believe Calvinism best reflects the Bible. I am convinced that a significant percentage of people who become Calvinists do not know what Calvinism really entails. To accomplish this, I seek to present both Calvinism and Extensivism in language that is precisely and consistently reflective of the commitments each perspective claims regarding God's sovereignty, salvific love, foreknowledge, and man's freedom.

When there is a lack of clarity and consistency in applying the actual meaning and entailments of each perspective, it establishes an insurmountable barrier to an honest and forthright biblical evaluation of these significantly different viewpoints. I love my Calvinist friends, but I do not appreciate either witting or unwitting misrepresentation (my assumption is the latter until proven otherwise) of the true meaning of ideas such as compatibilism and its entailments. I appreciate when Calvinists provide biblical interpretations that truly reflect the teaching of Scriptures, which clearly depict man as having otherwise choice and God providing and desiring all to be saved. I do not appreciate Calvinists' lack of clarity regarding how such biblical interpretations are inconsistent with the major doctrines and entailments of Calvinism. Such practices only serve to obscure the true beliefs of Calvinism.

Further, the oft-given answer "it is a mystery" to defend a Calvinist belief that generated the mystery in the first place is an unacceptable defense of Calvinism. We may always disagree, but we should at least agree that we will write and speak so that others may know what we believe because of our commitment to compatibilism or libertarianism. Doing so will clarify our differences so the true nature of our beliefs and disagreements are elucidated, thereby facilitating a more informed decision by anyone regarding whether he should consider himself to be a Calvinist or an Extensivist.

Within Southern Baptist life, the term Traditional most closely approximates the approach of Extensivism. The Traditional Southern Baptist theology, a position I endorse, is outlined in the Traditional Statement and explained and defended in the book; *Anyone Can be Saved*. I have chosen to use the term Extensivism for several reasons, one of which is that in its broadest application, it serves as a positive descriptor for non-Calvinists both within and beyond Southern Baptist life. In some ways, it is also a tertium quid for Arminianism and Molinism.

I only concern myself with mainstream Calvinist beliefs as articulated within four or five-point Calvinism, the former rejecting limited atonement (see Authorial Glossary, Tulip). I understand unconditional election to be the defining doctrine of whether one can properly be designated as a Calvinist. The acceptance of the doctrine of unconditional election is essential to mainstream Calvinism, which means that one's position regarding the other four points is more a matter of consistency.[1] Since I do not seek to address Hyper-Calvinism, one cannot dismiss my evaluations of Calvinism as only being relevant to Hyper-Calvinism. While I may quote a Hyper-Calvinist with regard to subjects like moral freedom or predestination, my point will be reflective of mainstream Calvinism.

Since I neither claim to be Arminian nor defend Arminianism, Calvinists' attempts to summarily dismiss my arguments or parry my point by labeling me an Arminian undermine fruitful discussion. I may at times speak consistently with or even draw from Calvinism, Arminianism, or Molinism, but my points should be specifically addressed as stated, and I will seek to do the same with the one whom I am actually interacting with on the given point. For full disclosure, I may very well be arguing a point similar to an Arminian without even knowing I am doing so since I have spent my entire Christian life studying Calvinism and not Arminianism.

My pilgrimage from Calvinism to Extensivism is nothing new. Although written in the eighteenth century, the following reflects my conclusion about Calvinism. In the book, *A Solemn Caution against the Ten Horns of Calvinism*, by Taylor Thomas, 1738–1816, the author writes to the Rev. Mr. John Wesley referring to himself as having been sympathetic to Calvinism, then questioning some of the teachings. Thomas refers to himself in the third person. He says, "Cole on 'God's Sovereignty' was put into his hands to clear his dull head, and make him quite orthodox; but still he could not see how God could be just in condemning men for exactly doing what he had decreed them to do. After many conflicts, your little piece, entitled, 'Predestination Calmly Considered' fell into his hands; he read it over with that attention which both the doctrine and performance deserve; and never had a doubt, from that day to this, that God is loving to every man."[2]

---

1. Calvinists often argue total depravity (TD) is the basis for the other four points. Accordingly, many non-Calvinists make the mistake of rejecting TD because they think this is the essence of Calvinism. I intend to demonstrate that one need not reject a biblical view of TD to reject Calvinism. I do reject Calvinism's definition of TD but not TD biblically defined since to do so leaves one believing in some sort of partial depravity.

2. Thomas, *A Solemn Caution*, par. 1.

My love and respect for my Calvinist brothers and sisters are not at issue, but rather a clarification of Scripture, Calvinism, and Extensivism. I deeply desire that we communicate our beliefs in such a way that those who so desire may truly understand the actual teachings and entailments of our positions. May our Lord Jesus permit this book to contribute to that end.

1

My Journey from Calvinism to Extensivism

I WAS A CALVINIST for over thirty-three years and was unabashedly so for the first twenty. I spent the last thirteen years of my time as a Calvinist probing deeper into my accumulated questions and concerns regarding the harmony between Calvinism and Scripture and only doffed the label Calvinist in the final months of that journey.

Although I continued to study Calvinism and rely on Calvinist commentaries on my pilgrimage out of Calvinism, I did spend those thirteen years evaluating what Calvinists said, what I had said as a dedicated Calvinist, and the entailments of Calvinism in light of a simple reading of soteriological Scriptures (Scriptures related to salvation). I always sought to let the simple reading of Scripture be my guide to studying Scripture. However, looking back now, I believe I inadvertently failed to faithfully follow this practice when it came to soteriology. It seems to me now that given many of the commitments and entailments of Calvinism, one cannot be a consistent Calvinist and let the simple reading of Scripture be the guide, at least in soteriological verses. At least that is what I now believe even though such seemed to be the very opposite when I was immersed in Calvinism. I will elaborate on the reason Calvinism cannot consistently do this in the following chapters. By simple reading of Scripture, I mean evaluation of the text based on context, grammar, history, and congruence with other Scriptures. Consequently, this is quite different from a simplistic approach.

As a matter of practice when I was in my questioning stage, I would consider a particular verse or passage as Calvinistically understood as I had done for well over two decades with little thought that such might be wrong. I was a doughty Calvinist. This stage included consultation with solid Calvinist theologies and commentaries at my disposal. Then, the questioning part of this process meant that I would focus exclusively upon the text, without even the remotest desire to either disestablish my Calvinist understanding or harmonize the passage with anything other than itself. Meaning

I focused intently on what it actually said. Progressively, once I was assured I was accurately noting what the passage said, as well as what it did not say, implicitly or explicitly, I would then seek to consider the verses in light of the totality of Scripture.

My discovery consistently revealed inconsistencies between the straightforward simple reading of the clearest verses in Scripture and Calvinism. I was confident I was not misreading the text because of what the text explicitly said; at this point, the interpretation was not in play but only what the text said and did not say. Additionally, my understanding was bolstered by reading significant Calvinist commentaries and preachers who often explained the text exactly as it clearly seemed to me, even though when everything is considered such reading was disharmonious with Calvinism.

This is not to say many did not feel compelled to mention unconditional election or some other theological belief unique to Calvinism that was simply not in the text. I was not reading books that were adamantly opposed to Calvinism, wherein one might expect a reading or comments that were inconsistent with Calvinism. This point was significant to me. I was reading other Calvinists say what I was seeing, even though their interpretations undermined the core beliefs of Calvinism.

This simple process of letting the text say only what it said even if it seemed to undermine significant beliefs of Calvinism like unconditional election, compatibilism, efficacious calling, and a good faith offer, for a Calvinist like me, had the effect of revealing serious incongruences between what I as a Calvinist believed and what the text actually said. Often, in the clearest and most unambiguous verses, the passage said precisely what is incompatible with some of the doctrines and entailments of Calvinism. That is, these Calvinistic doctrines are not gleaned from the text, but rather they are artificially superimposed upon the clear declaration of the text.

Within Calvinism, the reconciliation of such inconsistencies is managed repeatedly by the creation of extra-biblical reconcilers (such as the good faith offer, the two-will theory, the supposed or intimated dissonance between God's salvific love and his glory, or the Calvinistically-generated "mystery") and what I non-pejoratively describe as double talk. Double talk is a rhetorical practice that obscures, elides, or simply misrepresents the harsh realities and inconsistencies found in Calvinism, which I do not believe are found in the simple reading of Scripture. Regrettably, and quite sadly for me personally, I had to face my own consistent double talk when I was a Calvinist. For example, I would seek to extol God's love or desire for everyone to have a meaningful opportunity to be saved when in truth, such is absolutely precluded by the doctrines of unconditional election, limited atonement, and the selective internal efficacious call to salvation. Actually, once I came to grips with Calvinism's need for and my own fluency in this pervasive practice, it troubled me greatly. This inescapable reality fueled my quest for truth and truth alone.

Here is an example of double talk. Matthew says of Judas, "It would have been good for that man if he had not been born" (Matt 26:24). I wrote publicly that this is true of all the non-elect if Calvinism is true; the gospel is therefore, not good news. One Calvinist responded, "True of any man who freely chooses like Judas and a whole host of others to reject the gospel." Another said, "They cannot be saved if they will not leave their sins in repentance. They will not since they love darkness rather than light and so are condemned." One said, "Calvinists hold that the sole reason why sinners are in hell is because of their chosen sin and nonbelief of the truth." Similarly, another responded, "People in hell will forever regret being born for rejecting the gospel of God's sovereign grace. Calvinism saves."

Such comments more rightly reflect Extensivism than Calvinism. These Calvinists seek to make one's eternal destiny dependent *solely* upon one's choice and will, implying that each could have chosen differently, or that everyone gets an opportunity to believe or not believe. However, this is simply double talk. That is speaking in such a way that obscures the real reason why the non-elect are in hell, which is because they are the non-elect—reprobate, and that pleased God. In Extensivism men cannot be saved because they *will* not believe, whereas, in Calvinism, men will not be saved because they *cannot will* to believe, as decided by God. The only difference in the sinners in heaven and sinners in hell, according to Calvinism, is that God was pleased to save some and reprobate some.

In Calvinism, the ones who did believe could not have chosen to disbelieve and the ones who disbelieved could not have chosen to believe. That is the insurmountable reason for one's eternal destiny and any articulation of Calvinism that obfuscates that truth is double talk. It is not a matter of deserving hell because everyone deserves hell. It is the matter of why some who deserve hell go to heaven and others do not. To intimate in any sense that the sole reason for different outcomes in Calvinism is due to whether one exercises faith, loves sin, or because of a mere act of the will is misleading indeed.

In my quest, I sought to bow to the simple declaration of Scripture in the most simple and obvious passages, which clearly did not say what Calvinism needed them to say. It was living with the inconsistencies necessitating double talk and extra-biblical concepts, without which the clearest of Scriptures did not coalesce with the essentials of Calvinism, which haunted me. For example, within Calvinism, unconditional election is the ubiquitous program that runs in the background of every interpretation of every verse, even those which clearly present God's salvific love for all or portray scenarios where everyone can and should obey the gospel or command of God. Unconditional election is at times elided by the Calvinist interpreter when facing verses that unambiguously declare the very opposite, but the need to reconcile is omnipresent. If just one verse can be shown to demonstrate real otherwise choice with regard to salvation (or in any area for that matter), Calvinism fails to be a coherent system. I believe there are numerous such Scriptures; consequently, the Calvinist default to extra-biblical concepts and double talk only obscure the clear meaning of such Scriptures and the irreconcilability of the Scripture and Calvinism.

Calvinism's commitment to decretal theology and compatibilist freedom makes any suggestion of the slightest possibility of choice between accessible options or minimizing its micro-specific determinism misleading at best because such is impossible within compatibilist freedom (see chapter 7 for a full description of compatibilism and libertarianism).[1] Decretal theology and compatibilism entail that everything, from beginning to end—including every one of my own choices and yours—is as it can only be. Yet, when preaching, writing, praying, and talking Calvinists repeatedly either explicitly say or imply such choices do exist. If someone is disinclined to believe Calvinists quotidianly communicate so as to be understood by the listener as believing in otherwise choice, just ask the listeners. While I do believe much of this is the result of Calvinists not fully understanding compatibilism and libertarianism, it does not seem that all of it can be.

I am not addressing the issue of motive, but only the practice. As mentioned, I began to consider soteriological verses and passages without Calvinist theological importations. Accordingly, I would simply ask myself if I do not read this verse as a Calvinist, what does it actually say—before asking what does it mean. Quite unsettlingly to this long-term Calvinist, I would discover it did not say what we said it says when viewed through Calvinism. Of course, this practice unraveled a tightly woven rope of correlated ideas and left me with many disturbing theological loose ends, but I did choose to let Scripture say what it said. I chose to live with the certainty of what pivotal Scriptures said and did not say while concomitantly wandering in the desert of thinking through these clear revelations that were dissonant with Calvinism.

My experience gives me compassion for Calvinists who truly seek to evaluate their commitment to Calvinism. These were years of theological

---

1. Decretal theology reflects Calvinism's belief that God decreed (determined) who would be saved and who would not be saved. People are not saved because they exercise grace-enabled faith, but solely because God decreed them to be saved. See Appendix 1 on the Order of Elective Decrees.

isolation and confusion as I watched the columns of my Calvinism decay, crumble, and fall, eventuating in the systemic collapse of the system, at least for me. I know others godlier, smarter, and more used of God than me see it quite differently, but this is how it appears to me. My experience is not meant to cast doubt upon the heart, sincerity, or motive of those who see Calvinism differently than me, but this is my experience. My theological thoughts and considerations are intended to motivate all to consider the beliefs and entailments of consistent Calvinism.

Based on my experience as a dedicated Calvinist, and my journey out of Calvinism, I believe a departure from Calvinism is highly improbable unless the definitions of terms or concepts used in Calvinism are considered as well. If one accepts the definitions employed by Calvinism, one will become and remain a Calvinist because it is a system of assumptions and definitions that leads only to the system of Calvinism. This is why it is absolutely inexplicable to most Calvinists why everyone is not a Calvinist or why anyone would leave Calvinism, at least for noble reasons. The inability of many Calvinists to evaluate those who disagree with them without filtering such through Calvinistic definitions and assumptions prohibits valuable dialogue, much less the plausibility of anything being more consistent than Calvinism. In my journey I would ask myself, are the assumptions and definitions that we Calvinists employ the only way or even the clearest and best way to define such terms in light of Scripture? My answers led to the conclusion that very often they were not.

Additionally, one cannot think through such concepts by merely reading a particular verse or even several because thinking through some of these ideas and related Scriptures leads to philosophy and speculative theology. The more I studied the soteriological Scriptures by the methods I have described above and considered Calvinism's philosophical and speculative theological commitments, the more I became convinced that Calvinism depended upon philosophical concepts and definitions that were biblically inadequate and philosophically inferior to alternative perspectives. For the record, I do believe there is a legitimate place for the study of philosophy and speculative theology, and I actually enjoy such study.

I have spent a significant amount of time thinking about and studying through concepts like compatibilism, libertarianism, foreknowledge, predestination, and election; this includes seeking to distinguish between what is entailed and what is not. This all played a part in my clearer understanding of what I believe to be deficiencies in Calvinism and how to address some of the tough questions posed by Scripture and Calvinism. Although I seem to know so little, God is very good to continue teaching me.

In my meandering departure from Calvinism, I first chose the label Minor-Calvinist in contradistinction to my prior commitment to being a Major-Calvinist, technically I was a four-point Calvinist. Then, after having rejected Calvinism totally, I referred to myself as a Disenchanted Calvinist which highlighted my journey away from Calvinism. I now refer to my soteriological position as Extensivism.

2

In Consideration of Calvinism

Since the publication of my book *Reflections of a Disenchanted Calvinist* (2012, updated 2016), I have been involved in countless conversations with many Calvinists through writing, e-mails, and talking one-on-one. I have enjoyed many of my discussions with my Calvinist brothers and sisters during this time. I can only pray that my thoughts have been even minimally as helpful in contributing to their knowledge and love of God as theirs have been for me. However, I must admit I have found *some* interactions with Calvinists quite frustrating because of the great difficulty I have often experienced in trying to discuss a particular point without being misread. These brothers will often provide me with only a standard response (one I used to give as a Calvinist) that is the very response I am trying to move beyond in our consideration of Calvinism and Extensivism. Or they simply neglect to engage my specific point and scurry to something I am not even addressing.

For instance, I have given precise examples of various disquieting realities of Calvinism only, at times, to have them either distortedly generalized, which, ipso facto, moves the discussion off topic, or summarily dismissed as what they characterize as merely emotional arguments. This is unfruitful for the Calvinist and those who do not understand the seriousness of the entailment mentioned. Because while these disquieting realities do often affect us emotionally, they are not merely emotional arguments to be so easily dismissed. They actually have for their substance the very nature of God, his plan, and the nature of man as portrayed in explicit Scripture. Consequently, I thought it might be helpful to identify three distinct levels of consideration I find helpful in properly evaluating Calvinism. These distinctive levels do operate as a synergistic unit, but contemplating them separately seems to be helpful in the process of consideration.

Level one is to illumine the disquieting realities and double talk within Calvinism. This must be accomplished in order to elucidate the actual beliefs and entailments of consistent Calvinism so both Calvinists and Extensivists can evaluate Calvinism more accurately. To fail at this point is to enter into the discussion ill-equipped to thoroughly examine Calvinism. This includes encouraging Calvinists to speak, pray, and write in such a way that these beliefs and entailments are neither elided nor easily misunderstood. Extensivists must not permit them to double talk. If we do, then we will continue to permit Calvinists to evade having to face such realities as well as prevent others from being aware of their existence.

Disquieting realities are often lesser-known inescapable unbiblical, harsh realities, the sine qua non, or entailments of consistent Calvinism. An example would be, the inescapable dilemmas that are created by their commitment to compatibilism in areas such as the origin of sin, God's character, and meaningful choices between options. Disquieting realities can also include Calvinism's extraordinary definitions of ordinary terms such as love, responsibility, choice, freedom, evangelism, and whoever. Additionally, I would include Calvinism's unduly narrow definitions of such biblical concepts as sovereignty and depravity, as well as its significant reliance upon speculative theology, philosophical assumptions, and general hermeneutical approach to soteriological Scripture.[1]

By double talk, I *specifically and only* mean thinking, praying, writing, or speaking in such a way that obscures the disquieting realities of consistent Calvinism. I believe much of the double talk is unintentional but unfortunately it does not seem that all of it is. If a person accepts and clearly and unabashedly articulates these realities, then he can be a knowledgeable and consistent Calvinist; if one is unwilling to do so, he cannot be a consistent Calvinist. Since I use the term double talk in this specifically limited way, the problem of inconsistencies that I am addressing cannot be ameliorated by referring to inconsistencies due to the frailty of man that may be present in others' approaches to Scripture—as well as in Calvinism.

Additionally, I am not calling anyone a double talker nor is my use of this term intended in any sense to be personally depreciatory, but rather I use it in order to draw attention to this rhetorical reality. Without properly dealing with this reality, it seems to me the fruitful and detailed evaluation of the essence of Calvinism remains inaccessible to honest appraisal and consideration. What is left is simply a partial evaluation that masquerades, quite successfully, as a thorough evaluation of the merits of Calvinism as a system.

This first level *does not primarily* seek to determine whether Calvinism is biblically true or the most helpful system of soteriology (understanding God's salvific plan); even though that is the ultimate goal. This level is *mostly* concerned with spotlighting and transporting these lesser-known

---

1. This can include such things as unconditional election always running in the background, complicating simple verses to fit Calvinism, or seeing good faith offers where the text gives every indication of making a good offer of the gospel.

essentials of Calvinism into a common conversation regarding Calvinism in order to facilitate a more precise and thorough understanding of Calvinism. For the sake of argument, the system with the most disquieting realities *could theoretically* end up being true. What is not acceptable is any obscuration of such disquieting realities that either facilitates or encourages one to embrace or espouse Calvinism without a true understanding of them. Any serious evaluative or comparative discussion of Calvinism necessitates a clear understanding of the terms being used by everyone involved and the entailments of Calvinism's beliefs and chosen terminology.

I have been challenged on the legitimacy of placing this step prior to determining whether Calvinism is true, the more biblically reflective system. This would include beginning with and focusing on Scripture. I understand the sentiment. However, it seems to me, it is impossible to properly evaluate whether Calvinism is biblical without an accurate understanding of its core concepts, definitions, and view of moral responsibility, sovereignty, and God's foreknowledge. We simply end up quoting the same verses, speaking of man freely choosing, God foreknowing the future and being sovereign, yet meaning mutually exclusive things.

This lack of clarification of terminology in both the written and spoken word allows Calvinists to continue to claim to be Calvinists without having to come to grips with consistent Calvinism. Further, those considering Calvinism make their choice based upon a very inadequate understanding of consistent Calvinism. It permits Calvinists to resolutely defend such ideas as decretal theology and compatibilism and ridicule those who believe in libertarian freedom while being able to speak as though all things are not determined when convenient. Such a formula leads to very little understanding and is fodder for misunderstanding and clichés. We owe each other more than that. We surely owe God more reverence.

Level two is to examine whether Calvinism's interpretation of Scripture, necessary concepts, assumptions, and entailments offer the most biblically helpful approach for knowing God, understanding the gospel, and comprehending his eternal plan as revealed in his Word.

This second level *primarily* seeks to determine whether Calvinism, with all of its disquieting realities, definitions, and assumptions, is biblically true, the most helpful system of soteriology, and the best hermeneutical approach. Only with a clear understanding of core Calvinist beliefs, entailments of those beliefs, and philosophical assumptions that come from those beliefs can one make a consistent and substantive evaluation of Calvinism's internal consistency and consonance with Scripture. Without the painstaking illumination of the disquieting realities and double talk as described in level one, this level is doomed to result in either an insubstantial or inaccurate evaluation of Calvinism as a plausible system.

The following is something I have experienced countless times. One can take the most prominent Calvinist commentaries on both the Old and New Testaments and read the handling of various soteriological passages, only to note they frequently interpret them just as Extensivists do. That is they speak of such things as true otherwise choice, God's extensive salvific love, and a genuine accessible offer of the gospel. The problem is that our differences are real and their interpretation is often in irreconcilable conflict with consistent Calvinism, even though the Scripture does say what they are communicating at that moment. At times the Calvinist commentator will accurately interpret the verse only to end by interjecting the concept of unconditional election, regeneration preceding faith, or other concepts essential to Calvinism, which is absolutely absent from the passage. Not only are these Calvinistic concepts absent, but both the passage and their comments are in direct conflict with such concepts.

For example, *The Bible Knowledge Commentary* on John 3:16, written from a four-point Calvinist perspective says, "This verse . . . is God's Word and is an important summary of the gospel. God's motivation toward people is love. God's love is not limited to a few or to one group of people but His gift is for the whole world."[2] While I do believe the commentator is correct in his interpretation of the verse, it is in absolute contradiction to unconditional election. Unconditional election's declaration is that God does not salvifically love everyone. The whole working of unconditional election and selective regeneration is indisputable proof that, according to Calvinism, God does not salvifically love everyone. Four-point Calvinists do maintain that Christ died for all (unlimited atonement) but that does nothing to assuage the reality of unconditional election. That is to say, they can tell everyone that Christ's death paid for their sins (something the five-point Calvinist cannot do), but they cannot legitimately say God's salvific love is available to everyone. This is because it is in fact limited to a few by unconditional election, selective regeneration, and the selective internal efficacious call (sometimes that latter two are used interchangeably).

Commenting on Matthew 11:20–24 D.A. Carson says, "Notice that Jesus expected his miracles *alone* to cause people to repent. How much more his preaching of the good news, which these towns had enjoyed"[3] (italics added). While I do believe Scripture is teaching what Carson says, this teaching is absolutely inconsistent with Calvinism's unconditional election and

---

2. Blum, "John," 282.
3. Carson, et al., eds., *New Bible Commentary*, 919.

the requirement of a selective internal efficacious calling of God, without which no one will be saved even if he is an eyewitness to a million miracles daily. This is a simple but poignant reminder that understanding the ideas delineated in level one are essential to successfully navigate level two.

Level three is Extensivists must offer a more biblically reflective alternative that neither elides the perplexities of some Scriptures (election, predestination, foreknowledge) nor complicates (as Calvinism does) the massive amount of simple and lucid Scriptures regarding the nature of God and his salvific plan being inclusive of sufficient provision so that anyone and everyone may be saved by faith in Jesus Christ (John 3:16; Titus 2:11).

This approach seeks reliance upon a simple (not simplistic) reading of Scripture. It recognizes that the deconstruction of one perspective must include a biblical alternative. To wit, it is dreadfully inadequate to merely highlight what one finds fault with (although necessary) without giving consideration to a better alternative. Better does not mean it is or will be accepted by all, particularly by committed Calvinists. Nor should it seek to fit within biblically unnecessary and Calvinistically-nuanced definitions that necessarily presuppose and lead inexorably to Calvinism. Rather, better simply means more congruent with the entire warp and woof of Scripture. Additionally, it seeks to reflect the unambiguous teachings of Scripture consistently and comprehensively.

Many Calvinists not only believe their approach to interpreting Scripture is the best way, they do not even properly evaluate whether any other approach could be considered biblical, much less right. This seems due to either an unwillingness or inability of *many* Calvinists to consider an alternative without doing so through the grid of Calvinism, with all of its very restrictive presuppositions, definitions, and causal understanding of scriptural concepts and the reality conveyed therein. This results in Calvinists evaluating whether the opposing view is consistent with Calvinism rather than Scripture, and these are not the same.

When I was a Calvinist, I viewed objections to Calvinism through the same grid for twenty years; thereby precluding objective evaluation of contrary claims. Many Calvinists would deny they do this. As a Calvinist, I would have denied the practice as well (I do not attribute malice to any present Calvinist or myself). Nevertheless, upon reflection, I did believe so strongly in Calvinism that I unwittingly did view counterclaims through the lenses of Calvinism, which is the order of the day within Calvinism.

I began to face the disquieting realities of Calvinism, and this included rejecting double talk as a satisfactory way of palliating these disquieting realities, along with interpreting both the difficult and simple Scriptures without the presuppositions of Calvinism. I gradually became convinced that while Calvinism did seek to handle some of the perplexities of Scripture, it resulted in biblically unwarranted and unsustainable assumptions about God, man, the gospel, and a host of unambiguous Scriptures. This was due in part (as it seems to me) to Calvinism's reliance upon biblically unnecessary philosophical assumptions, definitions, and strained reinventions of the clearest verses in Scripture. This would include such things as compatibilism and excessively causal sovereignty along with strained readings of rather straightforward passages like John 20:30–31.

The nurture of my eventual disenchantment with Calvinism was due almost exclusively from reading Scripture and Calvinist authors. They helped me through over a decade-long process to realize there was a better way that did not require additional mysteries (generated solely from Calvinism and not Scripture), did not require me to defend very harsh and unnecessary entailments (which disappear when one doffs the spectacles of Calvinism), and did not obscure the beauty of clear Scriptures and the fullness of God's attributes.

As I have stated many times and in many ways, I respect *most* Calvinists, especially the ones who are straightforward about Calvinism's entailments, disquieting realities. I have interacted with some who seek to do that. I believe most Calvinists as well as those who reject Calvinism are seeking to know and represent God accurately. I have met personally and communicated through writing with knowledgeable Reformed five-point Calvinists. Our meetings were both delightful and spiritually rich. In light of that, I believe we all benefit by accurately portraying our own beliefs as well as those with whom we disagree. During the past few years, I have found myself not only engaging Calvinists but also either clarifying Calvinism's actual claims or defending my love for Calvinists to some of my Extensivist brothers and sisters.

I desire to portray Calvinism accurately so people can make a more informed decision about whether to don the Calvinist label. This includes Extensivism seeking to evaluate the claims of Calvinism in light of Scripture, and the internal consistency of Calvinism as articulated by the Calvinists themselves. Correspondingly, Calvinists must consider Extensivism in light of Scripture and its internal consistency as articulated by Extensivism and not merely through the assumptive grid of Calvinism.

3

Why I Chose the Term Extensivism

HERE IS MY PARTICULAR definition of Extensivism: The belief that man was created in the image of God with otherwise choice and that God's salvation plan is comprehensive, involving an all-inclusive unconditional offer of salvation and eternal security of the believer; reception of which is conditioned upon grace-enabled faith rather than an exclusive plan involving a limited actual offer of salvation to only the unconditionally elected, or any plan that, in any way, conditions salvation upon merely a humanly-generated faith.

Applied more *generally*, I use Extensivism as a positive term in place of non-Calvinism. It may have some things in common with Arminianism, Molinism, or even Calvinism, but Extensivism does not rely exclusively upon any of these. Further, similarities do not equal sameness. Extensivism seeks only to present a comprehensive, consistent system of soteriology that is reflective of the warp and woof of Scripture, which may have shared beliefs with other systems of soteriology, but Extensivism seeks to neither be consistent with nor defend other belief systems.

I use the term Extensivism to encapsulate my soteriological (salvational) understanding. I gave considerable thought to choosing the term. It does seem to be free of negative connotations and appears to me to be a suitable parallel for discussing soteriology within this Calvinist/Extensivist theological milieu. The appropriateness of the term becomes evident anytime Extensivists and Calvinists are engaged because consistent Calvinism is soteriologically exclusive. This is evident in Calvinism's commitment to God's limited *salvific* love, unconditional election, internal efficacious call for only the unconditionally elected, limited and selective regeneration, and limited atonement (that Christ's death *did not actually* atone for the sins of every person in the world *in the same way* so that anyone and everyone can believe and be saved).[1]

In contrast, we who disagree with that exclusive approach do so because we believe Scripture teaches an extensive salvation plan. This includes

---

1. This speaks of all five-point Calvinists but does not include four-point Calvinists.

universal salvific love, conditional election comprehended in God's creation of man with otherwise choice, the sufficient call of the gospel for all, grace enabled faith in the gospel resulting in regeneration, and unlimited atonement (that Christ's death *did actually* atone for the sins of every person in the world *in the same way* so that anyone and everyone can believe and be saved). Extensivism speaks to the sufficient provision of God's salvational plan so that every single person can and should believe and be saved.

As seen in my definition above, I employ the term in two ways. Broadly, I use it to include all who believe that God salvifically loves everyone and has evidenced such by provisioning sufficiently for everyone to have an opportunity to believe and be saved. This includes Traditionalists, Arminians, and Molinists with all their variations so long as they believe anyone can be saved. In this sense, it serves as a positive term for non-Calvinists. More particularly, I use the term to express precisely my view regarding some of the specifics of how God accomplishes his salvific work of love and grace as well as answering tough questions posed by Scripture and Calvinism. This may be a little different or worded differently than others who agree with me, broadly speaking.

I do not profess to be an Arminian, which is evident from my perspective regarding the eternal security of the believer. This disagreement between Extensivism and Arminianism is based upon more than referencing various Scriptures or recognition that someone may be an Arminian and believe in eternal security. Rather, it includes differences which consist of variations within the understanding of libertarian freedom, and most particularly, what is the nature of a saved individual and his God-given range of options after salvation. Additionally, while all orthodox perspectives believe God's grace must precede faith to be saved, Extensivism's approach may use some distinct features to explain the process and application of grace to the question of whether salvation is accessible to all.

The distinction between Extensivism and Arminianism is important because Calvinists greatly depend upon utilizing Arminian ideas, which do not include the security of the believer and are not essential to the idea of libertarian freedom, to dismiss any and all who reject Calvinism.[2] Lastly, I have spent my entire Christian life studying Calvinism, and I am, therefore, unqualified to argue from an authentic Arminian position. Although I do not desire to limit what God may do, it seems to me at my age, I may not have another thirty years to brief myself on authentic Arminianism prior to engaging Calvinism.

---

2. Examples of such are legion, but one may see this in Lewis Sperry Chafer's *Systematic Theology*, vol. 3, chapters 14–17, specifically page 279.

I may write another book on Extensivism in order to more fully expound on the biblical and logical rationale for my soteriological beliefs. I intend to continue probing into the underlying endemic problems with Calvinism as I see them (theological, philosophical expressions, assumptions, and entailments), which I believe are irreconcilable with Scripture. These difficulties and the lack of clear answers and disclosure by Calvinists played a significant role in my disenchantment with, and ultimate departure from, Calvinism. They continue to serve as fecund soil for inconsistencies within Calvinism. My disagreement with Calvinism is at its most basic and non-negotiable fundamental level. This means I reject all five points of the TULIP and more as properly defined by Calvinism (including its significant assumptions and definitions regarding the nature of God, sovereignty, and created man) that lead to their understanding of the TULIP.

It is my practice to seek to only deal with mainstream Calvinism (what I label as Major-Calvinists, those who embrace four or five points of the TULIP) and leave hyper-Calvinism to others. I seek to evaluate their system of beliefs based on what they say and believe rather than what others may say they believe. This becomes very precise when I am engaging an individual, and more encompassing of the general teaching of Calvinism when dealing with only a particular topic. Even when dealing with the latter, I most often seek to engage a specific Calvinist and thereby employ both a broad and specific engagement. In spite of their weaknesses, I do find labels helpful so long as they do not cause one to engage what a particular individual is not saying (beyond consistency within their chosen system). For example, some of Millard Erickson's views are different from Charles Hodge's; consequently, when I engage Erickson, I seek to do so based upon what he says about his own specific belief even though both Erickson and Hodge claim to be Calvinists.

One of my frequently expressed concerns is that of inconsistency within the system of Calvinism as expressed in the communication of Calvinism by its adherents. My increasing awareness of and concomitant dislike for the pervasive rhetorical practice of double talk within Calvinism stimulated my evanescing commitment to Calvinism. This customary manner of communication obscures the inescapable disquieting realities of Calvinism to both the Calvinist and the listener, and this whether it is done wittingly or unwittingly.

Until one is willing to face and communicate with inflexible consistency the harsh realities that double talk gauzily veils, one cannot truly evaluate the compatibility of Calvinism with Scripture. If one is willing to speak, write, and pray consistently with these non-negotiable essential ideas and entailments of Calvinism, he can be a thorough Calvinist, and I applaud him.

For example, one such often elided essential is the absolute micro-deterministic nature of Calvinism.[3] This indisputable bedrock of Calvinism is rarely communicated without a nearby attempted contrary palliative statement and may very well be impossible to live by; at least I can say I have never met anyone who lives and communicates consistently with his or her espoused belief in determinism. Thus, eventually, out of respect for God and Calvinists, I doffed the label. I must admit, after over thirty years that was a difficult and lonely time.

I have often mentioned I do not believe the designations of one, two, or three-point Calvinism are actually representative of Calvinism because to maintain such means the individual has so personalized his beliefs that they are not reflective of true Calvinism; usually modifying or rejecting one or all of the following: total depravity, unconditional election, limited atonement, or irresistible grace. Nor does it seem respectful or helpful in discussing the merits of consistent Calvinism. This is all too common in Southern Baptist life where Extensivists and Calvinists serve the King side by side.

Many staunch Extensivists don the label one, two, or three-point Calvinist. I believe we must disabuse ourselves of this practice if we are to rewardingly proceed. This is not to say anything against the godly men and women who use such terms, but rather that it is not obvious how the employment of designations that include the term Calvinist by individuals who are not Calvinist is either accurate or helpful. Unfortunately, I used all three designations for brief periods to describe my fluid perspectives during my migration from being a steadfast four-point Calvinist to my final rejection of Calvinism. I think such designations misrepresent true Calvinism, confuse the discussion, and unjustifiably make Calvinism the standard for theological and dialogical parameters. The question simply becomes what kind of Calvinist are you?

I base this conclusion upon the reality of the mutually exclusive understanding that exists between Calvinism and one, two, or three-point perspectives regarding some of the core concepts. Such concepts include both theological and philosophical ideas that are determinative in whether one is actually a Calvinist or an Extensivist. The different perspectives regarding such concepts as the nature of man's freedom, God's sovereignty, and foreknowledge, which if properly understood and consistently applied, illumine the substantive and irreconcilable dissimilarities between true Calvinism and one, two, or three-point perspectives. Such nuanced

---

3. See Appendix 2, Theological Determinism, for an example of determinists' logic.

positions are actually more reflective of Extensivism than Calvinism. Accordingly, I suggest when a person reaches that level of personalizing of Calvinism, for the sake of clarity and maintaining an accurate portrayal of true Calvinism, he discontinue using the term and accept that he is not truly a Calvinist. Of course, this is my opinion, but I think I will demonstrate that to be true in this book.

I believe if one accepts unconditional election, one can claim the title of Calvinist. Once a person accepts unconditional election, the question correctly becomes whether the individual is a consistent Calvinist. By unconditional election, I mean as it is defined by mainstream Calvinism. This understanding includes inherent determinism in man's freedom, God's foreknowledge based upon determinism, as well as what God can know and be sovereign over. If one does not accept unconditional election, I do not believe one can rightly claim to be a Calvinist, and the label actually becomes a detriment to understanding the substantive and pervasive differences between Calvinism and Extensivism (broadly speaking). Again, I am well aware of a number of people who are not Calvinists, and yet employ the descriptive of one, two, or three-point Calvinist to describe themselves; a practice I believe should be abandoned.

I think it is helpful in discussions between Calvinists and Extensivists to evaluate one's beliefs in light of what the particular individual claims to believe. For example, when I reason for libertarian freedom, this engenders all kinds of questions in the Calvinist's mind. I believe as an Extensivist, I need to answer these questions so that they are consistent primarily with Scripture and secondarily with Extensivism. As I ask questions of Calvinists, the same applies. They need to provide answers that are consistent with Scripture and Calvinism, e.g., compatibilism.

The breakdown in dialogue often surfaces when we ask questions of Calvinists in which we seek answers that comport with an Extensivist soteriology rather than being consistent with Scripture and Calvinism. Similarly, the same breakdown of communication occurs when Calvinists ask Extensivists questions in which they seek answers that comport with Scripture and Calvinism. I have found, both when I was a Calvinist and now as an Extensivist, Calvinists are quite often either unable or unwilling to even consider a perspective with which they disagree without filtering it through the deterministic lens of Calvinism (determinism as entailed in their compatible view of moral freedom and decretal theology); thus, they are foiled in their attempt to properly evaluate whether a competing perspective, although not deterministic like Calvinism, is biblical or not.

For example, since Calvinists believe man is endowed with a compatible freedom, Extensivists need to evaluate whether Calvinism is consistent with compatibilism in its proclamations, rather than whether or not their statements are consistent with libertarian freedom, which knowledgeable Calvinists reject. Conversely, since Extensivists believe God endowed man with libertarian freedom, Calvinists need to evaluate whether Extensivism is consistent with libertarianism in its proclamations, rather than whether or not our statements are consistent with compatible freedom, which we reject. Moreover, all evaluations on both sides must preeminently include evaluating each perspective, as defined by the adherent, in light of Scripture. Then we are better situated for accurate and helpful comparisons between the two perspectives. But first, we must understand what the other is claiming from their perspective and whether it is even consistent with that.

To wit, I do not engage Calvinists in order to seek only answers that are consistent with Extensivism, nor should they seek to evaluate Extensivism in light of their system. I am not ambiguous. I am not a Calvinist, and I actually reject the underlying essentials of the system systemically. This means that I not only reject the TULIP but also the soil (philosophical assumptions and definitions) from which the TULIP blossoms.

My engagements with Calvinists are not principally to convert them to Extensivism per se. Rather they are to challenge them to be consistent within Calvinism to the Scripture and their chosen system in all points when they speak, write, and pray (including living their daily lives). I challenge them to do so in order that not only can they understand their system more accurately, but those who hear them are enabled to do so as well. If they cannot, I would advise them to abandon Calvinism. I do not mind challenges for me to do the same. My approach is based on the belief that we should speak so that *everyone* can understand the beliefs and entailments of our perspective, and if that is achieved, many will abandon Calvinism.

One point of clarification is in order. When I speak of the pervasive inconsistencies within Calvinism, I am not referring to inconsistencies in light of Extensivism, nor the inconsistencies due to the frailty of all men. Rather, I refer to the inconsistencies within their own system and between their doctrinal beliefs and their writings, preaching, and prayers, for which I find the perennial rejoinder *it is an inscrutable mystery* to be symptomatic rather than resolvent. I do applaud *consistent* Calvinists for seeking to be clear about all their beliefs and the entailments of those beliefs (disquieting realities), even though we disagree theologically.

4

Why Some Extensivists Identify as Calvinists

WHILE MANY DON THE designation Calvinist because they have endeavored to learn all the aspects of Calvinism and are thereby convinced that it provides the most cogent, comprehensive, and consistent grid through which to understand Scripture, others adopt the label less nobly. Of this latter kind, it seems to me many assume the title of Calvinist because they like certain components of Calvinism, which they are led to believe are unique to Calvinism. Such conclusions may arise from their exposure to the claims of some Calvinists, the inadequate explanations or responses of those they are familiar with who reject Calvinism, or even from their own subjective assumptions. Such aspects are exampled by God's sovereignty, the preeminence of God's glory, or the total depravity of fallen man.

Additionally, many who are exposed to the teachings of godly Calvinists are understandably impressed, which readily leads them to not only accept some of their teachings but also inclines them to identify more closely with the individuals themselves; accordingly, they embrace the designation Calvinist for themselves. This assimilation into the fold of Calvinism is quite frequently without an adequate understanding of the philosophical assumptions, entailments, or what I term *disquieting realities* of Calvinism.

A fast track to this imprudent adoption is readily detectable in places where Calvinism is either the only or the dominant position of the constituents. And yet, we are able to find another less obvious inspiring path for becoming a naively inconsiderate Calvinist in our own Southern Baptist Convention (SBC). This is because Calvinism, to an unhealthy degree and by default, is granted the position of being the unofficial standard from which even those who are not *actually* Calvinists (and readily admit such) find their own personalized descriptive. The dearth of more instructive terms to describe this vast group or the various subgroups within (who find the term Arminian unsuitable) results in many leaning too heavily upon a modified Calvinistic designation, thereby occasioning virtually everyone to seemingly be either a Calvinist or merely a derivative. Accordingly, the practical question becomes, "What kind of Calvinist are you?" Some are trying to correct the absence of terms with suggested terms as Traditionalist, Savabilist, or my term Extensivist. The most popular by far is the term Traditionalist. The Traditionalists' beliefs are codified in a formal document and explained in a book.[1]

Once the doctrinally Extensivist person chooses to embrace the title Calvinist, he may begin to exclusively study these godly teachers. Of course, this path further exposes him to more of the admirable teachings and seemingly correct assumptions, definitions, and conclusions of Calvinism. However, along the way, he also encounters teachings within the structure of Calvinism he does not believe are consistent with the clear teachings of Scripture. At various junctures along his journey of descending deeper into Calvinism, rather than totally disavowing Calvinism because of these Calvinistically-generated contrarieties (mysteries), which disavowal seems to be psychologically equivalent to renouncing the godliness of these men as well as biblical doctrines such as sovereignty, he chooses instead to embrace only what he deems to be consistent with the clear teachings of Scripture. Of course, these are usually the most readily accessible, palatable, and definitionally unencumbered aspects of Calvinism, even if such understanding is definitely inconsistent with the deeper and more precise teachings of Calvinism.

In contrast, the less palatable teachings and entailments are ostensibly resolved by the development of an increasingly personalized understanding of these objectionable, yet actual essentials of Calvinism. He then morphs his position into not only an inadequate reflection of Calvinism but more specifically into a corruption of such. I refer to such personalized Calvinism as Minor-Calvinism, which is in contrast to Major-Calvinism.[2]

Major-Calvinists include both four and five-point Calvinists. The major distinction between them is the rejection of limited atonement by four-point Calvinists. I sometimes include both under the general term Calvinist when I am not speaking specifically about the atonement. Both are categorized as

---

1. Traditionalist beliefs are codified in the document, "A Statement of The Traditional Southern Baptist Understanding of God's Plan of Salvation," which is available to read and sign at http://connect316.net/the-statement/. The full explanation of the document is available in the book, *Anyone Can Be Saved: A Defense of "Traditional" Southern Baptist Soteriology*. Other terms used instead of non-Calvinist within SBC life are Arminian, Molinist, Biblicist, and just Baptist.

2. See David Allen's helpful definition of High-Calvinist that includes five-point Calvinists as well as Moderate-Calvinists. Moderate-Calvinists include four-point Calvinists as well as those who "reject a strictly limited atonement, [and] believe God's saving design in the atonement was dualistic." "The Atonement," 64. For a fuller description of these terms, see Allen's book *The Extent of the Atonement*, xxviii.

Major-Calvinists because both believe in unconditional election, irresistible grace, and God's predetermination of the eternal destiny of everyone.

A Minor-Calvinist so individualizes his commitment to Calvinism (seeking to keep what he likes and reject what he sees as clearly unbiblical and objectionable entailments of Calvinism) that his perspective is actually reduced to piratical Calvinism—illegitimate. Knowledgeable Calvinists are correct to reject such personalized and inchoate Calvinistic portraits as representative of true Calvinism because Calvinism, as all theologically sophisticated Calvinists know, seeks to be an internally coherent and comprehensive system. Even though many Calvinists readily count people who espouse such an incomplete view as Calvinists when referring to how many people are Calvinists.

I do not believe the linchpin of Calvinism is total depravity (TD), as is often proposed by Calvinists and understood by many. Rather, it is their understanding of depravity based on their deterministic perspective of human freedom, known as compatibilism. This distinction means a person can embrace total depravity as the condition of mankind because of the fall, as I do, so long as it is based upon a libertarian understanding of freedom. My perspective includes the inability of the individual, subsequent to the fall of man in the garden, to make a spiritually restorative decision prior to God's pre-conversion work of grace enablements. It does not include or require a work of creating a new being (regeneration, quickening, rehabilitation) prior to the exercise of faith or a determinative act of grace, which is true of Calvinism and compatibilism. See Authorial Glossary for a list of grace enablements.

In my opinion, the actual question is not whether man is totally depraved (extensively speaking, i.e., affecting his total being) or not but whether God created man with libertarian freedom or compatible freedom. It seems to me, it is defining man as possessing compatible freedom along with a supposed concomitant determinative solution that makes Calvinism's definition of TD unacceptable and not TD per se—biblically speaking. I find the relinquishment of the term *total* depravity to the Calvinists to be unwise since it seems clear to me the Scripture teaches TD and not a *partial* depravity, which is what one is left with having abandoned the word, *total*. I believe the preeminent essential element of Calvinism is its belief in unconditional election. Without unconditional election, one cannot legitimately claim to be a Calvinist. Unless one properly understands these two aspects (compatibilism and unconditional election) and is willing to embrace them and the entailments of such concepts, he should doff the designation of Calvinist.

What often keeps many Minor-Calvinists (one, two and three-point) clinging to their claim of being a Calvinist rather than totally rejecting the designation can be: an unawareness of the irreconcilable inconsistencies produced by such positions, a willingness to live with such incongruities because of what they deem to be sufficient benefits for doing so, the lack of a suitable designation other than a negative like non-Calvinist, or even an unwillingness or fear of leaving the security that being in the fold of Calvinism provides. I am not against self-chosen labels because it does appear to me soteriological discussions are enhanced by more specific terms than just Christian or Biblicist. However, the incongruences created by one, two, or three-point Calvinism make them inaccurate and, therefore, unhelpful in either properly reflecting or evaluating Calvinism.

Minor-Calvinists often seek to palliate their inconsistent position by unwittingly embracing the double talk that seems to launder these unacceptable provisions. This rhetorical practice, coupled with a simple trust that some knowledgeable Calvinists have adequate answers for these biblical incongruences and dilemmas arising from either their personalized Calvinism or true Calvinism, appears quite satisfactory to many. The dreadful news is that truly knowledgeable Calvinists do not have an answer that vanquishes these Calvinistically-generated anomalies. They too live with these disquieting realities and ideas contrary to even the clearest of biblical passages with the aid of the perennial retreat to *double talk or it is a mystery.*

Calvinists frequently claim to be more comfortable with the idea of a mystery than the rest of us (those unwilling to embrace developed Calvinism). They may ask me why I am not comfortable with the idea of mystery. My response is I am quite comfortable with biblically generated mysteries such as the full knowledge of the Trinity, what actually (in all of its details) took place upon the cross when the Father judged the Son for our sin, or how it is that the triune God lives within his people. What I am unbearably uncomfortable with are Calvinistically-generated mysteries.

The difference between the two classes of mysteries is gleanable by asking oneself if I were not a Calvinist, would this particular mystery being suggested actually exist? If not, it is a Calvinistically-generated mystery rather than a biblical mystery. For example, would there be a mystery regarding the reconciliation of unconditional election and Scriptures that explicitly teach God's salvific love for every person if one were not a Calvinist? If the answer is no (experienced by a *temporary test run* disavowal of unconditional election) then it is a Calvinistically-generated mystery rather than a biblically-generated mystery. Therefore, it should be summarily and permanently disavowed in favor of the clear teaching of the most straightforward reading of Scripture.

Lastly, I have found Calvinism's tactical argument that says people with my soteriological position have "the same problem" (as used in various scenarios, which, if existed, would lessen Calvinism's conundrums) to be based on a misunderstanding of the precise position of those who disagree with them.[3] While in glaring contrast, the problems within Calvinism necessitating the non-resolving resolution of the inscrutable mystery are based on a precise understanding of Calvinism, which is evidenced by its pervasiveness in Calvinists' theological writings.

Therefore, unless one is willing to embrace Major-Calvinism and work as arduously at consistently proclaiming all the tenets and entailments of such as Calvinists are in seeking to promote the merits of Calvinism when contrasting it with what *some* portray as the tawdry man-centered Extensivism, one should doff the title Calvinist. Such a decision enables a person to freely interpret the clearest verses of Scripture without the obscurant program of unconditional election always running in the background. It honors true and knowledgeable Calvinists and helps to enhance more enlightened conversations regarding the different positions, thereby enabling more informed decisions of whether to don the designation Calvinist.

---

3. An example of the same problem argument can be found in chapter 30 with regards to the availability of the gospel.

5

One Man's Suggestions for Calvinists and Extensivists

ALTHOUGH I NO LONGER don the Calvinist label, I do continue to recognize the system of thought as an option within historic Christianity as well as Southern Baptist life. Further, I have no interest in personally attacking my Calvinist brothers' and sisters' devotion, piety, or love for God and his word. I do *sincerely* believe *most* Calvinists are truth seekers. I do not wish to expel Calvinists nor to be expelled by them from SBC life but rather to suggest and take some substantive steps to help all of us know God better. I assume that is what the vast majority of those of us in this discussion truly desire; although, there is obvious disagreement on how to accomplish this quest.

In order to continue to move our discussions toward lucidity in both articulation and understanding of our various theological perspectives, I would like to suggest the practice of the following ideas within Southern Baptist life. My suggestions are drawn from my Christian life as a Southern Baptist, which includes both the perspective I gained during my years as a Calvinist and now as an Extensivist. While I view my suggestions as necessary, I also view them as partial and modifiable. I believe some of the steps should be implemented immediately, while others are clearly long-term goals that may take years. I offer my suggestions with no more credentials than being a rather obscure but concerned Southern Baptist.

I trust that if we speak with grace and listen with humility, which some on both sides of the discussion do, we can learn from each other. I genuinely believe if the following suggestions are not implemented, the future of the SBC may not be as bright as it could be; although, one may easily find sufficient grounds to view my suggestions dismissively since I do seem to have an extraordinarily unimpressive record as a prophet. As a Calvinist, I loved, respected, and worked with those who were not, and now that I am no longer a Calvinist, I hold that same love, respect, and desire to work with those who are.

Calvinism's challenge: Face its *disquieting realities* and unabashedly seek to elucidate them to the masses by speaking clearly, often, and consistently about the full implications of Calvinism.

Disquieting realities are the cold, harsh, inescapable implications and conclusions of consistent Calvinism, which I do not believe comport with the warp and woof of Scripture. I mention only two examples. First, according to Calvinism, God desires for the vast majority of his creation to burn in hell forever; meaning the gospel is *actually* that God loves to save *some* sinners and equally loves to damn *most* sinners to eternal torment. To retreat to saying things like "it is a mystery," "God is sovereign," or "all people deserve hell and to save one is grace" does nothing to assuage this austere understanding of God, which I believe is fundamentally inconsistent with the panoply of Scripture and a biblically-balanced view of the attributes of God. The response of some Calvinists that God desires all to be saved according to his revealed will but only desires to save some according to his decretal will is an equally vacuous response since the existence of another will that contradicts and *eternally overrules* his revealed will in Scripture necessarily exiles his revealed will to a permanent state of meaninglessness.[1]

Second, in Genesis, God commanded Adam not to eat of "the tree of the knowledge of good and evil" (Gen 2:17); according to Calvinism's compatible view of man's nature, which limits the range of *actually accessible* choices to one, God did in point of fact *desire*—not cause—Adam to sin, and this with full knowledge of all of its ensuing torturous horror; of which we are all both perpetrators and sufferers. This desire is not the same as the necessary desire for God to create, without which nothing would exist. This desire is unique to Calvinism. It means that within God's desire to create he also desired to create man with compatible freedom so that man could only ultimately choose to sin. This in light of the fact that, consistent with compatibilism, God could have created man, had he so desired, so that man would not choose to sin. Both of these concepts are inextricable components of Calvinism and, therefore, cannot be dismissed by discussing the order of decrees or declaring *it is a mystery*.[2] I appreciate and applaud my Calvinist brothers who shamelessly seek to proclaim these essentials of Calvinism.

I only ask of those who believe Calvinism to be correct, which necessarily entails believing it pleases God to withhold salvation from an untold number of persons whom he created, to please be no more reticent in proclaiming these realities as often, loudly, and consistently as one does the more palatable concepts of Calvinism. At least Calvinists should be as forthright

---

1. See chapter 19 "Does God Have Two Wills?"
2. See Appendix 1 on the Order of Elective Decrees.

to declare these inescapable conceptions about God as they are to speak of God's glory or sovereignty, and this without *double talk*. Actually, these realities are as much a part of Calvinism's understanding of the gospel as is "who calls upon the name of the Lord shall be saved" (Acts 2:21). In point of fact, the latter is only *trivially* true in Calvinism since only the *unconditionally elected "who"* can indeed call upon the name of the Lord.

By *double talk*, I *specifically and only* mean thinking, praying, writing, or speaking in such a way that obscures the *disquieting realities* of Calvinism. This rhetorical practice of *many* Calvinists makes substantive conversations regarding the essence of Calvinism so that both Calvinists and the sincere enquirer can fully understand these *disquieting realities*, frustratingly improbable. If a person accepts and clearly and consistently proclaims such realities, then he can be a knowledgeable and consistent Calvinist; if one is unwilling to accept and unambiguously proclaim them, he cannot be a consistent Calvinist.

I am not labeling anyone as a double talker nor is my use of this term intended, in any sense, to be pejorative but merely descriptive. I only intend to highlight one of the issues that I believe, if left unresolved, dooms the otherwise potential fecundity of our conversations. Additionally, I truly desire to contribute to a more clear understanding of Calvinism so that individuals can make a more informed choice of whether to either embrace or remain in Calvinism. Anything less than a total repudiation of dissembling communication on both sides will simply perpetuate befogging the issue.

The inconsistencies of which I speak are not the inconsistencies that are endemic in the frailty of all human ideologies merely because we are human; thus, my concerns cannot be justly dismissed by noting that everyone is inconsistent unless the inconsistencies referred to in others are *essentially similar* to the inconsistencies I am addressing. To wit, these inconsistencies must include language that obscures or euphemizes the insufferable and inescapable corollaries of their position. Further, I come to this understanding primarily by reading Calvinist theologies and commentaries and listening to their declarations and messages as opposed to being schooled in Arminianism.

> **Extensivism's challenge:** Develop systematic theologies and comprehensive systematic interpretive approaches that seek to explain the soteriological perplexities of Scripture biblically, consistently, and comprehensively. This includes answering the tough philosophical questions regarding libertarian vs. compatible human freedom.

There are already many such works available. This challenge is not intended to depreciate nor ignore these works (particularly some superb individual books addressing various aspects of Calvinism), but rather to draw attention to the need for considerably more to be done.³ I am thinking primarily of theologies that can be used in SBC theological training of students and pastors.

It seems clear to me that Calvinists have, quite admirably, written voluminously in this area in contrast to those who cannot be properly classified as Calvinist or Arminian. I think this is a grave shortcoming. Further, I believe the written systemization of such beliefs, readily available in Calvinism, is very appealing to people who value systematic thinking. That was a particular draw for me. I could actually see the systematic outlay of the interrelationship of individual concepts.

It has been my experience that professors who clearly demur to being called a Calvinist are left to rely far too heavily upon Calvinistic theologies while merely noting their disagreements with such. This approach offers only a *personalized* Calvinism rather than a coherent alternative. It seems obvious to me that Calvinist theologies voluminously outnumber comparable works by those of us who rightly shun being labeled Arminian or Calvinist. While correcting this deficit will clearly take time, it is nevertheless essential that it is corrected. There are many exceptionally qualified theologians to admirably accomplish this task if we can disabuse ourselves from an unhealthy reliance upon easier paths, which can only perpetuate the status quo.

Following are some of the characteristics of the approach I am suggesting. First, this approach moves beyond *merely* the deconstruction of or noting disagreements with Calvinism. By this I am not suggesting the abandonment of serious critiques of Calvinism, but rather, along with exposing its weaknesses, much more time must be given to constructing thorough and systematic biblical alternatives for our schools, pastors, and serious laymen. Particular attention must be given to soteriology. Because while analyzing the weaknesses of Calvinism is essential, alone it is a woefully inadequate theological destination. For example, it is one thing to biblically critique Calvinism's view of predestination, but it is quite another to offer a biblical alternative as a part of a thorough systematic approach.

Second, this approach does not rely merely upon Calvinism, Arminianism, or Molinism, nor does it shun an explanation of Scripture that is associated or compatible with any of them merely because it is so associated.

---

3. Examples of recent works include *The Extent of the Atonement: A Historical and Critical Review* by David L. Allen, *Anyone Can Be Saved: A Defense of "Traditional" Southern Baptist Soteriology* edited by David L. Allen, Eric Hankins, and Adam Harwood, *Whosoever Will: A Biblical-Theological Critique of Five-Point Calvinism* edited by Steve Lemke and David Lewis Allen, *The Potter's Promise: A Biblical Defense of Traditional Soteriology* by Leighton Charles Flowers, *The Spiritual Condition of Infants: A Biblical-Historical Survey and Systematic Proposal* by Adam Harwood, and *Determined to Believe? The Sovereignty of God, Freedom, Faith, and Human Responsibility* by John Lennox.

Simple agreement with certain components of a theological system neither makes nor necessitates one being identified with that system—all such dismissive labeling notwithstanding. Preferably, theological designations (Calvinist, Arminian, Molinist, Traditionalist, or Extensivist) should be determined by the adherent rather than by his adversaries. Then, we can freely and respectfully engage one another's biblical fidelity and internal consistency based on a person's chosen identification.

The only exception I would suggest is that if a person is unwilling to embrace the label that undoubtedly describes his position because he does not want to reveal it, then it may be prudent for non-adherents to label him. For example, I was called by a pastor search committee member on one occasion regarding a candidate who said he was not a Calvinist. He also claimed to agree with everything John Piper believes. I took the liberty of telling the committee he was a Calvinist. In order to help pastor search committees avoid being confused about whether the pastoral candidate is a Calvinist or not, I wrote a guide for them to follow. See Appendix 3, A Guide for Determining a Pastoral Candidate's Level of Commitment to Calvinism.

Third, this approach develops *positive* theological designations to replace popular *negative* terms such as non-Calvinist, and one, two, or three-point Calvinist. As mentioned earlier, some are seeking to do this with terms like Traditionalist, Extensivist, and Biblicist without an adjective, which is not to say a person cannot be a Calvinistic Biblicist.[4] It is to say, just because one chooses to reject being a Calvinistic Biblicist or Arminian Biblicist, one should not be banished from using the designation Biblicist.

As mentioned in chapter 4, I have identified those who claim to be one, two, or three-point Calvinists as Minor-Calvinists. Although I once accepted such designations as valid and helpful, I no longer see them in that light. I used such designations to describe myself during the latter days of my migration away from Calvinism. I now believe these designations to be invalid since they represent such a custom-made Calvinism that they become incapable of correctly reflecting the essence of Calvinism; consequently, they obscure what true Calvinism teaches, and thereby obscure the disquieting realities of Calvinism. Because of this, they necessarily facilitate the dialogue to nowhere.

I think the following problems are inherent in using non-Calvinist or one, two, or three-point Calvinist as a theological designation. First, they make Calvinism, ipso facto, the standard (or starting point) from which all perspectives are derived and evaluated. Second, they are by their nature

---

4. Traditionalist as defined in "A Statement of the Traditional Southern Baptist Understanding of God's Plan of Salvation," http://connect316.net/the-statement/. The full explanation of the document is available in the book, *Anyone Can Be Saved: A Defense of "Traditional" Southern Baptist Soteriology*.

negative appellations, which seem at best to be a somewhat lethargic way to describe one's biblical perspective. Third, they perpetuate an unnecessary and prejudiced trajectory toward Calvinism within Baptist life. For example, when one becomes a Baptist or enters into ministry, the only question to be decided is what kind of Calvinist one is or is to become. Lastly, they are fecund terms for *double talk*. These problems beckon the discontinuance of them.

As I grew to see such terms as unredeemably problematic, I looked for another descriptive. After moving from seeing myself as a Minor-Calvinist, I began to use the term *Disenchanted Calvinist*. Though this term worked for a brief time, I began to recognize while it was sufficient for emphasizing my migration from Calvinism, it was inadequate as a long-term designation. After some thought, I chose the term *Extensivist* as a descriptive term for my soteriological position.

One final thought, and I am not seeking to be overly reductionistic. Alluded to earlier, it does seem quite clear to me if someone rejects unconditional election, he *cannot* be an actual Calvinist, for that is at the heart of Calvinism. If a person accepts unconditional election, then he can rightly don the title Calvinist, which then moves the question from one of legitimacy to one of consistency.

I do not even believe four-point Calvinism really addresses the most troubling aspects of Calvinism because it maintains the concept of unconditional election. At first glance, it seems to overcome Calvinism's gospel problems because of its rejection of limited atonement. The acceptance of unlimited atonement is argued to free up the four-point Calvinist to offer the gospel to all without having to face the dilemma caused by limited atonement. Scripture's clarity on Christ dying for all, and all seeming to receive a genuine offer of salvation is what actually led me to adopt four-point Calvinism instead of five-point. However, I now believe it only *appears* to offer the gospel freely and honestly to all because so long as one maintains unconditional election, as four-point Calvinism does, the gospel is no more accessible to the non-elect than if one believes in limited atonement. Consequently, the four-point Calvinist can say to anyone and everyone Christ paid for your sins, which the five-point Calvinist cannot say. But, like the five-point Calvinist, the four-point Calvinists cannot legitimately say God salvifically loves you and wants you to be saved because he believes in unconditional election.[5]

---

5. Reliance upon the idea that God desires all to be saved in his revealed will but only the unconditionally elect in his decretal will, which eternally supersedes his revealed will, is, minimally, the quintessence of double talk.

6

The TULIP: The Petals *and* the Leaves

Before you make the TULIP your flower of choice, consider it in full bloom. TULIP is used acronymically to succinctly point out the major emphases of Calvinism. I well understand the use of the TULIP does not fully illustrate the depth and breadth of Calvinism. I do understand some believe the acronym has outlived its usefulness. However, it still enjoys popular usage among Calvinists and Extensivists alike. I find this to be particularly true among those seeking to explain Calvinism to people who may demonstrate some interest in understanding Calvinism or as a simple tool to convince young people of its biblical and systematic cogency. I am not considering this acronym in order to portray Calvinism either simplistically or inaccurately. Rather, I use it in the manner described by Roger Nicole when he said, "The five points provide a classic framework which is quite well adapted for the expression of certain distinguishing emphases of Calvinism."[1]

Now admittedly, I do want to call attention to some of the frequently ignored or suppressed essentials of the TULIP in order to augment our understanding. In other words, I wish not only to consider the petals but the leaves as well, so to speak. I consider the leaves, these lesser-known beliefs, premises, and entailments to be biblically unsustainable and, therefore, crippling to the seemingly more palatably related beliefs demonstrated by the TULIP.

First, I will give a brief normal understanding communicated by Calvinists, which will be in italics. Second, I will include *some* of these infrequently presented and, therefore, lesser known beliefs and entailments associated with each particular petal.

1. *Total Depravity: The whole of man's being is corrupted by sin and he is, therefore, incapable of doing any eternal spiritual good.*

    Calvinism's understanding of total depravity includes a compatibilist view of human nature, unconditional election, and limited and

---

1. Nicole, *Five Points of Calvinism*, preface 7.

selective regeneration. This means the only interpretive option Calvinism permits for God to be able to redeem such a compatibly defined totally depraved person is that God must give him a new nature (variously called quickening, regeneration, or restoration), which he is pleased to do only for the limited unconditionally elect; thereby, guarantying their subsequent free exercise of faith.

Viewing man from a compatibilist perspective means that while fallen man freely chooses to sin, he cannot freely choose to believe in the gospel unless God gives him a new nature and past that assures he will freely choose to exercise faith in Christ; however, in either state, man cannot choose to do other than he did choose because while freely choosing, he has no salvific choice.

Although it seems most Calvinists in the SBC do believe in regeneration prior to faith, it is true not all Calvinists depend upon regeneration preceding faith. Nevertheless, they all do depend upon on a preceding determinative work of God that changes the elect's past. This work of God changes their nature from what it was before to something different after the work. This is due to their commitment to compatibilism. Technically, compatibilism requires that given the same past, man cannot choose, in the moral moment of decision, other than he did in fact choose.

Consequently, while some may seek to avoid reliance upon a new nature preceding faith, if they are going to be consistent compatibilists, they must believe God works determinatively in the unconditionally elect so as to change man's past in order that he can transition from only being able to reject Christ to only being able to accept Christ. Therefore, regardless of what term they choose to employ, it never changes the deterministic nature of salvation nor its limited accessibility. This pre-faith work necessary to exercising faith is intentionally withheld by God from the non-elect.

Further, while defining man compatibly may include that God is not the *proximate* cause of man's depravity, it also absolutely includes that he did in fact *desire* it.[2] This is evidenced by his choice to create man with a compatibilist free will, which *guaranteed by design* that Adam would freely choose (*be the proximate cause*) to sin and equally

---

2. Efficient cause is the idea that one need look no further than the individual for the cause of the action, i.e., moral responsibility; this is characteristic of Extensivism, and libertarian freedom. That is not the case in compatible freedom. Efficient cause is "An agent that brings a thing into being or indicates a change," *Oxford English Dictionary*, s.v. "Efficient Cause." Aristotle considered the efficient cause to be "the primary source of the change" for making physical changes. See Clark, *Thales to Dewey*, 137.

assured that he *could not* have done otherwise than what he did in fact do. To wit, if God had *desired* man to not sin, he would have given him a different nature, i.e., past.

Some Calvinists seek to avoid this dilemma by contending that God created Adam and Eve with libertarian free will (the ability to choose to eat of the tree or refrain), and man only became compatibly free (unable to choose to act or refrain in the moral moment of decision) after the fall. This contention fails because it treats moral freedom as extraneous to the nature of man, when in fact, it is intrinsic to the nature of man as man. God endowing man with moral freedom is not the same as God putting a coat on man and then taking it off and putting on a different coat, which leaves humanity unchanged.

Rather, the kind of moral freedom God created man with is essential to what it means to be human. If one proposes a change in this essential component from pre-fall to post-fall man, it is to change the very nature of man. This to the point that the man who fell in the garden is not the same (essentially) as mankind after the fall; to wit, the being before the fall may be classified as human, or the being after the fall may be so classified, but they both cannot be so classified since they are *essentially dissimilar*. We can understand one of them as being human but not both of them since their natures are mutually exclusive. The significance of such a change in *essentially disimilar* moral capacities further means the ones God is redeeming are not *essentially the same beings* as the ones who sinned in the garden, thereby meaning God's salvation plan is a failure; therefore, Calvinism cannot extricate itself from God's desire for man to sin as evidenced by God creating him with compatible moral freedom.

Moreover, the use of the word *desire* as a deterministic desire in Calvinism is *essentially dissimilar* to Extensivism's use of the term. Extensivism maintains God always desired man to choose holiness but permitted him to choose to sin when he could and should have actually chosen to not sin. God permitted man to so choose and knew he would choose against his desire for him to remain holy. He comprehended that eventuality in his creation-redemption plan. Desire spoken of here is also not merely the desire to create because we all agree had God not desired to create something, nothing could exist. Rather, Calvinism's meaning of desire speaks specifically and only about what God desired to create man to choose to do as a compatibly free individual, which was to sin.

Therefore, if a person believes Scripture teaches the following, he cannot be a Calvinist: God's only *desire* for Adam was for him to be holy because God is holy and always desires holiness (Gen 2:17; Lev 19:2; 1 Pet 1:15); God created Adam with true otherwise choice so that he could have chosen to sin or chosen not to sin, and whatever he did choose he could have *actually* chosen otherwise; God is able to be sovereign over beings with otherwise choice and to grace enable totally depraved fallen man to have free choice to either believe the gospel or not believe the gospel without resorting to a compatibilist (deterministic) view of moral freedom; and whatever choice someone makes with regard to the gospel, he could have chosen otherwise. Other biblical approaches but not Calvinism embrace these truths.

2. *Unconditional Election: God chose for some to be the objects of his unmerited favor, and salvation is totally a work of God.*

   Calvinism's understanding of unconditional election includes God's choice to give the salvifically required new nature to only *some* of his vast created humanity even though all are in equally desperate need of such in order to experience salvation. Accordingly, it has pleased God to select *some* of his created people to experience incomprehensible eternal bliss while being equally pleased to withhold this experience from the vast majority of his humanity, thereby ensuring the people of this latter group equally incomprehensible eternal suffering in the cauldron of inescapable torment of pain and the absolute loss of love and hope in hell.

   This doctrine is maintained with full awareness that God could have just as easily chosen to provide such favor upon any and all of his humanity, but it pleased him to select only a few, comparatively speaking, to be so favored. These inextricable realities of unconditional election are neither explicated nor moderated by retreating to phrases like, "God is just to send all to hell" or "God is gracious to save even one sinner" or "God loves the non-elect differently" because none of these contribute one whit to either explaining how this is perfect infinite love, mercy, and compassion or explaining the scriptural portrayal of God's exercise of such. I find all Calvinists' attempts to assuage the reality of these entailments as dreadfully troubling and actually serving to enfeeble the doctrine of unconditional election.

   Therefore, if a person believes Scripture teaches the following, he cannot be a Calvinist: God salvifically loves all of his humanity and has graciously provided for everyone to be able to receive the treasures of the gospel by simple faith. Just as God is perfect holiness and would, therefore, never be pleased to act unholy, he is also perfect love and mercy and would, therefore, not be pleased to withhold the offer of salvation from billions of his creation, thereby delightfully assuring their eternal doom in hell when he could have just as easily offered them salvation. God is not pleased to predestine the incomputable majority of his humanity to spend forever in the crucible of hell's torment, which torment, by comparison, makes the most shuddering, gruesome, ghastly, and torturous woes of crime or natural catastrophe nothing more than trifling annoyances. Other biblical approaches but not Calvinism embrace these truths.

3. *Limited Atonement: Christ's death is of infinite value, but he died salvifically only for the unconditionally elect.*

Calvinism understands limited atonement to mean Christ's death did not in any *eternally meaningful* way pay for the sins of the non-elect. Thus, there is not even the remotest possibility of even one of the non-elect experiencing salvation in spite of such opportunity being so lucidly and compellingly commanded and presented in the simple call of the gospel for everyone to repent and believe. Correspondingly, this point, along with the aforementioned points, gives rise to the need for and creation of the extra-biblical *good faith offer*.

Four-point Calvinists reject this point in order to avoid trying to reconcile the idea that Christ salvifically died only for the sins of the elect with what they believe to be the clear, consistent, and undeniable teaching Scripture; Christ's death paid for the sins of the human race. This rejection is believed to free the four-point Calvinist to make an *actual* offer of the good news that Christ paid for the sins of every person in the world as is so vividly portrayed in the gospels. As a result, the position of four-point Calvinism is often understood to reduce the need for some of the guarded language of five-point Calvinism even though a good faith offer is still required as opposed to a good offer.

Nevertheless, if a four-point Calvinist believes in the previous two points as defined by Calvinism, it seems to me their offer to the non-elect is as salvifically hollow as is the offer of the five-point Calvinist. They may be free to speak more consistently with the gospel's message of Christ dying for the sins of every person, but they still offer no real hope to the non-elect. This is particularly true, and I believe unavoidably true, for anyone who embraces unconditional election (even if they call themselves a one-point Calvinist and the one point is unconditional election).

To state it differently, if a person does not fully embrace unconditional election (where unconditional really means unconditional), he should doff the title Calvinist. Limited atonement is organically related to God's pleasure in limiting his salvific grace, love, mercy, and compassion. I do not believe any reference to God providing temporal grace, in things like rain, temporal life, or other earthly blessings, or the defense that "God loves the lost differently" allay this reality in the slightest—voluminous attempts notwithstanding.

Therefore, if a person believes Scripture teaches the following, he cannot be a Calvinist: God really does salvifically love each person that comprises mankind as evidenced by his declarative statements; God gave his Son to die for the sins of the world, all humans, so that the sins of every person were atoned for in the same way (John 3:16); the gospel is his power unto salvation for everyone whether they are Jew or Gentile (Rom 1:16); he sent the church to every nation with this gospel because he truly loves and desires everyone who hears it to repent and be forever forgiven and delivered from their just deserts (Matt 28:18–20; 1 Tim 2:4; Titus 2:11); Christ passionately desires for everyone whom he commanded "repent and believe in the gospel," to do what he commanded them to do; in addition, believes all these scriptural attestations quite obviously disallow the likelihood that the God who does these things also devised a plan that inviolably precludes the remotest possibility for the vast majority to obey his gospel. Other biblical approaches but not Calvinism embrace these truths.

4. *Irresistible Grace: The Holy Spirit efficaciously applies salvation to those unconditionally elected sinners whom he personally calls to Christ.*

Calvinism believes the general call of the gospel extends to everyone, but the internal efficacious call of the Holy Spirit that is both required and inexorably results in salvation is only extended to the unconditionally elect. The nature of these two calls is the former can *only* be rejected and the latter can *only* be accepted. That is to say, the non-elect can never do anything but reject the preaching of the gospel, and the elect will do the same until they receive the internal efficacious call (irresistible grace), which they can only respond to by believing.

Regeneration is monergistic (God alone), and man is totally passive until regeneration is accomplished. After God regenerates an elect individual, then and only then does man become active, cooperative, in the relationship. Calvinism's understanding of God's work of regeneration (sometimes referred to as or included in the concept of the efficacious call) necessarily involves *irresistibility* in purpose, *availability* to the unconditionally elect only, and the *inevitability* of a subsequent free exercise of faith.

Worth noting is the adjectives general and efficacious in both order and description are not explicitly taught in Scripture but rather are understandings of Calvinism. I would suggest the term general call be replaced with the much more biblically congruent term sufficient call, which is available to all who hear the gospel and can be accepted or rejected; additionally, the efficacious call (if there is such a thing) be understood as consummating (securing) salvation for all who accept the sufficient call rather than initiating salvation for the unconditionally elect.

It is important to understand while, according to Calvinism, the act of faith that follows regeneration is a free act; the act of regeneration which inescapably leads to this free exercise of faith is *forced* upon the totally passive and depraved unconditionally elect (monergism and compatibilism). This means the free act of faith is more accurately defined as an eternally predetermined free act of choosing, which excludes any idea of having choices—compatibilism. This eliminates even the remotest possibility for the elect to do other than what he did in fact do and the non-elect the same end. While this is Calvinism's portrait of the inner workings of the gospel, I do not believe it is the picture of the gospel painted by Scripture.

God's choice to ration his salvific grace to only the unconditionally elect necessarily means the lack of faith and the unflinching resistance to the gospel by the non-elect is as equally and inviolably a predetermined free act as is the predetermined free exercise of faith of the unconditionally elect. Therefore, the offer of salvation to *some* and the withholding of salvation from the *incalculable majority* was predetermined by God's good pleasure, thereby making the gospel the most unfathomably ghoulish and macabre news for the great majority of God's humanity.

Therefore, if a person believes Scripture teaches the following he cannot be a Calvinist: the gospel is good news for everyone who hears the words "whoever" or "who wishes take the water of life without cost" (John 3:15; 4:14; and Rev 22:17 respectively) and not merely *some* who hear these words. God has grace enabled all who hear the good news to receive his forgiveness by faith in the gospel. Other biblical approaches but not Calvinism embrace these truths.

5. *Perseverance of the Saints: This includes both preservation by God and perseverance by the saints. The Westminster Confession says, with regard to the truly elect, they "can neither totally nor finally fall away from the*

state of Grace."[3] *J.P. Boyce notes in his Abstract of Systematic Theology*, "It is not merely preservation by God, but also perseverance of the believer, in faith and holiness, unto the end."[4] *Within Calvinism, God's preservation of the truly elect is standard, while there is variation in understanding of how eternal security, internal and external assurances, and warning passages of Scripture relate to knowing one is elect in this life.*

This petal is not a simple affirmation of the eternal security of the believer. Since there does seem to be such acceptable variance in defining perseverance of the saints as long as one does not question the security of the elect, this point can be seen as not being as biblically problematic as the other four petals—a point with which some disagree.

Therefore, if a person believes Scripture teaches the following, he cannot be a Calvinist: anyone who hears the gospel can, by God's grace, will to accept the gospel by faith, and thereby become eternally secure in the safekeeping of God (one of the elect); those so saved do demonstrate evidence of such, as well as believing Scripture does *not* teach the other Calvinistically defined petals of the TULIP. Other biblical approaches but not Calvinism embrace these truths.

---

3. Westminster Confession, 17. 1.
4. Boyce, *Abstract of Systematic Theology*, 431–32.

7

Compatibilism or Libertarianism?

IN ORDER TO UNDERSTAND the actual contrast between Calvinism's belief about the nature of God, his sovereign rule over his creation, and his salvation plan with Extensivism's view of the same, one must understand the two position's vastly different perspectives of what it means for man to be free to choose and be responsible for his choices.

The following is intended to precisely clarify the two positions. While Calvinists adopt and defend a compatible view of freedom, their frequent imprecision in defining it and regularly speaking inconsistently with the actual meaning of compatibilism, including its entailments, obscures its real meaning. This has the effect of leading many to think Calvinists and Extensivists mean basically the same thing when we say man is morally free and responsible, or when Calvinists defend their belief that man freely chooses.

If one adopts Calvinism with its compatible view of freedom, I can respect that. But, I cannot abide the continued attack on libertarian freedom, which is often based upon an erroneous understanding of libertarianism while neglecting or suppressing the micro-deterministic nature of compatibilism. This perpetuates confusion and places meaningful dialogue outside the circle of rhetoric. To the question, did God endow man and woman with the ability to choose? The Calvinists and Extensivists both answer yes, but our answers have very different meanings. Regarding man's freedom to choose and moral responsibility for his choices, there are three primary options from which to choose. They are determinism, compatibilism, and libertarianism.[1]

The definitions of the three perspectives regarding the moral responsibility of man are not dependent upon a Christian worldview. They are philosophical in that they explore the metaphysical nature of man and his freedom. One of the perspectives may be held by someone who is a Darwinist, Atheist, Theist (but not Christian), or a Christian. The fundamental

---

1. In philosophy there exist other variations, some of which are quite minor, such as free will deniers and pessimists, but they are not relevant to considerations of Calvinism and Extensivism.

definitional meaning of each is the same regardless of who holds the position. Consequently, the application to Christianity, references to God, sin, and salvation are not inherent in the nature of the perspectives but only in their application to Christian theism. Additionally, while it is proper to apply a particular one to Christianity, it is invalid to use the application to obscure or negate the core idea of the concept.

Determinism

Man is determined; therefore, whatever he does, he could not have done otherwise. Accordingly, he is not morally responsible for his actions.[2] Sometimes this perspective is referred to as hard determinism, whereas compatibilism is referred to as soft determinism. These are designations coined by William James.[3] This perspective says determinism and moral responsibility are *not* compatible. Neither Calvinists nor Extensivists hold this perspective.

Compatibilism

Determinism and moral responsibility *are* compatible; hence the name. This compatibility is not achieved by compatibilism being less deterministic than hard determinism. Rather, it is achieved by defining free choice to mean as long as a person chooses according to his greatest desire, he can be considered to have made a free choice for which he is morally responsible; even though given the same past, he cannot choose differently in the moral moment of decision.

Consequently, the difference between compatibilism (soft determinism) and hard determinism is not to be found in the levels of the deterministic nature of each because they are the same. Rather, the difference is compatibilism simply contends people are morally responsible for their choices if they are made according to their greatest desire, and hard determinism says they are not. Therefore, moral responsibility is the product of defining free choice as a person acting in accordance with his greatest desire even though the desire is determined. I frequently find Calvinists who affirm soft determinism and disavow hard determinism because they

---

2. Some may argue he is, but generally that is not the case because that is more precisely the position of compatibilism.

3. An American philosopher and psychologist (Jan. 11, 1842–Aug. 26, 1910).

think soft is not as unflinchingly deterministic as hard; that is based upon a misunderstanding of compatibilism.

In addition to quotidianly speaking inconsistently with compatibilism (leaving the impression upon the listeners that man chose between two accessible options), Calvinists often seek to define or represent it as meaning moral responsibility is compatible with God's sovereignty. D.A. Carson says, "In the realm of philosophical theology, this position is sometimes called *compatibilism*. It simply means that God's unconditioned sovereignty and the responsibility of human beings are mutually compatible."[4]

First, note that I am interacting with Carson's chosen term regarding moral freedom and responsibility. Second, it should be observed that Carson is using the philosophical term compatibilism, which is precisely what I am using and have defined according to its proper definition; therefore, I am not misjudging Carson, but rather challenging his improper definition, which subtly substitutes his *belief* that compatibilism is the superior biblical option for the *actual definition* of compatibilism. Unless one is sufficiently familiar with the actual meaning, such conflation then becomes the adopted, albeit, erroneous definition for many.

Commenting on Carson's practice of improperly defining compatibilism, Paul Gould notes, "As [D.A.] Carson sees it, compatibilism teaches the following: God is utterly sovereign, but his sovereignty never functions to mitigate human responsibility. Human beings are morally responsible creatures, but their moral responsibility never functions to make God absolutely contingent."[5] Gould then says, "Notice, what Carson means by "compatibilism" is just that freedom is compatible with divine sovereignty (not determinism). In other words, he is restating the fact that Scripture upholds both divine sovereignty and human responsibility (and freedom). But, importantly his "compatibilism" isn't compatibilism."[6]

There are two fundamental problems with Carson's definition. First, he presupposes compatibilism in his definition because libertarian freedom, rightly understood, is also compatible with sovereignty.[7] Second, he has

---

4. Carson, *Difficult Doctrine*, 51. See also Carson's book, *A Call to Spiritual Reformation*, 148.

5. Gould, "Why Theology Needs Philosophy," par. 5.

6. Gould, "Why Theology Needs Philosophy," par. 6.

7. Calvinists often juxtapose compatibilism with libertarianism by characterizing libertarian freedom as proffering man having absolute freedom that can, in some degree, operate contrary to God's sovereignty, or libertarian freedom must always have the full range of options, i.e., one can do anything or it does not exist. Neither are actually true as demonstrated in this chapter. Thus, their argument is invalid.

confused his belief that compatibilism is consistent with divine sovereignty with the actual definition of compatibilism, and they are not the same.

According to compatibilism properly defined, determinative antecedents (one's past) provide the desire from which one freely chooses; therefore, it is a predetermined free choosing without a choice between accessible options in the moral moment of decision. Given one's past, one could not have chosen differently than he did in fact choose. This means at the moral moment when a person chooses to love God, hate God, tell the truth or lie, commit rape or rescue a woman from rape, that person acts freely so long as that is his greatest desire, but he cannot act differently given the same past. It is a predetermined free choosing without a choice between accessible options.

In an attempt to parry such undesirable entailments of compatibilism, a compatibilist may say had a person desired to, he could have chosen differently. This is merely a hypothetical otherwise choice rather than an actual otherwise choice.[8] While it is trivially true that if he had desired to act differently he could have, that response does not truly answer the specific question. The real question is, could a compatibly free being have chosen differently in the moral moment of decision given the same past? The answer is no. This is because, given one's past, he could not have had a different greatest desire from which freely to choose differently in the moral moment of decision. For example, could Adam, given his same nature and past have chosen to not sin? No!

Calvinists understandably attempt to maintain the biblical perspective that God does not cause evil. They seek to accomplish this by maintaining that God stands behind good and evil asymmetrically.[9] That is to say, God is related to the presence of evil so that it is not morally chargeable to him but always to secondary causes; conversely, he is related to the presence of good so that it is always morally chargeable to him and only to secondary causes or agents because of his grace. All of which happens within his sovereignty. D.A. Carson writes, "I alone am responsible for that sin . . . God is not to be blamed. But if I do good . . . God's grace has been manifest in my case, and he is to be praised. If this sounds just a bit too convenient for God, my initial response . . . is that according to the Bible this is the only God there is. There is no other."[10]

---

8. More formally known as a hypothetical analytical otherwise choice vs. an actual otherwise choice.

9. Carson, *Divine Sovereignty*, 37. Compatibilism fails to convincingly present this asymmetrical relationship, which libertarianism easily does.

10. Carson, *How Long*, 189.

I agree it is indeed the biblical position that God does not cause sin. I would also contend he does not even desire it in those whom he has created (beyond the desire to permit man the freedom to choose evil), but this biblical position is irreconcilable with Calvinism because of Calvinism's commitment to compatibilism. Since compatibilism entails that the desire from which Adam freely chose to eat of the tree was predetermined by his past—nature—when one continues to trace his past back to its beginning, it leads to God as the one who is *ultimately* responsible for Adam choosing to sin. Although Adam's decision was a free decision reflective of his greatest desire, according to compatibilism's definition of such, he is not the originator of his past from which the desire emanated because that is from God.[11] According to compatibilism, had God not desired for Adam to sin, he would have created him with a different nature and past. Therefore, compatibilism may accomplish leaving man *proximately* responsible for his sin, but it leaves God being *ultimately* responsible, which problem is avoided with libertarian freedom.

This is the position of Calvinism even though not all who don the label Calvinist fully understand compatibilism and most (maybe all) do not speak consistently with its unflinching determinism. For sure, virtually no one lives and talks so that everyone understands the micro-determinism of Calvinism with its compatible view of moral freedom.

Following is a list of what compatibilism includes and excludes (entails)

1. Includes
    a. Voluntariness—one acts freely if he chooses according to his greatest desire.
    b. Man is morally responsible because he freely chose according to his greatest desire.
    c. Micro-determinism—given one's past, no actual accessible options are available other than the one chosen in the moral moment of decision because the greatest desire emanates from determinative antecedents.[12]

---

11. This is not to say that Adam's decisions were not a part of his determinative past because they were, but each of them was also as determined as every other part of his past.

12. The determinative antecedents, and particularly the genesiacal determinate antecedent (ultimately responsible action/actor) may be different in Darwinism, Christianity, or other worldviews, but the degree of determinism is constant.

d. One may have an *experiential sense* of deliberation in decision-making (feeling and thinking he is actually able to choose between options).
   e. The determinism of compatibilism extends to every choice of every person.
   f. Guaranteed outcome—God knows what will happen because he predetermined everything so that everything would be precisely as it is; thus, everything is as God desired.[13]
2. Excludes
   a. Origination—the ability to change the future sequence of events or create alternative possibilities.
   b. A sense of deliberation that includes the possibility of *actually* choosing between accessible options.
   c. Actual possibility in the moral moment of decision to have chosen differently than one did choose—otherwise choice.
   d. Actual range of accessible options—alternative possibilities.
   e. Reliance upon character-influenced choices in order to lessen the deterministic nature of the choice because for one's character to accomplish such necessitates that the person made at least one or more previous choices between accessible options, which is absolutely disallowed by compatibilism.
   f. Being sufficiently defined to mean moral responsibility is compatible with sovereignty. This may be what an individual believes to be true, but it is not the definition of compatibilism.
   g. The individual is *ultimately* responsible for his choice because *ultimate* responsibility must be found at the origin of the beginning of determinative antecedents. From a Christian worldview, the origin is God.[14]

---

13. As noted earlier, the aspects of spiritual realities are not innate to compatibilism; consequently, secularism would exclude God.

14. I first ran across the concept of ultimate responsibility used in the discussion about libertarian and compatible freedom when reading a chapter on this subject by philosopher Robert Kane, "Some Neglected Pathways in the Free Will Labyrinth," 407.

Libertarianism

Man is not determined. He has the actual ability to choose between accessible options, at least in some scenarios. Libertarians contend determinism is *not* compatible with moral responsibility. Man possesses actual otherwise choice and can, therefore, act or refrain in the moral moment of decision, given the same past within a given range of options. Extensivism would argue God endowed man with this ability, which is an aspect of being created in the image of God. God determines the range of options. Adam's range of options prior to the fall was greater than mankind's options after the fall. The range of options present prior to the fall was the result of creative grace.

Fallen man can still choose between options, but the range of options is less than man had prior to the fall. This lessening includes losing the ability to make choices that are inherently righteous or spiritually restorative (making one right with God) based solely on creative grace. In order to make an inherently righteous choice or one that is spiritually restorative, God had to provision redemptive grace—grace enablements.

Regarding the problem of the presence of sin, while compatibilism leaves one with the problem of ultimate responsibility, libertarian freedom does not. First, sin is the result of man's misuse of his freedom, which God did not desire but did comprehend in his plan. Second, it may very well be, and I think it is, one cannot create a libertarian free human being with the option to sin and guarantee he will not misuse his freedom.[15] However, Scripture teaches us God overcomes this dilemma through his coextensive creation-redemption plan.

The following is a list of what libertarianism includes and excludes (entails)

1. Includes

    a. Voluntariness—man acts freely.

    b. Origination—choice can initiate a new sequence of events or alternative possibilities.

    c. One's moral choice may be influenced, even strongly, but not determined. If it is a determined decision, then the individual is not morally responsible for that specific decision.

    d. Efficient cause— "An agent that brings a thing into being or indicates a change."[16] It moves something from potentiality to actu-

---

15. This seems to be the consensus of the philosophical writings I have read on the subject. I am not aware of any who cogently argue it is possible.

16. *Oxford English Dictionary*, s.v. "Efficient Cause."

ality. It involves the idea that one need look no further than the individual for the cause of the action—*agent causation*.[17]

e. Contra-causal power—ability to do otherwise.

f. Actual otherwise choice in the moral moment of decision even with the same past.

g. At times, one's character may occasion substantial or sufficient influence for a choice, thereby lessening the need for as much deliberation as other decisions may require.

h. No guaranteed outcome—God knows contingencies because he is essentially omniscient.[18]

i. The problem of sin is answered in that it is the result of a free choice in which man could have and should have acted differently. Additionally, it may be impossible to create a libertarian free human being with the option to sin (in his range of options) and guarantee he will not misuse his freedom.

j. God overcomes man's misuse of the good gift of libertarian freedom with his coextensive creation-redemption plan.

k. God created man in his image with libertarian freedom; therefore, libertarian freedom is a force. Like all other forces, it is under his sovereign rule, which he can contravene at any time. He allows the misuse of freedom, but if such misuse goes too far, he can and does thwart it; we see this in Scripture in many ways, but particularly in his dealings with rulers like Pharaoh and kings like Nebuchadnezzar.

l. Man is responsible for all choices he makes apart from the use of force, e.g., held at gunpoint or when God overrides his freedom.

m. Only some choices of man must include otherwise choice, thereby allowing for some events to be determined.

2. Excludes

a. The idea that libertarian freedom means a person can do anything; freedom is absolute.

b. The idea that having one's libertarian freedom overruled results in a dispossession of libertarian freedom. God may overrule one's

---

17. Norman Geisler states, "So, I am the efficient cause of my own free actions, but the power of free choice is the means by which I freely act." *Baker Encyclopedia*, s.v. "Evil, Problem Of," 220.

18. Defined in the Authorial Glossary.

freedom in a given moment or man may be imprisoned by another; such actions, however, do not mean the individual no longer has libertarian freedom, but only that he is not morally responsible for that particular action.

c. The idea that libertarian freedom disallows *strongly* influential antecedents.

d. The idea that a change in the range of options eliminates the existence of libertarian freedom because while different seasons of life, birthplaces, familial dynamics, physical and mental capabilities affect the range of options available to the person, they do not necessarily affect the reality of libertarian freedom.

e. The idea man's choice is baseless or random. Libertarian choice may be influenced by reason, emotions, past, character, or circumstances, or a constellation of these, but the decision is not determined by them. That is the result of the free agent, which means he has reasons for his choice, but he is not controlled by them.

f. The idea that fallen man can choose to come to God apart from grace enablements.[19]

The two perspectives contrasted in the fall

Genesis 2 seems unmistakably clear in presenting Adam as having a choice between obedience and blessing (Gen 2:16) and disobedience and judgment (Gen 2:17). Then when Adam and Eve did eat (Gen 3:6), God rightly judged them and they died; consequently, they lost all the blessings God had granted them while living in the garden because he held them responsible for their actions (Gen 3:11–13, 16–19, 22–24).

According to compatibilism, Adam and Eve freely chose to eat of the tree and sin. Equally true of compatibilism is that given their nature and past, they could not have refrained from sinning because the desire from which they freely chose was a predetermined desire given their past and nature (Calvinists often omit this component of compatibilism). Consequently, while God did not cause the sin, he did desire they freely choose to sin. This is evidenced by the fact he set in place their past and nature, from

---

19. As stated before, such spiritual things as this are not innate to the essence of libertarianism, but they are essential to the perspective of Extensivism I am describing and they do not change the core concepts of libertarian freedom. Further, the effects of the fall are such that Adam could not be restored to his right relationship with God had God not provided sufficiently for him to do so in his redemptive grace.

which inexorably emanated the predetermined desire to freely choose to eat of the tree and sin. Consistent with compatibilism, had God desired for them to refrain from sinning, he would have given them a nature and past emanating that desire from which to freely choose.

According to libertarianism, Adam and Eve freely chose to sin and eat of the tree. Equally true of libertarianism is given their past, which includes their nature, they could have and should have refrained from sinning because they had the ability to choose to eat or refrain, and whatever they did choose, they could have chosen differently. God's desire for them to refrain is evidenced in that he endowed them with the ability to live in holy fellowship with him, blessing them by placing them in the garden and warning them to not sin and of the consequence if they did sin. Even though he knew they would misuse their freedom and sin, he never desired that for them since he is essentially holy and good (1 Pet 1:15; 3 John 11) and is pleased when his creation acts righteously (Heb 13:16); therefore, he always desires holiness and righteousness.

The two perspectives contrasted in the "gospels"

According to compatibilism, given one's past and fallen nature, man can only freely choose to reject the gospel; he not only *will not* believe, he *cannot will to* believe. In other words, he will not believe because given his past, nature, he cannot believe. For him to be able to respond with anything but disbelief and rebellion, God must work graciously to restore the ability to choose freely to believe the gospel. In Calvinism, this restorative act is referred to by different names such as regeneration, new birth, quickening, or renovation; it is determinative.

God performs this grace work only upon the unconditionally elect through selective and irresistible regeneration (efficacious grace), which inevitably results in the person freely exercising faith. Accordingly, the restorative act of regeneration precedes and inescapably results in faith.[20] Once this regenerative work is accomplished, the person cannot disbelieve any more than he could have believed prior to the grace work. Thus, as with Adam, while the individual freely chooses, it is a predetermined free choosing without the possibility of choosing otherwise.

According to libertarianism, given one's past and fallen nature, man can only freely choose to reject the gospel; he not only *will not* believe, he

---

20. Some Calvinists do not believe that regeneration precedes faith, but they still believe, given compatibilism, there is a selectively provided determinative essential work of grace that must take place prior to the elect exercising faith.

cannot will to believe.[21] For him to be able to respond with anything but disbelief and rebellion, God must work graciously to restore man's ability to make righteous and spiritually restorative decisions such as choosing freely to believe the gospel. This restorative act of God is through grace enablements, which flow from God's redemptive grace. The work of restorative grace is provisioned for everyone and is not determinative. By this I mean, had God not provided for man's redemption, man's spiral to hell and judgment would have been unalterable.

Grace enablements restore fallen man to the point at which, while still in his sins, he is enabled to either believe the gospel or continue to reject the gospel, only now with a more full understanding of what he is actually believing or rejecting (John 12:35–36). Accordingly, God's gracious liberating work precedes faith, and faith is both a free and undetermined choice, which if exercised results in regeneration and salvation. Thus, as with Adam, God desires that man choose to trust him, but he can still choose to disbelieve and walk away.

In summary: Calvinism's work of grace is limited to the unconditionally elect, determinative in the outcome, and provides so that the elect will believe. This work of grace changes the elect's past or gives them a new nature that emanates new desires—compatibilism. Extensivism's work of grace is for every person, non-determinative in the outcome, and provides so that everyone may choose to believe or reject God's salvation while still in their sins. This work of grace restores man's ability to make spiritually restorative decisions; this was lost in the fall.

I suggest that everyone reading Scripture without theological importations sees the clear and ubiquitous message that people have otherwise choice, and God conditions blessing or judgment upon the choice a person makes. Extensivism contends this is a component of what it means to be created in the image of God. The libertarian perspective is the only view that consistently communicates that God redemptively loves all of his creation (John 1:9, 29; 3:16; Titus 2:11).

---

21. This is not essential to the philosophical definition of libertarian freedom, but it is according to what I believe about how libertarian freedom operates within Extensivism; because I believe the fall affected man so profoundly that his range of options changed from what man had prior to the fall. Someone else could believe in libertarian freedom and view the effect of the fall differently. Specifically, I believe in total depravity, by which I mean the fall affected man extensively, and thereby man is incapable of coming to God without God's redemptive grace—grace enablements—which God provides for all. This does not mean that man lost all sensibilities regarding God (Gen 3:8–13; Rom 1:18–23).

In consideration of the gospel of John 20:31

The Apostle John gave as his reason for writing his gospel "so that you may believe that Jesus is the Christ, the Son of God; and that believing you may have life in His name" (John 20:31). It seems clear that "you" includes anyone who reads John's gospel. Now, why would John write, or more importantly, why would God inspire him to write this in order for people to read, believe, and be saved if God knows the non-elect can never read and believe? Moreover, not even the elect can believe prior to regeneration since that is monergistic and man is totally passive? The Synod of Dort states, "Men are chosen to faith and to the obedience of faith, holiness, etc., therefore, election is the fountain of every saving good; from which proceed faith."[22] As a result, *no one* can merely read John's writings or any Scripture and believe unto salvation because prior to regeneration the process of salvation is monergistic—accomplished by God alone; faith is the freely exercised result of that work of grace.

Yet, Jesus continually called on people to believe so they would not die in their sins. "Therefore I said to you that you will die in your sins; for unless you believe that I am *He*, you will die in your sins" (John 8:24). The obvious conclusion to draw from this statement is that they desperately need to believe, Jesus truly desires that they believe and they can believe in order not to die in their sins.

This is contrary to the Calvinist secret that while it is true if one does not believe he will die in his sins, the corresponding truth is Jesus is telling them to do what he knows they cannot do unless they are the elect.[23] See also Matthew 11:20–24; 23:37; Luke 23:34; John 5:40–47; 11:42.

---

22. Canons of Dort, First Head of Doctrine, article 9.

23. Regarding unconditional election and selective regeneration, the non-elect really cannot be saved even though they hear "whosoever will may come." Calvinists often emphasize that is not something to be talked about with the unsaved. For example Lewis Sperry Chafer says, "The entire theme concerns those only who are regenerated and should never be presented to, or even discussed in the presence of, the unsaved." *Systematic Theology*, vol. 3, 172.

8

Can Human Acts like Prayers and Childrearing *Really* Affect Someone's Salvation?

BOTH CALVINISTS AND EXTENSIVISTS speak as though things such as prayers, trials, miracles, preaching, testimonies, child rearing, education, and other influences play a vital part in salvation; these, along with a host of other influences may be categorized as events. It seems as though we all really mean these kinds of events play a similar role in God's salvation plan. However, such is not the case. The only similarity is that Calvinists and Extensivists use the same words, but the way Calvinists use these words are essentially dissimilar to the way they are normally used and used by Extensivists. Calvinists themselves tend to obscure the real differences.

These events may be classified as either indefinite or definite. By indefinite, I refer to events in which human involvement can actually affect the outcome. This is in contrast to definite events in which God has predetermined that human involvement does not affect the outcome. Extensivism recognizes Scripture includes both definite and indefinite events, whereas Calvinism recognizes only definite—determined—events. The difference between these two viewpoints is Extensivism actually believes these indefinite events really do play a part in God's salvation plan.[1] Keep in mind, while it is quite common for Calvinists to speak libertarianly, Calvinism utterly rejects man having libertarian moral freedom. Speaking libertarianly is especially misrepresentative of Calvinism's determinism.

Calvinism's belief in unconditional election and compatibilism, wherein everything is micro-determined, necessitates a different meaning than is normally understood when speaking of the correlation between events and a person's salvation.[2] It requires understanding that while such events may be a part of the process of God's predetermined elective plan to bring his

---

1. Indefinite does not mean they are unknown to God, but only that these events are contingencies; they are not determined and, therefore, did not have to happen.

2. One may also add the other elements of Calvinism's decretal theology.

unconditionally elect into redemption, these events do not, in any way, play a role that includes the idea they could have been different or resulted in a different outcome. That is to say, all direct or suggestive talk by Calvinists of how pivotal events, someone's prayers, or a person's involvement in an individual's life played a non-determined role in someone's salvation is misleading. It misrepresents the true meaning of Calvinism. Unfortunately, and quite confusingly, that is how they are most often portrayed.

In contrast, according to Extensivism God comprehends libertarian freedom in his salvation plan so that these indefinite events can play an undetermined part; they can even play a part that actually affects the outcome. I refer to the relationship of these events as being *constitutionally, organically,* and *substantially* related. This is in contrast to Calvinism's determinism in which nothing *actually* matters in an effective way but unconditional election and its partner, selective irresistible grace. Here is the way I define the relationship of indefinite events in God's salvation plan:

Constitutionally related

Constitutionally related speaks to the *nature of God's salvation plan* wherein grace enablements are essentially, sequentially, and operationally incorporated into the structure of God's plan.[3] Since God's work of salvation is a grace work, every aspect of the plan exists and functions according to his grace; therefore, such things as prayer, witnessing, listening with understanding of the gospel, other indefinite events, and exercising faith are not reducible to purely human works or virtues. For them to be merely human works, they would need to exist outside of God's grace work of salvation. That is to say, they would need to be unconstitutionally related to his salvation plan. Since they do not so exist, they are grace components in God's redemptive plan (Rom 3:28; 4:1–5).

Organically related

Something being organically related speaks to the *complex relationship between libertarian freedom and God's pre-conversion grace enablements* that work according to his salvific plan of grace so that the choices of a libertarian free being really do matter in a person's salvation. They have a *systemic arrangement and interaction* with other parts of God's plan. Specifically, they

---

3. By grace enablements I mean things which God has to do in order to make salvation available to all. See an explanation of some of these enablements in the glossary.

play an actual non-determined and non-meritorious role in one's salvation. The outcome of this organic relationship is that many factors can actually be involved in the salvation of a person, salvation is available to every person, and man is saved by non-determined and non-meritorious faith (John 4:39–42; 11:42, 45; Eph 2:8–9).

For example, we may say the prayers of a grandmother were instrumental in a person's salvation; by this we mean if the grandmother had not prayed, which she could have chosen to do, the person may not have been saved at that time. The influence of the grandmother's prayers in the gospel encounter is solely because God included such non-determined components in his salvation plan. These components have an organic relationship to other aspects of God's salvation plan; they do in fact matter (John 17:20–21; Rom 2:4; Titus 2:1–11; 3:1–8; 1 John 2:2).

An example of such a constitutional and organic relationship may be illustrated by considering a flower. We give the name flower to a particular plant that includes certain and various components in its structure; being organic means there is a systemic arrangement and interaction between the various components. Included in these components are things such as roots, stem, bud, petals, sepal, stamen, and pistil. Some of these are *substantially* related so that if they did not exist, the flower would not exist.

Substantially (substantively) and insubstantially related

Substantially and insubstantially related speaks to the *relationship between things, people, personal experiences, and other events as part of the process and the process's final product*. Something substantially related indicates if it were not present in the process, the product would be different, or at least would likely be different. In contrast, components that are insubstantially related would not change the product by their absence. Given libertarian freedom, some events (indefinite events) may or may not be present because these relationships are not predeterminately fixed. In Extensivism some events are substantially related to salvation, but in Calvinism, all events are determined (there are no indefinite events but only definite) and can only be insubstantially related because they cannot change, nor can they change the process or the product.

To clarify, even though strictly impossible in a compatibly free world, if some events were not there, the product, such as unconditional election, would still take place in precisely the same way. It is unconditional. If Calvinism accepts that indefinite events exist and are substantially related to one's salvation, then things like unconditional election are really organically related to them so that election incorporates these grace contributors in the production of the end product. This means the abandonment of compatibilism and transforming unconditional election into conditional election.

In Extensivism, given libertarian freedom, some events are substantially related because if they were not a part of the process in the way they are (and that could have been the case), something different would be happening; therefore, the result could be different in various scenarios (Matt 11:20–24).

Calvinists and Extensivists may speak similarly about salvation, but this is because Calvinists are constantly speaking libertarianly about people being saved, praying, witnessing, and events substantially affecting one's life. I can only ask my Calvinist brothers and sisters to be as resolutely committed to speaking determinatively (so that all understand, including the Calvinist speaking) as they are in pedestaling compatibilism and denouncing libertarian freedom for depending on something other than grace.

Then, we can have meaningful discussions about the merits of Calvinism and Extensivism. And people listening can make a clear and informed decision about what label they wear.

9

Calvinism: Origin of Sin and Offer of Salvation

CALVINISTS BELIEVE MAN IS free to choose according to his greatest desire. For example, Jonathan Edwards believed in what he called "strength of the motive."[1] He said concerning such, "I suppose the will is always determined by the strongest motive."[2] Therefore, Edwards argued one freely chooses to act according to his "strongest motive." Regarding the nature of free choice, he also said it is "the ability to do what we will, or according to our pleasure."[3]

Consequently, according to Edwards, man's freedom to choose is determined by his nature and his desires. In other words, man is free to choose to do his greatest desire. Of course, this is the Calvinist view of free will as defined by what is now known as compatibilism. It is important to note three very important components of this view. First, the nature or past from which the desire emanates is not chosen.[4] Second, the desire is not chosen. Third, the unchosen desire is determinative of what the free choice will be.

The Calvinist believes man is free to choose according to his greatest desire but not otherwise. Therefore, his free choice is actually determined by his desire. For example, according to Edwards, sinful man will always freely choose to do his greatest desire, which is to sin. This greatest desire is a part of his nature. Fallen man will never choose to follow Christ without first having his nature changed to emanate new desires; this is the basis for the Calvinist position that regeneration precedes faith.[5]

---

1. Edwards, *Freedom of the Will*, 143.
2. Edwards, *Freedom of the Will*, 143.
3. Edwards, *Freedom of the Will*, 11.
4. Although compatibilists rightly claim their choices are a part of their past, they should also recognize all their choices were as determined as any other part of their past.
5. Such change may be called renovation, quickening, or regeneration.

This view of freedom highlights the compatibilist's inability to satisfactorily explain the origin of the first sin in a way that fully exculpates God. Because if man chose according to his greatest desire, and man chose to sin, then sin must have been his greatest desire. This leads to the disturbing question of where did the desire come from? It had to ultimately come from God since God created everything. As a result, according to Calvinism, God gave the desire (or one may say the antecedents that produced the desire), which unavoidably birthed the choice to sin. This desire, or at least its determinative antecedents, (as a part of creation) God called "very good" (Gen 1:31).

Therefore, God must have, in some significant sense, desired for man to sin or else he would not have given him a nature or past emanating such a desire (this desire being more than merely the desire to create, which all recognize). This is one of the disquieting realities of Calvinism. In the same way, when God desires people to be saved, he must choose to regenerate in order to give them a new nature with new desires so they will freely choose to exercise faith in Christ.

When the concept of compatibilism is applied to the first sin, the Calvinist quandary is equally apparent because it results in Lucifer choosing to sin because of his nature or his greatest desire before sin existed. His choice could not have been from preexisting internal sin nor a direct external temptation since both he and his environment were directly created by God, lest one posit God creating sin or tempting one to sin, which is impossible (Jas 1:13). Therefore, it seems inescapable that according to Calvinism, God gave Lucifer either an environment, nature, or past that would inviolably produce a desire to sin, from which would come the free choice to sin. If Calvinists respond that Lucifer (or man) could have chosen not to sin, then they are espousing libertarianism, and compatibilism becomes simply an incongruent post-fall development of Calvinism. With man, this would entail God redeeming a different being than the sinner in the Garden.

It is true Calvinists are often clear and passionate about their denial that God *caused* sin, which I appreciate; further, they are correct to deny Calvinism teaches God *directly* caused sin, which is consistent with a compatibilist understanding of freedom. Still, their answer to how this denial fully exonerates God, within compatible freedom, from being the *ultimate* cause and truly desiring man to sin is inchoate and unconvincing and leads to the Calvinist retreat, "it is a mystery." In other words, they do not usually want to implicate God in desiring, willing, or orchestrating sin, and rightfully so, but the logic of their system seems to inevitably lead to that inescapable reality. Some Calvinists are quite forthright regarding God's role in the first sin and sin in general by not only their belief system but their candid avowals as well.

For example, R.C. Sproul Jr.'s comment that "every Bible-believing Christian must conclude at least that God in some sense desired that man would fall into sin . . . I am not accusing God of sinning; I am suggesting that he created sin."[6] He further "describes God as 'the Culprit' that caused Eve to sin in the garden."[7] Then there is Gordon Clark's assessment, "As God cannot sin, so in the next place, God is not responsible for sin, even though he decrees it."[8] Again, Clark in response to Arminians asseverates, "I wish very frankly and pointedly to assert that if a man gets drunk and shoots his family, it was the will of God that he should do so . . . In Ephesians 1:11 Paul tells us that God works all things, not some things only, after the counsel of his own will."[9] Contrary to Clark, Ephesians does not say that God wills—determinatively desires—everything, but rather that "he works all things after the counsel of his will" (Eph 1:11).

William G.T. Shedd, writing about God's choice regarding the origin of sin and allowing sin to continue, says, "The permissive decree as related to the origin of sin *presents a difficulty* that does not exist in reference to the continuance of sin . . . *an inscrutable mystery*"[10] (italics added). Of course, the origin of sin is a "difficulty" and "inscrutable mystery" only because of Calvinism's compatibilist view of free will. I would add to this, their limited meaning and understanding of the nature and operation of foreknowledge with regard to salvation further influences their retreats to "it is a mystery".

The Calvinists' inability to reconcile satisfactorily their view of moral freedom, the origin of sin, God's election of the saved, and reprobation of the damned with the scripturally revealed character of God forces them to retreat to an incomprehensible judgment, i.e., mystery. But it is Calvinism that creates Calvinism's mystery. Calvinists' desire to make election unconditional and regeneration monergistic creates a God that is disharmonious with God as presented in Scripture, and once again their understanding of salvation is seen to be inextricably connected to their view concerning the origin of sin. I am denying the legitimacy of the Calvinists' response that Calvinism is true even though it is impossible to understand how God is not, in a serious sense, implicated in at least desiring the origin of sin and mercilessly predetermining *some* to spend eternity in hell who could have gone to heaven had God desired that for them. Calvin is unabashed in the defense of his views:

6. Sproul, Jr., *Almighty in Authority*, 53–54.
7. Sproul, Jr., *Almighty in Authority*, 51.
8. Clark, *God and Evil*, 40.
9. Clark, *God and Evil*, 27.
10. Shedd, *Calvinism: Pure and Mixed*, 95.

CALVINISM: ORIGIN OF SIN AND OFFER OF SALVATION

> Many professing a desire to defend the Deity from an invidious charge admit the doctrine of election, but deny that any one is reprobated (Bernard, in Die Ascensionis, Serm 2). This they do ignorantly and childishly, since there could be no election without its opposite reprobation. God is said to set apart those whom he adopts for salvation. It were most absurd to say, that he admits others fortuitously, or that they by their industry acquire what election alone confers on a few. Those, therefore, whom God passes by he reprobates, and that for no other cause but because he is *pleased* to exclude them from the inheritance which he predestines to his children[11] (italics added).

I maintain all consistent Calvinists inevitably believe in double predestination, arguments to the contrary notwithstanding, yet most shy from the forthrightness of Calvin. They either believe God actively predestined some to hell, as Calvin does, or he did so by choosing not to offer what would have surely delivered them from hell to heaven, which is unconditional election and selective regeneration. Calvin refers to this cold inescapable reality as the product of God's wish, pleasure, and counsel.[12] This is a disquieting reality of Calvinism.

All of the euphemizing in the world will not purge Calvinism of their unbiblical view that people are saved because God desired for them to be and people are in hell for the same reason. This is true even if *some* Calvinists continue to resist admitting it because according to Calvinism if God pleased, not only could everyone have been saved, but they would have been saved. Calvinism asks us to believe God chose eternal torment for the vast majority of his creation (Matt 7:13–14). They want us to rejoice in a God who desires and chooses for the vast majority of his creation to go to hell when he could have redeemed them.

I concede such understanding to indeed be God according to Calvinism, but utterly reject such a portrait being reflective of Scripture. Where is the plethora of Scriptures where God expresses his desire for the vast majority of his creation to perish in eternal torment, and this with *equal* clarity and abundance as those Scriptures declaring his indefatigable, sacrificial love, and desire that all repent and be saved? I suggest they do not exist and for good reason.

Regarding human freedom, R.C. Sproul's Calvinism sends him retreating to "it is a mystery." He says, "Predestination seems to cast a shadow on the very heart of human freedom. If God has decided our destinies from

---

11. Calvin, *Institutes of the Christian Religion*, 225–26.
12. Calvin, *Institutes of the Christian Religion*, 210.

all eternity, (unconditionally) that strongly suggests that our free choices are but charades, empty exercises in predetermined placating. It is as though God wrote the script for us in concrete and we are merely carrying out his scenario."[13] I must admit, although I adamantly disagree with his Calvinism, I appreciate and admire such candor.

Sproul unveils the truth of God's love for the non-elect saying, "It was certainly loving of God to predestine the salvation of his people, those the Bible calls the 'elect or chosen ones.' *It is the non-elect that are the problem. If some people are not elected unto salvation then it would seem that God is not all that loving toward them. For them it seems that it would have been more loving of God not to have allowed them to be born. That may indeed be the case*"[14] (italics added). This is what I mean when I argue that God's salvific love for the non-elect is virtually indistinguishable from indifference or hate. Various distinctions proffered by Calvinists that supposedly mitigate this reality are, eternally speaking, merely distinctions without a difference; how things play out eternally is what *really* matters.

Calvinists are very clear at times that sin entered into the world and people spend eternity in hell because God made a voluntary decision for them to be there, which means he could have chosen, if it pleased him, for them not to be there. Shedd says permission to allow sin "is one that occurs by a voluntary decision of God, which he need not have made, had he so pleased. He might have decided not to permit sin; in which case it would not have entered the universe."[15] Augustine, speaking of such permission, said, "And of course his permission is not unwilling but willing."[16]

They say nothing of God's decision to disallow sin in the universe necessitating the disallowance of the existence of man or Lucifer, an understanding which is harmonious with a compatible view of freedom. According to a compatibilist perspective, God could have created Lucifer, Adam, and Eve with different natures, emanating different desires, and they could have and would have existed without sin. Once more, the ever-present Calvinistically-generated impasse that God, to a serious measure, must have desired them to sin. Shedd does attempt to exonerate God from sin by saying, "Nothing but the spontaneity of will can produce the sin; and God does not work in the will to cause evil spontaneity. The certainty of sin by a

---

13. Sproul, *Chosen by God*, 37.
14. Sproul, *Chosen by God*, 21.
15. Shedd, *Calvinism: Pure and Mixed*, 94.
16. Shedd, *Calvinism: Pure and Mixed*, 94–95.

permissive decree is an *insoluble mystery* for the finite mind."[17] (my emphasis on insoluble mystery).

With regard to Socrates' reference to God and sin in *The Republic*, Shedd's belief that God must have desired sin to enter the lives of his creation is even more apparent.

> While evil in his [Socrates] view, does not originate in God, and is punished by God, it is not, as in Revelation, *under the absolute control of God, in such sense that it could be prevented by him.* The *power to prevent sin* is implied in its permission. No one can be said to permit what he cannot prevent. *Sin is preventable*, by the exercise of a greater degree of that same spiritual efficiency by which the will was inclined to holiness in creation. *God did not please to exert this degree in the instance of the fallen angels and man*, and thus sin was possible[18] (italics added).

He does not require of God that angels and man would not have been created as moral beings in order to preclude sin, but only God choosing to grant "a greater degree of that same spiritual efficiency." Once again, it seems according to Calvinism, God desired preventable sin. Even without such statements, this truth is entailed in a compatible view of moral freedom. Shedd says, "The reason for the permission of sin was a manifestation of certain divine attributes which could not have been manifested otherwise."[19] Then he lists things like mercy, compassion, the suffering of Christ, justice, and holiness, all to the glory of God. Similarly, D.A. Carson attempts to distance God from being responsible for sin:

> If compatibilism is true and if God is good ... then it must be the case that God stands behind good and evil in somewhat different ways; that is, he stands behind good and evil *asymmetrically*. To put it bluntly, God stands behind evil in such a way that not even evil takes place outside the bounds of his sovereignty, *yet the evil is not morally chargeable to him: it is always chargeable to secondary agents, to secondary causes* ... In other words, if I sin, I cannot possibly do so outside of the bounds of God's sovereignty ... but I alone am responsible for that sin ... God is not to be blamed[20] (only asymmetrically is italicized in the quote).

---

17. Shedd, *Dogmatic Theology*, vol. 1, 420.
18. Shedd, *Dogmatic Theology*, vol. 1, 420–21.
19. Shedd, *Dogmatic Theology*, vol. 1, 421.
20. Carson, *How Long*, 189.

I commend him for noting the biblical teaching that God is related to good and evil asymmetrically. Nevertheless, such a recognition and declaration does nothing to demonstrate how such is the case, ultimately speaking, if compatibilism is true. If compatibilism is true, the best that can be hoped for is man is justifiably proximately responsible, which leaves God inarguably being ultimately responsible. The reliance upon secondary causation to exonerate God is only successful in a libertarian scenario where man is the efficient cause with the actual ability to have chosen differently than he did in the moral moment of decision.

Therefore, the inescapable truth of Calvinism is God could have prevented sin, and while he may not have been the proximate cause—or direct cause—he inescapably desired it and, therefore, sin exists. This is because within a compatible system of freedom, reliance upon secondary, tertiary, quaternary, or even quinary causes fails to palliate or remove the fact that God by free choice is ultimately responsible for man's choice to sin, which could have been different had such pleased him.

Therefore, he desired all the horrors of sin, rebellion against him, untold ghastly violence, dreadful death, and the drowning sea of tears deluging the lives and homes of his creation; such desire is not satisfactorily explained by resorting to his permissive will because the activities of his permissive will are as determined in Calvinism as any other aspect of his will, given decretal theology and compatibilism.

10

Extensivism: Origin of Sin and Offer of Salvation

EXTENSIVISTS BELIEVE SCRIPTURE TEACHES God gave Adam and Eve the true ability to choose to sin or not to sin. God gave that freedom, which is good, and man misused it, which is a sin. Man is a libertarian free moral agent with the ability to choose to sin or not to sin, which means he is the efficient cause of sin. This understanding avoids the intrinsic revelatory problems of Calvinism and compatibilism with regard to the origin of sin and God desiring people to sin or be in hell.

While man, nor anything else for that matter, would not exist if God did not desire to create him, the desire of God that plagues Calvinism is not merely the desire to create so that man and things can exist in time. Rather, it is in regard to what precisely God's desire to create included, including the state and nature of man. According to Extensivism, God's desire to create man included a desire that man would not misuse his freedom to sin, but God provisioned sufficiently for such a reality. God always knew man would sin, and fallen man would continue to misuse his freedom, but God always desires man to walk in holiness. Knowing man would sin, God out of love provisioned for that eventuality in his coextensive creation-redemption plan for everyone, which further evidences his desire for all of his creation to live holy lives.

God chose to create man in his own image, which includes giving man the ability to choose otherwise. To wit, whatever Adam did choose in the moral moment of decision, he could have chosen differently; he could have acted or refrained. The same is true today within the still available options. Furthermore, the meaning of concepts like love, mercy, compassion, worship, and righteousness are inextricably connected to otherwise choice and consequently emanate from the freedom to act or refrain. We reject the notion that deciding is synonymous with desire as illustrated in the life of Paul. He said, "For what I am doing, I do not understand; for I am not practicing what I *would* like to *do,* but I am doing the very thing I hate. But if I do the very thing I do not want *to do*, I agree with the Law, *confessing* that the Law is good" (Rom 7:15–16).[1]

It is the essential foreknowledge of God, which includes exhaustive eternal knowledge of contingencies in time that resolves the problem of how to establish the certainty that man would sin even though he had been created in holiness and did not have to sin. God's foreknowledge can assure certainty without Calvinism's causality and eternal necessity.[2] For the question, "If God knew we would sin with otherwise choice, why not create man without free will?" The answer is that man created without libertarian free will is not man created in God's image. God's love toward man is a free choice—God could have chosen not to create man with whom to share his love—in like manner, man is designed by God so that he may choose to love, worship, or follow God or not.

To say man freely chose to love and worship God but actually could not choose to do otherwise is contrary to the most obvious teaching of Scripture as well as human understanding and application of those terms in real life. Imagine a wedding with a groom standing at the altar by his bride. The pastor says, "In taking this woman you hold by your hand to be your lawful wedded wife before God and these witnesses, do you promise to love her, cherish her, forsaking all others and cleave only to her so long as you both shall live?" Then the man responds, "I do, but of course that is all I can say; I must say yes because that is my nature." Besides everyone being aghast, I suspect the honeymoon would lack some honey. But that is the nature of Calvinism and compatibilism. The choice is free to be sure, but it is equally a determined free choice

The very thing that makes love so romantic, mercy so tender, compassion so endearing, marriage so enchanting, and commitment so noble is the reality that the person could have chosen to do otherwise. The groom could have loved another, but he chose this woman; mercy could have been withheld, compassion denied, marriage rejected, and commitment forsaken. Defining free choice in a manner that excludes otherwise choice in the actual moment of decision is almost indistinguishable from animal instinct. The only differences are concepts like the experience of deliberation, which

---

1. Commentator C. E. B. Cranfield said, "The more seriously a Christian strives to live from grace and to submit to the discipline of the gospel, the more sensitive he becomes to . . . the fact that even his very best acts and activities are disfigured by the egotism which is still powerful within him—and no less evil because it is often more subtly disguised than formerly." *Commentary on Romans*, vol. 1, 358.

2. Eternal necessity in the sense that within Calvinism, God knows what man will choose because he knows and governs by deterministically making everything in time to happen precisely as it does.

in reality does not affect the choice set by determinative antecedents any more than if one compares it to determined instinct.

I contend Scripture teaches and humans quotidianly act in concert with libertarianism and not compatibilism. This truth is even pervasive in Calvinists' writings that are often reticent to lucidly display the essence of compatibilism. Similar to the aforementioned question, some then ask, why did God not create man so he could not sin? The answer is because to create man in such a way so as to guarantee that he *would* not sin (so long as sin was within the range of options) or *could* not sin means that God would not have created man as man—endowed with libertarian freedom.

There are many reasons the possibility to sin does not exist with God, but suffice it to say, Scripture teaches this truth (Jas 1:13), and God's nature makes such an actual impossibility. If God sinned, he would not be God, and if God can cease to exist, he was never God. Dissimilarly, man can sin and still be man, albeit unrighteous man. God has no part in creating sin, creating a past that inviolably predetermines a desire to sin from which man will freely choose to sin, creating sin's eternal necessity, or an environment conducive to sin, but rather always desires righteousness (Hab 1:13; Heb 6:18; Jas 1:13 and 1 Pet 1:15–16).

God created man in his image as a free moral agent with true freedom to choose righteousness or sin. Therefore, God created freedom, and by every measure, freedom is good (Gen 1:31). It is the misuse of freedom that birthed sin (Gen 3:1–6). That does not make freedom evil or the one who gave it responsible for evil or even desirous of such eventuality in light of other *actual* possible eventualities. Man is the efficient cause of sin, which means from a libertarian perspective it is nonsense to ask who or what caused man to sin; however it is highly relevant in light of a compatible perspective. Norman Geisler succinctly says, "God made the *fact* of freedom; we are responsible for the *acts* of freedom."[3]

Quite unlike Calvinism, under the terms of which God must have in some regard beyond the desire to create man desired man to sin, Extensivists contend God desired to create man as a truly free moral agent, with otherwise choice as God has; desiring only that he would choose to live righteously. God never did nor does he now desire sin. He is holy and only and always desires holiness. God's choice to permit sin temporarily was not God's true desire for man any more than it is his desire for man to continue in sin, but neither is God's desire for righteousness to be thwarted or overcome by man's sin.

---

3. Geisler, *Chosen But Free*, 23.

In God's desire to create a truly holy man, he knew free otherwise choice was required. This is because holiness and sin are the results of a choice between two accessible options rather than a consequence of a predetermined free choosing in which man could not have chosen differently. Accordingly, God knew man would sin, although he did not desire for man to sin in the beginning nor does he desire him to sin now. What he did and does desire for man is as a free moral agent, man would choose to live righteously rather than sinfully, which is the only real kind of righteous choice since merely instinctively driven beings do not choose righteously or sinfully since they have no *actual* choice. Therefore, God created man with an eternal redemptive plan in mind that affords fallen man a real free choice between accessible options, whereby man may choose to remain in his sin or by faith in Christ choose to be truly righteous, loving, and worshipful.

The serpent's temptation of Adam and Eve gives every indication of being one in which man could obey or disobey God, and God desired obedience (Gen 2:17). It also seems clear the serpent's effective temptation was a direct challenge to God's call for man to live by faith which was based on God's worthiness and the essential dissimilarity between God and man; God knows everything infinitely. This includes even the nature of sin, although he has never sinned. In contrast, man only knew about sin by trusting what God said prior to choosing to sin (Gen 3:5). This limited dimension of man's knowledge could also include knowledge about death (Gen 2:17), sin's temporary pleasures (Heb 11:25), and the deceitfulness of sin (Heb 3:13), as well as all of the immitigable suffering from sin and death; these things God knows exhaustively without needing to experience sin.[4]

Extensivists contend the desire of God was to create man in his own image, a man who would express true love, righteousness, and compassion as God did to man. God knew that unlike him, man would not choose to do that but rather he would use his freedom to sin, which God did not desire. God's redemption plan from eternity past included his determination to provide salvation for all through the death of Christ, grace enablements, and providing man a real choice between following Christ or remaining in his sin.

Theologians and philosophers recognize there seem to be things that are truly impossible even for God; these fall into two categories. The first is that which is logically impossible, and the second is that which is contrary to

---

4. In heaven, after having experienced sin and redemption, man will be more like God having learned what God already knew about sin. This process includes God's protective work (John 10:28) and a change in the range of options available to man. Then man will use his freedom only for righteousness and never misuse free will again. See chapter 22 "Is Libertarian Free Will Eternal."

his nature. Shedd says, "God can do anything that does not imply a logical impossibility. A logical impossibility means that the predicate is contradictory to the subject."[5] Regarding those actions that are contrary to God's nature, Shedd comments, "Again, God cannot do anything inconsistent with the perfection of Divine nature. Under this category fall the instances mentioned in Heb. 6:18, 'It is impossible for God to lie;' 2 Tim. 2:13, 'He cannot deny himself;' and James 1:13, 'God cannot be tempted.'"[6]

Others, with whom I agree, would add to Shedd's list the impossibility of creating true human freedom with otherwise choice with the guarantee that man will not use it for evil (when that option is available as it was in creation). Another actual impossibility is to force man into heaven against his will because to do so would destroy man as God's image bearer; therefore, the redeemed would not be the same created being who freely chose to sin, thereby making God's redemption only a partial redemption of man.[7] In part, this is why it is fallacious reasoning to argue people would, in the end, be glad if God forced them into heaven because forcing them into heaven means they would cease to be human.

As a part of his free will defense, Alvin Plantinga argues what he refers to as "transworld depravity." He summarizes, "What is important about the idea of transworld depravity is that if a person suffers from it, then it wasn't within God's power to actualize any world in which that person is significantly free but does no wrong—that is, a world in which he produces moral good but no moral evil."[8] He further notes, "It is logically *possible* that every person suffers from transworld depravity."[9] Regarding libertarian freedom, Peter Kreeft comments, "One gives a polish to a table, or a pony to a schoolboy, but one does not give three sides to a triangle or free will to a human being. Free will is a part of our essence. There can be no human being without it. The alternative to free will is not being a human but an animal or a machine."[10]

---

5. This can include things like making a material spirit or an irrational man. Shedd, *Dogmatic Theology*, vol. 1, 359. Other examples of actual impossibilities include things such as two mountains without a valley.

6. Shedd, *Dogmatic Theology*, vol. 1, 360.

7. In Calvinism, although man technically freely believes unto salvation, everything prior to choosing or acting is predeterminately forced upon man, which is undeniable according to compatibilism, monergism, unconditional election, and irresistible grace; all of which predeterminately precede an unalterable free exercise of faith.

8. Plantinga, *God, Freedom, and Evil*, 48.

9. Plantinga, *God, Freedom, and Evil*, 48.

10. Kreeft and Tacelli, *Handbook of Christian Apologetics*, 3.

Accordingly, people are in hell because they are born sinners, practicing sinners, and they rejected an accessible opportunity to freely choose to be delivered from hell to heaven (Luke 13:3). In the Garden of Eden, God provided an environment in which man could freely choose to walk in relationship with him or walk away from him. In like manner, God provides a salvific environment in which man can choose to accept an opportunity to come back to him or reject him (Rom 10:9). Man chose to leave his relationship with God, and man must choose to return; without such choice, what is redeemed from sin is not what was lost in sin. Man as man is destroyed and only an ersatz man is redeemed.

Calvinism's commitment to compatibilism means man chose to sin, but he could not have chosen not to sin; man is in heaven or hell because God desired—elected—him to be, and man could not have chosen otherwise. God's desire is the ultimate and sole determiner and the reason why man sinned and why man is saved. George L. Bryson sums up the essence of Calvinism thusly, "Calvinistically speaking, the lost will not be eternally lost for committing sins or being depraved, any more than the saved will be eternally saved for believing the Gospel or receiving Christ. That is, Calvinism asserts that the elect are eventually, ultimately and inevitably saved unconditionally, just as the unelected are eventually, ultimately and inevitably lost unconditionally."[11]

In contrast, Extensivism contends Scripture's clear and ever-present message regarding the nature of God and man (as well as the pervasive descriptive and prescriptive Scriptures depicting the interactions between the two) is that man is endowed with otherwise choice, which misuse includes the truth that man is both the proximate and ultimate cause of sin with all of its ghastly horror. Moreover, God provisioned for such eventuality so that the reason people perish in hell is because they reject God's genuine offer of salvation by faith in Christ, which they could have received by God's grace enablement. People are in heaven because they, as eternally unworthy beggars, received by faith via God's grace enablements what they otherwise could not have received. This provision is *solely* because "God so loved the world, that He gave His only begotten Son, that whoever believes in Him shall not perish, but have eternal life" (John 3:16).

---

11. Bryson, *Five Points of Calvinism*, 35.

11

Does Physical Birth Demonstrate That Spiritual Birth Precedes Faith?

Calvinists are clear on how they see the order of faith and the new birth. John Piper avers, "Faith is the evidence of new birth, not the cause of it."[1] Again, he states, "Except for the continual exertion of saving grace, we will always *use our freedom* to resist God."[2] In like manner, R.C. Sproul declares, "We do not believe in order to be born again; we are born again in order to believe."[3]

Commonly, when expounding upon passages regarding the new birth, particularly John 3:1–16, many Calvinists argue the new birth precedes and provisions for faith.[4] They seek to illustrate this truth analogically by arguing man did not contribute to his physical birth, and in like manner, he does not contribute to his new spiritual birth; hence, regeneration precedes faith.

I contend such a conclusion must be subjugated to the clear reading of both the historical example given by Christ in John 3:14–15, which refers to Numbers 21:4–9, as well as John 3:1–21; neither of which demonstrate their conclusion. Moreover, Christ's chosen illustration of the serpent incident (John 3:14–15) explicitly places faith prior to receiving new life.[5] The Calvinist suggestion in either place seems to arise out of a theological need to find it rather than actually emanating from the passages. I further find the Calvinist analogy to be both unnecessary with regard to the creation of life and irrelevant to the question regarding the relationship of faith to the new birth, which is the point of their analogy. Additionally, it is important to keep in mind as far as this passage is con-

1. Piper, *Desiring God*, 63–64.
2. Piper, "Irresistible Grace," par. 8.
3. Sproul, *Chosen by God*, 72–73.
4. The view that regeneration precedes faith seems to me to be the dominant view among Baptist Calvinists and is significantly prevalent throughout the Calvinistic spectrum, but not all Calvinists endorse that view.
5. For additional comments and exposition of this passage, see chapter 12, "Does Faith Precede or Result from the New Birth?"

cerned, the significance of the physical birth of Nicodemus seems to lie in the fact of its insufficiency for entering the kingdom.

First, I find the Calvinist analogy unnecessary with regard to the creation of life. It seems everyone would gladly agree with the Calvinist claim that man did not contribute to his human birth (creation) and, therefore, analogically he does not contribute to the new birth, the creation of his new spiritual life. The analogy at this point is cogent, and I agree because only God can create life, whether natural or spiritual. God is the efficient cause of the creation of life. Additionally, this reality is clearly present in Christ's chosen historical example of the serpent. Accordingly, the point of disagreement is not whether God alone creates life because no one contributes one whit to the creation of life. God is the creator, and we are the created. The precise disagreement is concerning the *reception* of the new birth (life), most particularly the sequential relationship of faith to the new birth.

Second, I find the analogy to be irrelevant with regard to addressing the sequential relationship of faith to the new birth. The suggestion that human birth somehow cogently illustrates faith follows the new spiritual birth is not only contradicted by the historical illustration given by Jesus in John 3:14–15 and is absent from the passage John 3:1–21 (in which there is not even the slightest hint or mention of such), but it is also not supported analogically since faith neither precedes nor inexorably results from physical birth.[6]

It seems clear the act of faith did not exist prior to physical birth since man, the one exercising faith, did not exist prior to his conception; consequently, faith's existence, or man's exercise of faith, was absolutely impossible prior to the first birth. This is not the case with the second birth, where man and the possibility of faith do exist, which is not only self-evident but is also evidenced by the repeated scriptural calls for man to exercise that faith. Contrastingly, one never finds a call for the pre-created Adam and Eve, or the preborn human to exercise faith or do anything for that matter.

The question is not whether one contributes to the creation of regenerate man in the second birth (no one does), but rather how one receives that new life. The human birth does not provide an analogical answer since everyone agrees it is an impossibility for man to have believed anything prior to his existence. In unambiguous contrast, Christ's use of the serpent illustration clearly demonstrates faith precedes the reception of new life (John 3:15).

To demonstrate the illogicalness of using the analogy of human birth, one needs only to think how absurd it would be for Christ to call on the

---

6. The context of discussion is salvational faith.

non-existent to exercise faith. Christ would never ask the non-existent to act. But with regard to spiritual birth that is precisely what he called for and commanded with severe denunciations for resisting. Such is never even intimated regarding the first birth because it is impossible. Therefore, it seems one cannot and should not seek to bolster the existence of a theological position in the actual world based on an analogy incorporating the non-existent world. To put it another way, one cannot use an impossibility (an act of faith before existence) to evidence the sequential relationship of faith and the new birth in the actual world.

Although this was a first-class opportunity for Jesus to introduce and utilize the human birth as illustrative of the second, he did not. Rather, he chose to use the wind (John 3:8) and the serpent incident (John 3:14–15). The wind clearly does not speak to the sequential relationship, whereas the serpent incident plainly places the reception of new life after and resulting from faith.[7] The serpent retelling also serves as the introductory and illuminative clarifier of the God-glorifying revelation of John 3:16. Maybe he did not choose such a readily available example as the parallel between the first and second birth because it is an impotent and invalid one.

Since the Calvinist's analogy can only demonstrate God is the sole creator of life, about which we all agree, and it neither demonstrates nor even suggests that faith results from spiritual birth, I for one believe we should put this analogy to rest. To allow the perpetuation of such a disparate example is to grant Calvinism an undeserved proof every time. This is due to the fact that it is an undeniable, foregone conclusion that faith did not precede the first birth since it did not exist. This is in absolute contrast to the existence of faith prior to the new spiritual birth.

---

7. I would suggest the wind illustrates the known and unknown qualities of both natural and spiritual birth and creation. Some believe it speaks to the mystery of spiritual birth. Others believe it is an example of how Christians appear to outsiders, or the sovereign creative moving of Holy Spirit. See the following for these perspectives. "John" in *The Bible Knowledge Commentary*, 281. *The New American Commentary: John 1–11*, 177. *New Testament Commentary: Exposition of the Gospel According to John*, vol. 1, 135.

12

Does Faith Precede or Result from the New Birth?

John 3:1–15

¹ Now there was a man of the Pharisees, named Nicodemus, a ruler of the Jews; ² this man came to Jesus by night and said to Him, "Rabbi, we know that You have come from God as a teacher; for no one can do these signs that You do unless God is with him." ³ Jesus answered and said to him, "Truly, truly, I say to you, unless one is born again he cannot see the kingdom of God."

⁴ Nicodemus said to Him, "How can a man be born when he is old? He cannot enter a second time into his mother's womb and be born, can he?" ⁵ Jesus answered, "Truly, truly, I say to you, unless one is born of water and the Spirit he cannot enter into the kingdom of God. ⁶ That which is born of the flesh is flesh, and that which is born of the Spirit is spirit. ⁷ Do not be amazed that I said to you, 'You must be born again.' ⁸ The wind blows where it wishes and you hear the sound of it, but do not know where it comes from and where it is going; so is everyone who is born of the Spirit."

⁹ Nicodemus said to Him, "How can these things be?" ¹⁰ Jesus answered and said to him, "Are you the teacher of Israel and do not understand these things? ¹¹ Truly, truly, I say to you, we speak of what we know and testify of what we have seen, and you do not accept our testimony. ¹² If I told you earthly things and you do not believe, how will you believe if I tell you heavenly things? ¹³ No one has ascended into heaven, but He who descended from heaven: the Son of Man. ¹⁴ As Moses lifted up the serpent in the wilderness, even so must the Son of Man be lifted up; ¹⁵ so that whoever believes will in Him have eternal life.

TO BE A CONSISTENT Calvinist, a person must believe the Bible teaches God limits his redemptive love toward his creation, and that limited love is more reflective of God being the sum of perfect love than God extending his salvational love to all of his creation. Of course, the perennial problem

DOES FAITH PRECEDE OR RESULT FROM THE NEW BIRTH?

with the Calvinist's perspective is the explicit claims of Scripture to the contrary. The encounter between Jesus and Nicodemus provides an example of God's universal salvational love and sets the context for probably the most well-known and beloved verse in Scripture, which explicitly declares God's universal redemptive love for all of his creation (John 3:16).[1]

I intend to set the context by briefly summarizing John 3:1–13. Then I will note some observations drawn from John 3:14–15. The illustration of John 3:14–15 serves a twofold purpose; first, it provides illumination for properly understanding some of the dialogue between Jesus and Nicodemus in John 3:1–13; second, it serves as Jesus's chosen introductory and illuminative illustration for John 3:16–21.

In John 3:1–2, Nicodemus acknowledges Jesus is a teacher. In verse 3 Jesus begins to teach Nicodemus about the necessity of being born again,[2] which is a spiritual or heavenly birth, (vs. 5–7), in contrast to a physical birth.[3] Nicodemus did not understand Jesus's teaching about the new birth (vs. 4, 9). Christ gives two examples to illustrate this great truth. First, Christ uses the wind (vs. 8) to example both the natural and supernatural (known and unknown) components of what he is saying.[4] Even though we know more about the wind today, the *ultimate* why and how the wind blows is only fully understood by God alone (creator), but man can know something about it by its effects.

The same is true with the heavenly birth, which is a work of God's creative power with observable effects.[5] Consequently, the message to Nicodemus seems to be a summons to trust Jesus's words that human birth, even if it included such recognitions as pharisaical standing or Jewish descent including privilege (Mal 2:10; John 8:39), is insufficient to make one right with God.[6] Even recognizing Christ as a teacher from God is in-

---

1. See discussion in various commentaries of whether Jesus continues speaking in John 3:16–21 or John is now speaking.

2. "The meaning of anōthen, frequently rendered 'again,' is an intriguing matter. The Greek word anōthen here is multidimensional and can mean 'again' or 'from above' as well as the less likely 'from the beginning.'" Borchert, *John 1–11*, 172–73.

3. One's position regarding whether water refers to physical birth or is conjoined to spiritual birth is not germane to my exposition, which focuses upon the sequential relationship of faith and the new birth. You may read many commentaries to find various views including arguments for and against baptismal regeneration.

4. The word wind and spirit are the same word in the original, *pneuma*.

5. The same can actually be said of physical birth. We know something about both physical and spiritual creation of life, but much like the wind, what we know includes some processes but mostly its effects.

6. Regarding the word "see," John 3:5 uses the word eiserchomai meaning "enter" or "enter into" for the same idea. "Often the verbs [see] mean 'to perceive' in such senses

adequate. For any person to experience the kingdom, salvation, God must create a new life. There must be a heavenly birth subsequent to the earthly birth in order to partake of God's kingdom, that is, be saved. This requirement confused Nicodemus for obvious reasons, but most importantly because it left him having to face the glaring inadequacy of what he was, all he had done, and with nothing he could do to rectify his lacking except to trust Christ's words. This truth left him with faith and faith alone, trusting God to do what Nicodemus could not do. This is the exact same place the gospel leaves everyone.

Calvinists are prone to see this as teaching regeneration precedes faith. For example, William Hendriksen says, "It is very clear, therefore, that there is an act of God which precedes any act of man. *In its initial stage*, the process of changing a person into a child of God precedes conversion and faith."[7] Actually if one pays close attention to the text, he will see Jesus's answer specifically addresses the question of *the essential* requirement (John 3:3, 5 "unless" and John 3:7 "must"). It does not explicitly address the *sequential* relationship of faith and the new birth. As a Jew, Nicodemus believed human birth or activities were sufficient, or at least a requirement, for rightly relating to God.[8]

It is that particular issue to which Jesus speaks. The *essential* requirement for experiencing the kingdom, becoming a child of God, requires a new creative act of God. This speaks to the ineffectuality of anything less than that for obtaining salvation rather than demonstrating being born again precedes faith. To wit, being born a Jew or Gentile is not what is either essential or sufficient. As far as the sequential relationship of faith and the new birth in this exchange, one only sees that when one realizes what Nicodemus must have realized, which is that dependence upon anything short of God's creative work cannot result in salvation.

---

as 'to experience,'. . . 'to realize,' 'to know.' Kittel and Friedrich, *Theological Dictionary of the New Testament*, 710. William Hendriksen, a Calvinist, notes the same meaning of see, "There must be a radical change. And unless one is born from above he cannot even see the kingdom of God; i.e., he cannot experience and partake of it; he cannot possess and enjoy it (cf. Luke 2:26, 9:27; John 8:51; Acts 2:27; Rev 18:7)." Hendriksen, *Exposition of John*, vol. 1, 133.

7. Hendriksen, *Exposition of John*, vol. 1, 133.

8. Nicodemus's confusion regarding the concept of the new birth may also be partly attributed to his unfamiliarity with this particular expression. We find this today even among Christians whose particular tradition does not use such terminology as regularly as others do, like Baptists. He would have been familiar with God working creatively in an individual, but this expression may have been one with which he was less familiar (Jer 31:33; Ezek 36:25–27).

That shocking and humbling revelation left Nicodemus where it rightly leaves everyone who is exposed to the salvation plan of God and desires forgiveness; it leaves every person, regardless of pedigree, to disavow everything else and trust God will do for man what man cannot do for himself. Rather than placing the new birth before faith, we see the opposite. First, we see Christ's revelation to man that he must experience a creative work that only God can perform before man can enter God's kingdom. Second, this revelation brings man to either reject the claim that his own righteousness is not enough, or *to trust Christ's revelation* and utterly reject his own righteousness and by faith trust in God's grace to bestow the needed righteousness in the new creation (Matt 5:3, 6; Rom 3:22; Eph 4:24; Phil 3:9). It is the revelation of the requirement of the new birth that precedes faith, which is the necessary response of man to experience the creative act of God in giving a new birth. If Nicodemus had refused to accept such a requirement by faith, a requirement that innately denies every other asset, he would not have experienced God's necessary creative act; he would not be saved.

This discussion says nothing to indicate one must be regenerated in order to exercise faith, rather it categorizes regeneration as an *essential* to becoming a citizen of the kingdom, experiencing salvation. What seems most clear is that revelation from God precedes faith and dependence on God to do what man cannot do for himself; thereby placing man in a position to believe or disbelieve his revelation. This is the same relationship that Adam and Eve had with God in the garden; they had to trust God's revelation (Gen 2:17) and that alone. When they did, they lived, and when they did not, they died. It is the same with the very nature of the gospel (John 3:16; 1 Cor 15: 2–3). It does not seem immaterial to note Jesus said nothing even remotely related to unconditional election or selective regeneration, which would have been exceptionally helpful if true.

In vs. 10, Nicodemus is scolded because the reference to wind should have also caused him to recognize that time spoken of by the prophets. "The Old Testament prophets spoke of the new Age with its working of the Spirit (Isa 32:15; Ezek 36:25–27; Joel 2:28–29). The nation's outstanding teacher ought to understand how God by his sovereign grace can give someone a new heart (1 Sam 10:6; Jer 31:33)."[9] In vs.13, Jesus makes clear he and he alone can reveal these truths about the new birth accurately and explain how man can enter the kingdom of God even though man cannot cause himself to be born again.

Israel, including Nicodemus, had become steeped in a works approach to God and the belief that being a Jew was in and of itself eternally

---

9. Blum, "John," 281.

superior to other lineages. Essentially, there are only two approaches to God; one is according to the wisdom of man (the broad road) and one according to the wisdom of God (the narrow road). The former leads to death and the latter simply trusts God's evaluation of the inadequacy of our human pedigree, and that he will do the work of salvation that leads to new eternal life (Matt 7:13–14).

The sequence of events: first, Christ's declaration that a creative work of God is necessary for salvation, which means whoever man is or whatever man can do is absolutely insufficient and noncontributory; second, the person must *trust* this inescapable judgment of God, resulting in man rejecting any dependence on himself; third, these can lead to man *trusting* God to do what only he can do, make man a new creation; fourth, God responds to this complete act of faith by man that his situation is precisely as Christ declares it to be (which leaves man helpless); therefore, faith actually precedes the new birth.

Jesus takes his second example from Israel's history, vs. 14–15. Nicodemus would have definitely been aware of this historical event. This example speaks to both the essential requirement (God giving new life) and the sequential relationship of faith (man's part) for receiving God's creative offer. It serves to further clarify the need for faith on man's part to trust God will work the miracle of providing new life to the dying in response to simple faith. The significance of this event is seen in that it is the incident that our Lord Jesus chose to provide an understanding of the preceding verses and, most poignantly, to rightly understand vs. 16–21, both of which maintain the same sequential relationship of faith and the reception of new life—salvation.

Jesus said, "As Moses lifted up the serpent in the wilderness, even so must the Son of Man be lifted up; so that whoever believes will in Him have eternal life" (vs.14–15). The degree to which Jesus used this historical event to illustrate the reality and purpose of his death on the cross is highlighted by the words: kathōs[10] translated "As" (meaning "just as"), *houtō*[11] translated

---

10. Καθώς sometimes functions as a comparative particle (1 Thess 4:13; 1 John 3:12), but most often as a subordinating conj. (cf. BDF §453), where the most important function is also comparison. Καθώς can therefore be translated (just) as and so far, just as. Balz and Schneider, *Exegetical Dictionary of the New Testament*, 226.

11. Οὕτως can refer to the foregoing, usually in a correlative construction... When used absolutely οὕτως means (with reference to the foregoing): thus / in this way, or accordingly / therefore; Balz and Schneider, *Exegetical Dictionary of the New Testament*, 549. Also, 3779. οὕτω houtō and οὕτως houtos; adv. from 3778; in this way, thus:—even so(1), exactly(2), follows(2), in such a manner(1), in such a way(4), just(2), like this(5), like(1), same(2), same manner(1), same way(5), so(125), such(2), then(1), thereby(1), this(1), this is the way(2), this is how(1), this effect(1), this manner(4), this respect(1),

"even so" (meaning "same way") vs.14, and *hina*[12] translated "so that" (meaning "in order that," i.e., for the purpose of) vs. 15.

Many have pointed out such things as the serpent was a type of Christ in that the serpent of brass was like the deadly serpents but without the poisonous venom, and Christ was like man but without sin (Rom 8:3; 2 Cor 5:21; Heb 4:15; 1 Pet 2:22–24). We know it pictured the cross of Christ most emphatically because Christ so states. In like manner, we know the illustration illuminates the purpose of his being lifted up and the process whereby the new life created by God is applied. John 3:15 tells us implicitly why the serpent was lifted up and explicitly why Christ must be lifted up. "So that" introduces the purpose of the lifting up. When Moses lifted up the serpent, it was *so that* people could look by faith and be healed, given temporal life. Looking in faith was an act of the people. Giving life was the act of God, which only he can do. Similarly, Christ is lifted up *so that* one can look to him in faith and receive deliverance (be given eternal life). Jesus's use of the historical example lucidly demonstrates the sequence of faith and reception of God's deliverance. Consequently, Christ's use of this illustration serves as the crucial interpretive grid for John 3:16–21.

Calvinists and Extensivists believe Christ was lifted up "so that whoever believes will in Him have eternal life" (vs. 15). The crucial difference is Calvinism believes only the limited unconditionally elect, exclusively atoned for, and selectively regenerated can do so because the non-elect not only will not but *cannot* believe unto salvation. In contrast, those who reject Calvinism believe God has unconditionally and unlimitedly grace enabled one and all to be able to look in faith and be saved. Essential to these two understandings is Calvinism believes a person receives new life (is born again) prior to being able to exercise faith whereas Extensivists believe a person exercises faith prior to receiving new life, and reception of the new life (being born again) is actually conditioned upon grace enabled faith.

Calvinists seem quite inclined to recognize only the similarities between this event and the death of Christ that are consistent with Calvinism as illuminative comparisons.[13] It is quite common for Calvinists to unneces-

---

this way(22), thus(7), way(7), way this(1). Thomas, *New American Standard Hebrew-Aramaic and Greek Dictionaries*.

12. ἵναa; ὅπωϲb[superscript b]: markers of purpose for events and states . . . 'in order to, for the purpose of, so that.'" Louw and Nida, *Greek-English Lexicon of the New Testament*, 784.

13. For example, Hendriksen says, "Now, in John 3:14 the words 'As Moses . . . so must the Son of man' clearly indicate that the event recorded in Numbers 21 is a type of the lifting up of the Son of man. This does not mean, however, that we now have the right to test our ingenuity by attempting to furnish a long list of resemblances between type and Antitype, as is often done. In reality, as we see it, only the following points

sarily limit the scope or meaning of words, verses, definitions, illustrations and theological concepts so they lead only to the correctness of Calvinism; a practice one must be aware of to effectively engage Calvinists. However, Jesus seems to emphasize a broader connection since he explicitly spoke to the sequence of faith and the reception of new life (vs. 14–15). This historical illustration speaks specifically and corroboratively to the sequential relationship of faith and receiving life so that the non-prejudiced obvious conclusion is that the grace revelation of the seriousness of sin and God's judgment (man's plight) occasions the opportunity of faith, which precedes the reception of life.

Both Jesus's words and this historical illustration are in harmony with the previously mentioned reality that the *only* recourse for man is either faith or disbelief once faced with the revelation that the seriousness of his sin requires a creative act of God, a new birth. This understanding is also in perfect harmony with God's universal declaration of love (vs. 16). Equally important, the historical illustration in vs. 14 clarifies who is included in the *whoever* of vs. 15–16, which was everyone at the historical time of the event. Consequently, Calvinism's disregard of these obvious aspects of the illustration which further clarify that everyone is included in the *whoever* and that the sequential relationship is one of faith preceding regeneration is unjustifiable and telling indeed.

What is clear is this: God's revelation precedes man's illumination of the actual reality. This illumination includes man being faced with the truth that everything up to the moment of revelation is irrelevant as far as securing or determining a person's salvation. Such irrelevancies include every component of privilege whether that is race, birthplace, wealth, intellect, rearing, how one has viewed himself with regard to his relationship with God, or historical proximity to relational godliness.

No less significant, this irrelevancy of the past includes every failure, the degree of sinfulness, nefariousness, black heartedness, cumulative sin, whether the sin was public or private, or the horrendous consequences of

---

of comparison are either specifically mentioned or clearly implied in 3:14, 15 (cf. also verse 16):

- a. In both cases (Numbers 21 and John 3) death threatens as a punishment for sin.
- b. In both cases it is God himself who, in his sovereign grace, provides a remedy.
- c. In both cases this remedy consists of something (or someone) which (who) must be lifted up, in public view.
- d. In both cases those who, with a believing heart, look unto that which (or look unto the one who) is lifted up, are healed."

Hendriksen, *Exposition of John*, vol. 1, 138.

the individual's sin upon others. It only matters whether the person accepts by faith God's adjudication of his sin and just deserts, that his plight requires what he cannot provide—a new him, that he needs a new life, and God is the only creator and giver of life. He has to trust this revelation with only a beggar's trust that God will in mercy provide what he needs by doing what only he can do. Therefore, he either trusts God's word that nothing can position him for anything but judgment and no degree of sinfulness positions him outside of the love and offer of a new life that only God can create, or he does not. He either trusts God or himself.

Faith regarding his plight is actually as essential as his faith that God offers deliverance. What man believes about his plight, at the moment of revelation, strongly correlates to his believing in the good news of God's provision of becoming a new person. The revelation to Nicodemus not only told him what he needed, something he could not supply, but it also told him where he will spend eternity based upon his own righteousness—outside the kingdom (vs. 3). Salvation is the acceptance of both by faith. Clearly, when one considers the four components of revelation, opportunity, faith, and new birth, it seems clear that opportunity follows revelation, which precedes both faith and the new birth. The opportunity, exposed by Christ's words, is either rejected by distrust or accepted by trusting what Christ says about our sin and deliverance from our sin. If the opportunity is seized by faith, God will respond by providing life.

These verses recall the incident in Numbers 21:4–9. Numbers 21:1–3 teaches God gave Israel a great victory over the Canaanite king of Arad. Numbers 21:4–5 tells us the Israelites became impatient with Moses, God's leader and, therefore, God, and were griping and complaining (Num 20:4). God then judged their ungratefulness and rebellion by sending poisonous snakes among them. If one of the serpents bit a person, he died, and many of them did die (Num 21:6). God's judgment prompted many to repent and plead for Moses to intercede for them (Num 21:7).

"Then the Lord said to Moses, 'Make a fiery serpent, and set it on a standard; and it shall come about, that everyone who is bitten, when he looks at it, he will live.' And Moses made a bronze serpent and set it on the standard; and it came about, that if a serpent bit any man, when he looked to the bronze serpent, he lived" (Num 21:8–9). This illustration seems crucial in determining if the Calvinists' or Extensivists' view is most reflective of the sequential relationship of faith and the new life, what Christ's death accomplished, and what God's love desires.

Following are some observations drawn from the biblical record of this event in order to provide a biblical lens through which to understand the relationship of revelation, opportunity, faith, salvation, and the required new birth. This approach seems far superior to Calvinism's superimposed limited interpretive grid of unconditional election. Keep in mind, Jesus chose to compare his crucifixion to this example.

1. God's judgment was already upon them.
2. God would have been just to let them all die because of their sin and rebellion.
3. Except for God's sovereign work of loving grace, they would all perish.
4. God is neither a minimalist in holiness (sin must be punished) nor love (deliverance is offered to all).
5. God's offer of deliverance to even one sinner is an act of grace.
6. God's offer of deliverance for all in need is an act of immeasurably more grace than if for only some.
7. God's grace alone provided sufficiently for all needy to trust and receive his deliverance.
8. God's promise was exactly what it appeared to be (real opportunity for all who hear).
9. God's redeeming love provided the pole, serpent of brass, opportunity to look, and the efficaciousness of the look of faith.
10. There was a mystery of how looking at a serpent of brass upon a pole could result in new life (like the wind illustration in John 3:8).
11. Not just any old serpent on a pole would result in healing, but only the one where God was at work.
12. God determined the time the offer was available.
13. What God required, repentance and the look of faith, each was able to do.
14. God made it personal by requiring that "when he looked" he would receive life.
15. God pre-determined to make the offer of deliverance unconditional and the reception of deliverance conditioned upon the look of faith.
16. The deliverance was truly accessible to "everyone" and "any man."
17. God did not exclude anyone under the sentence of death for sin from the offer of healing.
18. This was a good offer and not merely a good faith offer.

19. Only the number who needed deliverance restricted the quantity of the new life offer.
20. Any suggestion that God's extensive offer was trumped by a predetermination to preclude "everyone" or "any" from "looking" is eisegesis!
21. God gave new life after repentance and faith rather than prior to them.
22. The new life was the consequence of the look of faith rather than the cause.
23. God's judgment occasioned repentance and his love occasioned the opportunity for faith.
24. The look was prompted by believing the promise of Numbers 21:8
25. They had to choose between two accessible options (look and live or not look and die).
26. There was not a work to do but a promise to be accepted.
27. Helplessness occasioned and preceded the look of faith.
28. The dying people came to Moses and pled for intercession prior to receiving new life.
29. A dying glance was enough to deliver the judged and perishing.
30. There were only two classes of people: those who looked and lived and those who did not and died.
31. The look required faith but did not require a full understanding of God's work in making the perishing live.
32. There was only one way to access deliverance.
33. Jewish descent was not enough to save them.
34. Life given at the first birth was not enough to stay death and judgment.
35. Looking in trust was man's part, and giving the miracle of life was God's part.

In light of God's revelation regarding the nature and actions of man, and that many of those at the time of the incident had not been faithful to trust and obey God's promises for years, there may well have been some who rejected the offer because of pride, a sense of independence, a belief they would somehow survive, or maybe a doctor would find a cure. That is, they rejected God's offer of deliverance because they did not accept his description of their helplessness, which is the initial act of delivering faith.

Additionally, since the group was undoubtedly rather large, it is probable that some could not literally *see* the pole as clearly as others, maybe some were blocking the vision of others, some may have had cataracts, but they could all exercise a faith-prompted *look*. Maybe some were even far enough away that they heard of God's offer second or third hand. Regardless, while all may not have seen everything clearly and none could fully understand the work of God, all could look by faith and receive healing.[14]

Although earlier in his conversation with Jesus, Nicodemus was utterly confused, it seems quite plausible that this historical illustration played a part in Nicodemus's understanding of how to become a true disciple of God (John 19:39). It appears this example made the truth of John 3:16–21 compellingly clear to him, and when he saw Christ high and lifted up, his works leaving him hopelessly damned, he simply trusted God and left the business of the required new life to God his creator and deliverer.

Scripture affirms faith precedes and is the prerequisite for regeneration—being born again (John 1:12–13, 3:3, 3:15–16, 3:36, 5:24, 6:40, 7:37–39, 12:36, 16:7–14, 20:31: 1 Pet 1:23; 1 John 5:1, 4).[15] These and a host of other Scriptures all show spiritual life follows the sinner placing his faith in Jesus Christ.[16] Zane Hodges succinctly says, "It is the consistent testimony of the New Testament Scriptures that God's Word in the gospel is what produces the miracle of regeneration. It—and it alone—is the powerful, life-giving seed which takes root in the human heart when that Word is received there in faith."[17]

---

14. Like the vulgarization of the cross today (merely a piece of jewelry or an iconic symbol of darkness), some turned this act of God's grace into paganism (2 Kgs 18:4).

15. John 3:3 illustrates this in that Nicodemus had to trust that his physical lineage was insufficient, and it would take a new birth, which would require him to just trust that to be true prior to being born again.

16. See my response to Calvinists' attempt to moderate Calvinism's order of regeneration and faith in Appendix 4.

17. Hodges, *Absolutely Free!*, 48.

13

God, Creation, and Sin: Calvinism's Dilemma

THE BIBLE IS CLEAR that God loves righteousness and holiness, abhors sin, and desires his creation to choose righteousness and holiness. This is evident prior to the fall (Gen 2:17), immediately subsequent to the fall as seen in his swift judgment upon sin (Gen 3:14–24); the repeated calls for holiness prior to his covenant with Israel (Gen 7:1, 15:6, 18:19), to Israel (Lev 11:44, 19:2, 20:7), in the gospels (Matt 3:2; 5:6, 20, 48; 6:33; 11:20), and to the church (Eph 5:3–9; 1 Pet 1:15–16). Calvinists unwaveringly claim to believe this as much as Extensivists do. However, their commitment to decretal theology and compatible freedom of mankind with its resultant micro-determinism, upon closer scrutiny, does seem to eviscerate such obvious teachings of Scripture.

Their reliance upon secondary causes is insufficient to adequately distance God from being the ultimate reason for sin because if God endowed man with compatible freedom and man chose to sin, then God did, in fact, have to desire to create man to inevitably sin. To wit, while it is, according to compatibilism, technically true God did not *cause* sin, it is equally true he did *desire* for man to sin. At the outset, I am rejecting "it is a mystery" as a satisfactory answer to this inevitable dilemma generated by consistent Calvinism. Consider the following commitments in Calvinism.

Calvinism's commitment to decretive theology and compatibilism means God's foreknowledge consists of that which he foreordained rather than including actual contingencies of libertarian free beings (the results of otherwise choice). Given that Adam and Eve did choose to sin and God endowed them with compatible freedom, we can say God created them so they would unalterably freely choose to sin. This assurance is evident in light of a proper understanding of compatibilism. In point of fact, according to compatibilism and consistent Calvinism, God did *not* have to create them so they would freely choose to sin. Nevertheless, he did so choose to create them where they would inevitably freely choose to sin. This choice was by God's design to disallow the freedom to have *actually* chosen not to sin in the moral moment of decision, given the nature and past God gave to Adam and Eve.

Accordingly, Calvinists' references to Scriptures that teach God abhors sin, desires man to live holy and abstain from sin, and holds man responsible for his sin are, in a substantially significant way, inconsistent with the essential elements of consistent Calvinism. While Scripture does portray all of the aforementioned elements Calvinism proclaims, it also teaches man's choice to sin was *against* God's desire and will for him. This means man's sin is due to an incalculably egregious misuse of his freedom. Such is the result of God comprehending the permission to misuse libertarian freedom in his coextensive creation-redemption plan without desiring that man would so choose.

Calvinist William T. Shedd says permission to allow sin "is one that occurs by a voluntary decision of God, *which he need not have made, had he so pleased*. He might have *decided not* to permit sin; in which case it would not have entered the universe"[1] (italics added). We all agree nothing, including sin, is outside of the sovereign governance of God, and that nothing can exist apart from his will, which includes permitting things that are contrary to his consistent desire for holiness. The difference is in Extensivism, God created man knowing he would choose to sin but had so designed man that it was not predetermined that he would ultimately choose to sin. It also includes God surely did not desire for him to sin. In Calvinism, however, the word desire is determinatively impregnated well beyond God's mere knowledge of libertarian contingencies.

If one is unfamiliar with the unflinching determinism of Calvinism and the compatible freedom of man, this distinction can be easily missed when reading statements like the one above from Shedd. Consistent with compatible freedom, God could have created man without the possibility of sin if that would have pleased him. In other words, according to Calvinism because of its commitment to compatibilism, the reality of sin is not inextricably connected to the creation of man and the cosmos. This means Calvinism necessarily believes God desired to create and also desired his creation would be wracked by sin when he did not have to desire the latter. Importantly, note that Shedd says nothing of God's decision to disallow sin in the universe requiring man or Lucifer not be created. Such might be the case when the same consideration is made in light of man being endowed with libertarian freedom, but that is not the case if man is endowed with compatible freedom, as Calvinists believe.

---

1. Shedd, *Calvinism: Pure and Mixed*, 94.

In light of compatibilism, it seems Shedd is quite clearly advocating that God could have created angels and man without sin entering the universe. Such statement is an accurate portrayal of the presence of sin if man has a compatible freedom. That is to say, God desired to create beings so they would freely choose to sin, but they could not have chosen to refrain from sinning, given the nature and past that he gave them. Most precisely, Adam and Eve's sin, as well as everyone's, is the consequence of God's predetermined decision to create beings with compatible freedom, which inviolably leads to beings making a free decision to sin. It is true compatibilism entails the person does freely choose to sin according to his greatest desire that emanates from his nature or past. It is equally true of compatibilism that man could not have freely chosen to not sin in the moral moment of decision—given the same past. This is true both before and after the fall.

This is not to say Calvinists do not speak in terms that seem to argue the opposite, but rather that such talk is inconsistent with compatibilism. For example, Shedd says, "Leaving the unfallen will to its self-determination would not make its apostasy certain; because it was endowed by creation with a power to remain holy as created, and there was no punitive withdrawal of any grace given in creation until after apostasy. How, under these circumstances, a *permissive decree which does not operate by direct efficiency* can make the fall of a holy being certain, is an inscrutable mystery"[2] (italics added).

It is only a mystery because Shedd attempts to absolve God of involvement and proximation to sin contrary to the way that decretal theology (God's foreknowledge is of what he predestines rather than contingencies from otherwise choice) and compatibilism require; consequently, rather than resolving this dilemma, Calvinists neatly place their Calvinistically-generated quandary behind the veil of "inscrutable mystery." Because, if left unveiled, one must face the entailments of compatibilism and its incoherence with Scripture and the nature of God. This incoherence does not exist with libertarian free humans.

Discussions between Extensivists and Calvinists are impeded by the combination of two pervasive practices by Calvinists. First, they repeatedly denounce libertarian freedom (resulting in contingencies, which are non-determined outcomes) in multiple ways while simultaneously extolling decretal theology, compatibilism, and God's foreknowledge being virtually identical to foreordination.[3] (See Appendix 2, Theological Determinism,

---

2. Shedd, *Calvinism: Pure and Mixed*, 95.

3. "God's foreknowledge is not a reference to His omniscient foresight but to His foreordination. He not only sees faith in advance but ordains it in advance." MacArthur, *Romans 1–8*, 495.

for an example of determinists' logic.) Second, Calvinists constantly speak libertarianly in scenarios that expose the incompatible relationship between Scripture and God desiring sin, God as the ultimate cause of sin, and the congruence of God's universal salvific love and reprobation. This includes every passage in which God commands man to do one thing when (according to Calvinism) he has already predetermined him to do another. Such passages clearly and repeatedly indicating man is to make a real choice between two accessible options each with concomitant consequences; some of which God does not desire for man.

Commonly we find Calvinists contrasting compatibilism with libertarianism so that libertarianism is discarded as unbiblical and undermining of God's sovereignty. Then, sometimes in the next paragraph or within the same commentary upon a verse that clearly is in conflict with properly defined compatibilism, they seek to divest compatibilism of its unflinching determinism, or at least speak of it in such a way as to obscure its entailed determinism for most who read their comments.[4] Shedd suppresses the nature of compatibilism when he writes, "The answer is, that God's predestinating in election and preterition is his making the origin of holiness in an elect sinner, and the continuance (not origin) of sin in a non-elect sinner."[5] Additionally, Shedd refers to the meaning of the Westminster Confession with regard to the fall and the existence of sin preceding election and preterition when he says, "Election and preterition, consequently, have reference to the continuance of sin, not the origin of it."[6]

While he may desire to limit the range of compatibilism's determinism, it does nothing to explain how the same does not include the origin of sin in the household of compatibilism and decretive theology. Citing statements by others does not help because such inaccurate redundancy does nothing to explain how Calvinism's reliance upon compatibilism can be satisfactorily reconciled with God not desiring (in significant measure) man to sin, and such desire being distinct from merely desiring in a permissive way since desired outcomes are as determined as any other outcome in compatibilism. One must not merely explain the continuance of sin but also its origin.

Even when Calvinists make a distinction between God's desire and decrees, it does not satisfactorily address the issue because God desired the

---

4. An example is professor emeritus Terrance L. Tiessen's definitions of compatibilism that obscure the determinism of compatibilism as well as what libertarian freedom means and the mutually exclusive nature of libertarian freedom and compatible freedom, http://thoughtstheological.com/glossary/, accessed 7/13/17.

5. Shedd, *Calvinism: Pure and Mixed*, 91.

6. Shedd, *Calvinism: Pure and Mixed*, 92–93.

decrees also. Additionally, when the continuance of sin is reflected upon in a compatibilist sense (determined), one is still faced with God desiring every rape, murder, and act of disobedience of non-Christians and Christians alike. The only way to maintain an approach to Scripture based upon a compatibilism and decretal theology is to speak inconsistently which veils the true nature of compatibilism, thereby obscuring the heart of Calvinism.

Concerning the fall of the angels, which is the real beginning of sin in the universe, Shedd says, "When God placed some of the holy angels upon probation, and decided not to prevent their apostasy by extraordinary grace, they might, nevertheless, have continued in holiness, had they so willed. The origin of their sin is not, therefore, fully accounted for by the merely negative permission of God."[7]

There are two things to note. First, he says, "God . . . decided not to prevent their apostasy by extraordinary grace." This seems to mean God could have created angels to live in a holy state forever by simply supplying more grace; apparently, the same could be said of humankind, had God so chosen. That is to say, there is enough grace available for God to have created angels (and I assume mankind) so they would not sin, but sin happened because God decided against a universe with angels and mankind without sin and its inevitable suffering. Second, granting the angels who were tested by God could have continued in holiness if they "so willed" implies a libertarian view of free will, but Calvinism holds to a compatibilist view; they are mutually exclusive.

Therefore, minus the obfuscating language, Shedd is saying they could have continued in holiness "had they so willed," but the reality is they could not will to do so without God having created them with a past or nature that emanated such desires, according to compatible moral freedom. These are disquieting realities within Calvinism. In addition, it appears only some angels were put to the test, which I understand to mean granted the ability to choose apostasy. This seems to bolster the evidence of God's *desire* for freely chosen sin among *only some* of the angels.

Notice also God's *permission* to sin (according to compatibilism and decretal theology) does not fully answer the question about the *ultimate responsibility* for their freely chosen sin, which they could not by God's design have freely chosen not to commit. The idea of the permissive will of God within a compatibilist framework disallows any suggestion of otherwise choice; consequently, their ability to will to not sin is only *hypothetically* true and not *actually* true in the moral moment of decision.[8] Accordingly,

---

7. Shedd, *Calvinism: Pure and Mixed*, 419–20.
8. Formally called "hypothetical analytical otherwise choice."

once more, we see the ever-present Calvinistically-generated dilemma. God did, in fact, desire to create man to predeterminately freely choose to sin when he did not have to do so. Because if it had pleased God, he could have desired to create man to inviolably and freely choose not to sin, and both outcomes are reflective of compatibilism.

The explanation I am presenting is precisely consistent with compatibilism; consequently, it does not make the error of saying God "caused" man to sin, (i.e., that man did not freely choose) or that God does not employ secondary or tertiary causes. It simply explains the very nature of compatibilism and the reason there is the presence of sin in our universe. According to compatibilism, man freely chose according to his greatest desire and is, therefore, responsible, but in the moral moment of decision, he could not have *actually* chosen differently than he did.

This immediately raises the question of ultimate responsibility, which most plausibly seems to lead to only one place, and that is God. God's creation of man with compatible freedom evidences God's permission to allow sin and his actual predetermining desire for sin to happen to be synonymous; thus, the Calvinist's difficulty of expounding the origin of sin in a consistently understandable way that removes any and every sense of God's responsibility. They simply choose to remain compatibilists and declare such an "inscrutable mystery".

For clarity's sake, we all agree creation could only come about by God's desire (including even the permission for libertarian beings to choose to sin when they did not have to do so). The dilemma of Calvinism is the desire of God included the *unnecessary* dimension of his desire for sin and all of its horror to exist, which was neither necessary to nor included in the simple desire to create moral beings as understood by libertarians and evidenced in Scripture. Moreover, since God could have created beings with compatible moral freedom with a different past, he could have created man, according to Calvinism and compatibilism, in which man's greatest desire would have always been to not sin.

An element of confusion that compatibilists, and in our case, Calvinists, frequently employ is the idea of a *hypothetical* desire to do otherwise (as seen in Shedd's explanation). If I would have desired to choose differently, I could have. However, the use of this idea actually fails to extricate Calvinism from its deterministic quandary, but it does give the appearance of doing so to the unsuspecting.[9] An essential element of their claim is, that yes, *hypo-*

---

9. Regarding the use of the hypothetical or conditional "could have done otherwise," Bernard Berofsky says, "The first prominent philosopher of the twentieth century to advance a compatibilist solution to the free will problem based on a conditional or hypothetical analysis was G.E. Moore (1912)." Berofsky, "Ifs, Cans, and Free Will," 182.

thetically, the individual could have chosen to do other than what he did, in fact, do if he had so desired (because choosing according to compatibilism means that the actor is considered to be morally responsible when he freely chooses according to his desire). But in every situation of *reality*, his desire from which he freely chose was developed by determinative antecedents of his past. For that reason, in *reality*, his desire could not have been different given the same past; therefore, his choice could not have been *actually* different in the moral moment of decision.

What Calvinists should say because it is the actual meaning of their claim, if my past would have been different, I would have had different desires, and I could have chosen differently. But given the past I had at the moral moment of decision, I could not have chosen differently. These statements highlight the fact that the claim (could act differently) is only *hypothetically* true (if another state of affairs would have existed), and not *actually* true (given the exact same state of affairs). Additionally, had the past history, laws of nature, or God's determinative design been different, they not only could have chosen differently, but they necessarily would have chosen differently because they would have had a different greatest desire. Compatibilism's desires are always the result of determinative antecedents.

That being the case, if the hypothetical moves into the real, it will be as determined as all other choices within compatibilism. Grasping what is clearly meant is crucial to preventing the *hypothetical* from obscuring the unflinching deterministic nature of the *reality* of a decision being made in the moral moment of decision (such as Adam and Eve at that point in time).

Another way to see the hollowness of their claim is to point to a real person. Let us call him Tom, who, in a real situation, chose to steal Sally's watch. Then ask the compatibilist if Tom, given reality as it was (his past) at the moral moment of decision, could have chosen not to steal Sally's watch instead of what he did in fact do. If the compatibilist understands compatibilism, he will have to say no. Therefore, claims that rely on the *hypothetical* otherwise choice only mask the determinism of compatibilism and Calvinism but do nothing to actually mitigate it.

A better alternative to the Calvinist position, which necessitates that it pleased God to create man to determinatively freely choose to sin, is God created human beings in his image with otherwise choice (libertarian freedom). Such a state of affairs seems to include the reality that one cannot guarantee such beings will not use their freedom to sin so long as that possibility is within their range of options (which is essential to the concept at the point of creation and is not so at the point of eternity). By God's essential omniscience he foreknew everything, which included all contingencies of libertarian beings, one of which is that man would choose to sin.

His knowledge of such an eventuality was without his desire for that to be the choice of man beyond the desire to permit man to so misuse his freedom. God knew man would misuse his good gift of free will and choose to sin. He also knew he would overcome sin and all of its horror.[10] He freely chose to love, create, and redeem man by his coextensive creation-redemption plan. In view of that, we say God desired to create man in his image, with otherwise choice (capable of undetermined love, responsibility, blame, and honor) reflective of his own undetermined choice to create, redeem, and love.

Again I draw attention to Alvin Plantinga's concept of "transworld depravity" which is reflective of the concept that it may very well be impossible to create beings with otherwise choice and guarantee that they will not use such freedom for evil so long as such a choice is within their range of options at the time.

> What is important about the idea of transworld depravity is that if a person suffers from it, then it wasn't within God's power to actualize any world in which that person is significantly free but does no wrong—that is, a world in which he produces moral good but no moral evil . . . Obviously it is possible that there be persons who suffer from transworld depravity. More generally, it is possible that everybody suffers from it. And if this possibility were actual, then God, though omnipotent, could not have created any of the possible worlds containing just the persons who do in fact exist, and containing moral good but no moral evil.[11]

This is a similar way of presenting the same truth as I have argued in that God permitted sin, but never desired for man to sin and suffer the horrors of his own choice.

Accordingly, within Calvinism, as God's voluntary decision to not regenerate some could have been different if such would have *so pleased* him, in like manner, he could have created man so he would not have sinned had such been what God desired (so pleased him) as well; therefore, Calvinism entails the truth that not only could God have saved more than he did or even everyone, he also could have created man without sin. The only reason he did neither is because, according to the entailments of compatibilism and Calvinism, such simply did not please God, a disquieting reality.

---

10. See chapter 22 "Is Libertarian Free Will Eternal" for more on how libertarian freedom coalesces with man living without sin in heaven.

11. Plantinga, *God, Freedom, and Evil*, 48.

14

Is Reprobation Necessary for God to Demonstrate His Holiness?

ACCORDING TO CALVINISM, GOD voluntarily predetermined for some of the human race, the unconditionally elect, to experience salvation in order to display his mercy. He concomitantly predetermined for most of the human race to be passed over, leaving them to inviolably perish in hell in order to display his holiness and wrath, the reprobate. Oliver Crisp notes that according to Calvinism, both were necessary "in order that the essential attributes of God be displayed in the created order."[1] A frequently cited passage in support of reprobation is Romans 9:18–26. This is consistent with the Westminster Confession 3.3: "By the decree of God, for the manifestation of his glory, some men and angels are predestinated unto everlasting life, and others foreordained to everlasting death." William T. Shedd agrees:

> Reprobation is the antithesis to election and necessarily follows from it. If God does not elect a person, he rejects him. If God decides not to convert a sinner into a saint, he decides to let him remain a sinner. If God decides not to work in a man to will and to do according to God's will, he decides to leave the man to will and to do according to his own will. If God purposes not to influence a particular human will to good, he purposes to allow that will to have its own way. When God effectually operates upon the human will, it is election. When God does not effectually operate upon the human will, it is reprobation. And he must do either the one or the other. The logical and necessary connection between election and reprobation is seen also by considering the two divine attributes concerned in each. Election is the expression of divine mercy; reprobation of the divine justice. God must manifest one or the other of these two attributes toward a transgressor. St. Paul teaches this in Rom. 11:22: "Behold the goodness and severity of God (divine compassion,

1. Crisp, *Deviant Calvinism*, 104.

and the divine justice); on them which fell severity; but toward thee goodness."[2]

Again we see a conscious voluntary deliberate act of God to predetermine humans' damnation to hell by purposing "not to influence a particular human will to good," thereby designating them as reprobate. Significantly, every person who perishes in hell does so because it pleased God to withhold the very act from him that the elect who go to heaven are provided. The fact they do not deserve salvation is not the point, but rather that God's decision alone is why one person is in hell and another is in heaven. The general rationale provided for such a decision is the reprobates serve the purpose of displaying God's justice. They display to all that God hates sin and judges sin because he is holy and just. Consequently, when time is no more, all will know God is merciful and just.

Shedd further comments, "Consequently, whoever holds the doctrine of election must hold the antithetic doctrine of reprobation. A creed that contains the former logically contains the latter, even when it is not verbally expressed. Such creeds are the Augsburg Confession, Part 1, Article 5; the First Helvetic, Article IX.; the Heidelberg Catechism Q. 54. Ursinus, who drew up the Heidelberg Catechism, discusses reprobation in his system of theology founded upon it. The Thirty-nine Articles mention election, and not reprobation."[3]

The Canons of Dort assert concerning the non-elect, "but finally to condemn and eternally punish them . . . in order to display his justice."[4] Similarly, Jonathan Edwards expresses the quandary of Calvinism that leads to double talk, "The great and last end of God's work which is so variously expressed in Scripture, is indeed but one; and this one end is most properly and comprehensively called, 'the glory of God' . . . And though God in seeking this end, seeks the creature's good; yet therein appears his supreme regard to himself."[5]

Here the problem is not the irreconcilability of God simultaneously seeking his own glory and the "creature's good" (what I think Scripture teaches), but rather it is reconciling Calvinism's belief that God voluntarily damned the vast majority of his creation because it pleased him with God seeking their good. There does not seem to be a biblical reason to believe God's provision for salvation to all is somehow incongruent with the end of all things being God's own glory or how hell is congruent with God seeking

---

2. Shedd, *Dogmatic Theology*, vol. 1, 429–30.
3. Shedd, *Dogmatic Theology*, vol. 1, 430.
4. Canons of Dort, First Head of Doctrine, article 15.
5. Edwards, *God's End in Creation*, 530.

"the creature's good" unless one is willing to redefine hell as a wonderful end of life. It is manifestly unclear why God would be more glorified with fewer in heaven than with more.

We see Calvinists believe God did voluntarily choose to endow man with a compatible freedom, thereby ensuring that man would freely choose to sin. We also see of those affected by sin (everyone), God did voluntarily choose to elect *some* to salvation (the unconditionally elect). God did also voluntarily choose to damn the rest to eternal torment (the reprobate) when he did not have to. At least we can say he surely did not have to damn as many as it appears he did—according to Calvinism. Regarding the presence of sin, Augustine makes it clear it exists because of the voluntary permission of God. He says, "And of course his permission is not unwilling but willing."[6] Similarly, Calvin says, "God's permission of sin is not involuntary, but voluntary."[7]

When Calvinists use phrases like "not permit sin," it is easy to misconstrue them to mean, permit in the libertarian sense. But in Calvinism, it actually means if God would have chosen not to predetermine man to choose freely to sin (compatibilism). Implicit in such declarations is the fact, according to compatibilism, God could have created man with a different past or nature, and thereby man could have lived without ever sinning. Man chooses to sin simply because it did not please God to spare man the torture of sin and, for most, an eternity in hell.

To state it another way, God could have just as easily created Adam and Eve with different natures, emanating different desires, thereby determining they would have freely chosen not to sin; consequently, sin would not have entered the universe. This would have resulted in a world without rape, child abuse, death, murder, and every other nefarious sinful thought or act, but such a world God did not desire, according to Calvinism. Therefore, it seems undeniable, according to Calvinism, the presence of sin and every vile, sinful, and hurtful act by one of God's created beings pleases him in a way that is not true of Extensivism.

Although from a libertarian perspective this does not make sense, it is quite reflective of compatible freedom. Once more, we see the ever-present Calvinistically-generated quandary, which is God must have not only desired to create man but desired to create man to predeterminately freely choose to sin. This explanation is precisely consistent with compatibilism. It avoids the errors of saying that God caused man to sin (that man did not freely choose)

6. Shedd, *Calvinism: Pure and Mixed*, 94.
7. Shedd, *Calvinism: Pure and Mixed*, 95.

or minimizing or ignoring God's use of secondary causes. It simply explains the very nature of compatibilism and the presence of sin.

We all agree creation could only come about by God's desire (including even the permission of beings to choose to sin when they did not have to do so—libertarian freedom). However, the dilemma of Calvinism, unlike Extensivism, is that desire included the unnecessary desire (as far as revelation depicts) for sin and all of its horror to exist. This reality is neither necessary nor included in the simple desire to create as held by Extensivists.

The Extensivist's position is, God's creation of such beings includes some will misuse the gift of choice since it appears one cannot create a libertarian free being and guarantee he will not use his freedom to sin so long as it is within the range of options as we see that it is in creation. God, knowing that, chose to create man and to permit his choice to sin.[8] We rightly say God's desire to create man to be in his image, with otherwise choice (capable of love, responsibility, blame, honor, etc.,), is reflective of God's undetermined choice to create and redeem.

Calvinists' emphasis upon God's desire for countless people to perish simply because that end pleases him when it did not have to be is never difficult to find. Shedd writes, "Both Augustine and Calvin had particular reference, in this connection, to the first origin of sin in angels and men. But their statement holds true of the continuance of sin in angels and men. When God passes by all the fallen and sinful angels, and does not regenerate and save any of them, it is by a positive voluntary decision that might have been different had he so pleased. He could have saved them. And when *God passes by some fallen and sinful men and does not regenerate and save them, this also is a positive voluntary decision that might have been different had he so pleased. He could have saved them*"[9] (italics added).

Accordingly, as God's voluntary decision to "not regenerate" some could have been different if such would have "so pleased" him; he could have created man so he would not have sinned had such been what pleased him as well. Therefore, we see again Calvinists believe God could have created man without sin or saved all who sinned, but that simply did not please God, a disquieting reality.

Additionally, the determinism of Calvinism is best understood as micro-determinism because it is not limited to the area of salvation (including reprobation) but does, in fact, extend to *all* human decisions and actions. For example, Millard Erickson says with regard to God's foreknowledge, "He foreknows what will happen because he has decided what is to happen.

---

8. See chapter 22 "Is Libertarian Free Will Eternal."
9. Shedd, *Calvinism: Pure and Mixed*, 95.

This is true *with respect to all other human decisions and actions as well . . .* God's decision has rendered it certain that every individual will act in a particular way"[10] (italics added).

This is why I maintain Calvinism believes everything happens *necessarily* because human choice did not ultimately cause the predetermined outcome of any event nor could any event ever be altered in the slightest degree by the choice of humans. Rather than obscuring such determinism by contending decisions and actions only *certainly* happen, Calvinists should speak consistently with their view of man's freedom and decretal theology. Speaking of something being certain is reflective of Extensivism since many outcomes, which could have by God's design be different by the choice of humans, is made certain because of his foreknowledge which can include both divine determinative causality and divinely determined human contingency rather than determinism only.

Most often Calvinists will demur at labeling Calvinism's determinism as making events necessarily true, preferring the phrase certainly true. It seems to me that actually serves the purpose of obscuring the micro-determinism to which they are committed, thereby enlivening the confusion of many both within and outside of Calvinism regarding its omnipresent determinism. It is always important to keep in mind that compatibilism's determinism (sometimes called soft determinism) is no less deterministic than hard determinism. The only component that is different is compatibilism seeks to reconcile determinism and moral responsibility, but it does so by defining free choice as one acting according to his greatest desire rather than lessening the degree of determinism of compatibilism.

Calvinists are correct to reject the claims of those who portray Calvinism as believing the actions of man are necessary when the term is used to mean force or coercion.[11] That is not the way I use it, nor is it the only or even the best way. When contrasting compatibilism and libertarianism, it is accurate to say a compatible moral freedom makes every future choice necessary in that it cannot be different from the one that will be made given one's past. God knows what the person with compatible freedom will do because he determined such by giving him a specific past or nature from which his greatest desire will emanate. From this predetermined desire, man will freely choose. If one knows the past of a compatibly free person, he can also know every future decision because they all happen necessarily (not coercively) given one's past. This is because, while the choice is free, the greatest desire is determined by the past—determinative antecedents.

10. Erickson, *Christian Theology*, 326.
11. Shedd, *Calvinism: Pure and Mixed*, 92.

In contrast, one cannot know what decision a person with libertarian freedom will make based on the individual's past because while one's past may influence a decision, it does not determine it. It is the individual as created in the image of God that is the efficient cause of his decision. Given the same past, whatever he decides, he could have chosen to do otherwise.[12] Accordingly, God would know the future acts of libertarian beings not because of their past (determinative antecedents), but because he is essentially omniscient. If man would in the future choose differently than God knows he will, God would have always known that; not because it is necessary as to causation, but rather because God knows every future proposition, and he cannot be wrong. Calvinism includes the idea that man's actions are necessary given his past that determined his greatest desire; though he freely chooses according to his greatest desire. According to Extensivism, man's actions are only certain because of God's infallible foreknowledge since man could choose differently given the same past. This is an important distinction to maintain.

Calvinists are tenaciously committed to double predestination, which emphatically declares either God determined to send some to hell, or it happens consequently by his determining to offer a provisioned for salvation only to some. Calvin averred, "By predestination we mean the eternal decree of God, by which he determined with himself whatever he wished to happen with regard to every man. All are not created on equal terms, but some are preordained to eternal life, others to eternal damnation; and, accordingly, as each has been created for one or other of these ends, we say that he has been predestinated to life or to death."[13]

If Calvinism is true and man was created compatibly free, it seems inescapable that God could have created a world in which at least one more, many more, or even everyone could have been numbered among the elect and been saved. It appears at least one could easily conclude God would have been more benevolent since fewer or even no one would have suffered God's wrath. Additionally, it seems difficult to find biblical support for how that would interfere with him still doing everything for his own glory. It seems like such a plan would pedestal his omnibenevolence, resulting in at least as much glory as the plan according to Calvinism. I would argue at least based on what we know from Scripture, it does seem to be the case that people do *not* suffer hell so that God may show his glory in wrath, but rather for their own sin and rejection of his grace (Matt 11:20–21; Luke 13:3–5).

---

12. This does not mean the presence of libertarian freedom requires every choice include the ability to act or refrain but only that some choices do.

13. Calvin, *Institutes of the Christian Religion*, vol. 2, bk. 3, chap. 21, sec. 5, pg. 206.

I would also insist it is both biblically and logically unnecessary to conclude the following: first, God voluntarily chose to create beings who could not actually refrain from sinning but only such beings who could and, therefore, would only will to freely sin; second, God voluntarily chose to pass over most people in order to demonstrate his wrath and holiness. Such a conclusion is certainly not obvious, and it is not even necessary if one relies solely upon Scripture for his conclusion. Consider the following:

One, the desire for God to demonstrate his wrath, unflinching intolerance of sin, is more than eminently evident in his judgment of Lucifer and those who chose to sin with him. Scripture explicitly says that hell was created for the "the devil and his angels" (Matt 25:41).

Two, God's wrath and unflinching holy intolerance of sin could have been overwhelmingly displayed by simply creating man with otherwise choice; since, as mentioned before, it seems impossible to guarantee at least some libertarian free human beings, in a world where sinning is an option, will not choose to misuse that freedom and sin. Such a scenario is absolutely consistent with Scripture's claim that God truly desires that none would perish (2 Pet 3:9). Consistent with this desire for none to perish, he did abundantly provision so that those who perish do not have to perish (John 1:29). God's certainty of outcome is not dependent upon predetermination, but rather it exists because he is essentially omniscient; therefore, he knows many will choose to reject his loving offer of forgiveness. This seems to be the simplest and most consistent reading of the explicit teachings of Scripture.

Three, if Calvinism is true, it seems unnecessary for God to predetermine more than one person to be eternally damned in order to display his wrath and holiness. God's wrath upon just one sinner would sufficiently display God's wrath against sin. Resorting to the truth that everyone deserves hell is irrelevant to Calvinism's point that damnation is necessary to show God's wrath. Relying upon "it is a mystery" is a most evidentially insufficient response to this idea, whose insufficiency is repeatedly emphasized in light of the consistently and explicitly stated salvific plan and plea for all to be saved as portrayed in Scripture (John 3:16; Rev 22:17).

Fourth, preeminently and, therefore, most compellingly, is the fact that no humans had to perish in judgment in order to graphically and most incontrovertibly demonstrate God's unmitigated wrath because that was unsurpassably demonstrated when he judged his only begotten Son on the cross for the sins of mankind. Even if he dammed every single person he created a thousand times over, such demonstration of holy wrath would be massively dwarfed by the death of Christ on the cross.

This means based upon what we know from Scripture about God, for God to voluntarily withhold salvation from even one person with justification for doing so in order to be glorified by demonstrating his wrath seems incomprehensibly ghastly, unnecessary, irrational, and contrary to his benevolence. This is precisely the basis for the Universalist Calvinists belief in universal salvation.

Oliver Crisp makes the argument that according to the Augustinian view, all could be saved since no one need go to hell to demonstrate God's justice and wrath, so long as "the sin of all human agents is atoned for in the death of Christ."[14] Crisp then argues against the claim in Augustinianism that grace is only applied to some and the rest are reprobate. He says, "Contrary to popular belief, the central tenets of traditional Augustinianism (of which the Reformed are a species) are in fact compatible with a version of universalism . . . But, if Augustinianism is compatible with universalism, then this claim is false: all human beings are the objects of special divine grace and will be saved; none will be rejected."[15]

The Calvinist belief in reprobation once again disembowels repeated Calvinist endeavors to demonstrate God salvifically loves the lost. Actually, according to Calvinism, it seems God could be more loving in electing even one more person unto salvation. At least it is not obvious why God's provision to save fewer people is more loving than doing so for more people. Even this raises the question of why the one who is the sum of perfect love did not save more if the supposed reason was a need to demonstrate both his love and wrath. God's glory fails to answer this problem for Calvinism.

In Extensivism, the atonement is universal and the offer of accessible salvation is universal as well. By the grace of God, everyone who hears the gospel has a genuine opportunity to believe or reject the gospel. The elect is comprised of those whom God *always and innately* foreknew would, if grace enabled, choose to receive the offer of his work of salvation on their behalf. Scripture depicts man as making this choice while still in his sins (John 12:35–36). God did not acquire such knowledge by looking down the halls of history or in any way looking outside of himself because God does not know perceptively. Rather he always knew such because he is essentially omniscient. That is to say, it is impossible for God to either be wrong or not know about a future event.

Calvinism simply reminds us what was said of Judas is true of every one of the non-elect, "It would have been good for that man if he had not been born" (Matt 26:24).

---

14. Crisp, *Deviant Calvinism*, 113.
15. Crisp, *Deviant Calvinism*, 125.

15

Is Man Totally Passive Prior to Monergistic Regeneration?

IT IS COMMON TO hear a knowledgeable and *consistent* Calvinist contend the lost are totally passive in salvation until they are monergistically (God alone) born again.[1] James Montgomery Boice gives an example of this:

> In this sad and pervasively sinful state we have *no inclination* to seek God, and therefore cannot seek him or *even respond to the gospel when it is presented to us.* In our unregenerate state, we do not have free will so far as 'believing on' or 'receiving' Jesus Christ as Savior is concerned. In fact, such is our slavery to sin that we cannot understand our need of Christ until God first gives us spiritual understanding. Even faith must come as a gift because prior to the regenerating work of the Holy Spirit our depravity renders us impotent to cooperate with God's saving grace[2] (italics added).

The Westminster Confession states, "This effectual call [to salvation] is of God's free and special grace alone, not from anything at all foreseen in man, *who is altogether passive* therein, until, being quickened and renewed by the Holy Spirit, he is thereby enabled to answer this call, and to embrace the grace offered and conveyed by it"[3] (italics added).

Therefore, according to Calvinism, God's grace leaves man absolutely incapable of responding to the gospel or even perceiving anything about

---

1. Some Calvinists use quickened or renovated. Some Calvinists do not believe the new birth precedes faith. Millard Erickson is an example of this perspective. See Erickson, *Christian Theology*, 330. However, they all, including Erickson, believe God determinatively and monergistically works to bring the unconditionally elect to exercise a free act of faith, compatible style. Bruce Demarest is another example of this perspective, *The Cross and Salvation*, 264–65.

2. Boice and Ryken, *Doctrines of Grace*, 30.

3. The Westminster Confession of Faith, Chapter X, Section II. I am specifically dealing with Calvinists who accord with Boice and this confession in that salvation is monergistic until the quickening is accomplished—consistent Calvinists.

the gospel, his need, or being influenced toward the gospel by anything; anything includes what anyone does prior to God causing him to be born again—quickened. Since man is totally passive and salvation is monergistic until after regeneration (one is born again) is accomplished, we must see every gospel offer, acceptance or rejection of the gospel, pleading, persuasion, shed tear, sense of urgency to receive the gospel, or biblical condemnation for rejecting the gospel in light of this tenet of Calvinism. This is because none of these have a meaningful relationship to a person's salvation prior to regeneration.

Any suggestion of or inclination toward believing some activity such as faith, prayers, witnessing, evangelism, love, or devoted parenting has any effect on a person's salvation is an illusion. This is because a person cannot be active and passive at the same time and way in salvation. Monergism prior to regeneration absolutely excludes man's active participation in any way because that would be a cooperative relationship. Any speech by Calvinists that obscures this harsh reality is misguided and problematic.

As an Extensivist, I believe God's sovereignly predetermined salvation plan provides sufficient grace for man's organic participation so that such things as faith, prayers, witnessing, the gospel, and choice precede and are inextricably and substantively related to election and being born again.[4] God organically uses pre-conversion workings, the conviction of Holy Spirit, and the power of the gospel, which allows man a grace-enabled choice to accept or reject the gospel. God's eternal salvation plan accomplishes the salvation of individuals by comprehending these activities so they are constitutionally related to election, faith, regeneration, and the entire grace work and process of salvation.[5]

The problem with Calvinism's belief that man is totally passive is that when one reads Scripture, without such secret knowledge, it clearly appears other realities such as testimonies, persuasion, miracles, particular sins, and the freedom to believe or not believe do actually exist and do *substantively* matter. To wit, they are related organically to whether or not someone exercises faith in God or withholds such trust at that time (John 4: 27-30, 39-42).

Calvinists often emphasize these things matter in Calvinism by noting God ordained the process. While it may be true he ordained the process, they still do not seem to substantively matter since Calvinism also argues that salvation, to the point of regeneration, is monergistic—God alone does something—and man is totally passive; man does nothing. It seems a

---

4. See chapter 8 and glossary for an explanation of the terms organic and substantively.

5. See chapter 8 and glossary for an explanation of constitutionally related.

person cannot coherently argue man is active in a substantive way while simultaneously and adamantly arguing God alone is active and man is totally passive prior to regeneration. This is also evident in unconditional election unless unconditional does not mean unconditional, which would mean regeneration is conditional. The emphasis on God using the process does not solve this dilemma if nothing means nothing. Aristotle reminded us of how nothing, nothing really is. He said, "Nothing is what rocks dream about."[6] If this is not what Calvinists mean by nothing, then they do in fact include *something* and are, therefore, not monergistic Calvinists.

In order to respect the emphasis of Calvinism's rejection of faith as a condition for regeneration because they deem such to be a work or virtue; to respect their love of extolling monergism (God alone) and man's passivity, and their initial belief in the gospel not happening until God via regeneration in the elect produces the will to believe, we must be equally careful to disallow any suggestion by Calvinists that anything influences man toward the gospel. Because that reality does not and cannot exist until God bestows the will to believe, and the lack of God's bestowal of the will to believe is the *only* deciding factor why others do not believe.

For that reason, according to Calvinism, people only *seemingly* reject the gospel because of the elevation of the traditions of man above Scripture (Matt 15:3 & 6), love of preeminence (Matt 23:6), respect of men (Luke 11:43), lack of miracles (Matt 11:21), love of riches (Matt 19:22–23), Satan's blinding (1 Cor 4:4), false philosophy (Col 2:8), or vain religion (Jas 1:26). In like manner, no one is even minutely inclined toward accepting the gospel because of such things as hearing about Jesus or the gospel (John 4: 27-42), seeing signs (John 20:30–31), witnessing the lives of godly parents, people praying for them, or any influence of Christian family or friends. If Calvinists do allow for such in any *meaningfully influential* way, then salvation is not monergistic and man is not totally passive until God causes him to be born again; one simply cannot have it both ways.

If Calvinism is true, one could throw bananas at the lost or sing the national anthem of Bangladesh in Swahili, and it would have the same effect upon the lost as praying, witnessing, or hearing the gospel. I recognize such would be against God's commands for the Calvinist to preach the gospel, witness, or pray and the Calvinist would be disobedient to such commands; however, that still does not help to extricate the Calvinist from the predicament, which is that in Scripture, the aforementioned things do seem to *meaningfully* relate to one's salvation.

---

6. This is commonly attributed to Aristotle but is not sourced.

Admittedly, these biblical realities in Extensivism do make God's work of salvation far more complex than the deterministic plan suggested by Calvinism, but I for one believe God is up to the challenge. Now, I do not mind so much that my Calvinist brethren disagree with me, but I do find it quite telling when they are unable to even entertain how a sovereign God could create man with otherwise choice and concomitantly comprehend that in his salvific plan without resorting to a works salvation. Additionally unsettling is they unequivocally contend for monergism, and yet they simultaneously and frequently speak, pray, and write in very synergistic terms. To say this differently, they resolutely contend for compatibilism and vociferously castigate libertarianism, but often and quite confusingly speak libertarianly.

Further, Calvinists can rightly affirm their belief in "whoever will may come." But they should be equally clear about their understanding of total depravity (requiring a new nature given to the elect in regeneration), their belief (faith) that man will only disbelieve because that is all he can do, and man's passivity prior to such time when God gives him the "will to believe". To wit, no amount of prayers, persuasion, compelling testimonies, a Christian living a life dedicated to Christ before a lost person, or rearing children in a godly home has even a micro whit of salvific benefit; that is, if man is passive, monergism is true, and unconditional election have any meaning at all.

Thus, in Calvinism, "whoever will may come" is only trivially true. In other words, yes whoever will may come if they had a different nature, which of course the non-elect do not and will not ever have, and that by God's good pleasure and design; even the elect cannot will to come prior to monergistic regeneration. Consequently, when a Calvinist attributes a person's rejection or acceptance of the gospel to anything other than God's deterministic salvific will, it is only trivially so (makes not one whit of *actual* difference in who believes and who rejects). This reality is inextricably related to their adamant unflinching insistence upon monergism and the passivity of man. Euphemisms or double talk will not assuage this truth except for the unsuspecting.

In contrast, I believe Scripture clearly teaches encounters with the gospel are reliable (they are what they seem to be) and involve accessible benefits which can be rejected or accepted by the hearer. They should be accepted according to God's grace through a spiritual paupers' trust (Eph 2:8–9) in order to escape our just deserts of incalculable eternal peril. For example, in John 4:39–42, Scripture explicitly states Jesus's words did influence the Samaritan woman to believe in him; at least that is her testimony (vs. 39). Equally clear is her testimony and words influenced the people of Samaria to believe in him, at least that is their testimony as recorded in

Scripture (vss. 39, 41–42), but not if Calvinism is true. If Calvinism is true, these explicit assertions are only incidentally true rather than essentially related to these individual's faith as indicated because faith cannot be considered to be even minutely related to anything other than, or even existing prior to, monergistic regeneration.

Accordingly, if Calvinism is true, they were all under a grand delusion, which Jesus did nothing to dispel; I fear we must all realize we too are equally deluded. This is not reading into Calvinism, but rather a serious attempt to respect their core tenets for which they brand those who reject Calvinism of being guilty of adding works to salvation, making salvation a work or virtue of man, undermining God's sovereignty, or giving God's glory to man (all of which, if true, are blasphemous).

Two other examples: first, John 7:17. Jesus actually made knowing the truthfulness and understanding of his words dependent upon a "desire to do His will," thereby placing man's will to desire prior to knowing; I desire and exercise faith in order to understand. Gerhard Maier says, "In an irreversible way it deduces understanding from obedience."[7] We see in the passage that some chose not to desire (vs. 30) and some chose to desire and believe (vs. 31). Second, in Mark 10:17–22, Jesus's encounter with the rich young ruler gives every indication of Jesus offering a real opportunity to follow him. The declination of such is explicitly attributed to the young man's unwillingness to follow because of his concern for his wealth (vs 22–23, 25, 28–30); an unwillingness that the passage indicates could have been otherwise. It is important to note vs. 21 says Christ "loved him." It seems unimaginably dreadful to believe Christ truly loved him and yet withheld the very enablement he needed to *obey* his commands (Rom 2:8; 2 Thess 1:8). Jesus's offer of "treasures in heaven" (vs. 21) in place of his treasures on earth seem to be made with the most sublime sincerity. One thing is certain, this pericope does not intimate in any sense Christ actually developed the plan that inviolably prohibited him from obeying the call to follow him and thereby inherit eternal life.

---

7. Maier, *The End of the Historical-Critical Method*, 54.

16

Does It Please God to Damn Most to Eternal Torment?

COMMENTING ON WHAT PAUL says in Romans 9, John Calvin candidly explains, "He [Paul] concludes that God has mercy on whom he will have mercy, and whom he will he hardeneth (Rom 9:18). You see how he refers both to the mere pleasure of God. *Therefore, if we cannot assign any reason for his bestowing mercy on his people, but just that it so pleases him, neither can we have any reason for his reprobating others but his will*"[1] (italics added). Calvin further says the reprobate are doomed in God's "hidden purpose" while simultaneously (and quite contradictorily) maintaining "so wonderful is his love towards mankind that he would have them all to be saved."[2] Calvin classifies God's good pleasure to doom this innumerable group of people whom he created to such an unalterable fate, which he did not have to so choose, as "incomprehensible judgment."[3]

Similarly, the Canons of Dort assert, "Moreover, Holy Scripture . . . further bears witness that not all people have been chosen but that some have not been chosen or have been passed by in God's eternal election—those, that is, concerning whom God, on the basis of his entirely free, most just, irreproachable, and unchangeable *good pleasure*, made the following decision: to leave them in the common misery into which, by their own fault, they have plunged themselves; not to grant them saving faith and the grace of conversion; but finally to condemn and eternally punish them"[4] (italics added).

In unmistakable fashion, consistent Calvinism believes that according to a conscious and voluntarily deliberate act, God did in fact unalterably predestine what appears to be the vast majority of the human race to eternal torment in hell because of only one stated reason: it pleased him. That they

---

1. Calvin, *Institutes of the Christian Religion*, Logos.
2. Calvin, *Commentaries on Second Peter*, 419.
3. Calvin, *Institutes of the Christian Religion*, vol. 2, bk. 3, chap. 21, sec. 7, pg. 211.
4. Canons of Dort, First Head of Doctrine, article 15.

deserved such an eternal existence fails to mitigate this truth one whit since everyone deserves damnation; alluding to such is merely an obfuscation. Moreover, even if the Calvinist seeks refuge in claiming to believe in passive or consequential reprobation, i.e., God simply was not pleased to elect them to salvation, the motive and purpose are the same.

This reminds us it is not merely the dreaded hyper-Calvinists who believe in double predestination. Rather the belief in double predestination encompasses everyone who is committed to the tenets of Calvinism. This in spite of one's position regarding the order of decrees, which actually change eternal destinies not one whit since God has predestined every person to heaven or hell either by divine decree or as a consequence of unconditional election wrought by selective regeneration. The eternality of every person is ultimately determined by only one thing and that is what pleased God; correspondingly, apparently, had it pleased him, he could have saved every one of the damned. This is a disquieting reality of Calvinism.

Shedd concurs with statements by Augustine and Calvin whom he had just quoted when he says, "When God passes by some fallen and sinful men and does not regenerate and save them, this also is a positive voluntary decision *that might have been different had he so pleased. He could have saved them*"[5] (italics added). I must admit I do weary of Calvinist forays into proffering supposedly palliative notions for such beliefs that creatively seek to portray God as salvifically loving the very ones whom it pleased him to damn (two wills, different kinds of love, inscrutable mystery). The truth is the Calvinist belief in reprobation serves to effectively eviscerate all Calvinist endeavors to demonstrate God salvifically loves anyone, or even significantly loves them for that matter, other than the unconditionally elected.

According to Calvinism, it does seem God would be more loving in electing even one more person unto salvation. Given the determinism of Calvinism, it seems obvious God's unconditional election of the number he has chosen is more loving than if he would have just chosen to save only half as many or even just one. As we have seen, the argument that some must perish in order to demonstrate God's holiness and wrath is impotent since the death of Christ serves as the quintessential display of God's abhorrence of sin. Even if God would have limited the preordained damned to just one person, that still raises the question why the one who is the sum of perfect love did not elect him as well if the only reason left is to demonstrate both his love and wrath and thereby set his glory on display (see chapter 14 "Is Reprobation Necessary for God to Demonstrate His Holiness?").

---

5. Shedd, *Calvinism: Pure and Mixed*, 95.

The unprejudiced truth is Calvinism does ascribe to the belief that God does *not* salvifically love everyone and truly desire everyone to be saved since if he did, according to decretal theology and compatibilism, they would be. Therefore, my modest request is that Calvinists be as forthright in all their writings, sermons, and prayers regarding this inescapable reality of consistent historic Calvinism as they are about Calvinism's more palatable aspects. If a Calvinist is reticent to do so, it might behoove him to reconsider his allegiance to a system of soteriology that indisputably does entail such beliefs. Moreover, a lack of consistent clarity in such a vital realm of doctrine is a monstrous impediment to meaningful brotherly dialogue so people can make an informed decision of whether to either embrace Calvinism or remain one if they are already a Calvinist.

Regarding this obvious reality, R.C. Sproul says, "If some people are not elected unto salvation then it would seem that God is not all that loving toward them. *For them it seems that it would have been more loving of God not to have allowed them to be born. That may indeed be the case*"[6] (italics added). Such reality makes the difference between God's salvific love for the non-elect non-existent and eternally indistinguishable from if he had indifference or hate for them. When time is no more and hell is populated to the full measure of God's design (according to Calvinism's view of what pleased God), will anyone inside or outside of hell be able to perceive an eternal difference between Calvinism's concept of God's love for the damned and if we simply called such his unmitigated hatred? I think not.[7]

---

6. Bryson, *Five Points of Calvinism*, 44.

7. Romans 9:18 deals with God's choice of how he uses people and not their eternal destiny. It particularly speaks of Pharaoh. Regarding Pharaoh in Romans 9 and the Old Testament narrative in Exodus, neither speaks to his salvation or eternal state. For a fuller treatment of Romans 9, and verse 18 particularly, see Chapter 31, What about Those Who Never Hear the Gospel: The Old Testament. See also my book, *Reflections of a Disenchanted Calvinist*, chapter 19, particularly pages 124–25.

17

Are We to Hope for the Hopeless and Blame and Reward the Determined?

CALVINISM'S DECRETAL THEOLOGY AND commitment to compatibilism create a host of conundrums that result in Calvinist's frequent visits to the storehouse of mysteries. This chapter includes two serious, albeit lesser discussed ones. One of these arises when Calvinists encourage others to have hope for people to be saved when their destiny, whether elect or reprobate, was eternally and unconditionally determined by God. On the surface, such encouragement seems meaningful, but that is only because such statements are almost always understood in a libertarian sense.

If they were understood in a compatible sense, it is not only meaningless, it seems to be glaringly misleading regarding the reality of Calvinism because it gives the unsuspecting false hope. In light of unconditional election and compatibilism, the only true eternal hope for anyone and everyone is that they are included in the group designated as the unconditionally elect. The second difficult problem involves the practice of expressing reward for certain behaviors and blame for others, none of which was the fruit of otherwise choice.

We are to have hope for those whom God desired and designed to have no hope

The Second Helvetic Confession states, "And although God knows who are his, and here and there mention is made of the small number of elect, yet we must hope well of all, and not rashly judge any man to be a reprobate"[1] (italics added). Reprobates are the non-elect, those whom God predestined to be excluded from heaven.

The declaration that we know God has predetermined the existence of the reprobate class raises the question from whence do we derive a

---

1. *Second Helvetic Confession*, 10.4.

legitimately God-honoring directive that "we must hope well of all"? This seems to direct God's people to hope in an eventuality that is undeniably discordant with God's desire, sovereign will, and good pleasure since some are reprobate by God's design; being so they are divinely deprived of a chance for "hope." Knowing this excludes even the remotest possibility of hope for them; why should Calvinists have hope for "all?"

Reliance upon a good faith hope fails just as a good faith offer of the gospel fails for the non-elect. Such is an illusion and an immeasurable cruelty since the call to believe and be forgiven is an unmatchable pretense of hope that is actually a predetermined, vacuous, hopeless, non-accessible offer. The reason we can say this is because we know most assuredly the reprobate class exists just as surely as we know the gospel provides no accessible entree or hope for them; not knowing who each of the reprobates is does nothing to assuage this reality. It would certainly not be less true to declare as forthrightly in gospel presentations the pleasure of God to save some and to damn many, and it would at least be more consistent with Calvinism's unique core tenets; accordingly, it would be more informative to the hearers, even the theologically unsophisticated.

It would even seem it would be far more applaudable to be honest with people and tell them to believe, but also to fear because there are apparently more reprobates than elect. Because the truth is, the person to whom the Calvinist speaks actually has a higher probability to have no hope than hope, and that state of affairs exists because God was well pleased to have created this massive reprobate class for which there is no hope. Consequently, when looking at a group of people, it seems more reflective of Calvinism to say most of you are probably not elect, although some may be; time will tell. I do not mean this sarcastically, but rather as genuinely reflective of the core tenets of Calvinism. At least this is closer to the truth than expressing a hope for all. You may say, this is extremely harsh. To which I respond, so is Calvinism.

Another thought is regarding the Calvinist who has a desire for a particular person to be saved when in fact (unbeknownst to the Calvinist) this person is one whom God chose to reprobate. Such desire might understandably be seen to make the Calvinist appear more benevolent than God. At least one must ask where such a desire originated. It most assuredly did not come from the Holy Spirit operating in the individual's life. That seems to leave only self or satanic deceptive influence. This desire is not a problem for Extensivists since we believe that God does in fact desire to redeem every person (Ezek 18:23, 32; 33:11; 1 Tim 2:4; Titus 2:11; 1 Pet 3:9).

Some Calvinists may respond if he has the desire for the person to be saved or to pray for a particular individual for salvation that is evidence the person is one of the elect, which demonstrates the desire is from God. This then leads to the important question: is the Calvinist sure enough to pass that valuable and comforting news on to the one for whom he just prayed? If he is not sure, then it seems we are back to the original dilemma: is the desire from self and, therefore, sin (caring more about a person's soul than God) or from God? If the person is a non-elect reprobate, we know most assuredly the compassion is not from God. The Calvinist may respond, well should we not pray and hope the best for people? My answer is yes, provided that is God's will for all people, which it is emphatically not according to Calvinism. Calvinists cannot simply borrow from Extensivism when it is convenient and most obviously contrary to one of their core tenets.

We blame and honor man for doing what God determined him to do

It is best to understand Calvinism as micro-determinism because it is not limited to the area of salvation (including reprobation). Well-known moderate Calvinist Millard Erickson, in contrasting Calvinism and Arminianism, says:

> Calvinists believe that God's plan is logically prior and that *human decisions and actions are a consequence*. With respect to the particular matter of the acceptance or rejection of salvation, God in his plan has chosen that some shall believe and thus receive the offer of eternal life. *He foreknows what will happen because he has decided what is to happen. This is true with respect to all other human decisions and actions as well.* God is not dependent on what humans decide. It is not the case, then, that God determines that what humans will do will come to pass, nor does he choose to eternal life those who he foresees will believe. Rather, God's decision has rendered it certain that every individual will act in a particular way[2] (italics added).

I must admit, it took me years to come to grips with the rigorous comprehensiveness of determinism that is innate to Calvinism—my first-grade teacher said I was a very slow learner, and unfortunately she was right. Erickson's words provide an example of why I maintain consistent Calvinism actually requires that everything happens necessarily because neither the predetermined cause, immediate antecedents to the choice, nor the ultimate outcome could be different than what has been pre-determined from

---

2. Erickson, *Christian Theology*, 326.

eternity; nor could it ever be altered by the choice of humans. Necessarily does not mean by force or coercion but only that given the person's past at the moment of decision or action, what comes to pass does so necessarily rather than just certainly.

Consequently, Calvinists should avoid obscuring such determinism by contending or even intimating that human decisions and actions are only certain to happen based upon God's exhaustive foreknowledge (a common practice). The latter claim is true of Extensivism since by God's design, many outcomes could have actually been different had humans chosen differently, which they could have in fact done in many scenarios. These are known as contingencies. They are not the result of God's predetermination, but rather God's predetermination to permit humans to make choices that could have been different than they are.

Unlike Calvinism, Extensivism provides a place for scenarios resulting from human choice, which can originate a new sequence of events and possibilities that would not have existed had the person chosen differently. It also provides a place for scenarios that God *caused* which either do not include human freedom to choose or that override human freedom to choose for an intended outcome. The latter does result in God being solely responsible for that particular decision rather than the individual.

In Scripture God does at times override the will of a king in order to stop the king from using his freedom in a way that would disrupt the continuance of his plan of salvation (Deut 10:14; Ps 10:16, 22:28, 103:19). Calvinism permits in actuality only divine determinism (things happen necessarily), whereas Extensivism permits both divine determinative causality (things happen necessarily) and divinely comprehended human contingencies that he foreknows (things happen certainly). That is to say, God has determined some scenarios are temporally necessary while others are not and yet still are temporally certain.[3]

Granted, Calvinists seek to call their decisions certain rather than necessary because the latter seems to imply the absence of a free decision. If the term *necessary* is used to deny free choice as defined by compatibilism, then they are justified in their rejection. However, I am not using it in that way.

---

3. The only thing that is necessary about man's libertarian free choice is: first, if man would have chosen otherwise, God would have known that choice because God knows everything and cannot be mistaken; second, the action is temporally necessary as related to God's knowledge since he cannot believe a false future tense proposition. In contrast, it is only temporally certain as to causation in that the action was not necessary as to causation but could have been different in time and space had the person, the libertarian efficient cause, chosen differently. Therefore, it is temporally necessary as it relates to God's knowledge, but it is only temporally certain as it relates to man since man could have chosen differently even with the same past.

According to libertarian freedom, one may choose A over B or B over A. Given the same past, whatever he did choose, he could have chosen differently in the moral moment of the decision; consequently, his decision was not caused by anything beyond himself—agent causation.

In contrast, while one may choose freely according to compatibilism, the agent does not have otherwise choice. His choosing is free so long as it is according to his greatest desire, but the desire is in fact determined by his past. That is, if one predetermines or controls one's past, in this case God, he controls what desire will emanate in the person from which the person will freely choose; therefore, without negating compatibilism's free choice, we can say the choice happens necessarily. It is always important to remember the inherent determinism of compatibilism (sometimes called soft determinism) is no less inviolable than the determinism in hard determinism. The ultimate desire from which one freely chooses is what it is because of determinative antecedents—nature, past, and all of the choices that made up one's past were themselves the result of determinative antecedents. Hence, free decisions are in fact, given one's past, not only certain, they are necessary due to the individual's past—or you do not have compatibilism.

Accordingly, in the final analysis, all of the sophisticated linguistic and philosophical endeavors of Calvinism that seek to elevate God's hatred of sin, desire for man to choose holiness, and his salvific love for those who ultimately perish to a place of biblical fidelity are found wanting. The truth is once this essential reality of Calvinism is disrobed of erudite and elaborate explanations, and removed from residing insufficiently scrutinized within the gauzy shawl of an inscrutable mystery, we find this unsettling and unbiblical truth. According to Calvinism, every single person's thinking, motives, choosing, and acting are exactly as God desired and designed them to be.

This includes every civilly kind thought or act extolled by God and appreciated and rewarded by man. It includes every evil, horrifying, and malevolent act condemned by God and terrifying to man because they all happened in every minute detail as God desired, intended, and predetermined them to be. Every person's rescue from evil such as rape and murder, as well as every person's abandonment to rape and murder are precisely as God desired. Every child being sexually molested, innocent being brutalized, aborted baby, and every other unimaginably gruesome act of barbarism are precisely as God determined them to be. Whether one sexually and physically abuses a small child or rescues such a child is the same in the sense that neither could have chosen differently. Which raises the question, why blame one and reward the other? You say, we sense, intuit, know the abuse is wrong and the rescue is noble. But in a Calvinist system of decretive actions and compatible freedom, those thoughts are equally determined regardless of our conclusion.

I do give credit and even admire the candor of some Calvinists regarding this. Consider Gordon Clark's comment in response to Arminians as he asseverates, "I wish very frankly and pointedly to assert that if a man gets drunk and shoots his family, it was the will of God that he should do so."[4] I appreciate Clark's candor and even applaud it. If more Calvinists spoke clearly about the beliefs and entailments of their system, I think Calvinism's popularity would wane on its own accord.

The reliance upon secondary or tertiary causes (or for that matter quaternary, quinary, senary, septenary, octonary, nonary, and denary causes) fails to assuage this determinative exactness one whit because according to compatibilism, everything is exactly the way God desired. It makes every impression of due punishment or praise having any relationship to what the doer *ought to have done* to be nothing more than a distraction from reality. Apply this to every single thought or act that people have. It makes our deepest understanding of life, liberty, responsibility, right, wrong, reward, and punishment to be no more than the effects of their determinative antecedents. Such as a piece of paper being printed because we clicked print on our computers, only supposedly with experiential deliberation and moral responsibility.[5] There is no more chance of anyone choosing differently than he did choose than the paper, which is obviously none since the paper has no choice. Yes, compatibilism argues that determinism and moral responsibility are compatible, but it is only so in a meaningless world in which every awareness of ought is a delusion.

As Clark exemplifies, some Calvinists do own up to this, and I do respect and appreciate them for doing so. However, my experience indicates most do not. Most either fail to sufficiently or consistently own up to this essential of their system along with the entailments of such determinism. In doing so, they become the ones who obscure this reality of Calvinism by the employment of hollow distinctions, distinctions without an ultimate difference, which actually obscure the micro-determinism beyond recognition for the vast majority of detractors and adherents of Calvinism. Calvinists can be remarkably pellucid in exalting God's determinism through decrees and compatibilism. Yet, with the same sophistication they are unintelligibly cryptic about the deterministic nature of Calvinism when they live, pray, write, and speak libertarianly.

---

4. Clark, *God and Evil*, 27.

5. I say experiential deliberation because it is not actual since it cannot result in a different outcome than what happens given the same past.

This minute determinism does not end at salvation (who gets saved and who does not). It is the only actual factor in producing every effect of even the redeemed. Everything else is essentially the conduit through which the effect travels from determinative antecedent to experience. Everyone who prays or does not pray is equally determined to do so. Everyone who is unfaithful, in any sense, is no less determined to be so than those who are faithful. Such differences are absolutely devoid of a non-determinative element. Any thought of change from determinative antecedent to effect brought about by an otherwise choice involving should or should not is itself the effect of a determined delusion.

Yet, Scripture is clear, as is human life. The ability of people being able to act differently is essential to make sense of Scripture and life. Without this, the Pharisees and people of faith are nothing more than determinatively different, quite unlike that which is portrayed in Scripture (Matt 23; Luke 7:9; Rom 1:18). Warnings given to false prophets and deceivers are not actionable admonitions that are affected by otherwise choice (Matt 6:1; 7:15; 16:11). Determinism makes nonsense of commands calling all to pray (Eph 6:18; Jude 20), and be faithful (1 Tim 1:50; 3:11; 6:12; 2 Tim 2:22; Titus 1:9). Because whether a person prays or does not, is faithful or not, is the outcome of God's determined plan for that person. That cannot be changed by anything other than God's appointed determinative antecedents. Any explicit or implicit idea that one can choose to imitate Paul or God, or choose not to do so (1 Cor 4:16; 11:1; Eph 5:1) is misleading at best. Correcting others to make a change that includes the idea they may not make the change without the correction, or that otherwise choice on the part of the corrector or corrected is objectively involved, is nonsense (Eph 6:4; 1 Cor 4:21; Titus 1:13).

Rewards for faithfulness are, in truth, non-inspiring examples of an unattainable determinism for the determined less faithful (Luke 12:42; 1 Tim 1:12). Even extolling faithfulness (Eph 6:20; 2 Tim 2:2; Heb 11) or denigrating faithlessness (Eph 6:21) is reduced to being nothing more than mere descriptors of their predetermined life (Eph 1:1; 6:21; 1 Tim 1:19; 4:17). No warning or sense of loss can be gleaned from hearing that some will leave the faith (1 Tim 4:1). Even God's promise of faithfulness to believers is less than what it appears to be since the effects of his faithfulness are not what they claim to be. Paul promised the Corinthians God's protection in temptation, and yet every succumbing to temptation is irrefutable evidence of the plan not to protect per compatibilism (1 Cor 10:13). We should not regard those that hear "well done good and faithful slave" (Matt 25:21) any more rewardable or faithful than those who hear "depart from me you who practice lawlessness" (Matt 7:23, 25, 41; Rev 21:8); they are merely doing only what they could do, what God determined them to do. That is to say, they were each as minutely acting according to what God made them to be and do—what God willed them to only be able to do.

Those who serve and sacrifice for the kingdom like the apostles and countless saints through the ages are only acting as they could act according to the determinative plan of God. Those who martyr the faithful, betray the faith, or vulgarize the holy are doing no less than what God desirably determined them to do. Those who praise God and those who blaspheme are the same in the sense that they are doing only what they can do because God determined them to. Any feeling or thought of there being a choice between doing one or the other or that the evildoers ought to have done differently, is a fabrication. Compatibilism argues the determined are morally responsible, but neither Scripture nor life makes sense in that understanding. Apply this to every thought and act as a Christian and that is Calvinism, their muddling statements notwithstanding. The reliance on a person's relationship to God becoming synergistic after monergistic regeneration does nothing to mitigate this because everything is as determined after salvation as before, given compatibilism.

I submit the only way these and a galaxy of other Scriptures, even the very story of Scripture, make sense is if God endowed man with libertarian freedom. This is why Calvinists do not speak consistently with complete determinism. For then, they would have to face the nonsensical and God-degrading logic of their system. Neither Scripture nor life makes sense if man does not have libertarian freedom. Such micro-determinism does indeed make the Bible's ubiquitous commands given to the saved and lost, obedient and disobedient, ultimately meaningless. That is the unavoidable end of theological fatalism. Yes, we do disagree on soteriology, but our preeminent disagreement really harkens back to this; who and what kind of God do we serve?

18

Does Unconditional Election Include a Forced Change, a Freely Chosen Change, or Both?

ONE OF THE MOST difficult tasks of evaluating Calvinism is being able to understand what is meant by the obscurant language that is often employed when they are seeking to present some of the most objectionable components of Calvinism in an attractive manner. If a person is not aware of these more biblically troubling ideas of Calvinism, one can settle into a very palatable but inconsistent Calvinism. I believe we should speak and write so as to be clearly understood. That is not to say all subjects are equally easy to grasp. Rather, we should not write and speak in a way that obscures what we are saying about the non-negotiables of our beliefs. With Calvinists, this usually involves eliding the entailments of the commitments and doctrines of Calvinism.

There are many examples of Calvinists' use of confusing language regarding man's free exercise of faith. The following provides an example of true Calvinism presented in Calvinistic code. In this example, Lewis Sperry Chafer responds to Arminians' rejection of the term sovereign grace and their charge that such coerces or annuls the human will. He writes:

> No step can be taken in the accomplishment of His sovereign purpose which will even tend to coerce the human volition. He does awaken the mind of man to spiritual sanity and brings before him the desirability of salvation through Christ. If by His power, God creates new visions of the reality of sin and of the blessedness of Christ as Savior and under this enlightenment men choose to be saved, their wills are not coerced nor are they deprived of the action of any part of their own beings. It is the unreasoned objection of Arminians that the human will is annulled by sovereign election.[1]

---

1. Chafer, *Systematic Theology*, vol. 3, 284.

This is quite obviously intended to explicitly confirm that the salvific process according to Calvinism does not require man's will to be forcibly changed in the outworking of the doctrine of unconditional election through irresistible grace (the efficacious call), monergistic salvation in which man is completely passive, and the free exercise of faith. To further clarify and strengthen his refutation against Arminians, he quotes Principal Cunningham who so deeply embeds the idea of compatible freedom (and thereby determinism) in his answer that unless one is thoroughly familiar with the idea, it will most assuredly go unnoticed. I will quote him at length in order to provide an example of how they obscure their commitment to determinism and to give the context of the particular statements I will address. Then, I will comment on his defense against Arminians. These kinds of engagements prepare Extensivists to be more skilled at seeing Calvinism for what it is regardless of the eloquence with which it is presented. In reference to the Arminians' charge against Calvinists, Principal Cunningham says:

> They usually represent our doctrine as implying that men are forced to believe and to turn to God against their will . . . This is a misrepresentation. Calvinists hold no such opinion; and it cannot be shown that their doctrine requires them to hold it. Indeed, the full statement of their doctrine upon the subject excludes or contradicts it. Our Confession of Faith, after giving an account of effectual calling, which plainly implies that the grace of God in conversion is an exercise of omnipotence, and cannot be successfully resisted, adds, 'Yet so as they come most freely, being made willing by His grace.' That special operation of the Spirit, which cannot be overcome or frustrated, is just the renovation of the will itself, by which a power of willing what is spiritually good—a power which it has not of itself in its natural condition, and which it could not receive from any source but a divine and almighty agency—is communicated to it. In the exercise of this new power, men are able to co-operate with the Spirit of God, guiding and directing them; and they do this, and do it, not by constraint, but willingly,—being led, under the influence of the news concerning Christ, and the way of salvation which He has opened up to and impressed upon them, and the motives which these views suggest, to embrace Christ, and to choose that better part which shall never be taken away from them. In the commencement of the process, they are not actors at all; they are wholly passive,—the subjects of a divine operation. And from the time when they begin to act in the matter, or really to *do* anything, they act freely and voluntarily, guided by rational motives, derived from the truths which their eyes have

been opened to see, and which, humanly speaking, might have sooner led them to turn to God, had not the moral impotency of their wills to anything spiritually good prevented this result. There is certainly nothing in all this to warrant the representation, that, upon Calvinistic principles, men are forced to repent and believe against their wills, or whether they will or not.[2]

Let me delve into this rebuttal for a moment. Remember according to compatibilism, one is considered to make a free choice when one chooses according to his greatest desire even though the desire is the product of determinative antecedents and one cannot choose differently at that moral moment of decision given the same past or nature; this means, according to compatibilism, every decision man is morally responsible for is both determined and free. Now, with this understanding in mind, one is equipped to detect the otherwise undetectable compatible view of moral freedom ensconced in his response to the Arminians.

First, he argues Arminians are wrong for accusing Calvinists of believing men are "forced to believe and to turn to God against their will." Provided this is an accurate citation of some Arminians, Cunningham is technically correct because neither Calvinism nor compatibilism teach man is "forced to believe."

Second, Cunningham says, "Our Confession of Faith, after giving an account of effectual calling, which plainly implies that the grace of God in conversion is an exercise of omnipotence, and cannot be successfully resisted," adds "yet so as they come most freely, being made willing by His grace." In this statement, he almost indiscernibly blends the effectual calling, which is irresistibly forced against man's fallen nature (man's fallen nature will never produce a desire to do anything but freely resist God), and the result of that unwanted, monergistic, irresistible work of God that produces a new nature (emanating new desires) from which man freely chooses to believe in Christ.

Notice this irresistible omnipotent act preceded man's free choice to believe, which he describes as coming after the lost man is "made willing by His grace." Although he meticulously avoids the term, this is basic compatibilism. To wit, at the precise time of this omnipotent work, man is spiritually passive, and God monergistically does a work of grace in changing fallen man's rebellious, sinful nature that can only disbelieve, so that from the completion of this irresistible divine work, man receives a new nature emanating new desires from which man now can freely believe. It is only after having been "made willing" that man transitions from being passive and

---

2. Cunningham, *Historical Theology*, vol. 2, 413–14.

incapable of believing or participating in any way to playing an active part in the process by freely believing. To engage the beliefs of Calvinism properly, one must recognize this sequential distinction.

It is prior to quickening or regeneration that man is totally passive. Man's passiveness is stated explicitly in The Westminster Confession. "This effectual call [to salvation] is of God's free and special grace alone, not from anything at all foreseen in man, *who is altogether passive* therein, *until, being quickened and renewed by the Holy Spirit*, he is thereby enabled to answer this call, and to embrace the grace offered and conveyed by it"[3] (italics added). This is the precise sequence laid out by Cunningham. I add to this the clarification that the sinner is not only "enabled," but according to Calvinism, he is enabled against his will; further, not only is he enabled to believe, but he is *made* to only be able to believe rather than choose between believing and not believing (this is because of Calvinist's commitment to compatible moral freedom). Therefore, the faith after the quickening is free according to compatibilism, but the quickening is forced upon a passive being.

Here is his argument stated slightly differently but using the same words so as to see his point. The last part says "they come most freely," but notice they come most freely only after they are "made willing by His grace." The specific grace that makes them willing is seen in his first statement. It comes upon the lost elect first. Of which he says, "the grace . . . cannot be successfully resisted." Calvinism is replete with arguments that all lost man can do is to resist. This work of grace upon the lost elect is resisted by the lost elect, but he is unsuccessful in his fight against it because it cannot be resisted; irresistible grace is the fourth component of the TULIP.[4]

It seems to me one simply cannot logically or scripturally argue man is *totally* passive and regeneration is *monergistic*—God working independently of the human will—on one hand, while seeking to maintain man has a simultaneously *substantive* role in the process, which Calvinists are prone to do. Man cannot both be active and passive at the same time in the same sense. A Calvinist may argue that man's actions are a part of the process, but he cannot argue that they are *contingently, substantively,* or *inextricably* part of the process, which in fact is the clear teaching and portrayal of Scripture. If one argues man's actions do have a *substantive* and *integral* role, then it seems Calvinism is positing either God foreknew this or he predetermined

---

3. The Westminster Confession of Faith, Chapter X, Section II.

4. Efficacious grace is used and preferred by some regarding this irresistible act of God; regardless which term is used, this act of God upon the elect is indomitable.

it, which seems to mean man is not totally passive and, therefore, regeneration is not monergistic.

Third, the following statement says precisely what I have said in my explanation of his words, albeit the compatibilism is far more concealed. He says, "That special operation of the Spirit, which cannot be overcome or frustrated, is just the *renovation of the will itself*, by which a power of willing what is spiritually good—a power which it has not of itself in its natural condition, and which it could not receive from any source but a divine and almighty agency—is communicated to it" (italics added). Observe the emphasis upon the irresistibility of this operation of the Spirit, which underscores again that fallen man cannot choose to believe given his nature and past, and yet he is also incapable of successfully "frustrating" this initial regenerative work of God; even though resisting the work of God is precisely the only thing he desires and is capable of doing at this point in the salvific process given his nature and past according to compatibilism. I would also include Calvinism's understanding of total depravity. This simply means at this stage in the process, the work of God is forced upon the rebellious sinner who hates God and everything holy. The transition from only being able to actively hate, resist, and blaspheme God to being able to believe and honor God is the result of an omnipotent act to which the unregenerate contribute nothing except their hostile and futile resistance; therefore, it is anything but a cordial transition.

He refers to this act of God as "the renovation of the will itself" which gives a "power of willing what is spiritually good." Up until the "renovation" the individual could not act (except in rebellion against God), participate, or believe, but subsequent to the renovation comes a new power to will what is "spiritually good." The renovation (some use regeneration or quickening) changes the person's nature from which emanates new desires. From these new desires, he now not only *can* will the "spiritually good" (believe in Christ), but he will necessarily and inviolably only will himself to freely believe. He can no longer choose not to believe given this new past. It is not that he *merely will not*; rather, he *cannot will to* disbelieve.

Fourth, in the next part he elaborates on this new power to choose "spiritual good," i.e., exercise a free choice to believe. Keep in mind this ability, as he has sequenced, comes only after the forced "renovation." He says, "In the exercise of this new power, men are able to co-operate with the Spirit of God, guiding and directing them; and they do this, and do it, not by constraint, but willingly,—being led, under the influence of the news concerning Christ and the way of salvation which He has opened up to and impressed upon them and the motives which these views suggest, to embrace Christ, and to choose that better part which shall never be taken away from them." Therefore, once man's nature has been changed in the forced renovation, then and only then, man is enabled to "co-operate with the Spirit of God."

Accordingly, the Calvinists are correct in denying they believe man is forced to believe in Christ because this free choice to believe is in fact what one does after the "renovation." Note the renovation was not something man freely chose or even actively participated in; actually, his only activity up to and at that point in the salvific process was rebellion. At the time of renovation, man is only active in rebellion and resisting the omnipotent work of grace—irresistible grace or effectual calling—which he cannot succeed in resisting. He is not cooperating spiritually or willfully in any sense because he is totally passive (in the sense of cooperating with God) until after the renovation. This renovation is imposed upon man against the exercise of his free will, free choice, which can only act in rebellion, emanating from the desires of his fallen nature. At this stage, the work of God is monergistic—God alone.

Only subsequent to having been renovated does his new nature emanate new desires enabling him to become a participant in the process by freely choosing to repent and believe in Christ. Notably, and often omitted in Calvinism's explanations as is done here, subsequent to renovation the person is no more able to choose not to believe than he was able to choose to believe prior to God's omnipotently imposed renovation. What is seen by examining Cunningham's statements is that because of these encryptions, one has to be very precise in order to expose the actual meaning and determinism of Calvinism, thereby avoiding being summarily dismissed by Calvinists as misrepresenting their perspective.

Fifth, the summarization of his remarks is precisely according to compatibilism as is my explanation of the meaning of his comments. He states, "In the commencement of the process, they are not actors at all; they are wholly passive,—the subjects of a divine operation. And from the time when they begin to act in the matter, or really to *do* anything, they act freely and voluntarily, guided by rational motives, derived from the truths which their eyes have been opened to see, and which, humanly speaking, might have sooner led them to turn to God, had not the moral impotency of their wills to anything spiritually good prevented this result." What his refutation of the Arminian charge does, in the final analysis, is only to point out an imprecision in their critique rather than liberating Calvinism from definite determinism.

As we look at this statement more closely we see at the "commencement" of the salvific process (up to and when the renovation happens), man is not "an actor" in the progression because he is "wholly passive," and this passivity continues until the "divine operation" is complete; an operation he neither sought nor desired because as a sinner he could only fight against any spiritual overture. Once the operation is complete and the "subject" has experienced the divine "renovation" (receives a new nature which emanates new desires), "they begin to act in the matter . . . they act freely and voluntarily." This is the component many are confused about, which makes them imprecise in their evaluation of Calvinism, leaving them legitimately open to the charge of misrepresenting Calvinism. Compatibilism includes voluntariness (the person acts freely) but excludes origination (the person can, given the same past or nature, originate a new sequence of events, i.e., choose otherwise in the moral moment of decision). This is precisely what we see in his defense of Calvinism.

Cunningham concludes, "There is certainly nothing in all this to warrant the representation, that, upon Calvinistic principles, men are forced to repent and believe against their wills." Once again, technically he is correct because the exercise of repentance and faith after the renovation is according to their new wills and desires. However, what is eloquently concealed in Cunningham's correction of the Arminians is that the free choice to repent is indeed a predetermined free choosing that emanates from God's irresistible (although it was indeed resisted by the lost man every step of the way) renovation. To clarify, the free choice to repent and believe after the renovation was as inviolably necessary and irresistible as the free choice of the sinner to resist God prior to the renovation. In each state, the individual did what he voluntarily chose to do, but he could not have originated a different sequence of events (chosen differently) than the sequence that happened in the respective states of the continuum.

Therefore, Calvinism's belief about man being endowed with compatible freedom does mean that every decision, from choosing to sin to accepting or rejecting Christ is a predetermined free choice. Man's choice is not based merely upon God's foreknowledge of what man *will* choose (libertarian freedom, contingencies), but rather upon what God predetermined man can *only will* to choose. Man being compatibly endowed *cannot will* himself to choose differently than he does choose. While he does possess voluntariness, he does not possess the ability to originate a new sequence of events; such possibility is absolutely absent from compatibilism and Calvinism.

This determinism is necessarily based upon the nature of compatibilism, microscopic to the point that if it were true, every biblical portrait of man choosing between accessible options of good and evil, your choosing to read or not read this book, and even whether you agree or not, was inviolably determined by your past or nature, which ultimately originated with God. Any sense of choosing between reading or not, agreeing or not, is a delusion—as is every sense of choosing between various seemingly accessible options.

Now to the question of this chapter, "Does unconditional election include a forced change, a freely chosen change, or both?" The answer is both. It is inaccurate for Extensivists to say Calvinists believe man is *forced to repent and believe*, but it is equally inaccurate for Calvinists to deny they believe the elect are *forced to freely repent and believe*. My prayer is that Calvinists would be more forthright in the conveyance of their compatibilist perspective on freedom and do so accurately.

A precise understanding of the issue regarding our different perspectives concerning the moral freedom and nature of man brings us to the real issue, which is the person of God. This is where the genesiacal and cardinal disagreement between Extensivists and Calvinists exists from which other disagreements emerge.

19

Does God Have Two Wills?

THE SIMPLE AND STRAIGHTFORWARD message of Scripture is God loves everyone and truly desires for everyone to hear the gospel and be saved by faith in Jesus Christ. This reality leads some Calvinists like John Piper to postulate God has a secret will in which he does not desire everyone to be saved.[1]

That is to say, by what we know from Scripture and the good news of the gospel, God wills for all to have an opportunity to be saved by faith in Christ. But according to Calvinists like John Piper, God secretly wills his public will, as revealed in Scripture, be superseded by unconditionally electing only some to salvation and choosing to pass over the rest of humanity. Therefore, we are to believe according to God's revealed will (Scripture), that God salvifically loves every person and desires for every person to be saved (Ezek 18:23, 32; 33:11; John 3:16–17; 1 Tim 2:3–4; 4:10; Titus 2:11; 2 Pet 3:9), but in his secret will, he only wills to make salvation *actually* available to the unconditionally elect.

Piper says, "My aim here is to show from Scripture that the simultaneous existence of God's will for 'all persons to be saved' (1 Tim. 2:4) and his will to elect unconditionally those who will actually be saved is not a sign of divine schizophrenia or exegetical confusion. A corresponding aim is to show that unconditional election, therefore, does not contradict biblical expressions of God's compassion for all people, and does not nullify sincere offers of salvation to everyone who is lost among all the peoples of the world."[2]

First, I note Piper's statement seems to be a rather clear admission that God's revelation to man does declare that he sincerely desires for every individual to believe upon the Lord Jesus Christ and be saved, which is the unabashed banner of Extensivism. Other Calvinists' attempts to limit verses like

---

1. Sometimes referred to as decretive will, see David Allen's book, *The Extent of the Atonement*, 787.
2. Piper, "Are There Two Wills in God?" par. 1.

1 Tim 2:4 notwithstanding.[3] If Piper's words are not such an admission, then the whole development of the two wills seems rather pointless.

In addition, there is no parallel conflict with Extensivism's claim that God created man with otherwise choice, always desiring for man to live a holy life while knowing he would sin, and in love, mercy, and forbearance provisioning so that every person may fulfill God's desire for him to live forever holy. Contrastingly, in Calvinism we have God's desire that all be saved according to Scripture while simultaneously revealing in his superior inviolable secret plan that he really precludes the provision for that to happen because his revealed will is actually subservient to his secret will and flatly contradicts it, all the while still declaring publicly he desires all to be saved.

John Murray and Ned Stonehouse, speaking of God's decretive will, said "It must be said that God absolutely decrees the eternal death of some wicked and, in that sense, is absolutely pleased so to decree. . . . Obviously, however, it is not his decretive will that all repent and be saved. While, on the one hand, he has not decretively willed that all be saved, yet he declares unequivocally that it is his will and, impliedly, his pleasure that all turn and be saved. We are again faced with the mystery and adorable richness of the divine will. It might seem to us that the one rules out the other. But it is not so."[4]

If one is not a Calvinist, the claim "it is not his decretive will that all repent and be saved" and "it is his will and . . . his pleasure that all turn and be saved" is nothing more than an egregious and absolute contradiction in which one does, in fact, rule out the other. Moreover, the elevation of God's secret, decretive, will that is in such irreconcilable conflict with his revealed will unequivocally undermines the trustworthiness of his revealed will in the Scripture on which we base our lives; no amount of elegant prose or theological sophistry can palliate that reality. It is not a "mystery" or "adorable richness"; it is a God-dishonoring absurdity! If this type of illogical

---

3. Related commentary on 1 Timothy 2:3–4 notes, "The antecedent of 'this' is the reference to prayer for all people in v. 1. Paul stated that God is pleased to see believers earnestly concerned for the salvation of all humankind and not simply for an elitist group . . . The relative clause of v. 4 provides the basis for the assertion in v. 3 that prayer for all people is pleasing to God. The goal of the prayers Paul urged is that all people be saved. Intercession for all people pleases the God who desires all to be saved. As Jesus did when he prayed for his disciples (John 17:9) and those who would believe (John 17:20) and that the world might believe (John 17:21). The term 'all' in v. 4 must refer to the same group as the reference to 'everyone' in v. 1. The petitions of v. 1 are to include all human beings, and the objects of Christ's death must include the same group. It would certainly include all persons without distinctions of race or social standing, but it also refers to all persons individually." Lea and P. Griffin, *1, 2 Timothy, Titus*, 88–89.

4. Murray and Stonehouse, *The Free Offer*, 127.

reasoning is used anywhere other than Calvinists' attempt to justify the unjustifiable, they would see it for what it is, bosh.

Second, in defense of his two-will theory, Piper draws upon the biblical reality of God's holiness and the presence of sin. He says, "The most compelling example of God's willing for sin to come to pass while at the same time disapproving the sin is his willing the death of his perfect, divine Son. The betrayal of Jesus by Judas was a morally evil act inspired immediately by Satan (Luke 22:3). Yet in Acts 2:23 Luke says, 'This Jesus [was] *delivered up according to the definite plan (boule) and foreknowledge of God.'* The betrayal was sin, and it involved the instrumentality of Satan, but it was part of God's ordained plan. That is, there is a sense in which God willed the delivering up of his Son, even though the act was sin."[5]

It seems to me Piper makes two mistaken assumptions. His first error is assuming the correctness of compatibilism and decretal theology so that everything is determined. Granted, if compatibilism is true, his problematic conclusion is understandable since there is a problem if God is "willing for sin to come to pass" in a determinative way via compatibilism, while simultaneously "disapproving the sin." Additionally, because of the deterministic nature of compatibilism even the very existence of sin is a problem because it entails God predetermining for sin to happen when he could have predetermined for it not to happen.

This means, since everything is determined according to compatibilism and decretal theology, God simultaneously desires holiness and sin in the same determinative sense, at the same time. Accordingly, this would mean God predetermined the individuals to sin precisely as they did and then condemns them for acting as he determined that they could only act. Piper is correct that the actions of Judas were sin and evil, inspired by Satan; it is his assumption of compatibilism where his confusion actually lies. From a libertarian perspective, the evil done by Judas and others is sufficiently and ultimately caused by their free acts as efficient causes, thereby eliminating the presence of conflict between God abhorring sin and permitting sin as the result of the free acts of man, which is not true of compatibilism.

From a libertarian perspective, God willed to permit man to sin and comprehended such in his creation-redemption plan. Note the verse says Jesus was "delivered up according to the definite plan and foreknowledge of God." Foreknowledge of God in Calvinism is basically the same as foreordination; to wit, God foreknows what he predetermines because he predetermined it to be so, whereas in Extensivism God's foreknowledge depicts his knowledge of not only what he predetermines (apart from human choice) but also

---

5. Piper, "Are There Two Wills in God?" par. 13.

contingencies that result from otherwise choice. The latter simply means that by free choice God delivered his Son and used the sinful free choices of those involved, without ever having to have ultimately caused or desired the sin of the individuals. Had they not freely chosen to sin in the way God prophesied, and they could have so chosen according to Scripture and Extensivism, he would not have used these particular people. He only prophesies future truths regardless if they come about by predestination or the otherwise choices of mankind. The latter he knows innately as a being who is essentially omniscient rather than determinatively or perceptively.

In contrast, according to Calvinism, the men acted sinfully because they could not have refrained from such behavior, and in that sense you have God both desiring and predetermining sin through compatibilism while quite contradictorily disapproving of the sin he desired and ultimately caused to happen; that he is not the proximate cause or that he used secondary causes does not mean he is not the ultimate cause in a deterministic system like Calvinism. In other words, as holy God, he commands man not to sin, condemns sin, judges sin, hates sin, and yet predetermines that man will freely choose to sin and cannot refrain from choosing to sin. That is true of the sin of Judas as well as every other person's sin. Consequently, God's causal relationship to the sinful acts of those involved in the crucifixion is problematic for Piper because of his commitment to decretal theology and compatibilism.

Another point of clarification regarding sin as a part of God's plan is because without the presence of sin there would be no need for a redemption plan. And since God is sovereign, we can be assured nothing happens outside his jurisdictional plan, and that includes all evil, sin, good, and holiness. I do not believe it is the recognition of this reality that is the problem Piper feels a need to address. The problem is why sin and evil exist. Piper's belief in compatibilism and decretal theology is why he has a problem reconciling the presence of sin and God's holiness.

Outside of decretal thinking, there does not seem to be anything in Scripture to forbid the congruence of eternal holiness and the temporary existence of sin. But according to compatibilism, you have God calling all to be holy while simultaneously predestining that they are not and cannot be apart from his limited elective purposes. This perspective leaves Calvinists with the compatibilist acts of Judas, as well as all the sinful acts of others involved in crucifying Christ, and God delivering Christ involving the same degree of determinism, only in slightly different ways, not degrees. That is a problem.

As a Calvinist, who views foreknowledge and foreordination as virtually the same, Piper understands the predetermined plan of God to include the reality that everyone involved was predetermined to do what they did. If, as Extensivists maintain, foreknowledge reflects the eternal knowledge of God as an essentially omniscient being, the problem is nonexistent. We simply have God working according to his predetermined coextensive creation-redemption plan that comprehended rather than predetermined the sinful choices of man. God predetermined to provide redemption for man which need was wrought by man's libertarian choices, which he did not have to make. God always knew man would sin; he always knew he would not simply leave his creation to its just deserts, but rather he predetermined to pay for the sins of man by giving his Son for the sins of man. This sacrifice included the sins of those who libertarianly chose to betray Christ in the crucifixion (Acts 5:31).

Piper's second error is seen in his statement, "That is, there is a sense in which God willed the delivering up of his Son, even though the act was sin." Now, while the work of Satan and sinful men in relation to the crucifixion is clearly sin, Scripture does not seem to support the contention that God either willing "the delivering up of his Son" or giving his Son to die and pay for the sins of mankind is sin. Although quite unsettling, it seems the act which Piper refers to as sin, is specifically, the act in which "God willed the delivering up of his Son" rather than the acts of man alone. The antecedent to "sin" is the act of God delivering up his Son.

While I acknowledge the actions of the humans involved was sin, I do not agree with the statement, "God willed the delivering up of his Son . . . was sin." Nor do I think anyone should even speak in ways that suggest such as a possibility much less explicitly say so. At best, he seems to conflate the sinful acts of men with the loving sacrificial act of God giving his Son. For such a claim to be valid, it would seem to necessitate an explicit assertion from Scripture for such being the case, and there does not seem to be one. It appears his commitment to Calvinism's determinism blurs this vital distinction.

Of course, sin occasioned the need for the cross, both in the original fall of Adam and Eve and in this passage, as is true of all sin. That is quite different from saying God ordained for man to sin, and he could not actually have chosen not to sin, both in the fall of Adam and here as entailed in Calvinism and compatibilism. What is clear from Scripture, and extricates us from the Calvinist conundrum is this. Both here and consistent with all of Scripture, God predetermined to create man with otherwise choice and permit him to choose to use his free will for good or evil; God also predetermined to overcome sin through his redemption plan, all for his glory.

As far as I can tell, Scripture is completely and compellingly consistent in declaring God's salvation plan, including most importantly the delivering of his Son to die for the sins of the world, as a selfless act of love, mercy, and unbounded grace flowing from God's very essence of love and omnibenevolence. Many Scriptures attest to the reality that everything he did regarding the death and provision of Christ's sacrifice is love and not sin (John 3:16; 14:13; Rom 5:8; 8:39; Eph 2:4; 5:2; 2 Thess 2:16; 1 John 3:1, 16; 4:9–10, 16, 19), mercy (Rom 11:30, 32; Eph 2:4; 1 Tim 1:13, 16; Titus 3:5; Heb 4:16; 1 Pet 1:3; 2:10), and grace (Acts 15:11; 20:24; Rom 1:5; 3:24; 4:16; 5:15, 17; Gal 2:21; Eph 1:7; 2:5, 7–8; 2 Tim 1:9; Titus 2:11; Heb 2:9; 4:16; 1 Pet 1:10).

Additionally, we are told Christ laid down his own life. Surely there is no biblical reason to view that decision and act as sin but rather a sacrifice of love for the most unworthy (John 10:11, 15, 17–18). In John 10:18 Christ emphatically stated, "No one has taken it away from me." Here he makes a clear distinction between what he was doing, freely giving his life as a sacrifice, and the sin of evil men who betrayed him (Matt 17:22). He was delivered by God for a holy and loving purpose into the hands of sinful men, which included allowing men to un-determinatively act sinfully (Matt 26:24; Luke 24:7). God's plan included the free choice of Christ to lay his life down, which was holy, loving, and sacrificial. He also allowed evil men to freely choose to act in concert with his plan, this according to libertarian freedom. Christ delivering himself up was not sin; nor was it sin for the Father to deliver him or use the libertarian free evil choices of sinful men for good, but the free acts of men in choosing to betray Christ is the sin.

I realize Piper believes God's salvation is born out of his love for us; however, he is the one who is failing to make an unambiguous distinction between God delivering his Son, an act of holy love, and man's sinful choice to betray him, an act of ungodliness. He seems blinded by his desire to defend unconditional election. Therefore, we may rightly say the action of the sinners was a sin, but God's creation of libertarian freedom, permitting the misuse of such freedom, and comprehending such in his plan, which involved the giving of his Son to die for man's sin, is not sin but rather infinite love and mercy.

Piper erroneously fuses the act of delivering up Christ by man and the act of Christ delivering up himself under one categorical act; seemingly leaving only two options. Both man's participation and Christ's act were holy, or man's and Christ's acts were sin, or at least somehow tainted by sin. His problem and argument seem to deteriorate under their own weight once libertarian freedom is accepted because there is an unambiguous demarcation between libertarian free sinful acts and God giving his Son for unworthy sinners; if he does make a demarcation, it is anything but clear. What I am saying is not to be understood as a slight against Piper's character or love for God, both of which I have high regard for. I am only addressing his Calvinistically-generated dilemma in which he fails to establish the *essential dissimilarity* between the sinful acts of man and the holy acts of the Father giving the Son and the Son giving himself; something Christ was clear about (John 10:18; 19:10-11).

With these distinctions in mind, we can see it is not Scripture that presents the problem mentioned by Piper. Rather the problem emanates from Piper's commitment to compatibilism and decretal theology. Meaning, he does not see that God comprehended the free otherwise choice of man in what he ordained to happen. Viewed from the libertarian perspective, in this passage specifically, God foreknew he would ordain Christ to be crucified, and he foreknew he would comprehend man's free otherwise sinful actions in the event known as the crucifixion. Accordingly, he neither caused nor predetermined the evil in the event because man's free choice accounts for that. God did ordain that he would permit it and overcome it by sending Christ to die for those as well as all sins.

To think about how contingent realities, which incorporate man's libertarian freedom, affect the certainty of prophecy and the assurance of God's word can be helpful. First, it is important to note when God speaks about an event that is still future (prophecy), it does not necessitate that he actually causes all or even part of it. Although, he surely may do so if he so pleases. If contingencies, actions, and results of morally free beings exist, then God can prophesy because either he will choose to cause every detail of the event (predetermine it) or because he intrinsically knows what the individuals will do because he is essentially omniscient. Given these realities, he also can prophesy of an event that incorporates both components, those he determined and those contingencies he comprehended in the prophecy that are known simply because he is omniscient. Often, we see both realities in biblical prophecy as I think we do in the passage under consideration (Acts 2:23).

Regarding the aspects that are the results of the actions of morally free beings, William Lane Craig says, "The temporal contingency of God's foreknowledge (and, hence, of prophecy) is counterfactual, not causal, in nature. Once a prophecy has been given, we can be absolutely certain that it will come to pass . . . If the relevant person were to refrain from doing what was prophesied, then God would have foreknown this fact and never given the prophecy in the first place."[6] By counterfactual, he means if the person acts a certain way there will be one outcome and if the person were to choose to act differently, there will be a different outcome; God's knowledge

---

6. Here Craig is arguing against a supposed mischaracterization by Molina of Ockham's position. Craig, *Divine Foreknowledge*, 198.

of such is not due to his determining it to be so, but because he is essentially omniscient and, therefore, knows all contingencies.

Additionally, the existence of libertarian freedom does not mean God cannot override one's freedom at any time he chooses or for any purpose he so chooses. He is sovereign over the force of otherwise choice as he is with every created force. It only means, since he freely and sovereignly chose to incorporate libertarian freedom in his plan and given his perfect foreknowledge of what man will do given the opportunity, he does not always have to override such freedom to accomplish his purposes. If he does override a particular choice of man so that it is not a free choice, man is simply not responsible for that particular choice.

To say one could act in such a way so as to bring about the reality God would have believed differently about a future state is not the same as saying one has the power today to influence God's past belief about today. It is not to suggest one can act so as to change the past (or the future once known by God). Rather, it is to say God's knowledge of *some* of the future is conditional—if people choose to act a certain way—and would have been different had the person used his God-granted freedom to choose differently. Such is the freedom that exists only because God sovereignly and freely chose to endow man with such freedom-producing contingencies in his plan. Libertarian freedom does not make God dependent upon man because God is the one who predetermined to create and comprehend otherwise choice in man.

Consequently, the Extensivist perspective demonstrates God's love in willing the death of his Son for the sins of all. It recognizes God did not causally predetermine the sin committed by the individuals; consequently, they did not have to choose to act sinfully in this particular way. This means God permitted their sin while non-contradictorily detesting their sin, yet comprehending it in his coextensive creation-redemption plan; therefore, Extensivism's libertarian perspective is disencumbered of Calvinism's dilemma which occasions the indefensible secret salvational provisioning for only some whom he really desires to be saved, a plan which categorically contradicts God's revealed will of desiring that all would come to repentance (2 Pet 3:9).[7]

Regarding the usage of the crucifixion as what Piper deems to be the "most compelling example" to demonstrate the cogency of his secret will theory, it seems actually to provide a glaring illustration of the weakness of the two wills theory; this is, in part, because it relies upon Christ dying

7. See John Calvin's contradictory defense of God desiring all to be saved while simultaneously by his "hidden purpose . . . the reprobate are doomed." Calvin, *Commentaries on Second Peter*, 419.

for the sin of man and God permitting the sin of man, both of which are revealed in Scripture. In other words, he uses *what is revealed* in Scripture to prove the existence of the *unrevealed* two-will theory that, in the end, contravenes and nullifies the revealed will of God. Given libertarian freedom, there is nothing inharmonious with the existence of a temporary state of affairs that includes sinful acts and what Scripture reveals about the nature of God. He is holy, merciful, and longsuffering. If this revealed truth about God was contradicted by a secret truth, which revealed God was not holy, merciful, or longsuffering as portrayed in Scripture, then we would be speaking about a conflict that is analogical to the one in the two wills scenario. The truth of the secret will is it actually, in eternity, trumps the revealed will regarding salvation.

When the full range of God's attributes and the creation-redemption plan are unbiasedly considered, there simply is no conflict. What would be as problematic as Calvinism's revealed-secret will theory is if God's revelation taught his holiness permits sin only for a season and then must be judged, and his secret will precluded the presence of sin for any reason or any time. Alternatively, it would be as problematic as the idea that he permitted the death of Christ in his revealed will, but not in his secret will. Other than the existence of such irreconcilable ideas, the parallel Piper draws is nonexistent when considered from a biblical and Extensivist perspective.

Relying on examples that are clearly portrayed in Scripture, harmonized by the reality that Scripture undeniably presents sin as something God overcomes by his loving redemption plan, which cannot be eternally thwarted by a secret plan, actually undermines Calvinism's defense of another will that eternally supersedes God's revealed will. Rather than Scripture fostering such an enigma, it is actually Calvinism's soteriology that provides the dilemma. Calvinism creates the need for another will theory because Calvinism's whole soteriology teaches that all those God elects will be saved and those he rejects to elect cannot be saved. This is absolute. God willed this inviolable eternal outcome. Accordingly, the Calvinists' actual problem is their belief in pervasive determinism and unconditional election, which includes man being endowed with a compatible freedom because it imprisons God's revealed desire to save all in the gulag of his determinative desire not to save all.

The inescapable reality is that the two-wills concept is not explicit in Scripture, whereas, as cited by Piper, the express will for "all persons to be saved" (2 Pet 3:9) is in Scripture.[8] Both terms *thélō* (1 Tim 2:4) and *boúlo-*

---

8. Kenneth O. Gangel, commenting on 2 Pet 3:9, says, "The words not wanting (mēboulomenos) anyone to perish do not express a decree, as if God has willed everyone to be saved. Universal salvation is not taught in the Bible. Instead those words

mai (2 Pet 3:9) are used regarding God's express desire, will, for all to be saved. Calvinism's commitment to compatibilism and decretalism is where the real dilemma exists. This is because they mean God's will (what will happen) is precisely what he desires to happen, and there is not the slightest degree of deterministic difference between what God permits and what he decrees. When Calvinists make statements or employ such distinctions in their arguments, they are simply obscuring the true teaching and entailments of Calvinism because they are distinctions without a difference. One simply cannot conveniently deemphasize or elide the micro-deterministic nature of Calvinism; it is always present in unalterable force. Reliance upon secondary, tertiary, quaternary, quinary, or senary causes does nothing to palliate this reality.

I further find Piper's endeavor to be profoundly puzzling in light of his other writings. Piper says he is attempting to "show from Scripture that the simultaneous existence of God's will for 'all persons to be saved' (1 Tim 2:4) and his will to elect unconditionally those who will actually be saved . . . [and] that unconditional election therefore does not contradict biblical expressions of God's compassion for all people, and does not nullify sincere offers of salvation to everyone who is lost among all the peoples of the world." Yet, elsewhere he passionately argues[9] God's mission is not to take the gospel to the nations in order to save as many individuals as possible, but rather "to reach all the people groups of the world and thus to gather the 'sons of God' . . . and to call all the 'ransomed from every tongue and tribe and people and nation.'"[10] Accordingly, the argument is that the real meaning of the reading of any and every verse in Scripture that explicitly says or even graphically portrays God's salvific love for all mankind (John 3:16; 1 John 2:2) can only be gleaned by knowing God's secret will regarding unconditional election. Thus, the revealed will (Scripture) is insufficient to know God's *real* will, and I would say, it is even torturously misleading.

I do recognize there are secrets of God not revealed in Scripture (Deut 29:29), but since they are secret, how can Calvinists know what they are? Employing logical deductions in an attempt to reconcile explicit revelatory teaching with Calvinism seems to provide a woefully inadequate basis for a secret will on which so much is at stake, and this particularly when it undermines what God has explicitly revealed. This seems to be nothing more

---

describe God's wishes or desires; He longs that all would be saved (cf. 1 Tim. 2:4) but knows that many reject Him." "2 Peter," 876.

9. Piper, *Let the Nations Be Glad*, 204. See also 203, 222–23.

10. Piper, *Let the Nations Be Glad*, 203. Piper actually gives ten reasons why Matt 28:18–20 should not be understood to include every person, 203–4.

than double talk, and more importantly, it leads to an unreliability of the straightforward teaching of God's revealed will regarding salvation.[11]

Who is to say there is not another will (a third will) that supersedes this second will so necessary to Calvinism? Logically one may add, if God has a secret will that is contrary to his revealed will regarding salvation, then it seems quite plausible he may have a secret will affecting other areas like the doctrine of the church, prayer, or possibly every area, thereby making the revealed will of God pervasively untrustworthy. Moreover, if such reliance upon a secondary will is deemed admissible in order to justify a significant concept of Calvinism within orthodox Christianity, then who is to say other groups (like cults or Islam) cannot argue with equal validity for the existence of yet another will that supersedes or conflicts with the clear and ubiquitous teaching of Scripture in order to demonstrate the cogency of their extra-biblical essentials? Surely the Calvinists' endeavor to defend the two wills of God makes their claim of sola scriptura seem a frail stalwart for defending the sufficiency of Scripture against foes who employ the same tactics; it is an ineffectualness born and sustained by their own forays into the academy of secrecy to bolster their theology when it conflicts with explicit revelation.

David Engelsma, a strong Calvinist, says of this position and the Calvinists who retreat to mystery "that God is gracious only to some in predestination, but gracious to all in the gospel, and that God wills only some to be saved in predestination but wills all to be saved by the gospel, is flat, irreconcilable contradiction. It is not paradox, but contradiction. I speak reverently: God Himself cannot reconcile these teachings."[12] Therefore, I would ask that Piper simply accept the actual teachings of Calvinism without resorting to tactics that confuse the clear teaching of Scripture.

---

11. Double talk speaks of contradictory language and is not meant pejoratively.

12. Engelsma, "Is Denial of the 'Well-Meant Offer' Hyper-Calvinism?" under the heading "The Weight of Christian Tradition" par. 3.

20

A Better Gospel!

THE GOOD NEWS ACCORDING to Calvinism is to be proclaimed to everyone everywhere, but it is not good news for everyone who hears. I believe the gospel according to Jesus presents a better gospel.

To many, it appears Calvinists, Arminians, Molinists, and Traditionalists (the last three I refer to, broadly speaking, as Extensivists) all believe the same thing about the gospel while merely differing on tertiaries. Consequently, they quite understandably retort, "Why all of this divisive bickering; let us just preach the gospel." I wholeheartedly agree that we can all communicate the gospel message so that anyone and everyone who calls upon the name of the Lord will be saved. Consequently, we should do so and applaud all endeavors at such. I also believe both Extensivists and Calvinists can be evangelistic.

However, I do think it is incumbent upon Christians to make clear that even though these things are true, the differences between Calvinists' and Extensivists' perspectives regarding salvation do in fact influence the evangelistic and missionary endeavor. This influence is even determinative of what one can and cannot say to a lost and hell-bound individual and world when we communicate the gospel. These differences are not tertiary as some claim, for they do in fact change the *raison d'être* (reason for being or existence) of the gospel, the purpose for sharing the gospel, the language used in communicating the gospel, and the nature of our passion derived from the gospel. These dissimilarities are substantial. So much so they actually and unavoidably define the missiology of the church; accordingly, they are not tertiary. Our differences even affect our understanding of arguably the most well-known, lucid, humbling, and awe-inspiring verse regarding the gospel and mission of evangelizing (John 3:16).

John Piper asked the question, "What message would missionaries rather take than the message: Be glad in God! Rejoice in God! Sing for joy in God! . . . God loves to exalt himself by showing mercy to sinners."[1] My

---

1. Piper, *Let the Nations Be Glad*, 33.

answer to this question is the truth that when someone hears this glorious message that same someone has a chance, by the grace and mercy of God, to receive the truth of the message by faith. Further, without opportunity for all sinners to accept, Piper's message should be changed to say, "*Some* can be glad in God if he predestined you" or "God loves to exalt himself by showing mercy to *some* sinners." This rephrasing of his statement is not a mischaracterization of Calvinism, but rather it is the *actual* message of Calvinism, and everyone who understands Calvinism knows it. Unfortunately, it is popularly and ubiquitously stated in the manner cited by Piper (or similarly opaque phrases) that shield most from yet another disquieting reality of Calvinism. I would greatly appreciate Calvinists' due diligence to speak in such a way that all can be reminded of this reality (as some Calvinists are very careful to do). Any suggestion this distinction is tertiary is baffling indeed.

Some like John Owen postulate a covenant of redemption which limits the atonement to the elect. David Allen gives several problems with Owen's belief in the Covenant of Redemption. For example, "no such covenant within the Godhead is revealed in Scripture. . . . This shifts the focus from God's revealed will in Scripture to a focus on God's secret will in eternity."[2]

The two irreconcilable approaches to understanding the presentation of the gospel can be seen in these brief synopses. Extensivists affirm that salvation is entirely a work of God because he has provided everything necessary, even the gift of faith, by which every sinner can by faith receive the salvation of the Lord.[3] The offer of salvation is unconditional, whereas the experience of salvation by an individual is conditioned upon grace-enabled faith (Luke 24:47; Acts 2:38). Many verses attest to the accuracy of this understanding of salvation. Man's part in salvation is seen repeatedly in the book of Acts, e.g., Acts 2:37–41; 3:19–26; 7:51; 8:6–14, 22–23, 36–37; 9:35, 42; 10:34–35, 43; 11:21; 13:8–13, 38–41, 46–47; 14:1; 15:19; 16:30–34; 17:2–4, 11–12, 17, 30–31; 18:4–8, 19, 27–28; 19:8–9, 18; 20:21; 22:18; 26:17–20; 28:23–24. The epistles teach the same (Rom 5:1; Gal 3:26; Eph 2:8–9; Heb 11:6). In addition, God gave repentance as a grace gift (Acts 5:31; 11:18).[4]

---

2. Allen, *The Extent of the Atonement*, 217.

3. Spiritual faith is the ability to trust what God has said and is a gift given by God in creation as are all the endowments of man. It is also a gift in the sense that God restores the ability to exercise spiritually restorative faith as a sinner through the provision of grace enablements (John 12:35–36). It is not a gift in the Calvinist sense of being resultant of God's irresistible grace upon the unconditionally elect, understood to be so in part by a misreading of Eph 2:8.

4. Repentance and faith are inseparable. Repentance focuses upon turning from sin, whereas faith focuses upon turning in trust to the Savior. Repentance is neither a predetermined irresistible work of God upon the unconditionally elect only, nor is

In contrast, Calvinism generally argues the new birth precedes faith.[5] Piper asserts, "The native hardness of our hearts makes us unwilling and unable to turn from sin and trust the Savior. Therefore, conversion involves a miracle of new birth. This new birth precedes and enables faith and repentance. Nevertheless, faith and repentance are *our* acts. We are accountable to do them . . . God grants us the inclination we need."[6] The Synod of Dort says, "Men are chosen to faith . . . therefore election is the fountain of every saving good; from which proceed faith."[7] R.C. Sproul declares, "We do not believe in order to be born again; we are born again in order to believe."[8]

Such explanation creates an abstractness in Calvinism's understanding of the gospel, which results in a concomitant chilling unfriendliness of the good news when shared one-on-one. It is one thing to say God loves Africa and desires the gospel to go there, or that he desires for Africans to be saved. It is quite another for the missionary to look into the eyes of a lost and perishing African and say God loves you and desires you to receive the good news of the gospel, which is the friendliness of the gospel in Scripture. The former has an abstract quality about it that the latter does not have (like the difference between saying I love Africans and then really loving the one who moves in next door). A Calvinist can say, "Believe in Jesus for the remission of sins," but there is a secret aloofness embedded in the invitation for the vast majority of individuals who hear the gospel; an aloofness the Calvinist is very aware of and staunchly committed to.

Further, this abstract quality of Calvinism is the provenance of the good faith offer, which is reflective of Calvinism's different understanding of the gospel. I for one find neither this abstraction, with its secret indifference for the majority of individuals who hear the gospel, nor the suggestion of such a concept as a good faith offer in the scriptural presentations of the gospel. This abstract quality transforms the simple straightforward gospel as seen in Scripture from being *exoteric* (available to all) into an *esoteric* gospel (only available to some). The exoteric gospel of Scripture calls upon every individual with whom we share to receive the gospel and gives every indication that he *should* and *can* believe. It is authentically and dependably what it appears to be, the good news of God's love and compassion offered to all who hear.

---

it merely a humanly derived act. Rather, the ability to repent is given to all by God through grace enablements and is required by God for salvation.

5. See my answer to Calvinists' argument for only a logical relationship between faith and regeneration in Appendix 4.

6. Piper, *Desiring God*, 62.

7. Canons of Dort, First Head of Doctrine, article 9.

8. Sproul, *Chosen by God*, 72–73.

In contrast, the esoteric gospel according to Calvinism says everyone *should* come, but the secret is that while God has told Calvinists to tell all the lost to come, be forgiven, and flee the wrath to come, the inner circle—Calvinists—know it has pleased God to exclude a host of individuals with whom the Calvinist presents this message. This means if one is to be consistent with Calvinism, the gospel must be protectingly presented so that the hearer believes God loves him and truly desires for him to be delivered from the fiery cauldron of God's eternal fury; something no Calvinist can say to any particular individual unless God inspires him to intuit that the lost man to whom he is witnessing is one of God's elect. If God gives such enlightenment it behooves the Calvinist to share such glorious news with the individual, or so it would seem.

According to Calvinism, the gospel is good news for some, but inherent in their understanding of the gospel is that for most with whom they speak it is the ghastliest horror one could ever imagine (whether a sinner desires to believe or not does nothing to palliate this point). That being the case, one may rightly question the righteous legitimacy of indiscriminately declaring a gospel so construed that, in any way, intimates it is for all who hear because it is emphatically not; something every knowledgeable Calvinist knows. To wit, if a Calvinist shares the gospel in such a way so that all those who hear believe God loves them and desires for them to repent and be saved by faith in Jesus, the Calvinist has been true to Scripture but not to Calvinism. One must genuinely ask, is there not a point when a good faith offer is transmogrified into an ungodly deception? Calvinists can avoid this point by determinedly shunning any semblance of offering, via precisely chosen guarded language, what the Calvinist is convinced does not exist. Or is the concept of a good faith offer an unchallengeable and un-fillable reservoir for storing gospel secrets of Calvinism? I am simply asking Calvinists to be clear in presenting what they so resolutely believe to be the *whole* good news, and I do not think that is too much to ask.

David Allen, referring to 2 Corinthians 5:19–20, says, "Here we have God himself offering salvation to all. But how can he do this according to limited atonement since there is no provision for the salvation of the non-elect in the death of Christ? Furthermore, how can God make this offer with integrity? It seems difficult to suppose he can. Without belief in the universal saving will of God and a universal extent in Christ's sin-bearing, there can be no well-meant offer of salvation from God to the non-elect who hear the gospel call."[9]

---

9. Allen, *The Extent of the Atonement*, 786.

Extensivists follow the scriptural pattern of presenting the good news as good news for *everyone* who hears because, by God's loving grace, they should and can believe. If they choose to reject, which they do not have to do, they will forfeit being adopted as a child of God and succumb to a sinner's just deserts. This is based upon a clear, simple, and straight-forward reading of the clearest presentations of the gospel and the declared nature of God. Calvinism's understanding of the gospel disallows any meaningfully eternal difference in the gospel if they simply said, "God hates you and has a terrible plan for you because the elect will get saved and the non-elect will not." For Calvinists to respond that they are sharing the gospel out of obedience is not a solution to the problem I pose but rather it is symptomatic of it. Further, for a Calvinist to rely upon such an idea as a good faith offer does nothing to absolve God from intentionally obscuring his real plan.

In contrast to Calvinism, Jesus clearly warned those to whom he spoke to repent, with every indication they should and could, which warning he issued repeatedly (Matt 4:17; 11:20–21; Luke 5:32; 15:7; 24:47). The same can be said for the Apostles (Acts 2:38; 3:19; 8:22; 17:30; 20:21; 26:20). If Christ knew some of them could not repent because they were not the elect, his warning seems disingenuous and misleading. Some Calvinists will say Jesus was making a "good faith offer" (if there is such an idea) because as a man, he did not know who the elect were.

As an example of Jesus not knowing certain things, in his humanity, they reference Jesus saying "But of that day and hour no one knows, not even the angels of heaven, nor the Son, but the Father alone" (Matt 24:36). Of course, we all recognize as a human, Christ did not know certain things. However, this explicit statement of not knowing does not seem to justify the good faith offer since he gives every indication of speaking as forthrightly in presenting the gospel as he did regarding his second coming, consistent with the way things really are. There is really something to believe, he really as a human did not know the hour, which it seems all could choose to believe. There is no pretense. When he said he did not know, he really did not know, and they could believe what he said. They need not be cryptographically savvy.

Further, Calvinists' reliance upon this example assumes they are justified in presenting something so that those who hear believe they can act on it when Calvinists know they cannot. That seems to be an illegitimate deduction. Clarification of the way things really are would only take a moment when Calvinists present the gospel according to Calvinism. I do not accept leaving the listener believing he is receiving a good offer when he is really hearing only a good faith offer to be noble evangelism. Unless one is a Calvinist who needs to justify the extra-biblical concept of the good faith offer, I doubt one would be able to mine it from this passage on the second coming. There is a crucial difference between Jesus *not knowing* certain things due to his role as a servant and his *speaking forthrightly* things that are either misleading or not true—do not correspond fully to reality. Moreover, Jesus stated he did not know the hour of his coming, but he never says nor even hints that he does not know the gospel.

Additionally, there are problems with assuming Jesus's words were in any way misleading or ill-informed. First, Jesus would have to have forgotten all about unconditional election and selective regeneration. This seems unlikely since, as part of the Trinity, he would have had to help devise the plan of unconditional election, which would at least make his "good faith offer" a little less good than such an offer from your everyday Calvinist. While he did not know the hour of the second coming, he did know there was a second coming; to wit as a servant, he lacked precise knowledge of the event's time not of the event, which he detailed in Matt 24–25. Second, and more problematic for the Calvinist, is that Jesus said he always did the will of the Father (John 4:34; 5:30; 6:38; 17:4) and spoke not of his own initiative but what the Father wanted him to speak (John 3:11, 34; 5:19; 7:16; 8:26, 28, 38; 12:49–50; 14:10, 24, 31; 17:8). Furthermore, the Holy Spirit was upon Jesus filling him without measure (Isa 61:1; Matt 12:18; Luke 3:22; 4:1, 14; John 3:34; Acts 10:38).

Consequently, even if Jesus did not know, the Father and the Holy Spirit did know; therefore, the Calvinist doctrine of selective regeneration makes the Trinity complicitous in this misrepresentation. The obvious truth is that Jesus commanded them to repent because he was not willing that any would perish and desired that all would come to repentance (2 Pet 3:9); something God has grace-enabled everyone who hears the truth to do.

The gospel according to Calvinism is the gospel that is commanded to be preached to all, presented as available to all with an urgency that it be received by all, and yet cannot be received by all who hear the message; even though its universal availability is the obvious inference any listener would draw based upon *most* Calvinists' carefully guarded presentation of the gospel (guarding the divulgence of the secret limitations of the gospel according to Calvinism). In reality, the doctrine of selective regeneration preceding faith dictates the gospel—good news— is really not good news *at all* because it cannot be received by *anyone* who just hears the good news, and this unavailability is just as true for the elect as the non-elect.

Reception of the Calvinistic gospel is divinely limited to the selectively regenerated; therefore, the primary good news of Calvinism is not the gospel, but rather that some to whom they speak are on the secret list of those who have been selected for regeneration, which results in receiving the good news— the gospel. That is to say, according to Calvinism, the gospel is not the good news to be received by *all* or *any* listener, but rather a description of the benefits that will be bestowed upon those on the secret list of the unconditionally elect. Simply put, the gospel according to Scripture is a better gospel than the gospel according to Calvinism.

21

Do the Doctrines of Grace Affect Evangelism?

SOME CALVINISTS CONTEND THAT ideas like *limited atonement, unconditional election,* and *selective regeneration* really make no difference in the nature of the evangelistic endeavor, meaning these doctrines are tertiary or irrelevant to the task of evangelism. In other words, God being secretly pleased to withhold salvation from a vast proportion of the humanity he created does not affect the nature of propagating the gospel.

Regarding God's will to deliver some by unconditional election, J.I. Packer says, "But this does not help us to *determine the nature of the evangelistic task,* nor does it *affect* our duty to evangelize universally and *indiscriminately.* The doctrine of God's sovereignty in grace *has no bearing on these* things"[1] (italics added). *Really!* Maybe it is due to my intractable obtuseness, but the claim that the *so-called* doctrines of grace do not affect the "nature of the evangelistic task" leaves me bewildered. With all due respect to those who believe such, that claim seems to me to be no more than a galactic ocean of nothingness.

It seems appropriate to ask if Calvinism's understanding of the doctrines of grace "has no bearing on these things," then why do Calvinists need a good faith offer? Why do Calvinists reject the straightforward meaning of verses like John 3:16, 1 John 2:2, and 1 John 4:14? That the doctrines of grace have no bearing on such verses is not evident when one is reading Calvinists' attempts to show they have no bearing. Why use such guarded language in gospel proclamations that secretly transform "whoever" (John 3:15; 4:14; Rev 22:17) into a calling out of God's elect. Why avoid saying to an individual (or the world at large) "God loves you and desires for you to flee the wrath to come and accept his forgiveness in Christ who died for you" as Scripture so compellingly and lucidly announces (Mark 10:21; John 3:16; 21:30–31)? Why say Calvinists believe "whoever will may come" while not revealing that it is only trivially true in Calvinism since only the

---

1. Packer, *Evangelism and the Sovereignty of God,* 97.

unconditionally elect can will to come; this in stark contrast to the simple straightforward declaration of such passages.

Furthermore, if these things are tertiary (have no real relevance to the nature and duty of spreading of the gospel), this seems to invite the question to whom are they tertiary? An unencumbered reading of a host of the simplest and most straightforward gospel verses does not so engender such a conclusion (John 3:16, 20:31). It does not seem to be tertiary to Jesus unless every person he addressed was elect (John 6:29). Clearly, such doctrines (unconditional election, selective regeneration, and limited atonement) are not tertiary for the sinner that hears Jesus speak of his mission and offer (Luke 18:10; John 1:29, 5:24). Relevance is not determined by whether one fully understands all related doctrines or the inescapable disquieting realities of such (for I am convinced many who don the title Calvinist do not fully understand these). Rather does it meaningfully relate to the subject at hand? In this case, we are talking about evangelism and the gospel, which fall under the theological heading of soteriology (doctrines of salvation)— exactly the same place we find unconditional election, selective regeneration, and limited atonement.

Additionally, relevance can be determined by whether or not the beliefs affect what is being offered, what is *actually available,* and whether such is determinative of the language used and not used in the presentation. Determining whether something is relevant or not can be illustrated by the answer we can give when someone asks, "Does God love me and want me to be saved?" I fail to grasp how a listener's lack of being a theological sophisticate and, therefore, unaware of a secret will of God that inviolably excludes him (if he is a non-elect) from accepting the offer before him (because such offer does not *actually* exist), or his obliviousness to the other speculative soteriological doctrines of Calvinism, makes these truths tertiary or irrelevant. I would suggest these details are not really even tertiary to the Calvinist, which is evidenced by the creation of the good faith offer. Every time an informed and consistent Calvinist shares the gospel, he is very aware of the other features that reduce the gospel presentation to merely a good faith offer as opposed to that of the New Testament, which gives every indication of being nothing less than a good offer.

The doctrine of regeneration preceding faith dictates that the gospel—good news— is really not *the* good news at all because it cannot be received by *anyone* who just hears the good news, not even the elect. The *real* good news, if Calvinism is correct, comes when one finds out his name is written on the secret list of the unconditionally elect. Then, and only then, come the hallelujahs. Such knowledge comes via selective regeneration followed by a predetermined free act of faith that results in receiving the promises of the gospel. Correspondingly, the gospel is reduced to announcing what people on the secret list receive. Moreover, the straightforward gospel, both definitionally and as biblically portrayed, becomes a mere phantom gospel—something of illusive power or efficacy—because the real power is in the secret list.

When speaking face to face with a lost person, a Calvinist's language is guided by these undisclosed truths; consequently, they are not merely disassociated tertiaries from the gospel. If I am perishing in a fire, and you offer me directions to a doorway which leads out of the fire, I can assure you that whether the doorway is actually accessible or divinely barricaded is neither tertiary nor even secondary but emphatically paramount. I do clearly recognize there are a host of secondary and tertiary issues related to various areas of Christianity. In this case, they may be associated with various theological headings such as Bibliology and Eschatology (doctrines regarding Scripture and end times respectively), but the matters to which we are referring all fall under the heading of Soteriology. We are considering the nature of God's plan of salvation and the faithful communication of his plan; such are not tertiary.

We are not interjecting concepts from other theological categories such as eschatological positions or nuanced ecclesiological positions (doctrine of the church). While they are clearly important in their own right, they are not primarily relevant to someone being saved, how we communicate the opportunity to be saved, or who can be saved and why. However, Calvinism's unique and speculative soteriology is inextricably connected to the nature of the gospel and their communication of it. It is extravagantly difficult for me to comprehend how a person who truly understands Calvinism and Scripture, and has witnessed to a variety of people who in turn ask a galaxy of questions, can really suggest these doctrines have *"no bearing on these* things."

The truth is without the extra-biblical concept of the good faith offer, there is no evangelism in Calvinism, at least as it is regularly practiced by Calvinists. The very idea incorporates the conclusion that Jesus merely made a good faith offer rather than a genuine offer to the rich young ruler whom he loved, *agapao* (Mark 10:21), and to every other person who asked him about salvation who were not the elect (John 6:28–29). The same can be said about the gospel offers of the apostles (Acts 16:31). It seems insurmountably difficult to find the good faith offer in a simple reading of the biblical presentations because they so indubitably seem to be what they appear to be, good offers!

Analogically, the fundamental difference between Darwinists and Creationists is the former say the cosmos *appears* to be designed, but *it is not*; whereas the latter says it *appears* to be designed because *it is*. Similarly, the Calvinists say the gospel *appears* to be simple and accessible to all, but *it is not*; whereas the Extensivists say it *appears* to be simple and accessible to all because *it is*. Allen says, "Anything that makes the preacher hesitant to make the bold proclamation that 'Christ died for your sins' is wrong. If one thinks it is true that Christ only suffered for some, preaching will be deeply affected. . . . Calvinists point out that they preach to all because they don't know who the elect are. Certainly true, but this misses the point. Belief in limited atonement puts the preacher in the difficult position of preaching to all people as if Christ's death is applicable to them even though all are not capable of salvation since the non-elect have no atonement made for them. This creates a situation where preachers operate on the basis of something that is not true in every situation."[2]

Suppose I extended the most gracious of all invitations for you and all of your families to come to my house for a meal of eternal life, which is actually the only *real* eternal meal in existence. What is more, I not only invited you, but I commanded you to come and warned you of dire consequences if you refused. If that were not enough, grace upon grace, I actually offered to afford you whatever you lacked in order to make the journey possible. I did this in spite of the fact that none of you deserved such an opportunity, and actually all invitees deserved to starve. I think we would all agree this invitation can only be seen as the sublime of loving and gracious invitations. However, in stark contrast to the invitations, I concomitantly masterminded a secret plan to make the road leading from *most* of your homes to mine absolutely impossible, resulting in eternal death for your spouses, children, and you. What would you think of me?

Now, would we not readily conclude it would have been more honorable for me to have told you the truth that I actually desired for most of you to perish rather than giving every indication I desired for all of you to live? When all the facts are known, it is undeniable I did not offer real love or opportunity to those who perished, although none could detect such from the invitations themselves. I dare say, rather than considering such to be a good faith offer or me an honorable benefactor, you would consider it nothing more than a cruel nefarious hoax of an unscrupulous ignoble blackguard.

This example or the biblical reality of the gospel has nothing to do with the invitees being undeserving (or incapable on their own) or the host being just in withholding from anyone or everyone, and for Calvinists to so answer is to evade the issue at hand. What kind of God devises a plan to secretly exclude the majority of those whom he invites in the most unambiguously

---

2. Allen, *The Extent of the Atonement*, 789.

loving and gracious terms, yea commands and urges? I for one find no such suggestion in Scripture. This helps to highlight the fact that while the good faith offer *may* provide *some* measure of serenity from the haunt of duplicity for the Calvinist, it offers not the slightest protection from duplicity for the Father, Son, or Holy Spirit who actually devised the plan.

The scriptural gospel is better news because it is a real offer of opportunity, by the grace of God, for everyone who hears. It is lexically described as "news that makes one happy, information that causes one joy, or words that bring smiles."[3] God's gospel is more *consistent* with the meaning of the word gospel, "news that makes one happy."[4] It is simple, straightforward, and dependable with its inarguable meaning of good news for anyone who hears it. What it means is good news from God to his creation, not merely good news for some and ghastly news for most (2 Cor 5:19).

---

3. Louw and Nida, *Greek-English Lexicon of the New Testament*, 412.
4. Louw and Nida, *Greek-English Lexicon of the New Testament*, 412.

22

Is Libertarian Free Will Eternal?

HUMANS ARE CREATED IN the image of God with soft-libertarian (incompatible) free will. This means humans can choose within the range of available options to act or refrain, and, whatever they do choose, they could have chosen otherwise. People have argued it is impossible to create such a human being and guarantee he will never use his freedom to do wrong; thus, God could not be in sovereign control, nor could he guarantee created man would never sin in either the Garden of Eden or eternity. It is obvious to all man did choose to sin, and all subsequent humans inherit a sin nature, with the exception of the God-Man our Lord Jesus Christ. Some have asked how can it be possible to guarantee those in heaven will never sin if Adam had libertarian free will and chose to sin? Stated a little differently, is it possible for God to create a human with truly *otherwise* choice who will never choose to sin? If it is possible, then why did he not so create Adam and Eve, which would have avoided sin and its consequences?

This dilemma is seen as an argument against man having libertarian free will and an argument for man having a compatibilist free will. Similar to what I have previously argued, I would suggest it may be impossible to guarantee a libertarian free human being, *who does not have experiential knowledge (either through personal experience or observation) of sin*, will never use his freedom to sin provided such choices are within his range of options as was clearly the case with Adam. This is precisely where Satan tempted Adam and Eve because while they had a *faith knowledge* of sin, they lacked *experiential knowledge* of sin (Gen 3:5). Even if the previously mentioned impossibility is the case (and I believe it is), God's coextensive creation-redemption plan assures that the redeemed in heaven will not be susceptible to the temptation to which Adam and Eve succumbed.

The redeemed in heaven will have experiential knowledge of sin and the consequences of sin, but they will have been redeemed from that and transformed in glorification (Rom 8:30). In view of that, it appears the redeemed and glorified man will have what is necessary to live forever and only use his freedom to choose righteousness. Of course, much could be said also about God's other protective promises and power (John 10:29, 11:25–26; Eph 4:30), which I believe are sufficient in and of themselves, but they also, in a certain sense, apply to Calvinism's compatibilism. Here I am simply addressing the consonance of libertarian otherwise choice and eternal righteousness. The angels appear to have demonstrated libertarian choice in that some chose to sin and some chose to not sin, and each could have done otherwise (unless one believes God created some who would inevitably choose to sin—compatibilism).

Consequently, it may be that *redemption* is not essential to guarantee every sort of created libertarian free being will always choose not to sin (although it may be essential for humans). It is possible the distinct nature of angels is that while redemption may not be necessary to guarantee the holy angels will not sin in the future, it may very well be that *experiential knowledge* of sin is essential, at least based upon the limited information we have. The holy angels did not personally sin, but they did and have continued to experience sin both consequently and observationally. This particular distinction between man and angels may be further illumined by the difference between the nature of the creation of angels who were created all at one time and humans, other than Adam and Eve, who were created through procreation, a process which infects all subsequent humans with personal consequences of the fall. That is to say, a human's first experience of sin after Adam and Eve comes from inheritance (procreation), which is not true of angels. Accordingly, a fundamental difference in fallen angels and fallen humanity is the former's first experience of sin is active and the latter's is passive. God solved the dilemma for humans through the plan to coextensively create and redeem man.

Although human illustrations do not fully capture spiritual realities, they can and do serve to simply and legitimately demonstrate various spiritual aspects, which is precisely what Jesus's use of parables sought to accomplish. Here I offer the example of a mother who may tell her little boy not to touch the hot stove. Each time she perceives his interest in touching, she warns him of the horrible pain, hospitals, surgery, and the loss of freedom to play, something of which he is so fond. Tragically, despite mom's severe warnings and heartfelt pleadings, one day, the little lad touches the fiery electric grill, and everything happens just as his mother had warned.

From that moment on, the little boy still has the freedom to touch the fiery hot stove, but he freely chooses to refrain for the rest of his life. He has no interest in touching it, and every inclination is to guard against even touching it by accident. The difference is not the loss of otherwise choice, but rather prior to his burn, he had only *faith knowledge*. His understanding was based on only believing his mother's words. Now, he has *experiential knowledge* coupled with an even greater faith in his mother's words. This demonstrates how one's experience can affect one's future desires to use free will. Add to this God's scripturally stated provisions and his exhaustively thorough foreknowledge and the problem of otherwise choice being used to sin in eternity is eliminated.

Additionally, God is not only the giver of otherwise choice, he is also the giver of the range of available options. Libertarian free will simply argues that an individual can choose between the various options God grants. Whatever God decides the available range of options should be, whether in Eden, post fall era, or heaven is entirely up to him. Even now, libertarian free will does not mean a person can do anything he wants, but rather that he can act or refrain within the range of options that are available to him. A person may choose to jump off a high cliff or choose not to jump, but once he has jumped, he curtailed his range of choices. A man may choose to commit suicide or not (God has given that option within the range of human choices), but man cannot choose to cease to exist because that is not within his range of choices.

God has libertarian free choice, but this does not mean God can or will sin. First, as God, sin is not within his range of options. God cannot be tempted with sin (Jas 1:13). God is omnipotent, but he cannot cease to exist since he is eternal and immutable (Ps 102:27). For the sake of argument, if God did sin or cease to exist that would prove he was not ever really God—the eternally holy self-existing one. Second, the inherent lack of knowledge and, therefore, initial susceptibility to sin in created beings with libertarian free will does not entail God having the same need or susceptibility because he is the sum of perfection. He is the eternal immutable holy one and has eternal, unchanging, infinite, *exhaustive* knowledge of every potentiality and actuality within himself. Therefore, he possesses libertarian free will, but he has never sinned; nor is there the remotest possibility he ever will.

Lastly, in my estimation, and to the best that I understand the relevant panoply of Scriptures, this is a far more biblical way to look at this matter than the compatibilist approach. Following are but a few reasons why I think this: first, this view provides an explanation that maintains God's sovereignty (he acts without any internal or external need or necessity in accomplishing his perfect holy and loving will). He does this without resorting to Calvinism's extreme causally-based sovereignty. Second, it maintains a balance of *all* of God's attributes such as holiness, love, justice, mercy, and omnibenevolence. Third, it reflects the simple story of Scripture that man sometimes *actually* chooses against God's perfect will for him (Adam and Eve, when they *could have* and *should have* done otherwise), and that man *should* and *can* accept God's gracious offer of salvation that extends to everyone. All of which is comprehended in God's perfect, sovereign, and infinite loving plan. Fourth, the Extensivism proposal seems to both reflect and be consonant with the teaching of both complex and simple passages of Scripture better than Calvinism's reinventions of the simplest of Scriptures in order to accommodate unconditional election.

These Calvinistic reinventions change the obvious meaning of such verses and passages so they do not mean what they so palpably say and seem to mean. This includes Adam and Eve freely choosing to sin against God's warning and *true* desire for them (Gen 1:26–31; 2:15–18, 20–24; 3:8–19, 22–24) to countless straightforward God-given pleas to fallen mankind to repent and be saved; all of which clearly imply he *desires* that end, that they *should* choose such, and that they *can, in fact,* choose such (Matt 4:17, 6:13, 11:20–24; Mark 1:14–15, 10:17–30; John 1:7–9, 6:28–29; Rev 22:17).

Fifth, it seems to explain soteriological perplexities better than resorting to strapping either God or man with a compatible will as Calvinism does, which entails a host of biblically unwarranted disquieting realities that are usually and quite unsatisfactorily dismissed by swathing them in "it is a mystery".[1] Sixth, regardless how fancy the theology, Calvinism's insistence upon compatibilism, if applied to God and man alike, means that both God and man ultimately choose (as defined by Calvinism), but do not choose among *accessible* choices.

I find the belief in compatibilism to not only be biblically unwarranted but a woefully dishonoring view of both God and man, particularly God. Because when one stands at the end of the causal chain of determinative antecedents of compatibilism, it seems more accurate to describe the moment of *choosing* or *acting* by man as merely a moment of *awareness* since the decision a compatibilist being will ultimately and unalterably make is determined prior to any conscious involvement of the individual; hence, the so-called decision is not really a decision at all (at least in the common understanding and biblical presentation), but merely an *awareness* of what the determinative antecedents have already established the individual is about to unalterably choose to do.[2]

---

1. At least some Calvinists argue for God having compatible freedom as well as man.

2. All the causal chain of compatibilism requires is that the determinative antecedents include free choosing.

23

Equally Lost and Equally Savable: No Distinctions!

> Even the righteousness of God through faith in Jesus Christ for all those who believe; for there is no distinction (Rom 3:22).

ROMANS CHAPTER THREE IS crystal clear in declaring the universal sinfulness of man. Although the Jews have advantages compared to the Greeks, such as having the oracles of God (Rom 3:1–2) and being born in the covenant God made with Israel that ended with the coming of Christ, they do not have a preferential relationship or treatment with regard to salvation. Rom 3:9 makes this very clear, "Jews and Greeks are all under sin." Both Calvinists and Extensivists recognize "all" clearly means every Jew and every Greek (every person) is under sin. Consequently, both the groups and "all" the individuals that make up the groups are included rather than *some* in each group comprising the "all." There are no exceptions.

Romans 3:10–18 reiterates this point by such phrases as "none righteous," "not even one," "none who understands," "none who seeks for God," "all have turned aside," "none who does good," "not even one," and "no fear of God." These phrases make the sinfulness of man inclusive of every person. Rom 3:19 says, "Now we know that whatever the Law says, it speaks to those who are under the Law so that every mouth may be closed and all the world may become accountable to God." This verse summarizes the state of "all the world" as under the law of God and, therefore, accountable to God. Obviously, every people group in the world is under the righteous law of God. Even more importantly this designation extends not only to people groups or some in the people groups. It includes every individual in every people group who has or ever will live. Every person fails to live up to God's standard of righteousness and, therefore, is held accountable to God. The Jews were under God's written law as given through Moses, and the Gentiles were under God's law written upon their hearts (Rom 2:11–15). For that reason, every person will be judged by God's standard of righteousness rather than merely every group with some exceptions.

Rom 3:20 says, "Because by the works of the Law no flesh will be justified in His sight; for through the Law comes the knowledge of sin." It is easy to see "no flesh" includes every person in the human race. Additionally, the law can declare the righteousness of God, and thereby reveal the sinfulness of man; it cannot save the sinful (Heb 10:1, 4). Salvation has always been by faith (Hab 2:4; Gal 3:11; Heb 10:38).

In Rom 3:21–22, God grants righteousness "through faith in Jesus Christ for all those who believe." All Christians agree that "all" who believe will be saved. The difference is not whether salvation is granted to all who believe, but whether *all can* believe unto salvation. The Calvinists say no (unconditional election). It seems to me the most reliable reading of this passage is that just as "all" in previous verses refers to all individuals being lost and in need of salvation, all here means all individuals in such need *can* and will be saved by faith in Christ. Understanding "all" as it has been used each time to include every person seems unstrained, natural, and most consistent with the passage. It seems to be a beacon of hope to the same all who are in need.

Just as there is no distinction such as some individuals are sinners and others are not in the preceding verses, it seems the "no distinction" in this verse 22 highlights the same with regard to salvation. To invoke a distinction at this point appears to originate from beyond the passage itself and to directly contradict the passage. That the promise is specifically to all who believe is obvious, but it also seems that no one would conclude from the passage that all cannot believe.

The idea of believing refers to individuals since only individuals can exercise faith. I do not see anything in the passage that would indicate this "all" is restricted to something like all people groups, specifically that there are some who can be saved from each people group. I do not think the passage even hints that this "all" is different from the "all" that included each person previously spoken of as under sin, of which "there is no distinction." This understanding corresponds precisely with its usage before and in the following verses.

Rom 3:23 says, "All have sinned," again clearly including every person. Therefore, if justification is going to happen, it must come about by God's grace gift (Rom 3:24). Once more we see "all" with no distinction. I would suggest any attempt to maintain "all" to mean *everyone* with regard to sin and judgment (unlimited lostness and judgment), and "all" to mean *some* from all people groups—unconditionally elect—with regard to savableness (limited savableness) seems to unwisely impose a distinction where God indicates none exists.

The human dilemma of needing to be perfectly righteous to rightly relate to God but incapable of becoming so by intrinsic worth or works and the divine dilemma of how to satisfy God's justice and be merciful to sinners is resolved in the death of Christ on the cross (Rom 3:24–26). Since Christ fulfills God's righteous and holy demands, God is thereby free to be just in declaring all sinners justified by simple faith in Jesus. By all indications within the passage, such includes any and every person, from the least to the greatest, without distinction. Kenneth Boa summarizes, "All men and women are made equal by three things: first, our equality in need (all are guilty). Second, our equality in what we receive (redemption is one gift; the same for all). Third, our equality in how we receive redemption (by faith; everyone receives it the same way)."[1] To suggest that some cannot be a part of the "all those who believe" is to suggest an eternal inequality in a passage that seems to be presenting the very opposite.

In conclusion, it seems the statement "for there is no distinction" (Rom 3:22) means just that. Romans 3:9–20 makes it lucidly undeniable that "all" means every single person has sinned and, therefore, each person is under the judgment of God; there is no distinction. Correspondingly, Romans 3:21–26 makes it equally clear that because of the work of Christ upon the cross, God is just in declaring any and all sinners justified based upon the merits of Christ; there is no distinction.

There seems to be no suggestion of a change with regard to who is the "all" being considered here from the "all" that are under sin (Rom 3:9) and "all" that "have sinned" (Rom 3:23); there is no distinction. Consequently, anyone and everyone, regardless of people group or sinfulness, can receive justification and be made righteous by faith (Rom 3:27–31) in Christ; there is no distinction. That being the case, any suggestion of limiting those who can believe to the unconditionally elect seems to be an inordinate contrariety, thereby creating a distinction where God has most clearly said, "There is no distinction."

All are equally lost and all are equally savable! This is the glorious work of God and the true nature of the gospel.

---

1. Boa and Kruidenier, *Romans*, 106.

24

The Exalted God of Scripture

THE NATURE AND ATTRIBUTES of God are seen not only in his person but in his creation as well. We are reminded, "For since the creation of the world His invisible attributes, His eternal power, and divine nature, have been clearly seen, being understood through what has been made, so that they are without excuse" (Rom 1:20). The Old Testament declares the same truth in Psalm 19:1. Calvinists' desire is to exalt, honor, and glorify God. However, Calvinism's endeavor to exalt God by emphasizing compatibilism, monergism, unconditional election, passive or active reprobation, and selective regeneration actually results in the antithesis of their desire.

As with God, the glory of a creator is not only seen in his attributes, but also in his creation. If I am shown the work of a person, I can tell a great deal about the person. For the excellence of such things as our creative ability, ethics, love, and purity have a way of being manifested in our work. An example of this is, while we have not met men like Bach, Da Vinci, or Aquinas, or may not have read their biographies, if we are introduced to their works, we immediately see their human genius and greatness. Specifically, one's works declare the greatness, talent, creativity, and often even the morality or stableness of someone at a particular time in his life; the latter being true of Picasso. H.R. Rookmaaker says of Picasso, "When he painted the woman he loved . . . he painted Olga in a 'normal' way . . . Again and again in his life we see Picasso returning to a more 'loving' and free expression when he loves a woman."[1]

While it seems to be true one can create something less than he is capable of creating, it seems impossible for someone to create something that is measurably beyond his capabilities. I would even argue that is true at any time since creating something by accident is certainly reflective of the accident, but not necessarily the ability of the creator. In any case, it is clear one cannot create beyond his capability with consistent intentionality. That being true suggests one simply cannot diminish the *work* of

---

1. Rookmaaker, *Modern Art and the Death of a Culture*, 152.

the Creator without concomitantly diminishing its Creator. But Calvinism does exactly this by strapping man (God's crowning creation) with compatibilism, whereby man was created to inevitably sin and be totally passive in regeneration.

It is often argued God cannot be sovereign if man has otherwise choice (libertarian freedom) and God cannot know contingencies (acts of libertarian free beings) prior to the act since the acts, so they argue, do not actually exist. Such reductionistic ideas from Calvinists and all determinists that are used to argue in support of the belief that man is endowed with compatible freedom tells us more about their, albeit unwitting, diminished view of God, who apparently cannot be in sovereign control of truly free beings with otherwise choice, than it does about their view of man.

It appears to me, if any view or system of thought is diminishing or humanizing God, it is really Calvinism rather than those who disagree with Calvinism's assumptions. One can see this in many areas in which we disagree with our Calvinist friends. As Extensivists, we believe Scripture teaches God created a more *sophisticated* man in his own image who had the ability to actually have chosen to not sin. We believe Scripture teaches God's sovereignty is more *complex,* in that he is capable of being sovereign over truly free beings with otherwise choice. We believe Scripture teaches God's plan is unique in that it is actually able to accomplish the otherwise seemingly impossible outcome of producing a human beings with otherwise choice who will one day, like God but not as God, always choose righteousness. He accomplished this through his coextensive creation-redemption plan. We believe Scripture teaches God's perfect love is more *comprehensive* in offering every person everything needed to be able to choose to believe in Christ and by that faith be brought into fellowship with him. This enablement is based on the sufficient sacrifice of Christ (1 John 2:2), the working of the Holy Spirit (John 16:8–11), the drawing of the Father (John 6:44) and Son (John 12:32), and the power of the gospel (Rom 1:16–17). We believe Scripture teaches God's salvation plan is more *inclusive* in that he does in fact *truly* desire every individual to be saved (Ezek 18:23, 32, 33:11; 1 Tim 2:4, 4:10; Titus 2:11; 1 Pet 3:8; Rev 22:17), and God's gospel is more *consistent* with the authentic meaning of the word gospel, "news that makes one happy."[2] This is the exalted God of Scripture.

---

2. Louw and Nida, *Greek-English Lexicon of the New Testament*, 412.

25

Good Faith Offer or Bad Deception?

CALVINISTS' COMMITMENT TO UNCONDITIONAL election along with believing in obeying the Great Commission to evangelize and make disciples (Matt 28:18–20) necessitates certain auxiliary concepts in order to harmonize these two; the good faith offer is such a concept. The simple explanation is that while the Calvinist is to preach the gospel to all so God can call out his unconditionally elect, every Calvinist is well aware that much of his gospel proclamation will fall upon the non-elect; who have no more chance of receiving the good news than a beaver does of being happy in a petrified forest.

Accordingly, the good faith offer is understood to free Calvinists to feel they can present the gospel to all as seen in Scripture and to exculpate them from appearing to be deceptive when they offer the gospel to all even though unconditional election inviolably precludes most from responding. Surely such an understanding does at least permit some legitimacy in thinking such could give the appearance of artificiality. Such an understanding may even prompt one to ask, is there a point at which this good faith offer is more accurately defined as a bad deception? I must admit, this question came to bother me greatly as a Calvinist.

Francis Schaeffer, in his book *He Is There and He Is Not Silent* says, "You have to preach the simple gospel so that it is simple to the person to whom you are talking, or it is no longer simple."[1] I believe our challenge is to not only "speak the truth in love" or merely proclaim the truth of the gospel but to do so with due consideration given to enabling the listener to understand the proclamation as it is understood by the proclaimer. A crucial endeavor of all who attempt to proclaim the glorious good news to the lost is that both in intent and effort, we seek to speak in such a way that our listeners truly understand what we are saying, what are their *actual* options, and what we mean by what we say. This seems so self-evident one could deem me foolish for broaching such a subject, but I think that would be imprudent.

---

1. Schaeffer, *Complete Works*, vol. 1, 285.

Based upon a Calvinistic understanding, God has eternally and unconditionally elected some to be the recipients of his loving salvation and has equally determined those for whom there is no hope. This is true for the latter group even if they heard the gospel from God himself and also could recite the gospel in every language in the universe. A point of clarification is that one's perspective regarding the order of decrees is impertinent to this reality. Regardless how one seeks to explain the plight of the non-elect, whether through discussing such concepts as decrees or that God either passively or actively does not afford them the grace to be one of the elect, all Calvinists believe this group not only *will not* but *cannot* ever be the recipients of God's salvific love; they cannot ever be saved, adopted into the family of God or forgiven of their sin.

As a result, remaining faithful to both unconditional election and the Great Commission requires Calvinists to knowingly offer what does not meaningfully exist for most of those to whom it is presented. In order to avoid glaring duplicity, there is a need to develop a concept, which in normal understanding would be simple and unabashed deception; the outcome of this line of reasoning is the good faith offer. Additionally, the coalescing of unconditional election, the Great Commission, and the good faith offer into an actual gospel presentation calls for yet another rhetorical tool. That is the employment of enigmatic phrases that seem to mean one thing to the listener but truly mean a thoroughly different thing to the Calvinist evangelist. His meaning is esoteric (for only the select inner circle), but the listener indubitably understands it as exoteric (for the masses).

It is this last device that leads every listener to believe he is unmistakably hearing the most loving message of hope one could ever conceive while still permitting the Calvinist to remain true to Calvinism. This requires the Calvinist to be extraordinarily chary in how he presents the gospel. For example, he speaks of God loving to save sinners, which actually can only mean he salvifically loves the unconditionally elect. He dare not say to the lost person to whom he speaks, "God salvifically loves you (entailing God has provisioned so you can be saved) and desires to save you" or "God salvifically loves the world." He may say, "If you believe you can be saved" (which is only trivially true in Calvinism, i.e., that is not the question people are asking), whereas he cannot in any way communicate that everyone who hears him can do so, or that God genuinely desires every person to do so.

Those Calvinists who insist they can tell every lost person God loves them by maintaining a distinction between the revealed will of God, Scripture, which says he does love and desire all to be saved, and his decretal will that he only desires and provisions for some fails to justify such communication. First, the existence of a secret will is not demonstrated in

Scripture. It is a construct of Calvinism; see chapter 19. Second, reliance upon varying degrees or kinds of love does not help because we all recognize the existence of different kinds of love; even human relationships demonstrate this with distinctions such as marital love, parental love, and love for a friend or even a pet. Third, I use the qualifier "salvific." This qualifier entails that this love means God truly desires the person to be saved as evidenced by Christ dying for their sins, the Father and Son drawing them, and the Holy Spirit convicting them. The absolute dissonance between God's supposed decretal will and his revealed will can only mean God does not *truly* desire the non-elect to be saved. Therefore, I utterly reject seeking escape into the darkness of a secret will that ultimately undermines God's revealed will as aiding the Calvinist plight.

I do not mind being considered too doltish to grasp how the good faith offer, which gives all the appearance of being a good offer, truly solves the problem of duplicity. Although it does seem to me to be in stark contrast to the gospel encounters in Scripture, which if read without theological importations, always seem to be making nothing less than simply a good offer. This is also the practice of the rest of the Christian world. This brings us back to the question, is there ever a point in which the good faith offer becomes the bad deception, or is the good faith offer by its very nature a bad deception? My answer is yes to both, in spite of a well-adorned theological need, Calvinistic consistency necessitating such, and the ever-present justifying asseverations. Upon serious, unprejudiced reflection, I find the adornment to do nothing more than gauzily veil a misleading message. This does not speak to the motive of the messenger, but rather to the nature of the message and the understanding of the listener. The motive seems to be correlated to each particular Calvinist's level of understanding of Calvinism; consequently, I leave that to the individual and am generally satisfied to think the best until proven otherwise.

Although I found solace for years walking arm in arm with the good faith offer, I did reach a point where the relationship began to deteriorate. This awareness did not surface because of the challenge of others or that the concept did not fit nicely into my Calvinism. No, for me, it was my constant engagement with Scripture and people that gradually turned my solace into a chronic theological uneasiness and finally into an intolerable acute disdain. When I read Scripture, offers always appeared to simply be good offers—what you see is what you get sort of thing. My regular and sometimes long-term engagements with people elicited an increasing sensitivity to my biblical responsibility to aid the listener in fully understanding the offer of the gospel, their *true* opportunity, and the consequences of rejecting God's grace.

This increasing desire led me to see that apparently (contrary to my surface thoughts and trite words), I really did not desire they understand too clearly or else I would doff the evasive language and tell them about my belief in unconditional election, limited atonement, the inefficacy of the external calling (proclaiming the gospel to all), and the efficacy of the internal calling, which is wrought by the Holy Spirit and reserved for the unconditionally elect. Rather than continue down this path of conflict, I gradually found biblical harmony by abandoning the good faith offer for the good offer. Seeking to make good offers as found in Scripture quite naturally resulted in continuing my evaluation of Calvinism's concepts that led to such.[2]

Since sharing the good news with the non-elect is a vacuous offer (cannot actually be received or worse yet, add that Christ did not even die for their sins), such reality is intentionally suppressed by guarded language so that the listener consistently leaves with a different understanding of the offer than that which truly exists. And such understanding is not due to the ineptness of the listener, but rather to the esoterically sophisticated presentation. This to the point that the conclusions of the hearer are irreconcilably contrary to Calvinism's full understanding of the gospel including precisely what options actually lie before the non-elect lost, and what they can really do about them. It seems to me something far less noble than a good faith offer is present.

Several years ago, I heard a pastor speak at the Southern Baptist Convention, and he challenged everyone to work together in proclaiming the gospel to the world. Anyone familiar with Calvinism could not miss his dedication to speaking Calvinistically about presenting the gospel. Specifically, speaking so that the uninitiated would not detect a difference between what the speaker said about the gospel and the Great Commission, and what those who reject Calvinism believe regarding the same. At the conclusion of his message, my wife, oldest daughter, and I were walking out. Being familiar with Calvinistic cryptography they both said; "He was a Calvinist wasn't he?" to which I answered "Yes." My daughter responded, "Why do they not just say what they mean?" I wish I could say the speaker was an obscurity in SBC life, but that would be glaringly inaccurate.

It may seem I have written this book in order to persuade people to leave Calvinism (I am pleased when that happens). More precisely, I am pleading with Calvinists to avoid speaking in such a veiled manner, thereby making their Calvinistically-endowed message clear to those to whom they

---

2. It is not that my acceptance of the good offer and the rejection of the good faith offer was merely experientially based, but rather that my experience of reading Scripture and evangelizing led me to undeniably recognize what my Calvinism's good faith offer obscured; the offers in Scripture were simply unsullied good offers.

speak. Then the listeners can truly decide for themselves. If a Calvinist is unwilling to consistently face his beliefs, entailments of those beliefs, and speak so that listeners understand as well, then perhaps he should evaluate his commitment to Calvinism and the need for such an appellation.

Here is a basic experiment anyone can perform to test the fairness of what I have written. Either accompany a Calvinist when he shares the gospel, or if a Calvinist yourself, share the good faith offer with some people. Then, ask the listeners to communicate what they heard and how they understood the message. To wit, each listener simply explains what the gospel means to him personally, based upon the presentation at that moment. If their understanding is not consonant with Calvinism's understanding of the gospel offer (a good faith offer rather than a good offer), then it seems safe to assume at least from the listener's perspective, it is neither a good offer nor a good faith offer but a very misleading and illusory presentation.

For everyone who is non-elect, it sounded like an accessible offer. It sounded like good news. It sounded like love, but when the language is unpacked, the message is anything but that. This minimally means while the Calvinist is seeking to be as forthright as he can and maintain Calvinistic integrity, the listener comes to realize he was led to believe he was offered meaningful forgiveness when he was not; unless of course he is one of the unconditionally elect. Which means once he is apprised of Calvinism's beliefs, his concern is not whether to accept the gospel, but whether he is elect or not. The truly good news embedded in Calvinism is not the gospel, but rather hearing that you are on the secret list of the unconditionally elect.

Here is the grand perplexity in all of this. Why are Calvinists so adamant about the superiority of their understanding of God's plan of salvation while concomitantly equally devoted to obscuring such superior qualities in gospel presentations? To respond that the Calvinist is simply following the command to preach the simple gospel invites the question of how is the gospel of Calvinism simple. To respond that these *essentials* of the Calvinist understanding of the gospel (unconditional election, selective regeneration, and limited atonement) are not relevant to the proclamation of the gospel raises the question, relevant to whom? This may seem true for the Calvinist, but I am quite sure the non-elect bystander would find it absolutely pertinent and alarmingly so.

For the Calvinist to say what we preach is sufficient for the elect to believe is indeed true; for example, "If you believe in the gospel you will be saved." It is equally true that it is unnecessary for the elect to understand such concepts as unconditional election, limited atonement, and efficacious calling in order to be saved. I say, of course that is true. As an Extensivist, I do not think it is necessary to understand all of God's salvific plan in order to be saved, or even for the hearer to have all their questions answered before hearing and receiving the gospel (John 12:34–37, 42). Correspondingly, what *must* be understood to be saved is not the question before us in this chapter. Rather, we are considering the integrity and responsibility of the speaker to speak in concert with what he truly believes about what he is saying, which seems to include assisting the listener as much as possible so that he understands the precise offer before him, and what he *can* and should do about it. With all due respect to honest politicians who disdain bunkum as much as the rest of us, *we are not politicians but rather brokers of truth.*[3]

A Calvinist may say such information is not germane. I for one must disagree. We must ask ourselves, at what point do the words of a speaker, implying through guarded language what he does not believe to be true, become deception? At least every listener is clearly on solid ground to infer that the Calvinist proclamation of *whoever will* means that he can will to come. Does such ever amount to deception? Calvinists scold the rest of us for not believing correctly; nevertheless, they work arduously to give the appearance that they are preaching the same message the rest of us preach, which is a simple and straightforward message that all who hear can and should will to come, as ubiquitously seen in Scripture. The Calvinist message gives the appearance of being an open invitation, which it is undeniably not.

When one sells a used car and tells the potential buyer everything works well, that is a good faith offer; provided to the best of his knowledge everything works well, and he is not holding any information back that might affect the buyer's understanding. This understanding affords the seller and the potential buyer precisely the same understanding of the offer, based upon all the knowledge the seller has. If the seller knows the car only works partially well, his offer is not good, nor is it even a good faith offer; at best it is a misleading presentation. Of course, if the car in question does not even exist, then what we have is even baser. Maybe we should ask the ones hearing the Calvinist presentation of the gospel (whoever will may come, believe, and be saved), after enlightening them about such doctrines as limited atonement, irresistible grace, and unconditional election, if they think the offer they received was good, simple, and straightforward. These do eternally affect the listener's understanding of the offer and their decision, do they not? Since they do, they are relevant.

Lastly, such obscurations cannot be justified by noting similar incompleteness in social niceties, such as when an acquaintance asks how you are feeling because such idioms do not even suggest that one should disclose every ailment. For in the case discussed in this chapter, the gospel is being presented, and the meaning of such by the speaker and listener is eternally

---

3. David Wells uses this phrase in his book *No Place for Truth*.

important and drastically different even though the listener thinks they are the same; whereas, social niceties, like a mere greeting, are thoroughly understood by passersby to preclude receiving an exhaustive recitation of one's infirmities. Proprieties of social graces are not at stake, but rather eternal destinies are being forecast (other reasons apply here as well). Paul preached, "Therefore having overlooked the times of ignorance, God is now declaring to men that all people everywhere should repent" (Acts 17:30).

I for one think the so-called good faith offer lacks being an offer since nothing is actually being offered to the non-elect; therefore, it lacks the quality of being good, at least for the non-elect. A potential redemption for the concept necessitates clarity on the part of the presenter that permits the hearer to understand the presentation as the presenter. Then the Calvinist can say his presentation is in good faith and clarity. It just seems palatably obvious that some reality of the thing offered needs to exist before the offer can be rightly called good. Such offer also needs to be disencumbered of intentionally secreting speech.

Why employ such befogging language that conceals Calvinism's inextricable components of what the gospel really is and means? Why not just say, "If you believe in Jesus for the forgiveness of sins you will be saved. God has unconditionally elected some to be able to do so by means of a select internal efficacious call. God is calling out his elect. You may be one of them. If you are, your calling as one of the elect will result in you believing the gospel. May God grant that you are the elect and make that known by granting you the gift of repentance and faith so that we can all rejoice in God's display of sovereign grace in your salvation."

I am not being facetious. This is the gospel as understood in Calvinism. This is the dynamic of the gospel encounter in Calvinism. God's sovereign grace in calling out the unconditionally elect and reprobating the rest is precisely what Calvinism's understanding of the nature of the gospel is all about. Yes, it includes believing in Jesus, but no more so than all these other Calvinist essentials. Sequentially, faith is not an option for anyone who hears the gospel, elect and non-elect alike. It seems obvious to me. Unless the hearer understands the gospel he heard was merely a good faith offer (just like the Calvinist understands it to be) and not a good offer, the offer lacks the quality of being good. For the Calvinist to respond that the presentation I have suggested is not what we see in Scripture is true, but this serves not as a defense of the good faith offer but rather a denial of it.

Our Lord Jesus said, "I tell you, no, but unless you repent, you will all likewise perish" (Luke 13:3, 5). Note the simplicity and clarity. *The simple dilemma,* people are perishing. *The simple message,* repent. *Simple meaning,* they should and can repent. *Simple concept,* good offer; thus, the gospel!

26

Rejecting Calvinism Does Not Require a Weak View of Depravity

SOME CALVINISTS ARE PRONE to chide those who do not don the Calvinist perspective for having a weak view of man's depravity, but that is not necessarily true.[1] As an Extensivist, I categorically reject such a claim. I do believe in *total* depravity.[2] More precisely, man's depravity is extensive (affecting every aspect of man).[3] Accordingly, since the fall, man is utterly and hopelessly *incapable* of exercising saving faith *on his own*. This ability (to be or continue in faith and fellowship with God) did reside in Adam prior to the fall, but it does not exist in mankind subsequent to the fall (Rom 3:10–18). Subsequent to the fall, God must provide everything necessary to enable sinful man to be restored to right relationship with him.

As a result, God is not only the initiator of salvation, but also the energizing power that empowers every aspect of the process, and the eternally sustaining power that protects the redeemed. Man's part, which is exercising faith in Christ as Savior, is possible *only* because of God's sovereign grace in affording man a real choice to either reject the gospel and remain in darkness or accept the light by grace-enabled faith. Fallen man is thoroughly incapable of exercising saving faith on his own, an incapacity that is overcome *only* by God's grace enabling, a part of which is the existence of the very gospel itself, which is caused solely by God's love—omnibenevolence (John 3:16).

Therefore, the difference between the two positions cannot be winnowed out by simply dismissing everyone who rejects Calvinism as being weak on depravity. This is because a lack of belief in the utter depravity and

---

1. Some who reject Calvinism may in fact have a weakened view, but that is not a required outcome when a person rejects Calvinism.

2. For example see my article "The Image of God in Man: A Proposed Working Definition" at https://ronniewrogers.com/2012/09/25/the-image-of-god-in-man-a-proposed-working-definition/.

3. This does not mean man has lost all sensibilities of God (Gen 3:8–13; Rom 1:18–23).

inability of man is *not* the real issue. Rather it is our disagreement regarding what constitutes the nature of man; this difference is where the conflict actually lies. It is this difference that regulates what needed work of grace is required, or permitted, and what is the intended outcome of such work in order to make man savable.

Calvinists believe man was created with a compatibilist free will.[4] As long as man chooses according to his greatest desire, he is exercising free choice. The essence of compatibilism is that determinism and moral responsibility are compatible. This means a person's every decision is free as long as he chooses according to his greatest desire, without external coercion, but his choice is not decided by choosing between two *accessible* options (compatibilism includes voluntariness but it does not include origination). Rather it is the result of determinative antecedents. Atheists, Darwinists, Theists, and Calvinists may disagree on what the determinative antecedents are (Darwinists argue they arise from nature only, whereas Calvinists would say they originate from God ultimately and man's God-given nature and past proximately). In compatibilism, otherwise choice—man choosing other than he did choose—is non-existent.

In view of this, from a Calvinist-compatibilist perspective, Adam freely chose to sin, but he could not have chosen otherwise without having a different nature than he had (or some other variation of determinative antecedents).[5] Accordingly, sinful man cannot believe without a new nature (regeneration) and having such he *will* believe; hence, Calvinism's view that the new nature precedes and provisions faith.[6] This is at the heart of Calvinism's understanding of freedom and depravity.

---

4. See chapter 7 in this book, "Compatibilism or Libertarianism?" and Jonathan Edwards, *Freedom of the Will*, 11, 15, and 413. God's predestination of all things complements this as well. John Calvin, *Institutes of the Christian Religion*, vol. 2, bk. 3, chap. 21, sec. 5, pg. 206. Every attempt to free Calvinism from its unflinching determinism seems to succeed only in providing an inconsistency within one's Calvinism or a slightly different path of terminology without substantive change in the deterministic nature of Calvinism.

5. Calvinists sometimes seek to avoid this reality by delving into discussions regarding such issues as man's moral and intellectual abilities, but these merely obfuscate the actual reality of compatibilism that Calvinism embraces. This is because the question being addressed is not whether Adam could intellectually or morally resist the fall, but rather could Adam, who possessed both moral and intellectual ability, resist the fall. The answer is no, not according to compatibilism. This is one of the disquieting realities of Calvinism, which is quite often obscured.

6. This perspective is held by many but not all Calvinists; it is to my knowledge the vastly dominant view among Southern Baptists. Regardless, given compatibilism, there has to be a determinative antecedent that changes one's past or nature prior to faith.

As an Extensivist, I unconditionally deny Calvinism's compatibilism, and I maintain the clear teaching of Scripture is that God endowed man with a libertarian free will. This simply means man acts freely when he is not coerced by external force or limited by internal inability. He is responsible for his decisions because he could have chosen differently than he did in fact choose. Using Adam again, what makes Adam's sin so damning is he actually chose to sin and walk away from the light when God had done everything within the framework of libertarian freedom to enable him to reject the temptation of the serpent, which he could have done.

In both the compatible and libertarian views, God knew what Adam would do but for very different reasons. In compatibilism, God knew because he gave man a nature that would ultimately result in man freely choosing to sin, whereas in libertarianism God knew because he is essentially omniscient; he foreknows everything that will come to pass—not because man was predetermined to do so. God knew, even though he had created man with the ability to not sin, man would choose to sin. Adam's sin, mankind's ensuing plight, and God's knowledge of all and love for his creation are expressed in his coextensive creation-redemption plan that overcomes the sin of mankind.

Extensivism's view regarding the severity of the fall is no less biblical or serious since both views require a comprehensive supernatural work in order to both provide and secure salvation. The true difference lies in our divergent understanding of man's nature and freedom. It is this understanding which occasions the difference between our answers to the question, *what supernatural work is required for God to place man in a savable position or save him?*

In Calvinism, a savable position leads inexorably to being saved (based upon unconditional election and selective regeneration). This means, in the end, being in a savable position is merely sequentially distinguishable but not qualitatively distinguishable from salvation. Whereas according to Extensivism, savable means to be enabled to have a real choice to either remain in love with darkness and one's sin, or to choose to receive the light of Christ and the gospel (John 12:35–36); consequently, being in a savable position is both sequentially and qualitatively distinguishable from salvation. Unlike Calvinism, Extensivism does not involve a selective deterministic trajectory that unalterably leads to faith for some and not for others.

Additionally, Scripture constantly speaks as though man has a choice between various accessible options, and man concomitantly senses that he can choose between believing and rejecting righteousness (once grace enabled). Humans quotidianly sense as a reality that we can choose from various options placed before us.[7] Even after such a decision is made, we often reflect on how we wish we would have chosen other than what we did, and this with every sense of reality that we could have.

In compatibilism, such sense is a delusion with regard to both the process of decision-making and the review of such decisions, whereas in the libertarian and biblical view, it seems like a reality because it is a reality. That is why man should and can come to the light and is judged for not doing so (John 3:16–21). Most Calvinists that I am aware of commonly obscure the unflinching determinism associated with every decision according to Calvinism because of its commitment to decretal theology and compatibilism. My observation of this reality is not to venture into the opaque domain of assigning a motive for doing so. I am only addressing what is objectively indicated. I try to assume the best of those who do speak with such inconsistencies. I attribute such to either not understanding fully the unflinching determinism entailed in Calvinism or simply collapsing under the unmanageable weight of actually speaking consistently with Scripture and real life when viewed through the lens of micro-determinism.

Regrettably, I did the same as a Calvinist, although it was done unwittingly. I assume the same for my Calvinist brothers and sisters until demonstrated to be otherwise. Unfortunately, even many who reject Calvinism, particularly its determinism, still tend to underestimate how deterministic Calvinism really is, and this far beyond the doctrine of salvation. It actually creates a world where man thinks, feels, and acts as if he and everyone around him are making decisions between accessible options every day. These options are either good or bad, and the ones that are bad should and can be rejected. Such is a phantasm in compatibilism. People read Scripture's commands and warnings with the self-evident understanding they are to make a choice between sin and holiness, faithlessness and faithfulness, hate and love, following self or Christ; yet, compatibilism means all such thoughts are delusional since the choice that one makes, whatever that is, has been determined from eternity. This reality speaks not merely to the nature of moral freedom but the nature of God as well.

With this in mind, it becomes apparent that it is fallacious to equate rejecting Calvinism with necessitating a biblically-weakened perspective regarding depravity. It is more precisely a rejection of the Calvinist belief that God created man with compatible freedom, which includes a disagreement regarding what grace act God must provision for someone to be saved rather than whether there is a requirement of a significantly

---

7. This does not mean man can do anything (fly, become an airplane, etc.,), but within the range of options actually accessible, he can choose to act or refrain; accordingly, man does actually have a choice rather than just a choosing.

essential grace provision. I believe God is sovereign enough to rule over truly free beings (possessing otherwise choice) and powerful enough to restore man to a place of savableness that does not deterministically result in salvation. This restoration enables man to have a real choice of whether to accept Christ or not and whatever man does in fact do, he could have done otherwise. This enablement is provided by God's loving and gracious pre-conversion work, which I often refer to as grace enablement or grace-enabled faith (see authorial definitions).

The truth is both Calvinism and Extensivism recognize the need for a sovereign pre-conversion work of grace, but we disagree on what is included in that work, and that is due to our disagreement regarding the nature of man and not merely biblical depravity. In compatibilism, total depravity might logically require a new nature before a person could be saved or savable, and such a change in man would inevitably result in a free exercise of faith; however, that is not essential to a scriptural definition of depravity, which is that man is so affected by sin that he is incapable of coming to God without God's sovereign enabling grace (Rom 3:10–18). Therefore, one can reject Calvinism without accepting a weak view of depravity. Moreover, one can reject the deterministic trajectory entailed in the change of nature of the individual that is a part of Calvinism (compatibilism) so that one can be restored to a non-deterministic state of savableness (libertarianism). One may surely reject Calvinism's idea that God limits his salvific grace to some, instead believing he provisions everything necessary for the salvation of every person.

This understanding makes it clear we do not necessarily disagree on the seriousness of sin, which is such that it requires God must not only initiate the salvific process, but he must provide every essential of such and continually be involved. What we disagree on (in this limited discussion) is the idea of compatibilism (and decretalism) versus libertarianism, and thereby God's sovereignty and love in a world so constituted. In Calvinism's determinism, God did ultimately desire (though not directly cause) Adam to sin, or else he would have given him a different nature (or other determinative antecedents). Accordingly, God evidentially and undeniably desires only for some to be saved or else he would have given all a new nature that inevitably results in saving faith—the attempted palliation or denial of such by some Calvinists notwithstanding.

In Extensivism, God did desire for Adam to remain in fellowship with him and not sin, although he permitted the latter. Equally, he desires the same for all of Adam's posterity. Therefore, as God provided Adam with the opportunity to remain in the light, he now works to provide a genuine opportunity for all of Adam's posterity to return to the light. According to

Extensivism, God always desired holiness in his creation, and he still does. Therefore, Extensivism does not proffer a weak view of depravity but rather a different understanding of God and the created nature of man.

27

Faith Is the Condition of Salvation and Grace Is the Work of Salvation

CALVINISTS TAKE SOLACE IN the claim that they believe salvation is totally a work of God. Frequently, they either imply or explicitly decry those who make salvation conditioned upon man exercising faith (in response to hearing the gospel prior to regeneration or forgiveness) as making it less than a total work of God, stealing some of God's glory in the work of salvation. According to Calvinists, this conditional nature of salvation, as opposed to monergism, is supposed to emanate from a lesser view of salvation by grace and God's sovereignty, which results in some sort of communal glory or credit between man and God for one's salvation. For example, J.I. Packer and O.R. Johnston say, "To rely on oneself for faith is no different in principle from relying on oneself for works, and the one is as un-Christian and anti-Christian as the other."[1] Wayne Grudem states, "Election based upon something good in us (our faith) would be the beginning of salvation by merit."[2]

Calvinists, as all determinists, are relentless in their reasoning that if one is truly regenerated and saved by exercising faith, then man is *ultimately* saved by his own works, virtue, or something innately superior in the ones who are thereby saved than that which exists in those who are not saved. That is to say, the essential difference between the one who is saved and the one who is not is ultimately based upon the work of faith that constitutes something better, nobler, or more rewardable in the one saved than the one who remains lost. As the argument basically goes, the lost hear the same gospel and receive the same sufficient grace to make them savable, but in the end, the saved make the better choice. Since they both have the same exact opportunity, the only difference is to be found

---

1. Packer and Johnston go on to say "In light of what Luther says to Erasmus, there is no doubt that he would have endorsed this judgment." Introduction to *Bondage of the Will* by Martin Luther, 59.

2. Grudem, *Bible Doctrine*, 287.

in the work of the individuals themselves rather than the work or grace of God; therefore, Calvinists argue Extensivism teaches a salvation based upon some element of human work or virtue.[3]

Reginald Garrigou-Lagrange wrote, "The singling out of one from another must finally be sought not in the human will, but in God who singles out one from another by His Grace."[4] He cites such verses as 1 Cor 4:7; Rom 9:15 and Phil 2:14.[5]

With regard to the free choice exercised in Molinism specifically, Garrigou-Lagrange provides a great example of this kind of reasoning. He said, "Let us suppose that Peter and Judas situated in equal circumstances receive equal prevenient grace; then God sees Peter consenting to accept that grace, and hence singling himself out from Judas who does not consent, not on account of the grace, for an equal grace is indifferently offered to each. Therefore it is because the will decides to accept the grace. Thus do all Thomists argue against Molina, and they thus affirm as revealed the principle that can be called 'the principle of predilection,' "namely, that no one would be better than another unless he was loved more and helped more by God.'"[6]

This is a basic argument used by Calvinists, against salvation being conditioned upon libertarian faith, because according to compatibilism (determinism), libertarian freedom evidences human works or virtue. My observations are as follows:

1. The principle of predilection highlights Calvinism's commitment to the deterministic inequality of God's love and grace (Peter could not have made a better choice without God providing him more love and grace than Judas). It implies a person *is* "better" than another because he *made* a better decision. As Calvinists see it, if Extensivism is true, Peter *is* better than Judas because he made a better decision. But simply making a better choice does not necessarily make or demonstrate the person doing so is essentially better than someone else; only that the choice is better than the contrasting worse choice.

---

3. Usually this is in the context of Arminianism specifically. This is an example of two things common to Calvinism, which must be grasped to successfully engage Calvinists. First, each concept, word and idea is defined to necessarily lead to Calvinism. Second, it is a prime example of begging the question because even the very construction and conclusions to be drawn are premised upon the correctness of Calvinism.

4. Garrigou-Lagrange, *One God*, 462. See also Thomas P. Flint, *Divine Providence, The Molinist Account*, 117.

5. See responses by indeterminists to his argument on the internet at *Theological Determinism Internet Encyclopedia of Philosophy, A Peer-Reviewed Academic Resource*, http://www.iep.utm.edu/theo-det/ accessed 1/3/16.

6. Garrigou-Lagrange, *One God*, 463.

Humans are created *essentially* equal (Gen 1:26–27), even the ones who make bad decisions. According to libertarian freedom, Peter is not saved because he *is* a better person even though he did make a better choice, which is precisely the nature of libertarian beings—choosing between options, some of which are better or worse than their counterpart. Sometimes, the better person, *non-essentially* speaking, may actually make a worse choice than his less noble counterpart within a given range of options. We see this when sometimes an atheist or thief may make a better choice than a Christian in the context of a particular choice, a range of options, and or an equivalent opportunity.

Once the better choice is made by Peter, the consequences of salvation do clearly make Peter an *essentially* better person, but obviously, that is only because of grace. According to Extensivism, grace both enabled the choice and the betterment resulting from the choice. That this does not fit Calvinism's determinism is neither necessary nor expected, only that it fits what we find in Scripture. Determinists seem unable to conceptualize God's plan being comprised of his *equal* love and help for *everyone*, including grace-enabled freedom to choose differently. We should not be surprised to find Calvinism's exclusivism here since it permeates the tenets of Calvinism—unconditional election, limited atonement, selective regeneration.

2. Garrigou-Lagrange relates the will to grace differently than seems best. Although he begins with equal prevenient grace, he then seems to move the will to a place that at least appears to be less dependent upon grace; saying it is "not . . . grace . . . . it is because the will decides to accept the grace." First, rather than say the will decides, I would say it is Peter and Judas as the efficient causes of their actions who decide;[7] they exercise their will.[8] Second, being created with libertarian freedom is solely a grace act of God in creation and, therefore, not some rogue force operating outside or contrary to the plan and grace of God. It would only seem to be so in a Calvinistically-determined system. Third, the ability to exercise their will in choosing is always by grace, regardless of their choice. Each is able to choose differently because it was the will of God for man to be able to do so.

---

7. This does not mean man is the efficient cause of salvation. God is the only efficient cause of salvation. He planned and provisioned salvation including making his grace enablements resistible, but Peter and Judas are the efficient causes of exercising their choices; that is by grace as well.

8. Man exercises his power of free choice as the efficient cause of his actions. Geisler, *Baker Encyclopedia*, s.v. "Evil, Problem Of," 220.

Consequently, Garrigou-Lagrange's issue seems to be with God's decision to endow man with libertarian freedom. What if God said to him, I chose the will to work libertarianly rather than deterministically as you teach. Would he say that cannot be? If so, does he believe God incapable of doing so? It seems clear to me that outside of a deterministic devotion, God seems quite capable of creating a world in which human choice affects some events.

3. Garrigou-Lagrange seems to contend that equal grace must result in the same outcome. This is to presuppose the correctness of determinism, which necessitates a rejection of otherwise choice. Looking at it in reverse, different outcomes necessarily demonstrate either an unequal grace opportunity or that something outside of grace is in play—here he appears to make it the will. It is essential to understand this unspoken (and biblically unjustified) presupposition by Calvinists when they make this argument. It looks like he is willing to accept libertarian freedom so long as it means one can only choose a certain action given the same past or opportunity—libertarianism compatibly defined.

This idea is either explicit or implicit in every argument I have encountered that contends if salvation is conditioned upon faith, the person who gets saved is either more virtuous or wiser than the one who does not; therefore, he is saved by a mixture of grace and human merit. Such can only mean man receives some of the glory or credit for his salvation. I contend the premise that equal grace must result in the same outcome is invalid. He presupposes God's granting of grace is only given to procure a certain choice rather than the certainty of otherwise choice. To wit, determinists make the only possible goal of grace to be a predetermined outcome, here salvation, rather than an outcome resulting from grace-enabled otherwise choice; he simply assumes determinism is correct.

It may be cogently argued that equal grace is the raison d'être for otherwise choice resulting in different outcomes, as Extensivism contends. Critiquing the libertarian position, he says Peter's singling himself out is "not on account of the grace, for an equal grace is indifferently offered to each. Therefore it is because the will decides to accept the grace." He assumes (via the belief determinism is correct) but does not demonstrate that if individuals can exercise their will differently, given the same grace, that cannot be the result of grace. But there is actually no reason, outside of a deterministic system, why the freedom to will different outcomes cannot be because of equal grace to choose differently.

He is simply limiting the purpose of grace to a certain outcome rather than to enable man to, at times, create different outcomes. This means his limitation is not imposed by Scripture, logic, the inability of God, or a deficiency of grace, but rather determinism's narrowness of reality that precludes such a state of affairs. He seems to have simply drawn his conclusions that equal grace did not include the will (technically the efficient cause) to be able to choose differently within the same grace, which is the essence of libertarian freedom. Therefore, he says that the singling out is "not on account of grace." But Extensivism contends the singling out is precisely because of grace that affords otherwise choice in an equal opportunity.

4. Garrigou-Lagrange seems to ignore the grace permitting Judas's choice. He notes only Peter's act "singling himself out." Of course, Peter's choice did single him out, but did not Judas, having the same grace opportunity, single himself out by not consenting to the invitation of the sovereign God? One may easily infer that his argument (about how libertarian freedom operates) includes the reality that Judas's act was not equally one of grace; at least if he does consider it to be, it is neither stated nor obvious. However, I maintain every sin, evil thought and act of defiance of the sovereign that does not lead to instant obliteration from the face of the earth and hurling into eternal torment is because of grace. One does not so choose and then continue to live because of some intrinsic merit or sovereign energy of the person. God's grace *pulls* one to salvation but it also *permits* one to resist or ignore that grace act. God permits man to trust his own works and reject trusting God's work of salvation, but God's work of salvation is intended to resistibly draw one toward salvation; such resisting of the sovereign is not grace pulling to resist but grace permitting resistance.

Libertarian freedom is given and operates only because of and in God's grace, and it is God's will that the person exercises his will. God does not desire man to choose evil, but he does desire man to make an actual choice between accessible options, which happens only in the context of grace. Libertarian freedom entails that different people, given the same opportunity, can make different choices because equal grace does not necessitate equal outcomes. Consequently, there is a sense in which Peter's choice to consent was no more a choice provisioned by grace than Judas's choice to not consent.

5. Garrigou-Lagrange indicates that Calvinism's compatible and decretal freedom is all grace but libertarian freedom cannot be designed by grace. Although I do not accept Calvinism and compatibilism, I do

believe if God did choose to so operate, it would be by grace; it is not something beyond the ability of God. Calvinists seem to either find it impossible, or they are unwilling to consider the same is true of libertarian freedom. Maybe because that requires thinking God is not limited to determinism.

It seems to me, whether God endowed man with a compatible free will or a libertarian free will, each would have been designed by God, and given by God. Therefore, each is, including all its entailments, by God's grace. According to compatibilism, the person chooses but does not have a choice; God decided this by grace. The result of the determined person's choice is a determined act of the grace-provided will. According to libertarianism, the person chooses between accessible options; God decided this by grace. The result of the non-determined choice is a non-determined act of the grace-provided will.

Garrigou-Lagrange's portrayal is that if a person can by an exercise of his will choose a better outcome than someone else, it demonstrates an unequal grace and love from God. This conclusion is true in Calvinism's determinism but not Scripture nor Extensivism's non-determinism. Extensivism contends that libertarian freedom and its entailments are *all* by grace. Properly understood, neither perspective is less dependent upon grace. I think we should be able to disagree about which perspective is most reflective of Scripture without unnecessarily limiting God.

Therefore, Extensivism argues the grace provided by God is equally sufficient for the salvation of both Judas and Peter. In Calvinism no such equality of grace exists since the grace for Peter would be efficacious and the grace for Judas inefficacious (evidenced by the outcome). The concept of equal salvific grace is foreign to Calvinism as is otherwise choice. In Calvinism, grace is given to produce salvation in the elect and withheld to prohibit salvation in the non-elect.

The position of Extensivism is that grace is given in order to *afford* the opportunity to understand enough to either believe or reject the gospel; if rejected, such decision includes more knowledge than the person had prior to this experience of grace. The choice to reject the gospel is because the individual chooses something else above God and in the face of God (sin). That he can do so and not be immediately and irrevocably judged is grace. The difference is one makes a spiritually beneficial choice while the other makes a human and temporary choice, but both are of grace. When sufficient redemptive grace is given to provide a genuine opportunity to believe unto salvation, and that grace is permanently withdrawn, the individual is said to commit the unpardonable sin (Matt 12:31–32). The creative grace given to Adam and Eve was sufficient for them to choose to eat or not eat of the tree, and that ability to make a spiritually beneficial choice in the offer of the gospel is restored by redemptive grace.

This perspective includes the concept, as portrayed throughout Scripture, that pre-fall man was created with otherwise choice and this according to creative grace. Similarly, as God endowed man in creation with such grace ability, he freely chose to sufficiently and redemptively grace enable fallen man to be able to choose to return to God or continue on the path of self-reliance. This means just as Adam chose to leave when he did not have to, man now must choose to return, but he does not have to do so. Both are by grace, which includes the ability to walk away from God. For if it were not for grace permitting such an option, not only could man not come to God, but neither could he walk away. Peter and Judas were enabled by grace to exercise their will according to their own reasons.

Before considering this matter further, let me address a few mistaken Calvinist ideas regarding man being able to choose to follow God or not by exercising his own free will. Various Calvinists frequently argue one or more of the following ideas.

First, some contend that giving man libertarian freedom elevates man to being sovereign in salvation. No! Man did not decide to give himself free will or make walking with God and salvation by faith; God sovereignly made that decision without the counsel of anyone else. Consequently, if God chose to create man in that way, then Calvinism's problem is not with free will, but the God who chose to create man accordingly. Additionally, free will is a force just like any other created force and is thereby always under the sovereign jurisdiction of God.

Second, some Calvinists say if everyone is not saved by God's salvific work then, in some measure, God failed, or at least he is beholden to man. The contention may also be stated thusly; if God sufficiently provisions salvation for some who do not ultimately get saved, then Christ died in vain and God's salvation plan failed. No! This conclusion presupposes God's plan is to *effect* salvation in everyone whose sins were paid for in the death of Christ rather than *provision* salvation for all. It further inaccurately assumes if man can resist the grace of God, then God's call is impotent—man is more powerful than God. That conclusion would be true if God determined to make his grace irresistible and men could resist it, but not if he freely chose to make it acceptable or resistible. Calvinism's confusion arises from their seeking to impose their understanding of the atonement and call of God upon Extensivism. Extensivism maintains God's creation-redemption plan was to *provide* everything necessary for everyone and anyone to be able to walk with God by exercising faith; in creation God endowed man with the ability to exercise faith, and he restored this ability in his pre-conversion work of grace (John 1:29).

This plan includes God's sovereign decision to enable man to choose between resisting or accepting his work of salvation and permitting all who desire not to believe to be able to resist his call of love and grace. Additionally, since God freely chose to create man in relationship with him, he quite consistently also designed man so that the choice of man to love God was of the same nature as God's choice to love man; it is one that did not have to be made, as evidenced with Adam and Eve. His eternal redemption plan was implemented subsequent to the fall of man, which included the restoration of man's ability to choose to believe or remain in disbelief. Since the reality of otherwise choice was included by God in his coextensive creation-redemption plan, the only way this plan can legitimately be deemed a failure is if God's intended provision for all to have the *opportunity* to be saved is found to be insufficient for that purpose. Fortunately, that is not the case.

William Lane Craig comments cogently on the companionable relationship between non-determinism and God.

> For my part, however, I do not see why the Christian theist should wish to adopt the view that God is the determining cause of everything that occurs or that He is impassible actuality. God's being the First Cause does not entail His being the universal cause . . . .the admission that God's grace is resistible would not seem to imply that God is, therefore, not the cause of a person's conversion. All that follows is that the cause is not efficacious so long as one refuses to allow it to act. One could maintain that the final, free consent of the human will is a necessary condition of salvation without holding that man thereby causes his own salvation, in the sense of being an efficient cause. God is the one who pardons and regenerates; he is the only efficient cause. Man must simply be willing to let the efficient cause do its work. Thus, the conversion of Paul was certainly God's work, since it was God who had set him apart, called him, and revealed His Son to him; all Paul did was not to resist (Acts 26:19). But in no way did God call and produce in Judas his betrayal of Christ; God's graces pulled in the opposite direction, and it was only by ignoring these and heeding Satan's temptation that Judas precipitated himself into his act of perfidy.[9]

---

9. Craig, *Divine Foreknowledge*, 271. That God is impassible is the idea that he does not suffer like humans or as a result of others. There seems to be a balance between the two positions, the other being that God is passible. That he is impassible can lead to God as detached, similar to Deism. That he is passible in a significant way can lead to

I would add that Paul's freedom to believe was an enablement of God creatively and redemptively.

Third, some Calvinists maintain if God *truly desires* all to be saved, and all are not saved, then God failed. No! God seems perfectly capable of creating a plan that affords everyone the magnanimous opportunity to be saved while simultaneously desiring that such plan encompass libertarian free will, the ability to resist. To wit, there is neither a biblical nor logical conflict in God desiring everyone to accept his love and salvation while concurrently desiring that such acceptance is conditioned upon a non-deterministic free will decision.

We see this parallel frequently throughout Scripture. For example, God both designed and desires marriage to be for life (Gen 2:18-24; Mal 2:16; Matt 19:8). Yet he also quite apparently desires to permit the freedom of those involved to choose to go against his desire for marriage (Matt 5:31-32; 17:7-8; 1 Cor 7:10-16). Similarly, Scripture is clear that God desires for all Christians to grow in the knowledge and holiness of Christ (Eph 4:15; 1 Pet 2:2). However, what we find in Scripture and the local church is the clear reality that God also desired to incorporate choice, which can result in some being unnecessarily immature and even remain so for long periods of time (1 Cor 3:1-3).

Does this mean God is not omnipotent? No, it means God created man with otherwise choice, which includes the God-granted freedom to actually choose between following or not following God. With this in mind, the reality is some people freely choose to remain immature, or they choose not to do the things that lead to maturity (such as regular Bible study, regular evangelism, regular prayer, and regular meetings with other believers). As a pastor, I can assure you this reality is painfully true and a great burden to every pastor who loves the flock. It would be a grievous error to conclude that because some choose to remain spiritually infantile neither God nor his shepherds desire them to grow.

In light of these examples, as well as countless others found in Scripture and life, it seems pointless and misleading to marshal examples that demonstrate events God desires to happen apart from human causation do happen because we all recognize some events are determined—definite events. That God has created a world in which some events are not determined (indefinite events) does not exclude the idea that some are determined. We can say God's will is always done, so long as one understands that to mean it was

---

Open Theism. However, Scripture does seem to include the truth that God is passible in degree. He feels and experiences suffering connected to his creation. Regarding the passibility of God, God feels and responds emotionally to events upon the earth: (Isa 14:1; Ps 38:3; Luke 19:41-42; Eph 4:30). Jesus was passible (Isa 53:3; Heb 4:15).

God's will to create man with otherwise choice, and that he permits such choice to be determinative in some scenarios, which can result in an event that would not be characteristic of God's highest desire. Rather, it is actually reflective of his desire to permit such state of affairs resulting from the free choice of man created in his image.

It is equally fruitless to contend such desires are necessarily competing or contradictory when there is nothing logically, or more importantly biblically, to evidence such to be the case. There does not seem to be a conflict between God's sovereignty and his desire to create a state of affairs that includes some events being the result of otherwise choice. Of course, I recognize such to be incongruent with Calvinism, but it is not incongruent with the ability of a sovereign God and what Scripture portrays. Therefore, it is perfectly consistent for God to desire all to be saved and equally desire that those who will be saved become so by choosing to believe when they could have chosen not to believe as others did, given the same opportunity. This is not to value free choice above salvation as some Calvinists are quick to quip. Rather, the place of choice is because of the chosen design of man by God; thus, the place of choice is due to the will of God in creation and salvation. Kenneth Keathley writes, "The message of the gospel is that a person is saved when he places personal trust in Jesus Christ as Lord and Savior."[10]

Part of Calvinism's difficulty in grasping this is their commitment to decretal theology and compatibilism, which necessitates that every event is actually a predetermined event. It is, in fact, a necessary event because God decreed everything to be as it is, even though they confusingly speak, write, and pray as though the events could be otherwise due to human involvement. This determinative necessity does not require exclusion of secondary causes, but rather that the event takes place as only it could take place. In contrast, Extensivism recognizes that some events are *definite* because they happen necessarily due to God's predetermination that such is the case without any possibility the event could happen differently. Such events are unaffected by human choice. Events like creation, the second coming of Christ, and the final judgment of God against all ungodliness are examples of this.

Extensivism also recognizes some events are, by God's design, *indefinite*. That is, God, determined to create man with otherwise choice and permit such ability to influence and change some events, thereby making them indefinite (not happening out of determinative necessity). God knows the *definite* events because he predetermined them to happen as they unalterably do. He knows *indefinite* events because he determined to incorporate

---

10. Keathley, "The Work of God," 696.

the force of free choice to shape outcomes, and he knows the free acts of man, contingencies, because he is essentially omniscient.

By describing an event as being necessary, I mean eternally in the mind of God such was *unalterably* determined to be a particular outcome in time; therefore, it is temporally necessary as to causality and God's foreknowledge, not merely certain. It is a *definite* event. By describing an event as certain, I mean eternally in the mind of God, such was *alterably* determined. It is considered to be alterable because God comprehended man's free otherwise choice as a sufficient influence upon the outcome in time. It is an *indefinite* event. This class of events could have resulted in different outcomes had the individual exercised his God-given freedom differently. They are not temporally necessary as to causality, but they are certain due to God's knowledge being incapable of error, which includes his infallible knowledge of future contingencies—free acts of man.

The Bible is unmistakably lucid in teaching salvation is totally a sovereign work of God and a reflection of his omnibenevolence. According to the unbeclouded teaching of Scripture, from conception to completion, God alone did the work of salvation and superabundantly provided everything necessary so he could legitimately and unconditionally offer it to everyone; it is truly accessible to all who hear the gospel. He is the efficient cause of salvation. He did the work of salvation, including sufficient provision and conditions. Accordingly, he did not condition the *work* of salvation upon faith, but rather it is more precise to say the *personal reception* of the free and full *work* God's salvation is conditioned upon faith. Even the act of faith is grace enabled—as opposed to somehow originating outside of God's design in either created or fallen man.

We may rightly say no outside force influenced either the development or procurement of God's plan of creation or redemption. God designed his plan of salvation so that the work and offer of salvation are unconditional. It is provided and offered to everyone regardless of anything beyond the desire of God, including whether a person will accept or reject it; further, he designed the work of salvation to include that the reception of salvation is conditioned upon grace-enabled faith.

By grace, God bounteously provides every essential for a person to be able to walk in relationship with him. This includes opportunity, necessary understanding, a free will to act, ability for all to respond or reject, and the basis for every sovereignly necessitated condition to exist in and emanate from the grace of God rather than the merit, virtue, or otherwise contribution of man. Both the conditions and the ability to meet said conditions exist because of what is in and provided by God's work of salvation rather than what is in or deserved by man.

God then graciously bestows these so that man's freedom of otherwise choice is simply an outcome of his sovereignly chosen and enabled precondition for enjoying his full fellowship. This is as true of Adam prior to the fall as it is of fallen Adam and his progeny after the fall. That a choice to receive God's blessings and walk in them is always conditioned upon faith is the pervasive and coherent teaching of Scripture (Gen 2:17; Rom 4:3). What changes from pre-fall to post-fall and then ultimately after glorification is what grace works God must accomplish and provide in order to make such blessing actually available and accessible. If a person seeks to taint faith with some logical deduction of human virtue, works, or bettering one over another then he has placed his reasoning above and in contradiction to explicit Scripture (Rom 3:21–31; 4:1–16). He has presupposed God is *incapable* of giving man a grace-enabled otherwise choice.

For example, God created Adam, placed him in an environment that was conducive to Adam being able to walk with him, while concomitantly being sufficient to provide Adam with the freedom to choose to cease walking with God. We can understand this as creative-grace enablement. That is the option God laid before Adam (Gen 2:17–18). Hardly anything could be more clear (Genesis 1 & 2). When Adam and Eve chose to use their God-given creative ability to walk away from God and go their own way (Gen 3:1–6), the opportunity for them to walk with God ceased to be available based upon God's creative-grace work. Unless God's eternal creation plan comprehended such an eventuality and accordingly incorporated additional grace provisions, man would never be able to walk with God in the same way that Adam did. This is true even though all of man's sensibilities regarding God were not obliterated by the fall (Gen 3:8–13; Rom 1:18–32); as a result of Adam and Eve's sin, the precise opportunity of Adam and Eve ceased to exist.

Thankfully, we all know God did not leave those he created irrevocably captive to their condign punishment. He always knew man would misuse his freedom, thereby eternally sequestering himself and his posterity from an intimate walk with their Creator. Correspondingly, God had eternally overcome such an egregious misuse of grace and freedom through his eternal coextensive creative-redemptive plan, which included not only creative grace but redemptive grace as well. This becomes immediately evident after the fall of Adam and Eve (Gen 3:21). It is encapsulated in his initial expression regarding the grander redemptive plan that included all of mankind (Gen 3:15), which, other than the triune God, becomes the theme of Scripture.

Man's freedom to exercise otherwise choice is a created force (libertarian free will), a work of God; therefore, God is sovereign over it, and he can contravene it at any time as he can any other created force. Consequently, whether this force is used for holiness or sin, it will not and cannot thwart his ultimate will as is seen in Genesis in that God was neither surprised nor ill-prepared. This force is neither foreign nor supplemental to his will or salvation plan (as is sometimes understood or portrayed by Calvinists), but rather it is an inextricable component of his creative plan of making man in his very own image unto his own glory!

Genesis, as well as the rest of Scripture, teaches God desired to create man with such power rather than limiting man to merely choosing what he only could choose through compatible freedom or being microscopically scripted by the precise decree of God. It seems God's creation of man with otherwise choice is the most obvious and unencumbered message of Genesis two and three if read without a Calvinistic theological necessity. Additionally, rather than this clear Genesiacal message evanescing with God's unfolding revelation, it actually becomes a captivating theme of Scripture.

Scripture is replete with examples of God giving man a choice between two accessible options and then either blessing or judging man corresponding to the choice he makes. It appears one would have to write a myriad of books, create all kinds of biblically foreign concepts, interpret simple verses in light of complicated ones rather than the reverse, and develop unduly narrow definitions in order to convince even a few that such is not the case. Further, to do so transmogrifies what began as revelation into a veiling only to be revealed by a few to a few.

I do believe since the fall, man is totally depraved (extensively); therefore, I do not believe in partial depravity. Calvinists are correct regarding depravity as affecting every part of man. They are tragically mistaken in their understanding of the nature of man being comprised of compatible freedom. Geisler succinctly says, "Depravity can be understood as an inability to initiate or attain salvation without the grace of God."[11] As a result, man is so affected by the fall that he, unlike Adam before the fall, must receive additional grace enablements beyond creative grace in order to have a genuine opportunity to choose to walk with God. This includes such things as God's redemptive love, Christ's payment for sin, conviction of the Holy Spirit, drawing of the Father and Son, and the power of the gospel. None of which were necessary for Adam and Eve prior to the fall because God's provision of creative grace was sufficient.

In Calvinism, faith is the predetermined result of God's creative and redemptive grace provision, whereas in Extensivism, otherwise choice is the predetermined result of God's creative and redemptive grace provision. This

---

11. Geisler, *Baker Encyclopedia*, 756.

means whatever decision is made, it arises from God's grace provision, and is, therefore, a grace choice rather than a meritorious or self-virtuous choice (Rom 4:16; Eph 2:8–10). Within God's options, he could have created man to be able to only *determinatively* exercise a free faith choosing, or he could have created man to be able to *deliberatively* exercise a free choice of faith; the latter is no less a work of grace than the former, Calvinists' asseverations notwithstanding. Rather than succumb to the insistence of Calvinists that this puts salvation in man's hand, somehow makes man deserving or participating in the *work* of salvation, or makes God dependent upon man, it actually is a strong point of Extensivism and poignantly highlights Calvinism's excessively narrow view of God's plan, man's creation, and resultant encumbering of the simple reading of Scripture.

I see no biblical problem believing if a person trusts Christ, he will not perish; if he does not trust Christ, he will perish (Luke 13:3, 5), and that God sovereignly, graciously, and determinatively provisioned for that choice to be available to everyone. Such choice exists without any contrary or cryptic programs running in the background known to only a few, which ultimately reduces the choice from true to trivially true—of course that choice is true but only the unconditionally elect can make such choice.

Upon reflection, it does seem quite odd that one can become more comfortable creating:

- Non-biblically attested-to covenants[12]

- Extra-biblical decrees that trump the simple meaning of revelation

- A two-will hypothesis, which secret soteriology will ultimately trump revealed soteriology

- A selective internal call for the elect only (making the preaching of the gospel a vacuous proclamation for most, and I would even say a misleading one)

- Election, as taught in Scripture, transmogrified into unconditional election (thereby making every passage that reflects opportunity and a need to choose a ghastly phantom)

---

12. For example, Charles Hodge refers to the covenant that God supposedly made with Adam, which is significant in Calvinism saying, "This statement does not rest upon any express declaration of the Scriptures ... Although the word covenant is not used in Genesis, and does not elsewhere, in any clear passage, occur in reference to the transaction there recorded, yet inasmuch as the plan of salvation is constantly represented as a New Covenant, new, not merely in antithesis to that made at Sinai, but new in reference to all legal covenants whatever, it is plain that the Bible does represent the arrangement made with Adam as a truly federal transaction." Hodge, *Systematic Theology*, vol. 2, 117.

- Substituting a good faith offer for the good offer of Scripture (offering what does not exist for the vast majority who hear)
- Having a salvific love for the unconditionally elect while only a temporal love for the rest of his creation (which if understood biblically actually appears to exist in concert with salvific love, not in lieu of it)
- Usage of such language in presenting the gospel that leaves every lost person who hears believing they can and should believe; all the while the Calvinist knows his words are actually an encryption for God calling out his unconditionally elect and have nothing to do with the non-elect except to further condemn them.

All of this dependence upon speculative theology might at least cause one to temper such hubris pronouncements as we hear from some Calvinists regarding those who disagree with them. When I compare Calvinism and Extensivism, just based upon the unclouded teaching of Scripture and apart from speculative theology whose fecundity of producing other such speculations is vast indeed, it results in recognizing God's decision to condition the restoration of man's walk with him upon grace-enabled faith. It seems so simple—apparently too simple for some.

The understanding of Scripture presented here simply means faith is the condition for receiving God's *work* of salvation, but faith is not the *basis* or work of salvation. The basis of Adam's relational ability and fallen man's relational ability (salvation) is always the love of God for his creation (John 3:16). This fact is the same as with Adam because he related to God by trusting God's word, which relationship was corrupted when he chose to distrust God's word (Gen 2:17–18). As the first man related to God by faith and broke his relationship by not trusting God, every subsequent person returns to God by faith (Acts 16:31, Heb 11:6) or remains separated from God for one reason: he refuses to trust God (Luke 13:3, 5; Acts 17:30), which is the ultimate sin of Adam. That dynamic has not changed. It further seems that since man will forever be finite, he will always relate to God by faith even though the range of options will change.

"If it is disagreeable in your sight to serve the Lord, choose for yourselves today whom you will serve: whether the gods which your fathers served which were beyond the River, or the gods of the Amorites in whose land you are living; but as for me and my house, we will serve the Lord" (Josh 24:15).

28

God Can Know the Free Acts of Man without Determinism

CALVINISTS OFTEN ARGUE THAT defending man as possessing libertarian free will not only places man's salvation in his own hands, but it also creates uncertainties that would mean God would not know everything because (as the argument goes) one cannot know an uncertainty for certain. On the other hand, the Calvinist idea is that all actions are predetermined by God through either decrees or compatibilism, and this makes everything definite and, therefore, knowable. This understanding makes the theological reality of libertarian free will an impossibility in Calvinism.[1] Fortunately, the impossibility is merely a Calvinistic impossibility rather than an actual one.

For example, Shedd argues that the undecreed (anything contingent) cannot be known, saying, "So long as anything remains undecreed, it is contingent and fortuitous. It may or may not happen. In this state of things, there cannot be knowledge of any kind."[2] He further summarizes the impossibility of such a state, "To know, or to foreknow an uncertainty, is a solecism [inconsistency or error]."[3] He continues to pose decrees as certain and man having otherwise choice as being contingent and uncertain, which means according to him, "There is, therefore, nothing knowable in the case. To know, or foreknow an uncertainty, is to know or foreknow a non-entity."[4] This type of argument is consistent with other forms of determinism as well.

Succinctly, Shedd is arguing that a contingency (the result of libertarian choice) is an uncertainty and, therefore, nothing; for that reason, it is unknowable, and it certainly cannot be known certainly. This understanding leads to the conclusion that for man to have the freedom to choose other

1. I say theological because Calvinists and Extensivists alike know that no one lives consistently with determinism; accordingly, libertarian freedom is obviously a real-world reality.

2. Shedd, *Dogmatic Theology*, vol. 1, 397. He is comparing Socinian and Arminian theology.

3. Shedd, *Dogmatic Theology*, vol. 1, 398.

4. Shedd, *Dogmatic Theology*, vol. 1, 398.

than what was predetermined is impossible because such reality undermines God's omniscience and sovereignty. Hodge states, "Because all events are included under the categories of the actual and possible; and, therefore, there is no room for such a class as events conditionally future. It is only possible, and not certain, how men would act under certain conditions, if their conduct be not predetermined, either by the purpose of God, or by their own decisions already formed."[5] As Hodge discusses the subject, he makes it clear Extensivists (non-Calvinists) are the ones who accept what is now termed libertarian free will and Calvinists are compatibilists.[6]

Regarding these two irreconcilable perspectives on moral freedom, Hodge states, "This is one of the points in which theology and psychology come into immediate contact. There is a theory of free agency with which the doctrines of original sin and of efficacious grace are utterly irreconcilable, and there is another theory with which those doctrines are perfectly consistent. In all ages of the Church, therefore, those who have adopted the former of these theories reject those doctrines; and, on the other hand, those who are constrained to believe those doctrines are no less constrained to adopt the other and congenial theory of free agency. Pelagians, Semi-Pelagians, and Remonstrants are not more notoriously at variance with Augustinians, Lutherans, and Calvinists, on the doctrines of sin and grace, than they are on the metaphysical and moral question of human liberty."[7]

Shedd considers the differing beliefs regarding the knowability of contingencies as held by Socinians and Arminians:[8]

> In respect to this point, the *Socinian is more logical than the Arminian*. Both agree that God does not decree those events which result from the action of the human will. Voluntary acts are not predetermined, but depend solely upon human will. Whether they shall occur rests ultimately upon man's decision, not upon God's. *Hence human volitions are uncertainties for God, in the same way that an event which does not depend upon a man's decision is an uncertainty for him.* The inference which the Socinian drew from this was, that foreknowledge of such events as human volitions is impossible to God . . . . The Arminian,

---

5. Hodge, *Systematic Theology*, vol. 1, 399.

6. Hodge later refers to the concept of libertarian free will variously as "contingency," "liberty of indifference" or "self-determining power of the will," although I do not find his definition to be accurate or precise. Hodge, *Systematic Theology*, vol. 2, 282–83.

7. Hodge, *Systematic Theology*, vol. 2, 278

8. Socinianism was a 16th and 17th century theological movement that claimed to believe in Scripture but denied doctrines such as the deity of Christ and the Trinity.

shrinking from this limitation of divine omniscience, asserts that God can foreknow an *uncertainty*; that is, that he can have foreknowledge, without foreordination[9] (italics added).

Thus, Shedd disagrees that contingencies arising solely from the free will of man exist but agrees with the Socinians that if they do exist, they are unknowable.

I would make the following distinctions. Contrary to Shedd, man does know differently from God since man is not omniscient and did not originate his ability to know or choose. God created man with otherwise choice (always knowing he would have such, which man did not know). He omnisciently always knew how such endowment could and would be used, which man did not nor does he now know. God's knowledge is particular, comprehensive, exhaustive, and eternal. Man knows and learns *perceptively*, whereas God knows because he is *essentially* omniscient. That is to say, God as God knows everything as an essential part of who he is (even free acts of libertarian freedom) and, therefore, does not look beyond himself for knowledge, i.e., learn perceptively. He does not look down the halls of history to know contingencies; he knows them essentially, as an attribute of being God. Conversely, man's knowledge is not of any such caliber either prior to or subsequent to the choices of others or even his own decisions.

The emphasis upon determinism stresses Calvinism's inability to perceive God as portrayed in Scripture. It seems to me, while neither side is heretical, our views of man reflect significantly different views of God. I think Scripture portrays God as more than capable of creating man with such freedom, restoring it after the fall, and still always knowing everything man would do. God is all-powerful and all-knowing. This includes the actual, potential, counterfactuals of otherwise choice (contingencies), what he will and will not cause or permit, and what he will make conditional even to the point of what option man will choose within the range he permits. He further knows what options flow from that and what man will subsequently choose out of that contingent range of options (new reality or sequence of events for man).

He knows our present and future thoughts, and he has known them eternally. His understanding is infinite. (Ps 94:9; Ps 139:1–18; Ps 147:5; Prov 15:3; Prov 15:11; Ezek 6:5; Matt 10:30; John 2:24–25; Acts 15:18; Heb 4:13). It is true Calvinists believe these verses, as well as the surety and infinitude of God's knowledge, but they do so for different reasons than Extensivists. This difference includes the nature and role of causality and even what is meant by the word know. Calvinists postulate God knows all because he

---

9. Shedd, *Dogmatic Theology*, vol. 1, 397–98. See also 313.

predetermined all, decretal theology and compatibilism, even though such causation may include determined secondary causes.

The following provides some examples of God's conditional knowledge (counterfactual knowledge). Matt 11:20–24 gives every appearance of teaching that had the people of Tyre, Sidon, and Sodom had the opportunity afforded Bethsaida, Chorazin, and Capernaum, they would have repented. Because of that, the judgment upon the cities Jesus was addressing would be more severe. Hodge, who seems troubled by this clear meaning, seeks to make this passage nothing more than "a figurative mode of stating the fact that the men of his generation were more hardened than the inhabitants of those ancient cities."[10]

Read without a Calvinistic necessity, it seems clear Jesus was truly excoriating the people of these contemporary cities for squandering what others would have embraced. He could make such a claim based upon his omniscience, which includes counterfactual knowledge (what if). Jesus says clearly "they would have repented." D.A. Carson says in reference to this judge (Jesus), "The Judge has contingent knowledge: he knows what Tyre and Sidon would have done under such-and-such circumstances."[11]

Hodge says regarding God as the sum of perfection, "Such a being cannot be ignorant of anything; his knowledge can neither be increased nor diminished."[12] On this, we can all agree. A difference Extensivists have with determinists is that we would argue there is nothing that would or could happen by either particular predetermination (which includes unconditional realities) or predetermined permission (which includes conditional eventualities) of which God has ever lacked infinite knowledge. Uncertainties in time and space and the mind and experience of man were never uncertain in the mind of God. Equating uncertainties of man to uncertainties of God, and in so doing making contingencies essentially nothing and consequently unknowable, is neither reflective of Scripture nor essential omniscience.

God's knowledge not only includes the significant counterfactual potentialities, but it even includes the mundane such as knowing every bird that falls from the sky and the number of hairs on everyone's head (Matt

---

10. Shedd, *Dogmatic Theology*, vol. 1, 400.

11. Carson, "Matthew," 273. Carson is a Calvinist, but he is forthright about the simple meaning of the passage, which I appreciate. As a Calvinist, if consistent, he would have difficulty with this statement and unconditional election. The Extensivist has no such problem since we teach everyone gets an opportunity, but we do not teach everyone gets the same opportunity to believe, which seems to be an absolute impossibility in a time and space continuum. Additionally, Carson is a compatibilist which means the contingency here is not the result of otherwise choice in man. See chapter 7, "Compatibilism or Libertarianism?"

12. Hodge, *Systematic Theology*, vol. 1, 397.

10:29–30). Both states are ever changing and rather unimportant, and yet God has eternally known everything about all of them because he is essentially omniscient; such neither entails nor even suggests he micro-causally predetermined each changing state. To separate God knowing himself exhaustively, including his intentions, which includes his intention to create libertarian beings from knowing the acts of such beings is artificial.

The Bible portrays many things as contingent upon man's choice, such as wisdom being conditioned upon seeking and asking (Prov 2:1–12; 4:5–7; 6:16; Jas 1:5). He grants grace to the ones who choose humility over pride (1 Pet 5:5). This genre of conditionality as well as the voluminous passages regarding the promise of blessing or cursing as contingent upon the decision of man (Gen 2:16–17; Deut 11:26–28) as well as salvation being contingent upon the choice of man and judgment upon same (Rom 10:8–11), give every indication of otherwise choice.

There is nothing contradictory nor deficient in understanding the biblical portrait of man's knowledge of contingencies being uncertain while God's knowledge is certain; as a matter of fact, that is the most lucid understanding. Man may in fact even be certain he will act a specific way at a particular time under a given set of conditions, and end up acting differently than he truly believed he would; God's knowledge of such a future event and choosing is not so uncertain. Peter offers us a well-known example of this truth.

Christ told Peter he would deny him, and Peter adamantly rejected such a notion (Matt 26:34–35). In the presence of Jesus, Peter could not imagine ever denying Christ; however, Jesus knew one day Peter would not be in his presence, and under the conditions of that moment, Peter would choose to deny Christ. This happened after Christ was taken prisoner. At the time of Peter's unthinkable denial, the conditions had changed and were far different than Peter could have imagined when he stood so strong in the presence of Christ. The point of denial came at night when Peter was alone, scared, and sad. Peter's emotions were disconcerted and a host of confusing and daunting uncertainties encapsulated him. In that crucible of temptation, he did what he previously exclaimed with certainty he would never do and what Christ said he would do. He denied Christ his Lord whom he loved no less at the temptation than at the time of strength. Christ, knowing all of that along with knowing Peter exhaustively, knew Peter would deny him. Peter's shock and regret over his failure to stand by his Lord are evident when Peter wept bitterly (Matt 26:75).

This uncertainty about Peter's decision was not uncertain to God. Christ always knew this, not because Peter was predetermined (the passage does not even hint at such), but rather Christ omnisciently knew the choice Peter would make before he made it, and this in spite of his determination to do otherwise. As God, Christ always knew what Peter would choose in different circumstances. Christ's knowledge of such does not necessitate predetermination, either by decree or otherwise, but it only requires essential omniscience. Accordingly, that man will act in a particular way is certain to God, but it is not necessary as to causality. Had Peter chosen to act differently, God would have eternally known that. Moreover, even if an uncertainty is nothing in time and space, that does not mean it is an absolute uncertainty (absolutely nothing), because uncertainty is a property of man's knowledge but not God's.

Hodge says, "In virtue of his omniscient intelligence, He knows whatever infinite power can effect; and that from the consciousness of his own purposes, He knows what He has determined to effect *or to permit to occur*"[13] (italics added). Again, I think we can all agree with this statement. The disagreement seems to reside in what we believe his "infinite power can effect." Can he be sovereign over truly free—otherwise choice—beings, or is that beyond his infinite power? For sure the disagreement resides in what we believe, "He has determined to effect . . . permit." Contrary to Calvinism, the biblical narrative depicts man created in God's image, which includes otherwise choice;[14] with such freedom, God "who works all things after the counsel of His will" (Eph 1:11) gives the range of options that are available to man. This freedom is not a potential thwarter to his plan and will. While it is a force, it is not a force external to his sovereignty. Rather, it is a vital component that bespeaks of his majestic power, wonder, and glory.

It is important to note the idea of God permitting something in Calvinism is quite different than the meaning when used by Extensivists, Scripture, and people in everyday language. In Calvinism, it is no less causally determined than anything else. It is either decreed or the predetermined result of compatible freedom. In contrast, Extensivists understand the idea of permit to be God giving freedom to do other than his holiness and mercy would desire one to do at that moment—i.e., freedom to do evil. While always desiring holiness, he permits contrarieties, yet such do not defeat him. Rather, all such rebellion is comprehended in his will and is ultimately overcome. This in contrast to determinism wherein God did desire such horror that he created a world in which such is predetermined rather than the consequence of man wrongly using the good gift of otherwise choice.

---

13. Hodge, *Systematic Theology*, vol. 1, 398.

14. I believe God has the ability to choose otherwise and that ability is included in his image in us. See my article, The Image of God: A Proposed Working Definition, https://ronniewrogers.com/2012/09/25/the-image-of-god-in-man-a-proposed-working-definition/

The Calvinist's determinism of everything is seen once more when Hodge says, "A free agent, it is said, can always act contrary to any amount of influence brought to bear upon him, consistent with his free agency. But if free acts must be uncertain, they cannot be foreseen as certain under any conditions."[15] Again we see the Calvinist puzzle being due in large measure to applying the uncertainty of man to God. The fallacy and problem arise from equating the actor's uncertainty as being equivalent to the Creator's uncertainty. Of course, the act is uncertain to the actor, but not to God. As to certainty and infinite knowledge, his knowledge of such seems no more discursive than decreeing something to be. Both are in that sense always known within God, intuitively, since he has always known everything—potential, actual, possible, and conditional—and he looks no further than himself for such knowledge.

Before further consideration of this issue, let me point out the statement Hodge makes "can always act contrary to any amount of influence brought upon him" is an inaccurate portrayal of libertarian free agency. God is the only sovereign; therefore, he can contravene free acts any time he so chooses. Not only can he, Scripture gives numerous examples of such (Dan 4:30–37). Libertarian freedom does not require every choice be unfettered, but only that some choices are the result of otherwise choice. The loss of the freedom to choose otherwise at different times, or in some areas, does not equal the loss of libertarian freedom. Libertarian freedom only entails that man is not responsible for the particular decisions wrought from other than agent causation.

Simply said, God has forever known, with inviolable certainty, what man could do and what he will choose to do from the God-given range of options. He knows this with the same certitude he knows those things he would predeterminately cause. God's knowledge of the actual, potential, and what potential realities he will actualize are inherent in his perfection and omniscience, which does not require the micro-causality of every act of man. This understanding is, in fact, a more biblically reflective and grander portrayal of God than the Calvinist painting. The God of Scripture can cause or permit (defining permit as allowing results derived from libertarian free beings), and he can know with certainty (without necessity) these contingent acts. He even knew the influences and the intricacies of the deliberative process of each free being. This represents man as having objective liberty in contrast to believing that man's liberty is merely subjective, as is the case in compatibilism (objective meaning that man's sense

---

15. Hodge, *Systematic Theology*, vol. 1, 399–400.

of deliberatively choosing between accessible options is *actual* rather than merely subjective, *imaginary*).

God's certainty of man's choice within the range of options given by God does not mean man could not have chosen to do other than what he did in fact choose. The act in time is both free and certain. It is free as to the choice between options afforded man in time, and it is certain as to God's eternal knowledge of what said choice would be. Some ask if God believed in eternity man would act a certain way, and then at the last second he acted differently, would God have believed wrong—been mistaken? The answer is no. Regarding man, William Lane Craig notes, "He has the power to act in a different way, and if he were to act in that way, God would have believed differently."[16] Lewis Sperry Chafer notes, "If the question be asked whether the moral agent has freedom to act otherwise than as God foresees he will act, it may be replied that the human will because of its inherent freedom of choice is capable of electing the opposite course to that divinely foreknown, but he will not do so. If he did so, that would be the thing which God foreknew. The divine foreknowledge does not coerce; it merely knows what the human choice will be."[17]

For that reason, God always knew what a person would freely decide (so the decision is free and could have been otherwise had the free agent so chosen), but the choice is certain in that God's knowledge of such choice is perfect. Had man chosen otherwise, God would have always known that. Extensivists believe man *will* act in a certain way, whereas Calvinists believe man *must* act in a certain way, albeit free from a compatibilist perspective. Extensivists believe man will certainly act in a specific way when he could have truly done otherwise; therefore, man's deliberative process, freedom, and liberty are objective.

The free act of man is certain due to God's omniscience, but it is not necessary due to causality. The only thing that is necessary about man's choice is that if he would have chosen otherwise, God would have known that choice because God knows everything and cannot be mistaken.[18] This is what I mean in saying the concept of liberty is objective rather than merely subjective. To reiterate an important point, the belief in libertarian free choice does not mean God cannot override man's freedom when he so chooses, and to postulate such is a glaring misrepresentation of libertarianism.

---

16. Craig, *The Only Wise God*, 71.
17. Chafer, *Systematic Theology*, vol. 1, 196.
18. See William Lane Craig's book *The Only Wise God* for a fuller explanation and illustration of certainty and necessity, pages 69–73.

Calvinism teaches God foreknows because he decreed man would act a certain way, and because of his decree, man necessarily acts a certain way and God can be certain of that. Extensivism says God foreknows because of infinite knowledge of the actual and potential (including new event sequences resulting from the otherwise choice of humans) as an essential property of his foreknowledge. In light of this, it seems Calvinism inadequately portrays and comprehends the biblical representation and facts regarding what man could, should, might, and will do, whereas Extensivism encompasses these in foreknowledge.

In both perspectives, there is never a nanosecond that God does not know with certainty every future act and the outcome of every future act. The difference is Calvinism contends God knows because he decreed such to be a certain way, whereas Extensivism makes liberty objective and known by God simply because he is God.[19] The latter is more reflective of the numerous biblical encounters between God and man wherein man is commanded to act a certain way, and blessed when he does or reprimanded and punished for not doing so. All of which clearly indicates man is endowed with otherwise choice and understandably responsible for his actions.

Such understanding does not make sense to a Calvinist. Part of the reason is their definitions are derived from and lead to micro predetermination. I understand God foreknowing everything as an innate property of his being does not fit the grid of Calvinism because I am not a determinist with all of its horrors; however, my argument is this understanding wherein God is essentially omniscient and not merely limited to knowing something because he determined it to be, without the otherwise choice of man, does fit Scripture. This understanding makes both foreknowledge and otherwise choice more consistent with Scripture without Calvinism's theoretical accouterments. Calvinists strongly demur to man possessing libertarian freedom, God being able to create such, and I understand their position. I would argue their conclusions are largely reliant upon speculative theology and unnecessarily restrictive definitions of terms, which require auxiliary

---

19. This flows from some things being logically prior. Craig, *The Only Wise God*, 74. Craig says of logical priority, "To say that something is logically prior to something else is not to say that the one occurs before the other in time. Temporally, they could be simultaneous. Rather, logical priority means that something serves to explain something else. The one provides the grounds or basis for the other. . . . This does not mean that there was a time at which certain events occurred without God's knowing about them. The priority here is purely logical, not temporal." *The Only Wise God* 127–28. See also where he demonstrates the fallacy of the fatalistic argument, *The Only Wise God* 72–74. I think substituting the term explanatorily prior for logically prior may be helpful. See also "God and Logical Priority" by J.W. Wartick, https://jwwartick.com/2010/06/13/god-and-logical-priority/ accessed 3/29/18.

concepts. In contrast, Extensivism seems to be more reflective of the biblical portrayal of God's knowledge and man's freedom than some speculation that God is incapable of knowing what he permits without necessitating such by predetermination.

It may help to remind ourselves when considering knowledge—finite vs. infinite—humility must be in order. God knows man's deliberative process, influences, and degrees of struggle. All of which have been eternally known by God before the event occurs in time and better than man knows his choices after the event. Consequently, neither the slightest aspect of the deliberative process nor the final choice is *ever* unknown to God. With man having true libertarian freedom, God could always have written Gen 3:1-6. Both the actualization of the event and Moses' writing of it were dependent upon the start of time, whereas God's knowledge of such is an eternally essential property of his being. Thus, foreknowledge establishes certainty without determinative causation.

Stated somewhat differently, God always knew he would create man with free will. He simultaneously knew this meant man would be the efficient cause of actions God would permit. He further concurrently knew results emanating from agent causation would establish new sequences of events. These new sequences are subsequent to the act of man, and, therefore, are dependent upon man. God's knowledge of his choice to create man, with all concomitant consequences, is dependent upon God's nature rather than necessitating God looking outside of himself to be informed by the choices of man. God always knew the interdependent nature of man's choice and new sequences. Because he always knew everything associated with such a creation, both particularly and exhaustively, there was never a point in the process in which he was ever informed by anything outside of his own eternally essential omniscience.

His eternal knowledge and his ability to know fully is not dependent upon anyone or anything outside of himself. To know future contingencies (the acts of libertarian free beings), God only needed to be exhaustively self-aware and always fully knowing his own intentions. Since he always intended to create libertarian free beings who could originate new sequences of events and possibilities, he always knew the choices and subsequent possibilities by knowing himself.

All human examples of God's foreknowledge break down at some point, which is due in part to the fact that humans never can know the future perfectly and humans know perceptively whereas God's knowledge is essential. The following is designed *only* to illustrate there is an essential difference between foreknowing and causing even though my example does not include essential or absolute foreknowledge. To state it differently, one may know something without being the cause of it just as a human may in fact inadvertently cause something to happen without ever knowing he was the cause until someone informs him—this is not reflective of God but only stating my point differently in order to further illustrate that knowing and causing are not necessarily the same.

I tell people that I know whom Gina (my wife for over 44 years) will vote for when she goes into the voting booth. I know this with mathematical certainty. I can tell you whom she voted for before I ever see her or talk to her after she has cast her vote. Why? Is it because I forced her, I coerced her, or that I somehow rigged the booth to cause her, or caused her to desire, to vote a certain way (so that her freedom and deliberation were merely subjective)? Is it because I performed magic so that while she thought she was making a choice between various accessible options, she was not. Absolutely not! I know how she will vote because I know her intimately. My knowledge of how she will vote actually has no bearing on her choice of whom to vote for, but rather I know because I know her. Simply put, knowledge and causation of certain actions are not synonymous. With regard to man, God's knowledge does not necessarily prejudice outcomes.[20] Chafer notes, "Divine prescience of itself implies no element of necessity or determination, though it does imply certainty."[21] God is not informed by looking beyond himself, nor is he informed sequentially even though he distinguishes the sequence of events.

---

20. "The action does not cause (chronologically prior) God's foreknowledge, but it is logically prior like 'four is an even number because it is divisible by two.' The word because expresses a logical relation of ground and consequent . . . Once we understand the logical priority of the events to God's knowledge of them, we can see more easily why the fact of God's foreknowledge does not prejudice anything.'" Craig, *The Only Wise God*, 73–74.

21. Chafer, *Systematic Theology*, vol. 1, 194.

29

The Dynamic of the Gospel Encounter

John 12:35-36

³⁵ So Jesus said to them, "For a little while longer the Light is among you. Walk while you have the Light, so that darkness will not overtake you; he who walks in the darkness does not know where he goes. ³⁶ While you have the Light, believe in the Light, so that you may become sons of Light." These things Jesus spoke, and He went away and hid Himself from them.

THIS PASSAGE IS ABOUT an encounter between Jesus and the Jews and Greeks. It provides a poignant insight into the intricate workings that transpire when people are confronted with the gospel of Jesus Christ.

Jesus had made his triumphant entry into Jerusalem (John 12:12–19), then in John 12:27, he begins to foretell his death. The news of Lazarus being raised from the dead had created quite a crowd of both Jews and Greeks (John 12:9, 17–22).

Christ's claims were met with more questions (John 12:34). He had previously proclaimed his glory (John 12:23), been hailed as king (John 12:13–15), and answered various questions. Now, the time had passed to answer more questions or demonstrate his power as he had done when he raised Lazarus from the dead. It was time to share the gospel, which always demands a response. This transition reminds us while there is a time to answer questions, questions can go on endlessly, thereby displacing the presentation of the gospel. Questions should be answered, but they should not be permitted to displace the presentation of the gospel.

This gospel encounter takes place in John 12:35–36, and gives a deep insight into the nature of the gospel encounter, which includes both the divine and the human side. The passage includes six elements of the gospel dynamic.

First, note the presence of the Light

The presence of the Light is seen in the phrase, "the Light is among you" (vs. 35a) and "you have the Light" (vs. 36a). Jesus is the Light of the world (John 8:12), and now they are in the immediate presence of the Light and truth as is anyone and everyone when the gospel is shared.

Second, notice the requirement in the Light

Two statements identify what they and all must do when enlightened. Jesus told them they need to "walk while you have the Light" (vs. 35) and "believe in the Light" (vs. 36). Even though they were enlightened by the presence of the Light of Christ and his truth (John 1:9), that was not enough. They had to act. The word believe is the same call for everyone who hears the gospel. This is the essence of all encounters with truth; one must "believe in the Light" who is Christ. That is the universal call of the gospel. This highlights the fact that being in the presence of the light of truth enables one to understand and receive salvation, but it does not secure one's salvation.

Paul, recounting why he was being sent to the Gentiles, said it was "to open their eyes so that they may turn from darkness to light and from the dominion of Satan to God" (Acts 26:18). They are not summoned by the gospel to believe after having left the darkness, or delivered by God from their darkness; rather the lost are summoned to believe while their sinful hearts are engulfed in the darkness of this world as seen here; the Light shines, the gospel summons, and God calls the sinner unto himself so that if someone is saved, he was truly called "out of darkness into His marvelous light" (1 Pet 2:9).

This is the sufficient call of the gospel, to walk while you have the light and believe in the Light, signifying a person should and can respond by believing. It is extended while people are in the darkness of sin, and this with every indication they can and should respond.

Third, the words "walk" and "believe" are commands

They are in the present tense and active voice. This command is for those listening, and they are to respond by walking and believing in what they hear. Additionally, all of the pronouns "you" are plural (vss. 35–36). Therefore, Christ is commanding every person within the range of his voice to act, decide, obey, and believe. As seen here, the enlightenment of the gospel is offered unconditionally, but the reception of the benefit of the gospel is indeed conditional. It is conditioned upon the listener's willingness to obey the command to walk and believe.

This is vital to understanding the dynamic of the gospel encounter. God enlightens, enables, commands, and summons (draws, John 12:32), and everyone who hears is commanded to believe, and should and can believe. The dividing line is not between the elect and non-elect, general external call and a particular internal efficacious call for the unconditionally elect, but rather it is between hearing only and hearing and believing. The writer of Hebrews reminds his readers of this very fact by saying, "For indeed we have had good news preached to us, just as they also; but the word they heard did not profit them, because it was not united by faith in those who heard. For we who have believed enter that rest, just as He has said" (Heb 4:2–3a). This refers to these first century Jews' ancestors who did not act in faith and wandered and perished in the wilderness, having never entered the Promised Land because of their unbelief.

Fourth, note the urgency of his message

The phrases, "For a little while longer" and "while you have the Light" and "while you have the Light" (vs. 35 and 36) communicate the urgency that is incumbent upon them and anyone who hears the gospel. The words "a little while longer" mean "briefly" or a "short time."[1] This pathos of Christ and the urgency seen here comport well with a temporal opportunity to believe and be saved, but it does not meaningfully do so within the doctrine of unconditional election. If unconditional election is true, there can be an urgency on behalf of believers to share the gospel in obedience to the command of Christ; however, there is simply no actual urgency on behalf of the hearer since the elect will be saved and the non-elect will not. To contend, as Calvinists often do, that there is still an urgency only produces a theatrical urgency rather than a real one since no amount of the passing of time can alter one's eternal state. The urgency to believe this while you can before it is too late and you cannot believe does not exist in Calvinism, given unconditional election. To suggest such does exists is misleading at best. If unconditional election is true, the passing of time does not affect the status of anyone, whether elect or non-elect.

This is a very urgent and moving moment. Being illumined by the gospel affords the command and choice to walk in the Light, but that time is

---

1. "Pertaining to a relatively brief extent of time—'a little while, for a little while, a short time, brief, briefly'." Louw and Nida, *Greek-English Lexicon of the New Testament*, 642.

limited and only God knows the length of opportunity. In this pericope, that time came very quickly (vs. 36) "He went away and hid Himself from them." Both the uncertainty of when one's death will occur and the unpardonable sin are haunting warnings that opportunity is only "for a little while longer" (Matt 12:30–32; 21:33–46).

Fifth, the Light overcomes darkness

This includes both the darkness of their fallen nature and their environment. This is evident in that Christ commands and calls upon each person there to believe and walk in the light. He extends this call while they are still in the bowels of the blackness of the soul, darkness of the world, and overshadowed by the canopy of judgment. Jesus said, "I have come as Light into the world, so that everyone who believes in Me will not remain in darkness" (John 12:46). While the gospel is presented, the hearers are in darkness, but if they believe, they will not remain in darkness; believing is the only thing that brings deliverance from the darkness of sin. John said, "In Him was life, and the life was the Light of men. The Light shines in the darkness, and the darkness did not comprehend it" (John 1:4–5).[2]

Edwin A. Blum commenting on John 1:5 says, "Light's nature is to shine and dispel **darkness**. Darkness is almost personified in this verse: darkness is unable to overpower light. By this, John summarized his Gospel record: (a) Light will invade the dominion of **darkness**. (b) Satan the ruler and his subjects will resist the light, but they will be unable to frustrate its power. (c) The Word will be victorious in spite of opposition."[3]

In man's sinfulness, apart from the grace of God, he can only wander aimlessly in the brume of his own sin (vs. 35b). Man on his own will never emerge from the darkness into the light because in the darkness he "does not know where he goes" (vs. 35b). On their own, people will walk the broad road of unlimited paths that promise salvation but ultimately lead to darkness and damnation.

The only hope for a person so encapsulated in the midnight of blackness is when the light shines into his hell-bound black heart and empowers

---

2. In John 1:5, the word is translated comprehend, *katalambano*, in the NASV, KJV and overcome in the ESV and NIV. In 12:35 it is translated "overtake." Both are appropriate because both are true. In this passage (12:35), it clearly means overtake or to conquer. "To gain control over—'to overcome, to gain control of.' καὶ ἡ σκοτία αὐτὸ οὐ κατέλαβεν 'and the darkness did not gain control over it' Jn 1:5. It is also possible to understand καταλαμβάνω in Jn 1:5 as meaning 'to understand.'" Louw and Nida, *Greek-English Lexicon of the New Testament*, 473.

3. Blum, "John," 272.

and shows him the way out. Then Jesus again spoke to them saying, "I am the Light of the world; he who follows Me will not walk in the darkness, but will have the Light of life" (John 8:12). There Jesus, as here, is speaking to the lost, while they are in darkness and says follow (present tense), which is the idea of becoming followers. This can only happen if they obey and believe. The call to believe, follow, walk, obey does not come after regeneration (new birth or an irresistible work of God), but while a person is in the cauldron of hell's darkness, on the precipice of eternal damnation. It is there God's delivering light, empowered by God's love, enables one to walk out of the darkest darkness into the light.

It seems this call to believe and walk in the Light is what it gives every indication of being, a genuine obeyable command and an accessible offer for everyone present to believe the truth and be saved. If it is not, then it seems to be nothing more than a cruel misleading command and a phantom opportunity, at least for the non-elect. What we actually see is that while in darkness, the Light of the gospel penetrates into the otherwise impenetrable darkness of death, and one is grace enabled to see the way out and can understand enough to walk out from the darkness by believing the gospel (John 3:20–21).

This grace-granted comprehension does not mean the person hearing the gospel and thereby given divine understanding grasps everything or even a lot. This truth can be seen in this passage in which they are called to believe and be saved while all of their questions have not been answered (John 12:34). Full understanding is neither possible nor necessary to be saved. The enlightenment is sufficient to convict one of sin, righteousness, and judgment (John 16:8–11) and grant understanding of God's offer in the gospel and exercise faith unto salvation.

I was saved at twenty-five years old. Because of my background, I had such a jejune understanding of God that, knowing what I do now and humanly speaking, I did everything wrong except believe. Thankfully, that is enough because the gospel enlightenment is sufficient for believing unto salvation, but not for having every question answered or understanding all of reality. Calvinism's commitment to unconditional election makes Jesus only *appear* to offer a real occasion to repent. Because if Calvinism is true, it is Jesus, as the second member of the Trinity, who developed the exclusive plan of salvation that inviolably precludes everyone but the unconditionally elected from repenting.

To say, as some Calvinists do, Jesus gave a good faith offer because as the man Jesus did not know everything and, therefore, he did not know they were not elect is to miss the point. For Jesus said, "The things I speak, I speak just as the Father has told Me" (John 12:49–50). No amount of relying upon a good faith offer can exonerate the Father from leading Christ to say and present such things as accessible for all if they were not true. Neither can one assuage the difficulty by saying this group was either composed of all elect or non-elect since some did not believe (John 12:37) and some did (John 12:42). The truth is Jesus spoke that way because the Father's plan included every provision necessary to give everyone who hears the gospel the grace-enabled choice to flee the wrath to come and be eternally saved.

Sixth, the two reasons one should believe and walk in the Light

We have seen the urgency of the gospel encounter, "while you have the Light," and now we graphically see the indeterminacy and the conditional nature of the gospel encounter in these two phrases. We see this in the two purpose clauses, which are indicated by the word *hina*, translated "so that." Negatively, "so that darkness will not overtake you" (John 12:35) and positively, "so that you may become sons of Light" (vs. 36). Read without importation of prior theological commitments, these two clauses rule out predetermined conclusions. They, as all who hear the gospel, are commanded to "believe," and "walk in the Light," "so that" they "may become sons of Light" believers, "so that" the "darkness" penetrated by the presence of the Light does not once again envelop them when the truth is gone.

Even though they are children of wrath imprisoned in spiritual darkness (Eph 2:3), at the moment of the gospel encounter, the cell door is opened, and the way out is illumined so they may become sons of Light, thereby avoiding being overtaken by total darkness again, left only to wander aimlessly. It is critical to see that as sinners before the enlightenment, we all wander aimlessly in the bowels of spiritual darkness. Here Christ commands them and all to believe so that "the darkness will not overtake" them.

This command of Christ clearly indicates at this moment of enlightenment, although still in the darkness of sin, they are grace enabled to believe and avoid being once again overtaken by the darkness of sin and judgment, and actually can become children of Light. What could be clearer than the truth that in the gospel encounter, God is so working to penetrate the darkness with the glorious light of the gospel that man is commanded to believe and free to do so?

As mentioned, all pronouns translated "you" (vss. 35–36) are in the plural form, which signifies all are addressed and commanded to act on the opportunity to become sons of Light and thereby avoid being once again overtaken by the darkness. Because in the gospel encounter, darkness looms portentously but not controllingly; like a mountain lion awaiting the right moment to seize its prey, darkness rushes in when the Light is withdrawn. In the presence of the Light of the gospel, blinding darkness is held in abeyance.

Overtake is the word *katalambánō*, which is an intensified form of *lambano*.[4] Here it conveys overtaking or gain control of. It bespeaks of an ominous imminent cloud of uncertainty, death, and irreversible judgment which shadows every person and their every breath. When it descends, the time for decision is vanquished because alone man is no match for the prince of darkness, the dark night of a fallen world, or the humanly impenetrable blackness of the human heart.

As already stated, sometimes this word is translated "comprehend" as the NASV does in John 1:5;[5] it is clear in this passage that it means to "overtake." Neither pure darkness nor one in pure darkness can comprehend nor overpower the Light. It is true the ruler of this world (John 12:31) leads world forces, rulers, and powers of this darkness (Eph 6:12); Satan does blind mankind to the gospel (2 Cor 4:4) and seek to keep man under his power (Eph 6:12) and, therefore, enslaved to darkness (Eph 2:1–3). He does so with unbreachable effectiveness against man on his own. But as is vividly portrayed here, in the dynamic of the gospel encounter, the darkness of sin and Satan is completely subjugated to the power of the gospel of Jesus Christ, the Light of the world (John 8:12)!

Crucial to understanding the dynamic of the gospel encounter is that it is obviously transpiring in the absence of a predetermined unalterable permanent work of grace for some and not for others. This warning is as meaningless as the offer of deliverance if unconditional election is true, Calvinistic creative claims to the contrary notwithstanding. As seen here, the word of truth is never to merely inform, but always demands a response of

---

4. "katalambánō; fut. katalépsomai, from katá (2596), an intens., and lambánō (2983), to take. To apprehend, attain, obtain, find. To lay hold of, seize, with eagerness, suddenness (John 8:3, 4) . . . . Figuratively of darkness or evil, to come suddenly upon someone (John 12:35; 1 Thess. 5:4; Sept.: Gen. 19:19; 31:23; 1 Kgs. 18:44) . . . To seize with the mind, to comprehend (John 1:5, the darkness did not admit or receive the light [cf. John 1:10–12; 3:19]). The darkness is here presented as being so thick that the light could not penetrate it. In the mid. to comprehend for oneself, perceive, find, followed by hóti (3754), that (Acts 4:13; 10:34); by the inf. and its subject (Acts 25:25); by ti (5101), what (Eph. 3:18)." Zodhiates, *The Complete Word Study Dictionary*.

5. Sometimes this word is translated "comprehend" as the NASV does in John 1:5, the NAS, KJV, and NKJV translates katalambano as "comprehend," and the ESV and NIV translate it "overcome it." It is translated by all of these as "realize" or "perceive" in Acts 10:34, and rightly so. This highlights the fact that in some contexts the word clearly means "overtake", and some "understand," whereas some contexts leave room for translating it either "overtake" or "understand" (John 1:5).

either acceptance or rejection. The invitation is essential to the proclamation of truth because its omission obscures the demanding nature of the gospel. The abuse of invitations, whether in personal witnessing or preaching, should not cause our disavowal of invitations any more than abuses of Christian love should cause us to abandon love. The invitation (call to follow Christ—John 8:12) is essential to the gospel. The gospel is not merely an informational message, but rather it is emphatically a divinely confrontational and transformational message.

In the crucible of conflict for the soul of man, the Light of Christ penetrates into the darkest corridor of Satan's power and man's sin, and frees man *provisionally* so that he may truly experience God's redemptive love *eternally*. Yes, a sovereign God is capable of such a dynamic work, and a loving God is dedicated to such a dynamic work of grace. This gospel encounter ends just as others both in Scripture and history end. Some believed by choice (John 12:42) and were saved, while others chose to reject the opportunity to become a follower of Christ and remained in their unbelief by choice (John 12:37). This is the nature of the gospel encounter.

30

What about Those Who Never Hear the Gospel: Analyzing the Argument

BASED UPON WHO GOD is and what he explicitly and repeatedly says, Extensivists believe God salvifically loves every single person in his creation; therefore, he understandably desires for everyone to be saved. This perspective is in contrast to Calvinism, which believes God only salvifically loves some individuals who are known as the unconditionally elect; therefore, he understandably desires for only those he selected to be saved, and nothing can prevent them from being saved. By virtue of Calvinism's commitment to unconditional election, they have already answered the question expressed in the title of this chapter.

In contrast, Extensivists are often challenged to provide an answer to the following dilemma. If God truly loves the entirety of lost humanity and correspondingly desires for every person to be saved, then what about all of the people who never hear the gospel, and therefore do not get the opportunity to be saved? Meaning, to claim Scripture does intend to express God loves every individual and does not desire any individual to perish, and yet God does not give everyone a chance to be reconciled to him, seems to make the claim at best hollow and maybe even misleading. If it can be demonstrated God says he desires all to be saved and the atonement of Christ is sufficiently provisional for all to be saved, but he simultaneously limits the availability of opportunity to believe, then he has, in fact, limited the number of people who can truly believe unto salvation. As a result, when the discussions and defenses are completed, both Calvinism and Extensivism believe God has an actual salvifically limited love.

Calvinists do not miss this apparent conclusion and are quick to analogize Extensivism with Calvinism—in this regard at least. If God does not give everyone an opportunity, then the only distinction between the two perspectives is not whether God limited salvation, but rather how God limited the number who could be saved. According to Calvinism, God limited the number by unconditional election, whereas according to Extensivism

THOSE WHO NEVER HEAR THE GOSPEL: ANALYZING THE ARGUMENT

God limited the number by never allowing them the opportunity to hear the truth and be saved.

As a former Calvinist, I have made this argument. Now as an Extensivist, I have encountered this challenge on a number of occasions when engaging Calvinists. I have attempted in this book to incorporate all the components of the challenges I have encountered in these exchanges. I will first summarize the challenge, and then in order to consider all of the various styles and components of it I have encountered, I will give the challenge in an expanded form. We can summarize the challenge like this, "What about those who never heard the gospel and perish in hell; how can it be said God salvifically loves them and desires them to be saved?" Following is the expanded version.

They contend, while it is true Calvinists have a problem regarding God's salvific love for everyone in light of unconditional election, Extensivists have a similar problem. We all worship a God who has structured the way of salvation in such a way that the vast majority of humanity will never even hear of his plan of salvation, much less have the chance to accept or reject it. We all know God allows untold billions of people to be born whom he knows will never hear the gospel, without which no one is saved. Extensivists can say God has a salvific love for everyone, but that love does not extend to actually giving every single person the opportunity to be saved. Since we know this to be the case, we see that God has limited the number of people who can actually be saved by withholding the opportunity to hear the gospel.

We all must admit God created the universe knowing his creation would rebel and most of the people whom he created would be lost forever. This is an issue for Calvinists and Extensivists alike. We all know there are people who die having never heard the gospel, and to say God salvifically loves them and the gospel is for them is meaningless since God did not give them an opportunity to hear and be saved. Consequently, according to Calvinism, God limited the people who could be saved by unconditional election. According to Extensivism, God limited the people who could actually be saved by never getting the gospel to them so they could be saved. Therefore, both perspectives have the same problem; God has provided a salvation that is limited to certain people he salvifically loves and desires to be saved.

This common challenge by Calvinists is serious enough that it deserves being addressed. The Calvinists do not have to answer this, but in order to meaningfully proclaim God salvifically loves and truly has provisioned for every single person to be saved, Extensivists must answer the charge. This should be understood as another Calvinist attempt to allay the harshness of unconditional election by making Calvinism and Extensivism essentially similar with regard to selective salvation. Unfortunately for Calvinism, it is not a valid comparison and, therefore, it fails to prettify the salvific portrait of Calvinism. As an Extensivist, I actually do believe God truly and salvifically loves every single person of the human race as the Scripture explicitly declares, and this salvific love is both costly and extensive; therefore, he does both desire and provision sufficiently for each person to be saved, including granting every person the opportunity to know him.[1] I intend to demonstrate the two views are not similar in this and the following three chapters in which I will address this issue from different vantage points.

Calvinists proffer an overly ambitious and mistaken statement. It is their claim that without hearing the gospel, "no one will be saved." In this specific discussion, such an unqualified statement is misleading, and unwarrantedly favors Calvinism; as I will seek to demonstrate. There is a difference between God structuring a salvation plan that intentionally prevents some from having an opportunity to be saved (Calvinism), and whether some never actually hear the gospel proper, a point I also plan to demonstrate. Lastly, believing God created a universe where most would reject a genuine salvific opportunity and be lost forever (Extensivism) is not equivalent to determining the same eternal result via unconditional election (Calvinism). The first permits God to have a genuine salvific love for everyone even though everyone does not avail themselves of his love. But unconditional election absolutely forbids such love, all attempts by Calvinists to demonstrate unconditional election is compatible with everyone having an opportunity to believe notwithstanding.

The remainder of this chapter will address the specific question, "What about those who never hear the gospel?" I will do so by responding to each of the components of the above argument.

First, the supposed similarity is false

The challenge is "Extensivists have the same problem." This conclusion refers to the problem arising from Calvinism's belief in such ideas as unconditional election, limited atonement, and the selective efficacious call, which all result in Calvinism being a salvifically exclusive perspective. Calvinists seek to make Extensivism have the same problem of exclusivism since, as the argument goes, everyone does not hear the gospel; therefore, everyone does not get an opportunity to be saved. This is characteristic of Calvinists' attempts to palliate the difficulties generated by their system while maintaining their perspective is the biblical one.

1. As will be demonstrated in this and the following three chapters, having an opportunity to know God in salvation is not *precisely* equivalent to hearing the gospel.

We begin considering this matter in light of two irreconcilable dissimilarities. The first one is, we each begin with a very different understanding of what Scripture declares. Extensivists begin by believing the wonderful and simple declarations of Scripture regarding God's salvific love for all are as clear as they seem to be. We believe, without theological prejudice, they declare God's unfathomable salvific love for every person. Calvinists read the same verses, but do so in light of unconditional election, which creates complexity where biblically there seems to be only simplicity (Ezek 18:23, 32, 33:11; Ps 86:5; John 3:16; 1 Tim 2:4, 4:10; Titus 2:10–11; 2 Pet 3:9).

We believe, considering the contextual and exegetical evidence of scores of such verses, they clearly mean more than people groups or some people in all parts of the world as Calvinists argue. Accordingly, we understand Jesus did come to enlighten humanity and take away the sin of the world, which means every sin of every person (John 1:9, 29; 1 John 3:5). The words *take away* mean just that. They signify Christ effectively dealt with sin in his sacrifice on the cross so that anyone and everyone in the world can be saved by faith.[2] We believe the Holy Spirit convicts the world, meaning every person comprised in humanity (John 16:8–11), Christ and the Father are drawing everyone (John 6:44; 12:32), and when Jesus commissions the church to go into all the world (Matt 28:18–20), it is to share God's love for each person with everyone. Jesus's ministry and life were dedicated to go about preaching (Mark 1:38), and he makes the offer of salvation not merely to groups but individuals (Matt 19:16–26; John 12:35–36).

Accordingly, God has throughout Scripture demonstrated his salvific love to the world in many ways. While we are aware words such as *all* and *world* do at times have limited meaning, they also regularly have a comprehensive meaning (John 3:16; Rom 3:23; Titus 2:11). Extensivists believe the same world of humanity that sinned and needs redemption, which includes every single person, is the same world for whom God gave his only begotten Son (John 3:16).[3]

Extensivism says when passages speak of God's love for the world (humanity) or all, these are the same people included in the all that have sinned (Rom 3:23), the same all for whom he died (2 Cor 5:14–15), the same all for whom he gave himself as a ransom (1 Tim 2:6), the same all for whom he tasted death (Heb 2:9) and paid for sins (1 John 2:2). It is the same all to whom Christ sends his church, to whom God may show mercy (Rom 11:32).

---

2. "To destroy, with the implication of removal and doing away with—'to destroy, to do away with.'" Louw and Nida, *Greek-English Lexicon of the New Testament*, 232.

3. See my evaluation of John Piper's argument to limit the word all to only meaningfully include the elect in my book, *Reflections of a Disenchanted Calvinist*, chapter 10, "World vs. Elect."

Passages such as Rom 3:9 cannot be limited to mean Jews and Greeks as a group (some in each), but rather do mean every individual in each group. Scripture is equally clear about the sufficient provision of salvation opportunity for each person in each group. We believe the passages that teach God's salvific love for every single person are as clear as those passages that teach that every person needs salvation (Rom 3:1–10).

The second related dissimilarity essential to understand in this discussion is that Extensivists believe God has endowed man with libertarian freedom, whereas Calvinism believes God has endowed man with compatible freedom. This difference is always, whether known or mentioned, a vital part of our discussions, and this time is no different. Our belief in libertarian freedom is an inextricable part of our understanding of God's plan. Accordingly, God can truly desire the salvation of every single person, and yet every single person is not saved. Their grace-enabled choice matters. This in contrast to Calvinism's compatible view of freedom, which means if God desired all to be saved (desire here being equivalent to the desire in Extensivism), they would all be saved; the process and salvific work required to save one is precisely the same to save all. Sometimes, Calvinism's lack of appreciation of this difference creates difficulty in true understanding or clearly communicating this concept.

This means according to Extensivism; the fundamental dissimilarity is God loves and desires the salvation of every individual. But being libertarian free beings, their choice to believe or refuse is actual and matters. The former results in salvation and the latter damnation. In contrast, Calvinism believes man has compatible freedom, and salvation is the product of unconditional election and damnation is the result of not being among the unconditionally elect.[4] That God does not salvifically love the world is evidenced by his exclusive plan of unconditional election. Moreover, although their choice to believe is considered free, per compatibilism, it is also determined by their past and is a consequence of unconditional election.

These distinctions make it clear the two views of salvation are obviously and *essentially* dissimilar, and therefore do not share a similar problem regarding the lost.[5] Not only are the two plans *essentially* different, but

---

4. This is not to negate that all have sinned and all deserve hell, but rather to note the crucially dissimilar process that determines who is saved and who is damned.

5. Things can contain similar and dissimilar components and still be essentially similar (the same with differences), but if the events or ideas contain essentially dissimilar components, they cannot actually be the same; although, on the surface they may appear to be. For example, a criminal shoots the storekeeper in a robbery, and a policeman shoots a man trying to murder a woman. They both have similarities (guns, someone shoots, and someone dies), but they are essentially different because of who did what and for what reason.

they also both proclaim mutually exclusive desires on the part of God. This is true even if we could not provide any plausible responses to how God accomplishes granting everyone an opportunity to know his forgiveness. Therefore, regarding both the plan and desire of God, the two views are essentially dissimilar and, therefore, mutually exclusive and irreconcilable; consequently, Extensivists do not have a similar problem.

Extensivists believe God does truly and salvifically love all of humanity; correspondingly, he both desires and sufficiently provides for each person to have an accessible opportunity to be saved. This belief is based, in part, upon repeated unambiguous declarations in Scripture to this effect such as Ezek 18:23, 32; John 3:16, 17; 1 Tim 2:4, 4:10; Titus 2:11; 2 Pet 3:9; Rev 2:21; all of which describe the nature of God as love (2 Cor 3:11; 1 John 4:8, 16), as well as merciful and omnibenevolent.

Charles Hodge says, "Goodness, in the Scriptural sense of the term, includes benevolence, love, mercy, and grace. By benevolence is meant the disposition to promote happiness; *all sensitive creatures are its objects*"[6] (italics added). Similarly, Millard Erickson says regarding benevolence, "By this we mean the concern of God for the welfare of those whom he loves. He unselfishly *seeks our ultimate welfare*"[7] (italics added). He then gives John 3:16 as an illustration of this benevolence, which indicates he includes people's salvific welfare.

I agree with Hodge that benevolence is the promotion of true happiness for all humans. I also agree with Erickson. But I would add the question to these wonderful explanations. Does not providing for the "happiness" and "ultimate welfare" of a person necessitate giving an opportunity to experience salvation? Does not this benevolent act tower exceedingly over all other promotions of "happiness" and "welfare"? Without such benevolence, with its concomitant eternal loss and damnation, all other blessings are doomed to eternal meaninglessness, and to talk otherwise is at least a massive distraction. That is to say, benevolence that provides only such temporal items as sunshine, food, and water is eternally meaningless because in the end, only salvation matters. Unfortunately, Calvinists often echo the sentiments of Hodge and Erickson, which confuse the issue because they are absolutely inconsistent with Calvinism's exclusive salvation; they are perfectly reflective of Extensivism.

Let me separate two issues that are often incorrectly conflated in order that we do not fall prey to another distraction as we think through the issue of this chapter. The first question asks, is everyone who hears the gospel

---

6. Hodge, *Systematic Theology*, vol. 1, 427.
7. Erickson, *Christian Theology*, vol. 1, 292.

sufficiently grace enabled to have a true chance to understand the message and either believe unto salvation or reject the gospel with ample grace-enabled understanding to know what in fact is being rejected? Does that same person have the opportunity to do the opposite of whatever he does in fact do? The second is the specific question we are addressing in this chapter. Does God salvifically work to provide everyone a genuine opportunity to be delivered from his condign punishment?

Regarding the first question, the Calvinist answer is no once the double talk is dispelled and the Extensivist answer is yes. Sometimes, when you ask a Calvinist the first question, he will respond by asking you the second, which is a distraction rather than a proper response. The question of whether everyone who hears the gospel gets a genuine chance to believe is substantially different than the question does everyone get an opportunity to hear the gospel. We should not let the Calvinist avoid answering the first question by posing the second.

Extensivists, Traditionalists, Calvinists, Arminians, and Molinists all believe God must do a pre-conversion grace work, but there is disagreement regarding the nature, purpose, and extent of the work. Consequently, with each perspective believing in such, one should not characterize another's position as one of works since each begins (in both the eternal omniscient mind and will of God as well as in time), is sustained by, and reaches ultimate sanctification through grace. If grace provides for all the details of salvation, then salvation cannot be justifiably dismissed as an accomplishment of works, merit, or virtue. To do so is to refuse to acknowledge the amazing grace of each perspective.

Second, the Calvinist overstates his case, which results in a misleading statement

The Calvinist says, "We all know God allows untold billions of people to be born whom he knows will never hear the Gospel, without which no one is saved." Their point is as God has limited the number who can be saved in Calvinism by unconditional election, God has similarly limited the number who can be saved in Extensivism by the simple fact he never gives them a chance to hear the gospel.

We must define the gospel. Paul said, "Now I make known to you, brethren, the gospel which I preached to you, which also you received, in which also you stand, by which also you are saved, if you hold fast the word which I preached to you, unless you believed in vain. For I delivered to you as of first importance what I also received, that Christ died for our sins according to the Scriptures, and that He was buried, and that He was raised on the third day according to the Scriptures" (1 Cor 15:1-4; see also John 1:29, 3:16; Rom 10:9-11).

Succinctly, by the gospel, we mean the good news that God loves the world, and Jesus Christ died for our sins so that by simple faith in him we can be delivered from our just desert and become children of God and possessors of eternal life. Now we know people were saved prior to the death, burial, and resurrection of Christ, and inarguably, they were saved without hearing the gospel. This includes all the saints in the Old Testament, some of which are referred to in the New Testament (Heb 11:1-40). The scriptural record is one indisputable proof that since the fall not every restored relationship with God was by hearing the gospel proper.

Although Calvinists frequently make such statements for the sake of comparison, they do recognize people have been saved without hearing the gospel. If a Calvinist makes the challenge we are considering, and I point out the salvation of the Old Testament saints who never actually heard the gospel, they immediately concede the point. Then one may fairly ask if everyone agrees on this, why make the point? Because they keep making their imprecise challenge, and many fail to grasp the overstatement of such a challenge. The salvific fact of Old Testament saints alone proves the statement as given, defined by the context of its purpose, is false. This limited falsification does not minimize the need to take the gospel to everyone in the world, nor the exclusivity of the gospel as declared in Scripture (John 14:6; Acts 4:12). Rather its purpose is to cogently demonstrate that this statement, without qualification, is invalid proof of God's limited salvific love.

Another example wherein people are saved who have never heard the gospel concerns babies and small children who die. Although there are differing perspectives within the Reformed tradition, there are those who believe children who die prior to exercising faith in the gospel go to heaven. Some believe pedobaptism accomplishes this; others believe elect children go to heaven without hearing and believing the gospel, while others simply believe all children go to heaven.

An example of a reformed perspective is in the Cannons of Dort, which says, "Children of believers are holy, not by nature but by virtue of the gracious covenant in which they together with their parents are included, godly parents ought not to doubt the election and salvation of their children whom God calls out of this life in infancy."[8] J.P. Boyce believes regeneration precedes faith, but he recognizes God gives children special salvation. He

---

8. Canons of Dort, First Head of Doctrine, article 17

writes, "Regeneration (as in infants) may exist without faith and repentance, but the latter cannot exist without the former."[9]

Extensivists believe children who die before being able to understand their sin, understand their need for a savior, and exercise saving faith as well as those who lack the mental capacity to exercise faith in the gospel are provisionally covered by the grace and love of God. This provision is made available through the sufficient work of Christ in dying for the sins of the world (2 Sam 12:20–23; John 1:29). The latter position particularly would argue since God loves the world of humanity (John 3:16), and his true desire is that no one would perish (1 Tim 2:4; 2 Pet 3:9), he would have comprehended this eventuality in his plan. With the reality of these two points, we see some people in Old Testament times, as well as today, go to heaven without having heard the gospel.

These two examples demonstrate God's grace has sufficiently comprehended certain and limited eventualities that permitted those for whom Christ died, and those whom God loves to come into his presence without properly hearing the gospel. This recognition does not minimize the command and need to take the gospel into all the world, nor the reality that everyone who hears the gospel and does not receive it by faith dies in their sin. Rather, it clarifies the place of the gospel in God's salvation plan, which is that while God has provisioned for the salvation of some who never hear the gospel, it is also true that no one is saved apart from the work of the gospel. That is to say, the gospel, the work of Christ, is always *ontologically* necessary for salvation, but there are undeniably exceptional circumstances where it is not *epistemologically* necessary.[10]

To allow the Calvinist to frame the issue with a blanket statement, such as no one can be saved without hearing the gospel, is misleading. Because without qualifications, it is an imprecise statement, which may be allowable in normal conversation, but it should not be allowed when marshaled to disprove God's genuine salvific love for the world of lost humanity. To do so is to permit a false argument that dishonors God.

---

9. Boyce, *Abstract of Systematic Theology*, 381.

10. Ontology is the study of the nature or essence of a thing. Epistemology is the study of knowledge. Applied here, the work or essence of the gospel, the death, burial, and resurrection of Christ, is always necessary for salvation, but sometimes the knowledge of that work, or even the name of Jesus as in the Old Testament, is not.

31

What about Those Who Never Hear the Gospel: The Old Testament

WE HAVE SUFFICIENTLY SEEN the argument often presented by the Calvinist fails to be cogent, but in order to further clarify and amplify upon God's salvific love for everyone, it is worth considering some of his salvific work in the Old Testament.

We can safely say, prior to the death of Christ on the cross, one was still saved by faith, and God was righteous to forgive one's sin based upon the merits of the gospel that Christ would die for the sins of the world (even though one could not as yet hear and believe in the gospel proper). This includes sins committed both before and after his death upon the cross (John 1:29; 1 John 2:2). As noted in the last chapter, this is because the work of Christ is ontologically necessary for the salvation of anyone at any time, even though it may not be epistemologically necessary. Charles Ryrie succinctly states, "The basis of salvation in every age is the death of Christ; the requirement for salvation in every age is faith; the object of faith in every age is God; the content of faith changes in the various dispensations."[1] Ryrie's summary reflects the nature of progressive revelation in God's salvation plan. It also dispels the incorrect notion that eternal salvation in the Old Testament was somehow dependent upon keeping the law.

Beyond the chosen nation of Israel, there were those known as proselytes and God-fearers. The latter two groups came to believe in the one true God and, in varying degrees, committed themselves to the Jewish faith. An article in the *Encyclopedia of the Bible* says, "The 'proselytizing,' or bringing into the covenant community of willing Gentiles, occurred most predominantly in . . . Jewish communities outside Palestine. Jews, living in most areas of the known world due to exile, commercial, or military reasons, naturally carried their religious faith and practice with them. . . . This . . . was attractive to many of the surrounding Gentiles. . . . The result was that many Gentiles attached themselves in varying degrees to the Jewish faith through

---

1. Ryrie, *Dispensationalism Today*, 123.

the life of the synagogue (see Isa 56:1–8; Mal 1:11)."[2] We find some God-fearers hearing and responding to the gospel in the New Testament (Acts 2:10, 11; 6:5; 10:2, 22; 13:16, 26, 43; 17:4, 17).

God's workings in dealing with Pharaoh is not demonstrative of his eternal state, as some would like us to believe. Rather it is indicative of a deliverance for God's people and an evangelistic endeavor for all, as seen in Rom 9:17–18, "For the Scripture says to Pharaoh, 'For this very purpose I raised you up, to demonstrate My power in you, and that My name might be proclaimed throughout the whole earth.' So then He has mercy on whom He desires, and He hardens whom He desires." These emphatically declare that God raised Pharaoh up to demonstrate his power. God gives the specific reason he wants to demonstrate his power, and that was so his name would be declared "throughout the whole earth." He is sovereign, not Pharaoh, and he can harden whom he desires. The hardening, in this case, was not an eternal hardening but one of mercy, an act of love and evangelism. God showed his power over the one who seemed the most powerful to all because he loves people and is not willing that any would perish. Christ similarly acted when he spoke repeatedly and lucidly about hell and judgment (Matt 5:29; Luke 13:3). God acted with compassion and mercy in Egypt when he exposed the vacuousness of the idea that one should look to and trust Pharaoh for the provisions of security and life. It was a self-declaration of God and a call for everyone to come to him.

The message was, Do not worship Pharaoh who cannot save you but worship Jehovah who is mighty to save. God cared about all who were there. He would prove to Israel he was the Lord who delivered them (Exod 6:6–7; 10:1–2; 13:14–16) and show Pharaoh he was the only God (Exod 9:14). He would show the Egyptians he was Lord (Exod 7:5; 14:4; 18) and that his name would be declared throughout the whole earth (Exod 9:16). We well know that God often works to demonstrate things, systems, false gods, and people are unworthy of our trust; for they shall all fail. To wit, God's compassion makes it known to all who will heed that he is the one true God who is alone worthy of our trust and devotion. His mighty acts in Egypt were acts of compassionate evangelization.

It demonstrated God's sovereignty by overpowering Pharaoh who was believed to be the sovereign. The news of this work of God spread to pagans in distant places like Jericho (Josh 2:8–14) and Gibeon (Josh 9:9). It spread to people like the prostitute Rahab in Canaan and "all the inhabitants of the land" (Josh 2:9). The message was clearly understood by Rahab because she believed and was saved. Donald Campbell notes,

---

2. Elwell and Beitzel, *Baker Encyclopedia of the Bible*, s.v. O.T. Proselyte, 1784–85.

"Then Rahab declared her faith in Israel's God: For the Lord your God is God in heaven above and on the earth below. Responding to the word she had received about the mighty working of God, Rahab believed, trusting in His power and mercy. And that faith saved her."[3]

Although we do not know how much fruit was born by this testimony of the mighty works of God, we do know it led directly to the salvation of at least one pagan outside of Egypt, Rahab.[4] I suspect many more. It should at least cause reverent pause to anyone who suggests our lack of precise knowledge about God salvifically working among a people is equivalent to the idea that he is not. For unless Scripture told us about Rahab, we would have simply met an unknown Canaanite in heaven who had heard of the mighty works of our God and believed unto salvation. Could there be others? I think so.

God's work in Egypt may provide an example of God overriding a person's libertarian freedom to accomplish his will, whereas if he did not do so, Pharaoh would use his freedom in that particular area to thwart God's ultimate will.[5] He would have continued beyond the permissive will of God. In this case, it was Pharaoh's unchallenged power, which not only prohibited the liberation of the Jews but also kept the Jews and Gentiles from being able to know Pharaoh is not God; God is God.

The redemptive power of God in this event has been celebrated ever since in the Passover celebration of the Jews as a testimony to their posterity and the world that God delivers people who trust him.[6] Regarding Rom 9:17, Berkouwer rightly says, "It is clear that Paul does not want to direct our attention to the individual fate of Pharaoh, but that he speaks of him in order to show his place in the history of salvation."[7] God tells us why he hardened

---

3. Campbell, "Joshua," 331.

4. For more comments regarding her genuine faith see "Joshua" by David M. Howard, Jr., 104.

5. That is if one concludes God hardened Pharaoh's heart prior to Pharaoh hardening his own. If God did in fact harden Pharaoh's heart first, it only serves to remind us that God can and does override libertarian freedom if one seeks to operate outside of what God's permissive will allows. Libertarian freedom is a force, but God alone is sovereign. The overriding of libertarian freedom does not mean the person is divested of libertarian freedom, but rather his range of options was either temporarily or even permanently altered.

6. Although the Gibeonites acted deceptively, they had heard of the mighty works of Jehovah in Egypt, which is approximately 200 to 250 miles from Gibeon. Their choice was that of Rahab's and all who hear of the mighty works of God; they can believe and be saved or disbelieve and continue to trust in one's self, even to the point of using God's gracious and mighty works deceptively.

7. Berkouwer, *Divine Election*, 212–13.

Pharaoh's heart, "But I will harden Pharaoh's heart that I may multiply My signs and My wonders in the land of Egypt" (Exod 7:3).[8]

God continued to delay in implementing his final phase of judgment in Egypt, but it was not from an inability or unwillingness, as it might seem to some. He did so to make his power known. It was to give place for repentance. Between the sixth and seventh plagues in Egypt, God said through Moses to Pharaoh that he could have already obliterated Pharaoh and his people (Exod 9:15). Then in Exod 9:16, God tells why he had not done so. "But, indeed, for this reason I have allowed you to remain, in order to show you My power and *in order to proclaim My name through all the earth*" (italics added). This Scripture and others remind us of God's withheld or measured judgments as acts of kindness so that man may repent, thereby avoiding his unmeasured final judgment.

Paul reminds us, "Or do you think lightly of the riches of His kindness and tolerance and patience, not knowing that the kindness of God leads you to repentance" (Rom 2:4)? He further states, "Whom God displayed publicly as a propitiation in His blood through faith. This was to demonstrate His righteousness, because in the forbearance of God He passed over the sins previously committed" (Rom 3:25). Peter says the same, "The Lord is not slow about His promise, as some count slowness, but is patient toward you, not wishing for any to perish but for all to come to repentance" (2 Pet 3:9). God is slow to anger. "The Lord is gracious and merciful; slow to anger and great in lovingkindness" (Ps 145:8). In God alone, as seen in Christ, "Lovingkindness and truth have met together; righteousness and peace have kissed each other" (Ps 85:10). Hendriksen says, "God is ever bearing with great patience vessels of wrath, to make known the riches of his glory lavished on vessels of mercy."[9]

There is only one name under heaven whereby we may be saved (Acts 4:12). However, in the Old Testament, the death, burial, and resurrection of Jesus was the basis of everyone's salvation, but not the content of their proclamation and faith. Today we preach the gospel, people are saved by believing in the gospel, and there is only one name under heaven in which to believe unto salvation. Before the cross, salvation was based upon the future work of Christ (Hebrews 10), but people were saved by faith in the

---

8. God is said to have hardened Pharaoh's heart in five places (Exod 9:12, 10:1, 20, 27, 14:8), and Pharaoh is said to harden his own heart in three places (Exod 8:15, 32, 9:34–35). His heart is just said to be hardened without mentioning who hardened it in four places (Exod 7:13–14, 22, 8:19, 9:7).

9. Hendriksen, *Exposition of Romans*, vol. 12–13; accompanying biblical text is author's translation, 329.

one true God. The Scripture is clear that God used Pharaoh to declare his message of salvific love for all, not to demonstrate his lostness.

Some of the Old Testament verses that declare God's concern about the world knowing him are Deut 4:6–8. Commenting on this passage, Jack S. Deere wrote, "One purpose of the Law was to give the Israelites a full life as they obeyed God (vv. 1–5). In verses 5–8 another purpose of the Law is revealed: to make Israel morally and spiritually unique among all the nations and thereby draw other nations to the Lord."[10] Joshua says, "That all the peoples of the earth may know that the hand of the Lord is mighty, so that you may fear the Lord your God forever" (Josh 4:24). The immediate purpose of the law was to help Israel follow God, but the broader purpose was so that all people of the earth might know about God.

God promised Israel victory over the Philistines saying, "This day the Lord will deliver you up into my hands, and I will strike you down and remove your head from you. And I will give the dead bodies of the army of the Philistines this day to the birds of the sky and the wild beasts of the earth, that all the earth may know that there is a God in Israel" (1 Sam 17:46). God was not just about destroying the Philistines or giving the Israelites a land but also had in mind his desire that all may know him. Regarding the last words of this verse, Robert D. Bergen comments, "Yet the Philistines would not die in vain. In fact, their destruction would serve a high theological purpose; it would be a revelatory event by which 'the whole world will know that there is a God in Israel.'"[11]

Solomon calls on the people to treasure the presence of God in their lives saying, "May the Lord our God be with us, as He was with our fathers; may He not leave us or forsake us, that He may incline our hearts to Himself, to walk in all His ways and to keep His commandments and His statutes and His ordinances, which He commanded our fathers. And may these words of mine, with which I have made supplication before the Lord, be near to the Lord our God day and night, that He may maintain the cause of His servant and the cause of His people Israel, as each day requires, so that all the peoples of the earth may know that the Lord is God; there is no one else" (1 Kgs 8:58–60). These words contain three blessings from King Solomon, and of the third, Paul R. House notes, "The king desires God to uphold Israel's cause. Why? Not for national prominence or royal pride but so 'all the peoples of the earth may know that the Lord is God and that there is no other.'"[12] We repeatedly see the purpose of Israel reaches far beyond following God and receiving a

---

10. Deere, "Deuteronomy," 269.
11. Bergen, *1, 2 Samuel*, 196.
12. House, *1, 2 Kings*, 148.

blessing from him. It is so that everyone may know the one true God. This so that the deception of idolatry will be demonstrated to be the ersatz religion it is and people will turn to the one true God.

Isaiah reveals the need to praise God, and the scope of that praise saying, "And in that day you will say, 'Give thanks to the Lord, call on His name. Make known His deeds among the peoples; Make them remember that His name is exalted.' Praise the Lord in song, for He has done excellent things; Let this be known throughout the earth. Cry aloud and shout for joy, O inhabitant of Zion, For great in your midst is the Holy One of Israel" (Isa 12:4–6). Notice that the message to "the peoples" is to "make them remember His name" which is to be made "known throughout the earth." God is always about people knowing him, not so that he may judge, but that he may save. Gary V. Smith remarks, "Through praise directed to God, his name is exalted in community praise and other nations are reminded of the greatness of God. This sounds like a practical formula for worship and evangelism. The focus is always on glorifying and exalting God, the method is to use singing and retelling of the story, the content focuses on God's great deeds and exalted name, and the results spread the good news of God to others."[13]

Jeremiah says, "Hear the word of the Lord, O nations, And declare in the coastlands afar off, And say, 'He who scattered Israel will gather him And keep him as a shepherd keeps his flock'" (Jer 31:10). Again, we see God's concern for the nations. F.B. Huey sums up God's concern, "Throughout the OT as well as the NT, the Lord shows his desire to be known by more than just Israel (Gen 1:28; 9:1; 12:3; Isa 12:4–6; 49:6; 52:10–15; 55:3–5; 66:18–19; Jer 1:5, 10; 3:17). His actions on Israel's behalf would demonstrate to all his compassionate grace as well as his sovereign power and holiness."[14]

We often hear people refer to Jonah as the great missionary book of the Old Testament. Jonah preached judgment, as did John the Baptist (Matt 3:11–12), the Lord Jesus (Matt 23–24), and later still John the Revelator. Just like his successors, the message of judgment was to warn with the hope of bringing the hearers to repentance. Jonah provides valuable insight into the missionary work of God that seems to extend well beyond the event of Jonah. That is to say that God sometimes works in extraordinary ways, with people we might not expect, with an outcome that could only come about by the grace of God. God not only procured everything necessary for every individual in Nineveh to repent and believe, but it appears from this book, as well as throughout the rest of Scripture and human history, that he will also do whatever it takes to get the message of deliverance to those he knows will

---

13. Smith, *Isaiah 1–39*, 283.
14. Huey, *Jeremiah, Lamentations*, 272.

believe if given the chance. Additionally, are we to think God would send the gospel to people he knows will reject it, as we know he does, and yet fail to get it to those whom he knows will be receptive? My answer is no, not the God of infinite power, wisdom, and loving compassion.

God called Jonah to preach judgment against Nineveh's wickedness (Jonah 1:1–2). Jonah's disobedience followed by God's mighty works of deliverance caused Jonah to vow to obey Jehovah. He cried out, "But I will sacrifice to You with the voice of thanksgiving. That which I have vowed I will pay. Salvation is from the Lord" (Jonah 2:9). Jonah then obeyed and preached in Nineveh the coming judgment of Jehovah (Jonah 3:4), and it appears the city, including the king, repented and believed in Jehovah God (Jonah 3:5–10). Jonah proclaimed the compassion of God for the pagan and debauched heathen, as we all were at one time (Jonah 4:2).

This book begins with a word of judgment from God against their wickedness, (Jonah 1:2), and ends with God's loving compassion for those who repent, "Should I not have compassion on Nineveh, the great city in which there are more than 120,000 persons who do not know the difference between their right and left hand, as well as many animals?" (Jonah 4:11). Surely God's compassion and desire for every person to repent and believe is present especially in light of the statement, "from the greatest to the least of them" (Jonah 3:5), which included the king (Jonah 3:6). The proclamation by the king and its language is all-inclusive (Jonah 3:7–10). It seems as though the number 120,000 bespeaks of the entire population.[15] At least we can say to interpret this missionary story as God merely calling out his selected ones not only lacks textual support but also seems quite incongruent with the entire event. In reality, it shows God's concern for all of his creation. God will judge sin, but only man utterly rejects compassion.

Regarding Jonah 4:11, Billy K. Smith comments, "God's question captures the very intention of the book. The issue is that of grace—grace and mercy. Just as Jonah's provision was the shade of the vine he did not deserve, the Ninevites' provision was a deliverance they did not deserve based upon a repentance they did not fully understand. God's wish for his creation is salvation, not destruction. He will work to accomplish salvation if there is willingness on the creation's part."[16] Commenting on the same verse, G. V. Smith said, "God will (and does) act in justice against sin, but His great love for every person in the world causes Him to wait patiently,

---

15. That the number 120,000 probably refers to the entire population. See Smith and Page, *Amos, Obadiah, Jonah*, 283.

16. Smith and Page, *Amos, Obadiah, Jonah*, 282.

to give graciously, to forgive mercifully, and to accept compassionately even the most unworthy people in the world."[17]

Regarding the message God sent to Israel through his working in and through Jonah, John D. Hannah writes, "First, one apparent message to Israel is God's concern for Gentile peoples. The Lord's love for the souls of all people was supposed to be mediated through Israel . . . Through Israel the blessing of His compassion was to be preached to the nations (Isa. 49:3). The Book of Jonah was a reminder to Israel of her missionary purpose. Second, the book demonstrates the sovereignty of God in accomplishing His purposes. Though Israel was unfaithful in its missionary task, God was faithful in causing His love to be proclaimed."[18]

The book of Jonah should serve as a perennial and poignant deterrent to those who limit God's salvific love for every person because they do not see or know about such works of God. It is one thing to say a certain people group is unreached—meaning by the missionary endeavor—or even to hear of people who say they have never had an opportunity to hear of the one true God. It is another to deem such as equivalent to God not giving them an opportunity. The truth is, if the work of God through Jonah was not included in the canon of Scripture, those inclined to limit the work of God to what they know (or think they know) would probably limit this incredible work by including them in the list of those overlooked by God. But we know otherwise because of the multitude of Ninevites that were saved. I believe we may safely assume there are many stories of the compassion of God which we know not because he is the sum of love, compassion, mercy.

Franklin S. Page provides this summary, "From the Book of Jonah we learn that the Lord's compassion extended even beyond his people Israel."[19] This compassion is the theme of God's grace in both the Old and New Testaments. He worked through Israel in the Old Testament, and when they failed, God did not fail to work mightily to make his name known to the nations, and the same is true in the New Testament. Regarding God's concern for the nations and individuals in the nations, see also 1 Chr 16:23–24, 31; Isa 45:22; Zech 8:20–23.

God raised up Cyrus to bring God's judgment on the nations and set the Israelites free so they could return to the land of Israel (Isa 45:1–5). God proclaims and demonstrates his sovereignty in both blessing and calamity (Isa 45:6–7). He exhibits his power and sovereignty through pagan kings like Pharaoh in Egypt and now Cyrus in Persia. He does so for the

---

17. Smith, *Prophets as Preachers*, 97.
18. Hannah, "Jonah," 1462.
19. Smith and Page, *Amos, Obadiah, Jonah*, 204.

benefit of Israel (Isa 45:4, 8; 46:13), but also so that every person may know he is the one true God and be saved. "Declare and set forth your case; Indeed, let them consult together. Who has announced this from of old? Who has long since declared it? Is it not I, the Lord? And there is no other God besides Me, A righteous God and a Savior; There is none except Me. Turn to Me and be saved, all the ends of the earth; For I am God, and there is no other" (Isa 45:21–22).

The display of his sovereign power is not merely so that all may know he is sovereign, for that day is sure to come in the day of final judgment (Isa 45:23; Phil 2:10). Rather he manifests his sovereignty before the final judgment as an act of mercy and love for his creation so that they may be saved before it is too late. God knows one day all will acknowledge him as the sovereign, for it will be undeniable. Equally true is, at that acknowledgment, the day of salvation will have passed. Since God desires all to be saved as stated here, he continually acts so that men will know he is sovereign and flee the wrath to come.

Consequently, since all will know God's sovereignty, such displays presently are not without purpose, and the purpose is explicitly stated; much of God's judgments, calamities, and workings are in large measure evangelistic. God is working to bring about his plan of salvation. If he truly desires the salvation of every person, he must provide an opportunity to know him, which he does in a host of ways.

The testimony of Rahab, the Egyptians, Nineveh, and countless others in the Old Testament declare in unison that God is aware and working in the (humanly speaking) strangest and most God-forsaken places to make himself known to every person. I dare say that is characteristic of John 3:16 and God himself desiring the holiness and happiness of his creation.

32

What about Those Who Never Hear the Gospel: The New Testament

THERE IS AMPLE NEW Testament evidence that God makes himself known to not just people groups, but to everyone in all people groups. This revelation is such that he can safely say he has so sufficiently made himself known to every single person that every single person is without excuse for not fleeing the wrath to come by acknowledging him. Paul makes this clear:

> Rom 1:18–23
>
> [18] For the wrath of God is revealed from heaven against all ungodliness and unrighteousness of men who suppress the truth in unrighteousness, [19] because that which is known about God is evident within them; for God made it evident to them. [20] For since the creation of the world His invisible attributes, His eternal power and divine nature, have been clearly seen, being understood through what has been made, so that they are without excuse. [21] For even though they knew God, they did not honor Him as God or give thanks, but they became futile in their speculations, and their foolish heart was darkened. [22] Professing to be wise, they became fools, [23] and exchanged the glory of the incorruptible God for an image in the form of corruptible man and of birds and four-footed animals and crawling creatures.
>
> "For the wrath of God is revealed from heaven against all ungodliness and unrighteousness of men who suppress the truth in unrighteousness" (Rom 1:18)

The first thing to note about God's wrath is that it is against ungodly people who "suppress the truth." Both the words "revealed" and "suppress" are present tense verbs. This signifies an action that is repetitive or continuous. The present display of God's wrath does not replace his foreboding eschatological judgment (Rev 20:11–15), but rather serves as an ever-present harbinger and warning of it.

It seems God makes his anger known because he desires the truth of his existence, deserved worship, and redemption to be known to all so that they will not suffer the final judgment because of their sin. He is angry with all who seek to suppress his self-revelation through his creation. Signifying, in part, that God is presently dispensing measured judgments upon people in carrying out his salvation plan. He reveals his wrath today in select and measured proportions on those who seek to suppress the truth about him. They may seek to suppress this truth in word and deed by seeking to operate beyond his permissive will to impede his ultimate will, thereby attempting to thwart his plan of redemption. God desires that he be known and worshiped and that men will be saved, so every attempt of man to undermine those desires angers a holy and loving God.

Those who continue suppressing the truth are led into greater spiritual darkness and often lead others into deeper darkness as well (Matt 23:13). At times, God may dispense measured judgment on some who may have rejected him for the final time, or those he knows will ultimately do so, in order to warn others of their ultimate fate while there is still time for them to repent. If this is the case, when all the facts are known, these measured judgments will be seen to be acts of righteous grace. As seen in the previous chapter, Scripture is clear that God often blesses and dispenses measured judgments to make himself known to everyone so that people might repent. All people are under the wrath of God before faith in Christ (John 3:18). God's tempered judgments are a constant reminder of God's abhorrence of sin and unrighteousness, and a foreshadowing of future judgment for those who suppress the truth.

He judges today in measured displays because fallen mankind continually works through a galaxy of ways such as idolatry, cults, occult, philosophy, and science, to suppress the truth of God. One lexicon puts it this way, "The people whose evil ways keep the truth from being known, Rom1:18."[1] God is continually demonstrating his wrath against sin. Man explains it away and seeks to suppress the truth of the existence of a holy and loving God, to whom every person will give an account based upon God's standard and not man's. Man seeks through a myriad of ways to suppress the contemplation of the final judgment in which no person will escape apart from the grace and mercy of God. The declarations of God so that man may know him are seen throughout Scripture and history. We also see the works of man to suppress such revelation, but they are unsuccessful (vs. 23). They are all so unsuccessful that God can declare, when all the facts are known, there is not one single person who can rightly say,

---

1. Louw and Nida, *Greek-English Lexicon of the New Testament*, 164.

"I did not know." Why? Because God's love is manifested to every single person so that "they are without excuse."

Mankind ever seeks to explain natural catastrophes in any way except the biblical way. Which is they are all a consequence of sin and God's judgment against sin. The biblical picture is that God's creation was totally life-giving and sustaining. It is when sin entered into his creation and sin required judgment that everything changed (Gen 3). All calamities, death, and destruction have as their ultimate cause God's wrath and sin. Knowing the ultimate cause is quite different than attributing each storm, earthquake, tragedy, or even human death to a direct and immediate act of God, even though at times that may very well be the case. Rather it is to say that death itself, as well as natural calamities, are ultimately the result of sin and judgment upon sin. The present judgment is declared by grace, tempered by grace, and escapable by grace. The final judgment is unmitigated and inescapable.

It is quite common to hear Calvinists explain the knowledge expressed in this passage as sufficient only to result in judgment, but not salvation. This juxtaposition incorrectly provides only two options. I believe there is a third alternative which seems more reflective of the passage. It seems while natural revelation provides sufficient knowledge for judgment while being insufficient for salvation, it may also serve as an intermediate step in knowing God. God has designed his plan so that people can come to know him through natural revelation (vss. 19, 21). If they accept that, God will get the gospel to them. In other words, he will see that those who do accept this light of creative revelation, that unmistakably testifies to his existence, get an opportunity to hear and receive the gospel so they may be saved and know him personally.

God knows who receives the light he has given and is accordingly receptive to more light. In the New Testament, providing them more light sufficient for salvation means taking the light of the gospel to those who receive the light of creation because he is not willing that any perish (2 Pet 3:9). This understanding seems to better fit the nature and working of God and the explicit declarations of Scripture (John 3:16). Even some Calvinists speak consistently with this meaning of the declaration; although, technically their understanding of the nature of man and God's exclusive soteriology prohibits any light leading to salvation for anyone other than those who are unconditionally elected.

John MacArthur comments regarding verse 19, "As Paul declares in the following verse, 'That which is known about God is evident within them; for God made it evident to them' (v. 19). His point is that all people, regardless of their relative opportunities to know God's Word and hear His gospel, have internal, God-given evidence of His existence and nature, but are universally inclined to resist and assault that evidence. No matter how little spiritual light he may have, *God guarantees that any person who sincerely seeks Him will find Him.* 'You will seek me and find Me' He promises, 'when you search for Me with all your heart' (Jer. 29:13)"[2] (italics added).

MacArthur recognizes all have this knowledge. He also says, "All people ... are universally inclined to resist and assault that evidence." I cannot be sure how he is using the word "inclined," but the word means to be disposed to, tend, or lean in a certain direction. I assume he meant it that way in light of his quote of Jeremiah 29:13, which, taken at face value, means man has a choice to either seek God according to his revelation or suppress his revelation. If that is how he is using it, I would agree. People are naturally inclined toward self and sin apart from God's gracious working of revealing himself through natural and special revelation.

However, according to Calvinism, people are not merely inclined to suppress, but they are actually predetermined to be able only to suppress the truth of creation or the gospel.[3] That is all anyone can do given the fallen nature of man who is compatibly free. No one will or can seek God who is not unconditionally elected, which seems contrary to the intent and wording of this passage. If MacArthur means to use "inclined" in a normal Calvinist sense, that such inclination is unalterable, that would be consistent with the idea that the revelation is sufficient only for condemning man, who is already unalterably predetermined to eternal condemnation. And then the point is?

The passage seems to indicate God desires the revelation of himself and his salvation before the final judgment and is angered by people who actively fight against him in suppressing his revelation through creation. It does not seem those who suppress *have to* but choose to do so. It does not seem to be saying God is angry with the ones who can only choose to suppress the truth about him because he predetermined them to do so. As we have seen in the Old Testament, God makes himself sufficiently known by miracles, witnesses, and displays of power, and judgment is not to judge or display his glory but that those who witness such works might repent and believe. If a person accepts the light of creation, God will get the truth to them so they can know him personally.

2. MacArthur, *Romans 1–8*, 67.

3. To say they suppress because they are depraved does not remove the determinism of Calvinism, where they are depraved because God endowed man with a compatible freedom by which man would make a predetermined free choosing to sin. He will always do the same unless he is the recipient of unconditional election, and even the elect will do so until they receive the efficacious call of God.

John A. Witmer suggests man has a real choice. "People had God's truth but suppressed it, *refusing to heed it*. And these wicked ones did this in an attitude of wickedness"[4] (italics added). Robert Mounce similarly comments, "Although the wrath of God is primarily eschatological, it is at the same time a present reality. The use of the present tense (apokalyptetai, 'is being revealed') indicates something that is taking place in the present. Furthermore, verses 24–32 describe divine wrath as currently operative in the lives of the ungodly. That God's wrath is present does not mean that it will not also be eschatological. God's present wrath anticipates *his final withdrawal from those who do not respond to his love*"[5] (italics added).

It is best to understand the passage as involving God working sufficiently to provide man with a choice to believe God's natural revelation as man believes God's special revelation. Those who choose to suppress that truth, including both the grandeur of creation and the reality of his abhorrence of sin as seen in the measured judgments in time, will suffer his unmitigated eschatological judgment. This understanding is congruent with what see in the Old Testament. God works sovereignly, judging the sin of those who seek to reach beyond his permissive will while the day of salvation is still present. He works in order to give more revelation that he is the one true God, and then for those who accept that light, he works to bring sufficient light to them so that they may be saved.

> "Because that which is known about God is evident within them; for God made it evident to them" (Rom 1:19).

The creative testimony of God is not limited to something one sees externally, but the knowledge of it is within the human mind and heart, and this knowledge is understood (vs. 20). Understood is the word *nous* meaning comprehend, understand, perceive.[6] God has overcome any barriers that might keep such truth from being comprehensible to sinful man. He made it evident, clear, to all. Regarding the second use of the word *evident,* one Greek lexicon defines it as "to cause something to be fully known by revealing clearly and in some detail—'to make known, to make plain, to reveal, to bring to the light, to disclose, revelation.'"[7] God makes it clear, demonstrably clear, and internally known and understood. God works comprehensively to

---

4. Witmer, "Romans," 442.

5. Mounce, *Romans*, 77.

6. "Rational reflection or thought, perceive, understand, comprehend (MT 15.17); (2) as perceiving through receiving sensory data, notice, think carefully about, recognize, consider (MT 24.15); (3) as mental conception imagine, conceive" Friberg, Friberg, and Miller, *Analytical Lexicon of the Greek New Testament*, 272.

7. Louw and Nida, *Greek-English Lexicon of the New Testament*, 337–38.

reveal himself to those whom he desires to be saved, which is everyone. God is not judging a man, holding him accountable for rejecting an unclear or inaccessible revelation, but rather God judges a person for rejecting what he has made undeniably evident and accessible.

Mounce comments on this particular verse and verse 20 saying, "Verses 19 and 20 tell why the wrath of God is being revealed. God, in his creation, has provided sufficient evidence of himself to hold accountable all who reject that revelation. What can be known of God is perfectly clear. God himself made it plain."[8] Consequently, man's indisputable comprehension of the connection between creation, creator, and man's accountability to him is not dependent upon the natural acuity of man, but rather it is due to the omnipotent revelatory power of God.

The warnings of this passage and his tempered displays of wrath are acts of grace. To see this, one only needs to think of heading for eternal judgment without any warnings, experiential deficiencies of this world, or current consequences of sin. Similarly, Scripture gives examples of Christ warning his listeners to repent or perish (Luke 13:1–5). Both God's tempered judgments against sin, as well as the experiential consequences of sin, are acts of grace, as is his patience because he truly desires the salvation of every individual (Rom 2:4; 2 Pet 3:9). He works in many known and, I assume, unknown ways to give man an opportunity to flee the wrath to come.[9]

The final judgment due to committing the unpardonable sin (Matt 12:32) is a spiritual darkness that was not present before that particular refusal in a person's life; so that one's spiritual state of blindness to the truth can be said to be individually self-imposed, leaving each person without an excuse. Like the Pharisees, some work arduously to suppress the truth so others are even more deceived (Matt 23). God's gracious work is such that it overcomes all cloaks of deception and darkness so that if a person desires, which he can do by grace, he can flee the wrath to come. If he chooses not to flee, he is without excuse for not turning to God. Mounce highlights this point by saying, "God has revealed to all humans something of his eternal power and nature. Yet people refuse to believe, and as a result, their understanding is darkened. To turn willfully against God is to move from light into darkness. The blindness that follows is self-imposed."[10] Mounce is clear that an individual's darkened understanding is the result of a refusal to

---

8. Mounce, *Romans*, 77.

9. Clearly Scripture does not contain every act of God or working in salvation (Deut 29:29; John 20:30).

10. Mounce, *Romans*, 77.

believe, and like their blindness, it is self-imposed; indicating natural revelation can be accepted.

The word "revealed" (vs. 18) signifies God is the revelator and being so, he is overcoming whatever obstacles may hinder fallen man from seeing the glory of God in creation and the sure wrath that awaits all who die while suppressing the truth of his creative revelation. Revealed is in the present tense; demonstrating it is a continuous action. It is being revealed. It appears God works so fallen man can have sufficient understanding to know by the witness of creation that God exists, that God will judge him, and that he should serve God. It is again important to emphasize this verse assures that even if man, because of his sinfulness, cannot on his own see God in creation, God works to overcome whatever may hinder man so that every man knows and can be said to have no excuse.

Of course, this revelatory work of God is not necessary for God to righteously judge sin, for that will surely happen in the eschatological judgment. God could be just and choose to shield mankind from any temporary revelation of mitigated wrath, man's sinfulness, condign punishment, or the connection between sin, wrath, and natural calamities. Such working as delineated here are not needed for God to enact his eschatological judgment. But as always, God in grace does everything to give man a chance to know him, even giving his Holy Son for sinful, wrath-deserving truth suppressors.

My heart resonates with the thought and words of John, "See how great a love the Father has bestowed on us, that we would be called children of God; and such we are. For this reason the world does not know us, because it did not know Him" (1 John 3:1). *Great is* the translation of a word that means what sort of, what kind of. The KJV says, "What manner of love." What manner of love indeed! God's continual revelation overcomes man's efforts to suppress the truth so all can know of the one true God. God works so the knowledge is not only in what they see (external creation) but in what they understand (internal knowledge). God works to assure that man internalizes this knowledge and understanding. Such comprehensive exposure to God's revelation in creation requires an active and intentional choice and concentration to be suppress it.

> "For since the creation of the world His invisible attributes, His eternal power and divine nature, have been clearly seen, being understood through what has been made, so that they are without excuse" (Rom 1:20).

This verse reminds us God has comprehended the eventuality of sin, man's lost estate, and the salvation of man in his plan. He has so designed creation, man's knowledge, and access to understanding of creation so that we can see his invisible attributes such as power and his divine nature in the visible reality of creation. The word translated "divine nature" is the word *theiótēs*. This "expression 'divine nature' may be rendered in a number of languages as 'just what God is like' or 'how God is' or 'what God is.' In Rom 1:20 'deity' may sometimes be expressed as 'the fact that he is God' or 'is truly God.'"[11] Another reminder that to question man's comprehension of these attributes of God is not to question sinful man's ability to do so, rather it is to question God's ability to communicate clearly and undeniably.

Some philosophers, skeptics, and scientists may question God's eternal power. People may blame God for man's plight, thereby attempting to exonerate man, as was true with Adam and Eve. They may even claim to not know God. Nevertheless, Scripture makes it undeniably clear that everyone, including those who make such charges and denials, does really know of God. They see in creation his invisible attributes, power, and character of holiness, love, mercy, and benevolence. They see "just what God is like" and that he is "truly God." It is a testimony of perennial clarity that can neither be missed nor ignored but requires either acceptance or continual suppression.

Any claim that creation insufficiently displays the one true God is false because whatever deficiency there might be with the raw facts of creation and fallen man's comprehension of such facts displaying the one true God are overcome by the revelatory power of God. This testimony of creation shows God's eternal power in the powers of nature and reveals God's very nature through the five senses. When man looks at nature, by God's design and work, he can see God's love, provision, goodness, and his own need for the work of the one true God in his heart. Man's response that he does not see evidence of God is due to man's suppression of the truth, not a lack of revelation on God's part (Rom 3:4).

Witmer, commenting on this verse says, "'God is spirit' (John 4:24), all His qualities are invisible to physical eyes and can be understood by the human mind only as they are reflected in what has been made, that is, in God's creative work . . . The word theiotēs, translated 'divine nature,' . . . embraces the properties which make God. Creation, which people see, reveals God's unseen character—the all-powerful Deity. An Old Testament parallel to these verses is Psalm 19:1–6."[12] Similarly, MacArthur says, "*Every person, no matter how isolated from God's written Word or the clear proclamation of His gospel, has enough divine truth evident both within and around him* (Rom. 1:19–20) *to enable him to know and be reconciled to God if his desire*

---

11. "The nature or state of being God—'deity, divine nature, divine being . . . his eternal power and deity' Ro 1:20." Louw and Nida, *Greek-English Lexicon of the New Testament*, 139.

12. Witmer, "Romans," 442.

is genuine. It is because men refuse to respond to that evidence that they are under God's wrath and condemnation"[13] (italics added).

In light of Calvinism's doctrine of unconditional election, and since MacArthur is a Calvinist, we are faced with the crucial underlying questions. Can anyone and everyone desire reconciliation with God? Is there sufficient love and grace from God to permit that opportunity? If there is not a genuine opportunity afforded to everyone by God's grace and love, then the truth is that the vast majority, by God's design, do not have enough divine truth to "to be reconciled to God." The non-elect cannot have a "genuine desire" to be reconciled. Any such talk of even a minuscule possibility within Calvinism is double talk. As MacArthur states it, one would rightly conclude God has provided so that everyone is enabled to desire to genuinely be reconciled with God. Of course, this is antithetical to Calvinism. If he means what his words indicate, he is speaking contradictorily to Calvinism. If he does not mean what his words say and seem to clearly mean (i.e., he actually means only the elect can genuinely desire God), then he should speak so as to be clear rather than implying God's love and provision is for all.

According to Calvinism, God judges those who ultimately die in their sin, which sin he predetermined they commit. He judges them for what they cannot actually do, which is repent and believe the gospel, and for what they cannot keep from doing, which is suppress the truth. Extensivism contends God judges the lost for their sin and what they by grace can and should do but choose not to do, which is repent and believe the gospel.

It seems by God's grace even fallen man can respond sufficiently to the light God grants so that he may ultimately be saved, an opportunity of choice harkening back to Adam. This is not to say there is enough general revelation for one to be saved, or that man on his own can, apart from redemptive grace, come to God in salvation. It is to say there is enough light in creation to assure that everyone can have sufficient knowledge about God and respond to that light; if they do, God will get the light of the gospel to them so that no one can say they did not have an opportunity to know God.

The passage makes it clear all have sufficient understanding that leaves them without excuse, and this knowledge is so clear that it must be actively and willingly suppressed. It makes it most assuredly clear that those who do suppress are the recipients of God's moderated wrath today; however, it does not seem to make the scope of the suppression unmistakable. That is to say, it does not say *everyone continually* suppresses this knowledge, which is the conclusion of some who argue general revelation is only sufficient to judge.

---

13. MacArthur, *Romans 1–8*, 68.

Rather it specifically says "men who suppress the truth." Given that it does not say all people, and suppress is in the present tense, I suggest it means that while all may at one time or another suppress the truth, not all continue or continually do so. This conclusion seems self-evident since surely some of the suppressors are eventually believers in the gospel. Something that is true for both Extensivists and Calvinists.

If unconditional election is true, it is unclear why God would make such a display of himself through natural revelation thereby leaving everyone without an excuse for not knowing. Also, if all man can do is to reject such knowledge, it is unclear why God would make such a display to justify his temporal and eschatological judgment because that is sufficiently validated based on the fact that everyone is a sinner and God is holy (Rom 3:23). The "without excuse" seems to correspond to the continual display of undeniable evidence of the reality of the one true God as seen through creation so that people are aware of the verdict now, and that they can flee such a verdict before the final unmitigated outpouring of the wrath of God in the final judgment (Rev 20:11–15). To wit, the revelation of creation leaves all sinners without an excuse for saying they did not have an opportunity to know God.

The following is what we see in the Old Testament as well. God worked to get more light to those who received the light given, even if his response requires extraordinary and miraculous undertakings, maybe even to the caliber of the people of Nineveh or Rahab. The New Testament appears to present the same loving God who will get the saving gospel to those who receive the light of creation.

MacArthur seems to concur, even if such is meaningless in Calvinism. He says, "It is evident within them as well as without them. All men have evidence of God, and what their physical senses can perceive of Him their inner senses can understand to some extent . . . All men know something and understand something of the reality and the truth of God. They are responsible for a proper response to that revelation. Any wrong response is 'inexcusable.'"[14] I agree, but the question still remains. Can all men make a "proper response"?

The indication of the passage, as MacArthur clearly suggests, is they can and should make a proper response, but some do not. However, we must remember the unambiguous claim of Calvinism does not even permit the remotest possibility of one of the non-elect making a "proper response." Moreover, the unconditionally elect cannot make a "proper response" before the quickening of the Spirit or some other equally determinative work of

14. MacArthur, *Romans 1–8*, 76.

selective grace upon the elect (for Calvinists who reject regeneration happening prior to faith); both of which are contrary to the verse. Thus, MacArthur's response elides the true teachings of compatibilism, Calvinism, and unconditional election. Because while they may, according to compatibilism, be held responsible for not accepting the light of God's natural revelation, they were also predetermined to only be able not to accept it; the very thing the passage teaches they have no excuse for doing.

Sometimes Calvinists obscure this reality by contending the place of people, things, and experiences within Calvinism's determinism are a part of the process, which could include natural revelation. While that may be true, they may only insubstantially be so; they are as predetermined as everything else. The end is predetermined and the elements along the way are only insubstantially related to that end. That is to say, if one, several, or even all of them were not there, the end, such as unconditional election, would still take place. It is unconditional. If such are substantially related, then things like unconditional election are conditioned upon them, and unconditional election becomes conditional election. Whereas, given libertarian freedom, some things are substantially related to salvation in Extensivism because if they were not a part of the process, something different would be happening; therefore, the result would be different in indefinite scenarios.[15]

A.H. Strong speaks of the balance between man already knowing and preaching the gospel, "The Scriptures . . . both assume and declare that the knowledge that God is, is universal (Rom 1:19–21, 28, 32; 2:15). God has inlaid the evidence of this fundamental truth in the very nature of man so that nowhere is he without a witness. The preacher may confidently follow the example of Scripture by assuming it. But he must also explicitly declare it, as the Scripture does."[16] As mentioned with regard to MacArthur's response, the same is true with Strong's. While creation may provide a witness, according to Calvinism, the non-elect cannot respond to the witness except with utter rejection. The same is true of the kind of response they can make to the gospel—only one of rejection prior to regeneration. Equally important is the text does not say that suppression is the only response or that every person responds to natural revelation that way.

It is far more accurate to understand this knowledge is more than merely a knowledge to which man should respond but cannot if he is not one of the elect, which reduces it to a knowledge that can only result in

---

15. Here we are talking about the place of the witness of creation, but other such processual things include people's testimonies, a host of events, other person's prayers, growing up in a Christian home, ad infinitum. None of which are substantially related to salvation in Calvinism. See chapter 8 and authorial glossary.

16. Strong, *Systematic Theology*, 68.

judgment without the possibility that it will lead to salvation. What this passage seems to present lucidly is the knowledge is within, without, constant, and ever so clear that it leaves no one with an excuse for not knowing God. Man cannot passively ignore it, but rather he must continually suppress the opportunity of knowing God. Witmer notes, "The witness to God in nature is so clear and constant that ignoring it is indefensible. Their condemnation is based not on their rejecting Christ of whom they have not heard, but on their sinning against the light they have."[17] Such words again seem meaningless if the person with such knowledge could not respond to the light of creation, which results in God getting the light of the gospel to those who receive the light given. Because of God's benevolent care for his creation, he has made this creative revelation clear and compelling enough to reveal his very nature. Such creative revelation is not the same as special revelation but is detailed enough to lead to more accountability, more light, and potentially salvation.

The revelation of beauty and power is so awe-inspiring that it reveals the very nature of God. It does this so clearly and persuasively that for men to resist the obvious conclusion and refuse to bow before God, they must work continually, creatively, deceptively, and arduously to suppress such overwhelming lucidity. The natural order gives every indication of someone existing outside the natural order who is far different in power and glory than the natural order. It does so with such intelligibility and power that it can lead to reverence for God and accepting the light of creation, which results in God getting the gospel to that person. It is so persuasive on its own that men must work at remaining in the dark.

Accepting the God-given light that leads to salvation is never forced, but man is responsible for how he responds to that light of creation because a proper response can result in more light. Creation leaves man sufficiently enlightened to lead to salvation and ultimately be saved. Mounce says, "The text says that people are without a defense for their unwillingness to believe. The Greek word translated 'without excuse' (anapologētous) suggests that from a legal standpoint people had been stripped of any defense. The age-old question about the salvation of the 'heathen' is clearly answered in this verse . . . Things visible call for a power that is invisible."[18]

> "For even though they knew God, they did not honor Him as God or give thanks, but they became futile in their speculations, and their foolish heart was darkened. Professing to be wise, they became fools, and exchanged the glory of the incorruptible God

17. Witmer, "Romans," 442.
18. Mounce, *Romans*, 78.

for an image in the form of corruptible man and of birds and four-footed animals and crawling creatures" (Rom 1:21–23).

These verses clearly reach back to the choices of Adam and Eve and those who might have lived soon enough after the fall that the knowledge of God was not as perverted as it has progressively become through the millennia. Additionally, it seems certain those referred to in these verses are the same people in verses 18–20. This shows a progression of man from the beginning. It also describes any person who refuses God's revelation both general revelation in creation and special revelation. The sin of Adam and Eve, though more glaring without the effect of sin, is committed throughout human history, which is to reject the love and grace of God in spite of the opportunity to receive it. It is to reject the well-known and understood truth that God is the creator, and man is accountable to him.

In the New Testament era, God works through the gospel, but not hearing the gospel is not precisely equivalent to the idea that the one who never heard the gospel did not have an opportunity to be reconciled with God. In our present era, belief in the gospel is the exclusive message by which one can find deliverance from the wrath to come for his sin. However, this passage demonstrates God is working through many ways, one being the perennial testimony of creation, to give people an opportunity, and there may be other ways of which we are not aware.

D.A Carson similarly says, "To be sure, God is sovereign in the communication of his grace as well as in its application, and he may at times choose to bring to people a knowledge of the gospel in ways quite *unforeseen and even unknowable to us*"[19] (italics added). He further states, "Paul makes clear that Gentiles in his day, and people who have never heard the gospel or read the Bible, have genuinely 'seen' something of God and who he is. But some people who receive that truth do not respond appropriately to it: rather than glorifying God or giving him thanks, they turn from the truth to embrace idolatry . . . all human beings have the capacity to receive such revelation because they continue to bear the divine image . . . No one, Paul makes clear here, can ever be saved on the basis of the truth revealed in nature by itself."[20]

Carson states that "some people . . . do not respond appropriately" to this revelation, which seems to imply, as the text seems to, that some people do respond. To believe otherwise necessitates believing that no saved person ever suppressed the truth revealed in creation before salvation. He is correct to recognize all humans have the capacity to receive because man still bears

19. Carson et al., eds., *New Bible Commentary*, 1122.
20. Carson et al., eds., *New Bible Commentary*, 1122.

the image of God. I think he is right to conclude natural revelation alone is insufficient for salvation. I would add the following to his comments. Since man has the capacity to receive this revelation, and it is not enough to save; since it is absolutely unnecessary to reinforce man's condemnation; and since God's righteousness to judge and surety that he will need no witness unless it serves as a warning and includes the possibility of avoiding his judgment against sin, it is best to see creative revelation as an intermediate act of grace that can lead to God getting the gospel to those who receive the light of natural revelation. It is truly another evidence of God's love in witnessing against sin and warning people to flee the coming judgment. It is reflective of the God of love (1 John 4:8). It is a perennial revelation of God so people can come to know him and live eternally.

This understanding means man is not merely given enough knowledge to confirm judgment, but rather enough to lead to salvation. Man cannot say God did not give him the opportunity to know him and flee the wrath to come. This understanding is consistent with what we see in the preceding and following verses. Rejecting truth brings God's judgment because mankind should have received his deliverance and worshiped and served him.

The unencumbered message of this passage is God's revelation of who he is through what he has done is so evidentially sufficient from without and within that it requires continuous and active refusal to refrain from accepting the undeniable. It is the refusal to believe when one could and should have that is the cause of judgment. God judges a man for refusing to believe the gospel (John 3:18); in like manner, God judges a man for refusing to accept the witness of God that would have led to him hearing the gospel.

Therefore, people are under the wrath of Rom 1:18 because God has revealed himself so clearly by and through his creation that they actually "knew God" (vs. 21). They choose to "suppress" that knowledge under the weight of "foolish speculations" (vs. 25), choosing to "exchange" the glory of God for the images created by man (vs. 23), exchanging the "truth of God for a lie" (vs 25), and finally God hands them over to what they desire (vs. 24). Suppressing the truth is never without consequence as we learned with the first sin in the Garden of Eden. Their quest for control leads to judgment and the bondage of sin—their pursuit to determine right and wrong results in exchanging the most natural of all created relationships for the most unnatural (Rom 1:26–27).[21]

Ultimately, it is an exchange of life for death. While God will get the gospel to those who receive the light of creation, he is not obligated to get

---

21. "It is the substitution of one thing for another; hence, 'exchange' rather than 'change' is the correct gloss." Louw and Nida, *Greek-English Lexicon of the New Testament*, 573.

the gospel to those who reject the light of creation to demonstrate that he salvifically loves them. A lack of the presence or knowledge of the gospel by some in the world does not necessarily demonstrate God did not truly desire for them to be saved and provide a sufficient opportunity for them to know him.

As a result, the difference between Calvinism and Extensivism is that Extensivism believes the simple declarations of God's love and desire for every person to be saved means just that. It means such love is proven in his comprehensive salvational provision, including the opportunity for all, as attested to in this passage and throughout Scripture. In contrast, Calvinism interprets all such passages through the prism of unconditional election, which can only mean God does not truly desire all to be saved. Calvinists cannot equalize Calvinism and Extensivism by using the same problem argument to deflect criticisms of their austere portrait of God; as seen in Calvinists' comments here, they do not even speak consistently with their own doctrines. Therefore, Calvinists' attempts fail.

Some accept and some reject the special revelation of the gospel. That pattern seems to be the same with regard to being exposed to general revelation. Some reject, which seems also to indicate some receive the light of the testimony of creation. That some reject special revelation does not mean all reject, nor is such a conclusion entailed in the fact that some reject general revelation. Even though with regard to creative light, we may not be privy to who does and does not accept it as gospel encounters make apparent.

While an acknowledgement of or even awareness of general revelation is not a prerequisite for receiving the gospel, "it is the power of God unto salvation" (Rom 1:16). We can say when a person does receive the light of general revelation, God will get the saving light of the gospel to him because he truly desires all to be saved (Jer 29:13). We believe that is what God is doing when he works in the heart of his people to share and go even to the remotest parts of the earth because there is one, or some, who upon hearing will believe and pass from death to life just like the Ethiopian (Acts 8:16–40).

We do find a clear promise that man can find God when he seeks him (Isa 55:6; Jer 29:13). We find examples like the Ethiopian (Acts 8:26–39) and Cornelius, who although a Gentile centurion in the Roman army, is described as "a devout man, and one who feared God with all his household, and gave many alms to the Jewish people, and prayed to God continually" (Acts 10:2), to whom God sent Peter with the gospel. "While Peter was still speaking . . . the Holy Spirit fell upon all those who were listening to the message," and they were "baptized in the name of Jesus Christ" (Acts 10:44, 48). Lydia provides another example; she is said to have been a "worshiper of God" and God did not leave her without sufficient witness, and upon hearing the gospel, "the Lord opened her heart to respond to the things spoken by Paul" (Acts 16:14).

It is true that man on his own will never seek God (Rom 3:11), but it is also true that God has not left man on his own. He works graciously calling, enabling, convicting, enlightening, drawing, and giving understanding, and both the Father and the Son seek man (John 4:23; Luke 19:10). Accordingly, he commands people to seek him (Matt 6:33) and promises that he will respond (Luke 11:9–10; Heb 11:6). He warns that many will continue to seek to come to God based on their own ideas and refuse to recognize their spiritual bankruptcy and need to repent and trust God. With that same warning, he commands the lost to strive to enter through the "narrow door" of repentance and faith (Luke 13:24). Robert Stein, commenting on this verse, says, "The main point of the verse centers on the need to make sure one is part of the 'few' who have through repentance and faith experienced God's mercy and grace."[22] Scripture teaches God's love, provision, and desire and gives us many examples of people responding to the light they had and God working to get the light of salvation to them.

In light of the entire passage, the evidence creation affords man seems far more valuable than evidence of God's reality for only the sake of judging man, which serves no meaningful purpose if one cannot escape the judgment. God always takes the initiative; man is never left without a witness of God through miracles, his presence, his witnesses, creation, and special revelation. God truly desires all to be saved and none to perish (2 Pet 3:9), and one may know that by pondering the many works God has done in order to make himself known to all people.

It seems biblically faithful and intellectually reasonable to believe those people who perish under the judgment of God who had never heard the gospel in this present era would have received light sufficient for salvation if they had received the light they had in creation. It is because men reject the light that leads to salvational light that God, in holiness, must and will judge them in their sin. I am not saying those who accept general revelation will be saved because salvation comes only through faith in the gospel. It is only to say the light of creation can serve as an intermediate step in the plan of salvation.

Scripture here and elsewhere reminds us God always has a witness (Acts 14:15–17). God makes himself known and graciously works so man can seek him and find him. Depending on this grace of God in speaking to the pagans, Paul could say, "He is not far from each one of us" (Acts 17:27).

---

22. Stein, *Luke*, 379.

MacArthur comments, "Every person has a witness of God, and therefore every person is accountable to follow the opportunity to respond to Him in faith."[23] "But if a person lives up to the light of the revelation he has, God will provide for his hearing the gospel by some means or another."[24]

The Bible proclaims God includes everyone in his salvation plan, and Extensivists believe Scripture gives us ample insight to know God works to give every person an opportunity to know him. In those places where we do not know the actual details, we may trust his revealed character and explicit declarations. The question then changes from, What about those who never heard to, How many times and ways must God say and show his salvific love for all of humanity before Calvinists will recognize his unbounded salvific love; that everyone or anyone can actually be saved?

---

23. MacArthur, *Romans 1–8*, 78.
24. MacArthur, *Romans 1–8*, 81.

33

What about Those Who Never Hear the Gospel: Foreordination versus Foreknowledge

As we have seen, Calvinists often claim Extensivists are in the same quandary as Calvinists in that God supposedly limited those who could be saved in Extensivism by limiting opportunity and in Calvinism by unconditional election. Another way to present this argument emphasizes the inarguable reality that both positions believe God created this world knowing many would not repent and be lost in torment forever. I have heard a Calvinist say, "We all worship a God who knowingly structured the plan of salvation and created a world in which the vast majority of humanity will never hear of his way of salvation much less have an opportunity to accept it and be saved." Or a Calvinists may say, "We all have to admit God knew his creation would rebel, and most of those he created would be lost forever in hell; thus, we all have the same problem." This form of the same problem argument is recognizable by its emphasis upon God's foreknowledge.

I think we can accurately portray this type of argument with this specific question. "Does God creating a world in which he knew many would perish pose the same problem for Extensivists as it does Calvinists?" That is the precise question addressed in this chapter.

Our Calvinist friends present these statements in order to demonstrate that both perspectives suffer from the *same problem*, thereby eliminating Extensivist's grounds for criticizing Calvinists for their view that God elects only some to salvation.[1] It is true both perspectives believe God created a world in which he knew most people would perish, but that does not mean Extensivism suffers from the same problem as Calvinism. The truth is, once we sort through the Calvinist gloss, we find these two statements serve to reveal significant differences between the two perspectives:

---

1. This is not an argument regarding supralapsarianism, but simply acknowledges that God being omniscient did, in fact, know that most would perish if he created the world as it is. All agree God, by his very nature, knew this.

first, the act of creation, second, the availability of salvation, and third, the eternal state of the lost.

We begin with an essential difference in Calvinists' and Extensivists' understanding of how God knows the future. Knowing (foreknowing) in Calvinism is based on God foreordaining what will be. He knows what will happen because he predetermined it to happen, and it will happen precisely and only as he determined it to happen. Speaking of this, Leigh Vicens says, "But if God knows the future exhaustively, theological determinists argue, then all future events must be determined, directly or indirectly, by God . . . It must be God himself who ultimately determines the event's occurrence."[2] Determinism means there are no contingencies. Contingencies are events that result from choices made by libertarian free humans. Extensivism contends the creator endowed man with libertarian moral freedom, otherwise choice. Because contingencies come into being by the choices of libertarian free beings, they are certain rather than determined events.

According to Extensivism, God can and does foreknow what he foreordained to happen. He also knows all contingencies, true free acts of man endowed with otherwise choice, which he freely predetermined to be an integral component in his creation. This means the reason there are contingencies in this world rather than everything being predetermined is that God predetermined to create a world with both events that are predetermined (human choice does not affect them) and contingent events (human choice does affect them). These often are referred to as definite and indefinite events. Definite events are known by God and happen *necessarily* because they are predetermined by God to happen and cannot be altered by human otherwise choice, whereas indefinite events are known by God and happen *certainly* because they can be altered by human otherwise choice.

Our understanding of the structure is quite different as well. According to Calvinism, God intentionally structured a plan that inarguably pedestals his desire that only some could, and therefore would be saved. According to Extensivism, God intentionally structured a plan that reflects his desire and provision for anyone and everyone to be saved. This plan includes God's desire to create man in his image with libertarian freedom, which decision substantively included a place for man's choice in his plan. With this in mind, we are prepared to look at our supposed similar dilemma regarding God comprehensively knowing the three interconnected parts of his plan for mankind.

---

2. Vicens, "Theological Determinism," under the heading "Arguments for Theological Determinism."

First, the act of creation

Extensivists believe God knew Adam and Eve would sin, and the whole of humanity would thereby be cast into a sea of sin and judgment. Each person after that would be born with a sin nature and become a sinner by practice, a state in which man would find himself hopelessly incapable of extricating himself from on his own. God always knew all of the suffering that would ensue because of the decisions of Adam and Eve. However, even though on the surface the problem seems to be the same for both perspectives, it is not. This is why.

Calvinism believes God only foreknows what he foreordains, and God created man with a compatible free nature. Either of these concepts leads to the idea that God created man where not only *would* he sin, but he *could not* resist sinning; although, Calvinists are quick to distance God from direct responsibility or causing man to sin by employing secondary causation. The inescapable fact is, even though the Calvinists' claim that man did freely choose to sin is correct, the corollary is equally true; the desire from which Adam and Eve freely chose was unalterably determined by their God-given nature and past.

As a result of these two components, Adam and Eve's decision was a predetermined free decision. Consequently, while it can be said God did not directly cause them to sin, he did predetermine they would freely choose to sin by endowing them with compatible freedom in concert with the past he established for them. Therefore, it is inescapable that God desired to not only create them but to create them so they would choose to sin because it is, given their nature and past, the only thing they could do. God knew they would sin because he predetermined that state of affairs by decree and by endowing them with compatible moral freedom.

This understanding is quite different from Extensivism, wherein God foreknew man would sin because he knows everything. He knew creating man with libertarian freedom would result in man misusing his freedom to sin. Although this result was certain, it was not necessary. This means, given man's nature and past, he could have chosen differently; therefore, the sin was neither necessary nor predetermined.

It was certain since God knows everything and God cannot hold to a false belief. Sin was not God's desire for man, but he did allow it. Allow or permit in Calvinism is indistinguishable from determined since even his permissive will is determined. Whereas according to Extensivism, permission includes the idea that God truly did not desire for man to sin and die, but he permits it within the context of his creation-redemption plan. God overcomes man's sin through his creation-redemption plan. This means the origin of sin was the misuse of the wonderful gift of being created in the image of God with libertarian freedom. According to Extensivism, God desired and provisioned man so that he could have and should have resisted the temptation to sin; whereas in Calvinism, God endowed man with compatible moral freedom, and man could not have done other than he did in the moral moment of decision.

According to decretal theology and compatibilism, God could have freely chosen to create man with a nature that emanated desires not to sin from which man would have freely chosen not to sin, and sin would not have entered man's world. In absolute contrast, the prevention of the presence of sin in the original libertarian free world wherein the option to sin exists seems to be an impossibility. In Calvinism, God knew he could have predetermined man to choose a path that would not have ushered in sin, whereas he could not have so predetermined man endowed with libertarian freedom, or it would not be libertarian freedom.

The two perspectives regarding the way God knows the future are as follows. According to Calvinism, God knows what he predetermined to happen. His predetermination includes every microscopic detail with exact precision. This is why there is actually little if any difference between what God foreknows and what he foreordained.[3] He foreknows what he foreordained, and he foreordained what he knows. Everything happens, including all human actions, precisely as predetermined. There is no such thing as indefinite events or contingencies, things resulting from otherwise choice. Every good and every evil, every help and every hurt is because God predetermined people to act the way they do in fact act. The fall of man was predetermined to happen by creating man with compatible freedom and a specific nature and past, which is the nature of decretal theology. God's predetermination includes the use of secondary causation but excludes the remotest possibility of even the minutest change in what he predetermined to be; what is, is, because God desired it and predetermined his desire to be actualized.

The two perspectives regarding God creating a world in which he knew everyone who would be saved and who would not are as follows. According to Calvinism, he knew because he predetermined whom he would save and whom he would not save without any consideration of, or the possibility of,

---

3. There does not seem to be a difference as far as what will happen in time. There may be a difference between what God foreknew he could have predetermined to be and what he actually did predetermine to be—foreordain—although I have read some who do not seem to allow for even this. They contend his present plan is all there could be since God only does what is perfect and their contention is that there is only one perfect plan.

humans affecting his plan. Everything is the result of God unalterably predetermining that outcome. It pleased him to select some unconditionally to be the beneficiaries of his grace. It equally pleased him to withhold the same grace (that would have most assuredly resulted in their salvation) from the majority of his creation. They are known as reprobates. Therefore, people do not choose to act differently because they cannot choose to act differently than God predetermined that they will act.

According to Extensivism, God knows everything because he is essentially omniscient (here we are specifically considering the future). God knows what he predetermined to happen. He predetermined to create a world that includes some predetermined, foreordained events (definite events) and some non-predetermined events (indefinite events). Some events are a mixture of both such as the crucifixion of Christ (Luke 22:22; Acts 2:23). Definite events are uninfluenced by human choice. Indefinite events are influenced by the human choice of libertarian morally free beings. The events that include both are simply mixed. It is the indefinite events (and mixed events) Calvinists reject since they believe God can only know predetermined future events. Extensivists contend God did not predetermine nor desire that man would sin, but as with angels, God knew man would sin because God is an essentially omniscient being.

To state the fact of essential omniscience negatively, God cannot fail to know. Stated more positively, God knows himself and his intentions exhaustively. God's knowledge includes his intent to create man with otherwise choice. Because he knows his intentions eternally and comprehensively, God innately knows the choices and actions of the man he would create, including the consequences of his choices. He does not look down the halls of history to see what man will do, nor does he even look outside or beyond himself. God knows innately rather than perceptively.

God does distinguish between the sequences of events (both definite and indefinite), but that does not mean he comes to know them sequentially. For example, he knew he would create the sun, and, consequently, the sun would produce sunlight from which would come warmth, the growth of plants, and countless other things; some of them have their own sequential relationships that in turn spawn other sequential relationships. Even by what we as humans know of this dynamic, it is truly incomprehensible how a being could know this from all eternity. I suspect there is even more he has always known about this one aspect of creation that we do not know. Now, multiply that by billions of sequential relationships, and we begin to contemplate what kind of being God is. The same is true of his knowledge of both determined and non-determined man, albeit with still more complexity. Multiply that times billions of individuals that are alive today or that have lived throughout history.

Both determined and undetermined man entail sequentiality. If God determined to create determined man, he would have always known he would. This choice would include always knowing every aspect of sequentiality—events taking place as entailed in that choice. If God determined to create non-determined man, he would have always known he would. This choice would include knowing every aspect of sequentiality. He would know either plan as he would know the sequentiality entailed in the creation of the sun. Therefore, the difference between the two is not in what or when he knows but rather in how he knows.

Determinism says God knows because he determined it to be, but there still had to be the knowledge of sequentiality. Extensivism says he knows because he is essentially omniscient. Being who he is, he could not have always known he would create a world with contingencies (acts of libertarian beings) and that knowledge be separated from his knowledge of what that entails. Regarding determinists' argument that contingencies do not exist until the libertarian being decides, and therefore cannot be known; I would respond that even though they do not exist in time, they do exist eternally in the mind of God because he would have always known he would create such a world, which entails knowing everything about that world. From an Extensivist perspective, the only predetermined requirement is that God predetermined to create man with libertarian freedom and permit some indefinite events. All God had to know was that he intended to so create man and by this, he would know what that entailed.

Extensivism's perspective allows God to genuinely desire that man would choose holiness, even though he knew he would not always so choose. Calvinism excludes such because if he had truly desired only holiness, he could have given man a different compatible nature and past. These distinctions make it clear that while it is true both views believe God knew man would sin, the process by which God foreknew in each perspective is vastly dissimilar. This dissimilarity reflects our differences, not only in the realm of soteriology but theology proper as well (the nature of God); hence, we do not have the same problem.

Why would God create man with libertarian freedom, knowing man would misuse it and sin? Such a state of affairs would have to do with God's eternal plan. If he desired to create beings who choose to love him when they did not have to do so, as he did not have to create beings to love, it seems that would necessitate those beings being able to choose to love him or not love him. God could have chosen to create beings to love or not create them at all. He could have acted or refrained.

In like manner, to receive the same kind of love from created beings would require they be endowed with otherwise choice; they could choose to love him or not. God's love is by free choice, and the loftiness of the relationship he has designed for man to experience seems to require undetermined love. The biblical portrayal, as well as our own understanding, of such concepts as love, valor, nobility, honor, compassion, and faithfulness are understood as including a choice between these and their evil counterparts, or not acting at all. We should not understand this as the *only* reason God created man or created man the way he did. Scripture gives the impression there may be many reasons such as: for his glory, to share his love, create loyal followers, or demonstrate his worthiness to others to name a few.

Second, the availability of salvation

We may summarize this component of the supposed similarity between the two perspectives in the following way. God created man knowing sin would affect every person in the human race, but he structured the plan of redemption so that only a very limited and specific number of people would ever have an actual opportunity to be saved. According to Calvinism, the only difference is that the number is selectively limited by unconditional election, whereas in Extensivism God selectively limits the number of people who will be saved by limiting the opportunity to hear the gospel. Let me point out three essential dissimilarities between the two views.

The first essential dissimilarity is the difference I have sought to demonstrate in the previous three chapters addressing this issue.[4] Extensivism believes God has sufficiently worked so that everyone has received enough light to know him. If they receive that light (which they can do by grace), he will get enough light to them to afford a genuine opportunity to be saved. This is not true in Calvinism.

The second essential dissimilarity is there is an obvious difference between Extensivism's contention that everyone who does hear the gospel does have an accessible opportunity to believe and be saved, whereas according to Calvinism they do not. Accordingly, believing that God knowingly created a universe where most would reject a genuinely accessible

---

4. Two things can have dissimilarities and be the same, whereas essential dissimilarities between them means they can only be similar; they cannot be the same. For example, you and I can both be human (same beings), even though we may be dissimilar in various ways; we still have humanness, created in the image of God. In contrast, a chimpanzee can be similar to a human (some abilities and physical characteristics), but a chimpanzee cannot be a human being because we are essentially dissimilar; they are not created in the image of God.

salvific opportunity sufficiently provisioned by grace enablements, and therefore be lost forever, is not equivalent to his knowingly determining the same eternal result via unconditional election in Calvinism. Unconditional election necessarily means God is actually pleased to damn most of his creation, something that is not true of Extensivism, given the nature of libertarian freedom.

The third essential dissimilarity I illustrate in this way. Let's suppose for the sake of argument, we were to consider a state of affairs in which all do not have an opportunity to be saved by the gospel. The two plans are still essentially dissimilar. Considering the comparison from this vantage point does mean both perspectives would preclude the possibility of everyone getting an opportunity to be saved, but that is as far as the similarity extends. The reason for this dissimilarity is because Calvinism's delimitation is clearly by intentional design, which it did not have to be. God could have elected everyone to salvation.

In contrast, not hearing the gospel in this precise Extensivist state of affairs would not necessarily require that to be reflective of God's desire. That is to say, not getting the gospel to everyone is not necessarily equivalent to unconditional election. It is possible, according to Extensivism, God could truly desire for all to be saved while also limiting his plan *exclusively* to the right exercise of libertarian freedom by his people to carry out his plan. In other words, he could have decided to inextricably connect the opportunity for the salvation of people *only* to the obedience of his people evangelizing. Such a plan would have God remaining genuinely desirous of the salvation of all, but incorporating only the free choices of his people to go and tell as well as those who hear to believe.

Now even though I believe libertarian free choice is an immense part of his plan to carry out world missions, I do not think this scenario represents the full story of his plan. But, had he limited the efficacy of his plan to just this, it still would not be equivalent to unconditional election. For according to unconditional election, it is impossible to defend the idea God genuinely desires everyone to be saved because if that was his true desire, all he would have had to do is elect everyone to salvation. As I have demonstrated, there are good biblical, experiential, and logical reasons to believe he does make sure, in our day, the gospel gets to everyone whom he knows will believe. However, he is under no obligation to get the gospel to those whom he knows will not believe even though he may and has done so many times.

To argue that because the gospel was not taken somewhere in the world necessarily means God did not give them the opportunity and so Extensivism has a sort of unconditional election of its own is totally without merit. We believe foreknowledge is God's side of the equation, knowing where to lead his people to go; someone feeling the call of God to go to a certain place as a missionary is our experiential side of the equation (Rom 1:8). This understanding in no way limits or minimizes the command of God for all of his people to go and evangelize their neighbors and the world. The failure to do so is disobedience to the gospel and the heart of God and does substantially affect the missionary endeavor. Nor does it in any way approximate Calvinism's idea in which man freely chooses, but he does not make a choice between accessible options of obedience or disobedience, believing or disbelieving.

Therefore, this attempt, as do similar attempts, to assuage the disquieting realities of Calvinism by showing we all have the same problem is meritless. There is simply an irreconcilable difference between a plan intentionally structured, so that sin and its consequences are extensive with an equally extensive offer of salvation compared to a plan of redemption that is a finely tuned exclusive plan that inviolably withholds salvational grace from the non-elect. While we may not know all of the details of how God brings sufficient knowledge to all, we do know that he does so based upon his revealed character, specific revelatory declarations, workings in both the Old Testament and New Testament, and testimonies of individuals. Based upon Scripture and God's character, we can be sure when God says he loves the world of humanity (John 3:16) and is not willing for any to perish (2 Pet 3:9), he will not sit idly by and fail to get the truth of salvation to those who have a willing heart. If we can figure that out, I am quite sure he is capable of doing so as well.

Third, the eternal state of the lost

In consideration of the last component of the "same problem" contention, Extensivism believes God created a universe where he knew most would reject a genuine salvific opportunity sufficiently provisioned through grace enablements and be lost forever. This scenario is obviously not equivalent to determining the same eternal result via unconditional election (Calvinism), which means God is genuinely pleased to damn most of his creation (Eph 1:11). Some Calvinists recoil at the suggestion that God is pleased that people go to hell, but it is an inescapable part of Calvinism, as is attested to logically and declaratively. Calvin commented, "We say . . . that God . . . determined once for all those whom it was his pleasure one day to admit to salvation, and those whom, on the other hand, it was his pleasure to doom to destruction."[5]

5. Calvin, *Institutes of the Christian Religion*, vol. 2, bk. 3, chap. 21, sec. 7, pg. 210–11.

The Canons of Dort assert, "Holy Scripture . . . further bears witness that not all people have been chosen but that some have not been chosen or have been passed by in God's eternal election—those, that is, concerning whom God, on the basis of his entirely free, most just, irreproachable, and unchangeable *good pleasure*, made the following decision: to leave them in the common misery into which, by their own fault, they have plunged themselves; not to grant them saving faith and the grace of conversion; but finally to condemn and eternally punish them . . . not only for their unbelief but also for all their other sins, in order to display his justice"[6] (italics added).

One may argue Extensivism is wrong, and Calvinism is right, but one cannot cogently argue the two perspectives have the same soteriological problems. To seek to expunge the essential dissimilarities of the two perspectives obscures the disquieting realities of Calvinism. Any attempt to soften the harsh realities of Calvinism leads to obfuscating double talk.

Given our look at these attempts by Calvinists to entangle Extensivists in their web of contradictions and misrepresentations of God's salvific love, we are better equipped to answer the question, "Do Calvinism and Extensivism have the same problem?" The only legitimate answer is *no*. Another way to see we do not suffer from the same problems is that unlike Calvinists, Extensivists do not require nor utilize phrases or double talk that ostensibly give the appearance that God truly desires the salvation of all, or he is truly sorry that some perish in hell when he undeniably does not desire all to be saved; nor is he sorry about those who perish. Because according to unconditional election, all he had to do was choose to elect everyone. Therefore, it is Calvinist's commitment to unconditional election that requires them to employ such verbal maneuverings.

In Extensivism, which substantially incorporates libertarian freedom into God's plan, the lacking is not the love of God nor the provision of God, but, rather, according to Jesus the lacking is his followers' lack of commitment. He said, "Then He said to His disciples, 'The harvest is plentiful, but the workers are few'" (Matt 9:37). We are to go, which is connected to people hearing the gospel and believing. Those hearing must harken to the words, "I tell you, no, but unless you repent, you will all likewise perish" (Luke 13:5). Therefore, we do not need special interpretive lenses to explain verses like John 3:16, whether we are speaking to a single person, group, or the world. The message is the same; God loves you and gave his Son for you so that you would not have to die in your sins. That is the difference.

---

6. Canons of Dort, First Head of Doctrine, article 15.

34

The Place of Creation in Witnessing to Pagan Gentiles

A GOOD PLACE TO start when witnessing to Jews is the Old Covenant. While that certainly plays a part in the grand scheme of witnessing to pagan Gentiles, it may not always the best place to start since they may not know or even care that there is an Old Covenant made with Israel. When witnessing to Gentiles, incorporating the witness of creation is often a better place to start because the witness to God in creation is available to every human. This practice is seen in the New Testament, particularly in Acts and Revelation. In the United States there used to be a basic common knowledge of and respect for Scripture, which made speaking from the Old or New Testament more relevant. But in totally pagan countries, and now often in the west with the pervasive influence of secularism and pagan religions, the wonder of creation can be a good place to start. We can witness from creation and the gospel, knowing that God is revealing himself through both; we are not without a witness of God. The place to begin is God's declaration that he reveals himself to everyone through creation rather than their appreciation or belief that he does (Rom 1:18–24).[1]

We find this practice in the New Testament. Paul and Barnabas called on people to repent by turning to the creator saying, "Men, why are you doing these things? We are also men of the same nature as you, and preach the gospel to you that you should turn from these vain things to a living God, who made the heaven and the earth and the sea and all that is in them. In the generations gone by He permitted all the nations to go their own ways; and yet He did not leave Himself without witness, in that He did good and gave you rains from heaven and fruitful seasons, satisfying your hearts with food and gladness" (Acts 14:15–17). Not only did they refer to God as

---

1. Some contend the arguments between Creationists and Darwinists are unimportant to our responsibility to evangelize and advance the kingdom. Such a belief does not seem to be consistent with the New Testament (Rom 1:18–24; Acts 14:15–17; 17:24–31; Rev 14 6–7).

creator, but also referred to his creation as being a perennial "witness" to himself. The witness of God's goodness in creation is so evident one must fight to suppress the obvious witness to the creator through philosophies, science, or one of the countless man-made fabrications.

We find this same reliance upon the testimony of creation when Paul preached to the Athenians:

> The God who made the world and all things in it, since He is Lord of heaven and earth, does not dwell in temples made with hands; nor is He served by human hands, as though He needed anything, since He Himself gives to all people life and breath and all things; and He made from one man every nation of mankind to live on all the face of the earth, having determined their appointed times and the boundaries of their habitation, that they would seek God, if perhaps they might grope for Him and find Him, though He is not far from each one of us; for in Him we live and move and exist, as even some of your own poets have said, 'For we also are His children.' Being then the children of God, we ought not to think that the Divine Nature is like gold or silver or stone, an image formed by the art and thought of man. Therefore having overlooked the times of ignorance, God is now declaring to men that all people everywhere should repent, because He has fixed a day in which He will judge the world in righteousness through a Man whom He has appointed, having furnished proof to all men by raising Him from the dead (Acts 17:24–31).

Similarly, we find the angels declaring the eternal gospel in the book of Revelation. They present the one to believe in as the Creator. It says, "And I saw another angel flying in midheaven, having an eternal gospel to preach to those who live on the earth, and to every nation and tribe and tongue and people; and he said with a loud voice, 'Fear God, and give Him glory, because the hour of His judgment has come; worship Him who made the heaven and the earth and sea and springs of waters'" (Rev 14:6–7). They warn of the swiftly coming wrath of God, which is the impetus for all to "fear God and give Him glory." Verse 6 refers to this as an eternal gospel, and verse 7 seems to explain what the eternal gospel is.

Based upon this passage, I believe the eternal gospel is the call of God to all people, in all dispensations, to "fear God and give Him glory" and to "worship" the creator and thereby flee the hour of judgment. It is the call to every person, but now in the time period of Revelation, there is an even greater urgency "because the hour of His judgment has come." God's call to repentance and faith had less specificity as we have seen in the Old Testament and in these verses as well as Romans 1:18–25. But the call to give him glory is consistent and the only way fallen humans can do that is by repentance and faith.

The eternal gospel is based upon the death, burial, and resurrection of Jesus Christ for the sins of man. Its efficacy in delivering people from their just deserts under the eternal wrath of God preceded the death, burial, and resurrection in time as undeniably attested by the salvation of those in the Old Testament who repented and placed their faith in God (Hebrews 11). They simply repented and trusted God and his plan over their own to the degree of specificity revealed at that point in the history of progressive revelation, which has been and will forever be true. Since the coming of Christ, the level of specificity is at its zenith. It appears that many in the tribulation will have heard the gospel of Jesus Christ, either prior to the onset of the tribulation or from the Jewish evangelists and their converts (Rev 7:4-8; 12:17; 14:1-5) and the two witnesses (Rev 11:1-12).

This gospel is eternal because it warns of eternal judgment upon all sinners, and it provides the only path of deliverance from eternal death to eternal life. It is eternal because God's redemptive plan of salvation never changes. It is based upon the work of Christ. The eternal gospel always calls upon every person to recognize he is a hopeless sinner, deserving of eternal damnation, and that God who is the creator of everything has provided the only way to avoid our just deserts by repentance and faith. Repentance and faith are always grace enabled and toward God, but the specificity of the content of our faith increases as God reveals more of his redemptive plan culminating in the coming of Christ.

Prior to the actual work of Christ, repentance and faith in Jehovah, the one true God, was sufficient, but since the work of Christ, it requires believing in the name of Jesus (Acts 4:10-12). The eternal gospel constantly declares the bad news, which is everyone is a sinner under the wrath of God (John 3:18). This along with the good news, which is God has sufficiently provided for everyone to find forgiveness and eternal life by believing this good news from the creator, and by repentance and faith anyone can be delivered from our condign eternal punishment and be given eternal life by the creator of all things.

It appears we find a form (the necessary components) of the eternal gospel even in the Garden of Eden. God created man to enjoy him and his creation, which was good (Gen 1:31; 2:9, 21-25). That is the first good news if you will. Man was created to relate to God and enjoy the blessings of creation that were conditioned upon trusting what God said as seen in the one prohibition against eating of the tree of the knowledge of good and evil (Gen 2:17). In creation, the good news preceded the bad; that is to say, God gave what was good but warned that a failure to give him glory by not trusting him as the creator would result in judgment, death. The message was to trust in the creator and avoid his wrath against sin.

We find Adam and Eve chose to distrust God. They chose to trust the deception of the serpent and their own assessment of reality over God's assessment. In doing so, they both sinned (Gen 3:1–6). They exchanged God's plan for their own plan of how they might relate to him and his creation. They continued on this path as they hid in fear and sought to rectify their situation through their own plan of redemption (Gen 3:7–10). Prior to sin, the eternal gospel conditioned blessing upon faith and placed blessing prior to the warning of judgment.

Subsequent to the choice of Adam and Eve to go their own way, distrust God's word and plan, we find the order of blessing and judgment reversed throughout both the Old Testament and New Testament. We find God pronouncing man under judgment for his sin (Gen 3:14–19, 22–24). Notice God does this even after man had implemented his own redemption plan (Gen 3:7). The eternal gospel always contains the components of faith in God, which gives him glory as creator, and the warning he will judge sin.[2] The only path to avoid judgment by God was for Adam and Eve to walk in trust of his word. The only way back from sin is to trust God's promise of restoration by faith in his salvation plan. This plan was given to Adam and Eve with sufficient specificity to call on them to repent and believe in God (Gen 3:15).

We have seen this same message throughout the Old Testament as we saw in chapter 31. In the New Testament, we see it in the preaching of John the Baptist when he said to the Pharisees, "Who warned you to flee from the wrath to come" (Matt 3:7), and his message was to repent (Matt 3:2). Jesus gave the same message to Chorazin and Bethsaida (Matt 11:20–24). It is seen when he denounced the Pharisees for their stubbornness that far exceeded pagan Nineveh (Matt 12:38–42). He gave the same warning to people when he referred to sinful Galileans and those upon whom the tower of Siloam fell (Luke 13:1–5). The components of judgment and giving God glory are seen in John 3:18 and the most well-known verse in Scripture, "For God so loved the world, that He gave His only begotten Son, that whoever believes in Him shall not perish, but have eternal life" (John 3:16).

The eternal gospel is eternal in that it is the only plan that grants man eternal life, and the essential elements of God's plan have never changed. Man is to "fear God and give Him glory" by repenting and trusting the creator of everything and by so doing receive eternal life, or he may reject the call of

---

2. Gives him glory means we recognize his glory; to believe and live so that we give all praise to him alone.

the creator and suffer his eternal wrath against sin. Every offer of receiving eternal life since the fall has been based upon the salvific work of Christ, and in this age, one's faith must be in Jesus specifically (Acts 2:41).

Paige Patterson notes, "Men are called upon to worship him who is the Creator God. There is a sense in which Gen 1:1 is the most important verse in the Bible. The simple statement, "In the beginning God created the heavens and the earth," establishes not merely the origin of all things but as such establishes both the ownership and the purposes of him who is the Creator .... If ... God is the Creator and owner of all that exists, then the only appropriate response of any human is to worship God, fear him, and give him glory."[3] Regarding the urgency in the call to give God glory, Patterson says, "Judgment is at hand, but even in judgment God is merciful and loving; and this fact is poignantly portrayed in the angel's crossing the heavens once again with the eternal gospel for all who live on the earth."[4] The call of the eternal gospel is always to repent, believe, and worship the Creator, and that judgment upon sin is certain and the time of such judgment is uncertain with man (Matt 24:38–39).

MacArthur poignantly comments, "God's natural revelation of Himself is not obscure or selective, observable only by a few perceptive souls who are specially gifted. His revelation of Himself through creation can be clearly seen."[5] Some commentators say the eternal gospel is just a message of judgment.[6] But that seems to require minimizing or ignoring the call of the angel for people to "fear God and give Him glory." The urgency of the message and the coupling of the call to "give God glory" is the same essential call given to all throughout time. Each time and in each revelatory season the call gives every indication of being one that can and should be obeyed. Subsequent to the death of Christ, one can only give God glory by repentance and faith in Christ; therefore, this is a call to repent and believe in Jesus Christ, the gospel.

The time of this declaration by the angel reminds us that even in the worst of times, God declares his message of deliverance for any and all who will repent and believe. R.C.H. Lenski says "The gospel is for all men. 'This

---

3. Patterson, *Revelation*, 290–91.
4. Patterson, *Revelation*, 291.
5. MacArthur, *Romans 1–8*, 79.
6. John Walvoord says, "Because of the word 'gospel,' some have felt that this was a message of salvation or the good news of the coming kingdom. The context, however, seems to indicate otherwise, for the message is one of judgment and condemnation. The angel announced, Fear God and give Him glory, because the hour of His judgment has come. So the 'eternal' message seems to be a message of God's righteousness and judgment rather than a message of salvation." Walvoord, "Revelation," 964.

gospel of the kingdom shall be preached in all the world for a witness to all nations' (Matt. 24:14) despite all that the devil can do."[7] Even though Lenski and others believe the angel to be Martin Luther, which I do not, they agree it is the gospel unto salvation.[8] As Calvinist Kistemaker says:

> The angel proclaims the gospel not necessarily as good news but as a reminder of God's abiding truth; the angel calls men and women to respond to God's message before the judgment comes. The expression 'every nation, tribe, language, and people' occurs repeatedly in Revelation and alludes to unrepentant residents on this earth who are inimical to God (compare 11:9; 13:7; 17:15) . . . and to people everywhere who are being called to repent (10:11). Here the angel addresses a message of repentance to all sinners who have been indifferent to God and his Word, as is evident from the angel's message.[9]

I disagree that the call to respond to God's message prior to his judgment is "not necessarily as good news." The call to give God glory is a call to salvation by repentance and faith in Jesus Christ because it is only then that a sinner can give God glory. It is a warning of impending wrath, which can be escaped only by repentance and faith; this is the eternal gospel found throughout Scripture. It is the good news that will one day cease to be proclaimed. So long as it echoes through the heavens and pathways upon the earth, it is good news which one can heed. Bow before the creator and give him his deserved glory; this is precisely what Adam and Eve failed to do in sin and prayerfully did do in accepting God's provisionary plan of redemption (Gen 3:15, 21). MacArthur states what I have sought to demonstrate.

> The eternal gospel preached by the angel is the same one proclaimed throughout all history. It is the good news of forgiveness and eternal life. He will declare that people are sinners, facing eternal judgment in hell, but that God has provided atonement for sins through the sacrificial death of the Lord Jesus Christ. That message of forgiveness was given even in Old

---

7. Lenski, *St. John's Revelation*, 428.

8. Lenski says, "The angel has an εὐαγγέλιον αἰώνιον εὐαγγελίσαι; the noun and the infinitive repeat and thus emphasize the gospel and the idea of good news. We need not ask what this gospel is, for its content is stated in v. 7. The older Protestants regarded this first angel flying in midheaven as a prophecy of Luther and his gospel, and to this day Rev. 14:6, 7 is the regular pericope for Reformation Day. Sometimes it was thought that Luther was prefigured by the third angel. The other two were thought to be Wycliff and Huss. When commentators reject this interpretation they do so without sufficient reason." Lenski, *St. John's Revelation*, 428.

9. Kistemaker, *Exposition of Revelation*, 407–8.

Testament times based on new covenant terms (Jer. 31:31–34; Ezek. 36:25–27). Its benefits were applied to all who truly repented and sought forgiveness and grace from God, even though the Savior had not yet died. In the purpose of God, the merits of the Lamb slain at Calvary have been granted to all true repenters in all ages.[10]

Creation serves not only as a witness to the lost but also to strengthen the saved. Ard Lewis is a theoretical physicist at Oxford University. When I was on sabbatical in Oxford during the summer of 2015, I heard him interviewed by Eric Metaxas. He spoke freely of his Christian faith and how his experience as a scientist increased his faith in God. He said about twenty of his colleagues in the physics department were strong Christians. After the interview, he told me the head of the physics department at Oxford was a strong Christian as well.[11] John C. Lennox, a mathematics professor at Oxford, states, "The beauty of the scientific laws reinforces my faith in an intelligent, divine creator."[12] David declared, "The heavens are telling of the glory of God; And their expanse is declaring the work of His hands" (Ps 19:1).

The heavens, creation, and the glory of the universe declare there is one outside of the universe more glorious. The power of nature declares there is one more powerful who gave nature its power. This message rings out to every nation, every person, every day, and it is a declaration by God to worship the creator and not creation. The message is so loud and clear it affords every person an opportunity to know him personally; an opportunity so compelling it leaves every person without excuse (Rom 1:20). It is a declaration so powerful that to resist it requires relentless suppression in a mental and spiritual sea of ungodliness (Rom 1:18–19). Men continually develop new plans and revive old schemes and false ideas in order to intellectually and spiritually suppress the truth. Even though it is true David was a believer, Romans 1:18–25 expands the accessibility of this knowledge far beyond believers to include every single person so that none has an excuse.

That Satan blinds people to the gospel and sin imprisons man in spiritual darkness does not thwart God's work of general and special revelation. God's light cannot be overcome by darkness (John 1:5). God reaches into darkness with the light of the knowledge of himself through the witness of his creation; if men accept that light, which they can do, God will get the

---

10. MacArthur, *Revelation 12–22*, 86.

11. The live event, called Socrates in the City, was hosted by Eric Metaxas in Oxford July 22, 2015.

12. Lennox, *God and Stephen Hawking*, 73.

light of the gospel to them, which penetrates the blinders of Satan and the darkness of sin (John 12:35–36).[13]

As the light of the world, Christ enlightens all men (John 1:9), Christ prayed for all, (John 17:20–21), and the Holy Spirit convicts all (John 16:8–11). Ezekiel reminds us, "'As I live!' declares the Lord God, 'I take no pleasure in the death of the wicked, but rather that the wicked turn from his way and live" (Ezek 33:11). God does not desire "for any to perish but for all to come to repentance" (2 Pet 3:9). God can, by grace, be found. The Lord promised through Jeremiah, "You will seek Me and find me, when you search for Me with all your heart" (Jer 29:13). Truly salvation has indeed appeared to all men (Titus 2:11).

---

13. This is not to say a person must wrestle with general revelation before he can be saved by the gospel. It is to say that if one accepts God's general revelation, which everyone can do because it is so compelling that it leaves everyone "without excuse" (Rom 1:20), God who desires all to be saved will get the gospel to him.

Appendix 1

The Order of Elective Decrees

THE TERM *DECREE* SPEAKS of what God from eternity past predetermined to be in time. As used here, it refers to what he predetermined with regard to his plan of salvation.[1] The arrangement of the decrees is a logical one rather than chronological. This means the full plan of salvation is one thought in the mind of God which includes a cause and effect relationship between the five decrees.

There are four approaches to the relationship of the individual decrees. They are *supralapsarian, infralapsarian, sublapsarian,* and *Arminian.* Various classes of Calvinists align with the first three. Arminianism is the same as *infralapsarian* but it includes faith as a grace-enabled act of man that is comprehended in God's elective plan so that election is not unconditional election.[2] The word *lapsarian* refers to one who believes in the doctrine that man is a fallen being.[3]

The Supralapsarian Perspective

This includes those who are often referred to as Hyper-Calvinists or Ultra-Calvinists. The order as defended by the supralapsarian is:

1. Decree to elect some to be saved and to reprobate all others.
2. Decree to create men, both the elect and non-elect.
3. Decree to permit the fall.
4. Decree to provide salvation for the elect.
5. Decree to apply salvation to the elect.

[1]. The decretal order of the four perspectives is taken from Chafer's *Systematic Theology*. For a more thorough explanation of the decrees see Lewis Sperry Chafer, *Systematic Theology*, vol. 3, 177–80.

[2]. I use grace enabled, but the more common term in Arminianism is prevenient grace.

[3]. Chafer, *Systematic Theology*, vol. 3, 178.

This perspective is deemed Hyper because it places the decree to elect and reprobate prior to creation.

The Infralapsarian Perspective

This view is reflective of those who are often called moderate Calvinists. The order as defended by the infralapsarian is:

1. Decree to create all men.
2. Decree to permit the fall.
3. Decree to provide salvation for men.
4. Decree to elect those who do believe and to leave in just condemnation all who do not believe.
5. Decree to apply salvation to those who believe.

Note the decree to elect some and leave others to damnation follows the fall, whereas according to the Supralapsarian perspective, election precedes both the fall and creation. Importantly, number (4), as understood in Calvinism is actually the result of unconditional election and the irresistible and efficacious call of God that is only extended to the unconditionally elect, which also precedes faith.

The Sublapsarian Perspective

This view is reflective of those who are also called moderate Calvinists. The order defended by the sublapsarian is:

1. Decree to create all men.
2. Decree to permit the fall.
3. Decree to elect those who do believe and to leave in just condemnation those who do not believe.
4. Decree to provide salvation for men.
5. Decree to apply salvation to those who believe.

Note the decree to elect precedes the decree to provide salvation. Lewis Sperry Chafer distinguishes this from infralapsarian saying, "Technically, the infralapsarians place election after the decree to provide salvation . . . The sublapsarians are identified by the placing of the decree to elect to follow the decree to permit the fall. In general, the sublapsarian order is a refutation of the supralapsarian order."[4]

The three schools of Calvinism all agree that election is the sovereign unconditional monergistic work of God in which the faith of man is consequent to unconditional election. Arminianism contends that election involves a requirement for man to exercise faith, which makes election consequent to faith.

Calvinism's commitment to unconditional election means the decree to elect those who believe and to leave in just condemnation those who do not believe is a belief that is consequent, and therefore subsequent to unconditional election and the irresistible and efficacious call of God rather than as it appears to be in the statements. The view that God elects or applies salvation to those who first exercise faith is true of Arminianism and Extensivism but not Calvinism. These two decrees of Calvinism are (3) in sublapsarians and (4) in infralapsarianism along with the decree to apply salvation to those who believe (5) in both sublapsarian and infralapsarian.

As an Extensivist, I argue that discussing the order of decrees more often than not simply confuses the dialogue between Calvinists and Extensivists. This is because, in all three Calvinists' perspectives, God is the sole determiner of those who are the unconditionally elect and those who make up the non-elect; this only because it pleased him to elect the ones he did and equally pleased him to reprobate others. To wit, eternal destinies do not depend one iota on man's faith, but rather exclusively on whom God wanted in heaven and whom he wanted in hell. Since he has always known this, it is accurate to say God created some, knowing they would spend eternity in hell, because he is pleased to have predetermined that end for them. The order of decrees does not affect who is in heaven and who is in hell because the eternal destiny of every person is unalterably determined by what pleased God.

Since God knows everything and salvation is one eternal thought in the mind of God, the order of decrees does not change or soften this truth. While the order of decrees may have some relevance in distinguishing one form of Calvinism from another, the order of decrees is not really helpful in determining the most pressing issues regarding the doctrine of salvation between Calvinists and Extensivists; it can actually be a hindrance if it obscures the reality of and place of unconditional election. Let me add, those who are not Calvinists do not believe man is saved by human merit or works, Calvinists' claims to the contrary notwithstanding.[5] Moreover, the order of decrees does

---

4. Chafer, *Systematic Theology*, vol. 3, 181.

5. Chafer says, "It will be observed from the foregoing that the differences represented in these various orders of decrees, though they seem highly speculative to some, do represent vital doctrine at its very foundation. The three schools of Calvinists

nothing to mitigate the reality that all consistent Calvinists believe in double predestination, not merely the hyper-Calvinists as is often thought.

---

contend alike that divine election is the sovereign choice of God which expresses His grace apart from every form of human works foreseen or actual; and that the Arminian school, by making election to be no more than foreknowledge of human merit, asserts that, in the end, man elects himself by his faith and obedience. The Calvinistic schools are the result of a faithful induction of the Word of God bearing on the elective decrees, whereas the Arminian school is an intrusion of human reason." Chafer, *Systematic Theology*, vol. 3, 182.

Appendix 2

Leigh Vicens on Theological Determinism

"But if God knows the future exhaustively, theological determinists argue, then all future events must be determined, directly or indirectly, by God. The reasoning they offer in support of this argument can be considered in two steps. First is the claim that for a future event e to be known at some time t (say, "in the beginning"), e must be determined at or prior to t. Otherwise, there would be no truth about e to be known at t. The second claim is that if all future events are determined from the beginning of time, they must ultimately be so by God since nothing else existed in the beginning to determine them. This is not to say that God's knowledge is causal, in the sense that simply by knowing something, God is the cause of that thing. Rather, proponents of this line of reasoning contend that God cannot know a proposition unless it is true; and the proposition that some event will occur cannot be true at some time, unless that event is determined by that time; but then if God knows that some event will occur when nothing but God exists, it must be God himself who ultimately determines the event's occurrence."[6]

Of course, this presupposes that God could not have always determined to create definite events (not affected by human choice) as well as indefinite events (affected by human choice) and necessarily knowing the entailments of such events because he is essentially omniscient. Extensivism argues that if God did always determine to create indefinite events, contingencies, God would know them as well as definite events because he determined they would exist in his eternal omniscience. He knows himself and his intentions exhaustively. He cannot fail to know himself, including his intentions. He eternally knows every potentiality and every potentiality that he intended to actualize in time and all that would include. While he apparently determined some definite events, the only determined thing required for God to create a world with contingencies, and know what those contingencies would be in time, is that he determines to do so. In which case, both types of events, and their entailments, always existed in the eternal mind of God.

6. Vicens,"Theological Determinism," under the heading "Arguments for Theological Determinism" par. 2.

Appendix 3

A Guide for Determining a Pastoral Candidate's Level of Commitment to Calvinism[1]

THE SELECTION OF A pastor may very well be the most important single decision a church makes. This questionnaire is designed to assist churches who seek to avoid calling a pastor who either is a Calvinist or has strong leanings in that direction, which is often referred to as Calvinistic. Determining whether a person is Calvinistic can be a difficult task for a pastoral search committee. The lack of certainty of a candidate's belief can result in Extensivist churches extending a call to a Calvinist candidate, which results in harm to the body of Christ. Such harm can be avoided by asking the right questions.

Although a certain level of precision is required in formulating the questions in order to avoid mistakes, unnecessary technical language has been omitted. Yes answers to the first six questions and the no answers to the last three questions reflect the general teachings of Calvinism. It is not uncommon to find those who embrace Calvinism to be inconsistent in their answers. This may be due to a lack of sufficient understanding of what a commitment to Calvinism includes or because of a lack of forthrightness in expressing his beliefs in the interview process.

I offer the following guidelines for using the questionnaire. First, the committee needs to ask, and repeat if necessary, the question *precisely* as written. Doing so will help keep the conversation focused on the question being asked. This will enable the committee to better understand the candidate's position; otherwise, the committee may find itself discussing topics not included in the precise question. Second, each question is written so as to be easily answered by a simple *yes* or *no*. In order to avoid a response that may fail to answer adequately the *specific* question, follow-up comments

---

[1]. The questions in this guide can also assess any person's level of commitment to the *actual* beliefs of Calvinism; a person may claim to be a Calvinist, but, in reality, is an Extensivist.

should be delayed until after the committee has obtained a clear *yes* or *no* answer. Third, the "Meaning" in italics listed under each question is to assist the committee in better understanding the nature of the question. Fourth, an Extensivist can readily answer *no* to the first six questions and *yes* to the last three. The degree of understanding and preference for Calvinism is best indicated by the number of times the candidate fails to answer as the questionnaire indicates an Extensivist would answer.[2]

1. Do you believe in unconditional election?
    i. *Meaning while all people have the responsibility to respond to the Gospel, only those whom God has sovereignly and unconditionally elected to salvation can or will believe unto salvation.*
    ii. Calvinists say Yes.
    iii. Extensivists say No.
2. Do you believe regeneration[3] is monergistic?[4]
    i. *Meaning until a lost person is regenerated he is totally passive with regard to exercising faith.*
    ii. Calvinists say Yes.
    iii. Extensivists say No.
3. Do you believe regeneration precedes faith?[5]
    i. *Meaning faith results from regeneration rather than preceding regeneration.*
    ii. Calvinists say Yes.
    iii. Extensivists say No.
4. Do you believe only the unconditionally elect will experience regeneration?
    i. *Meaning God selectively and exclusively applies regeneration to only the unconditionally elect.*
    ii. Calvinists say Yes.
    iii. Extensivists say No.

---

2. Extensivist is used broadly to mean non-Calvinist.
3. Usually understood to mean born again
4. This means God alone brings about regeneration in the elect without any cooperation or activity by man; consequently, being born again is not dependent upon man exercising faith.
5. Not all Calvinists ascribe to this, but most in SBC life do; all Extensivists reject it.

5. Do you believe there is an internal efficacious call of God extended only to the elect?[6]
   i. Meaning this is the essential and irresistible call given by God to the elect that inevitably results in salvation, and this same call is withheld by God from the non-elect.
   ii. Calvinists say Yes.
   iii. Extensivists say No.
6. Do you believe making regeneration or salvation depend upon a person's faith in Christ is equivalent to adding human works, merit, or virtue to salvation?[7]
   i. Meaning Calvinism's belief in unconditional election gives God all the glory (credit), and Extensivism's belief that salvation is conditioned upon faith gives man some of the glory (credit) for his salvation.
   ii. Calvinists say Yes.
   iii. Extensivists say No.
7. Do you believe both God's saving desire and his will *agree* that his salvation plan provides everything necessary for every single person to *actually* be saved by faith?[8]
   i. Meaning God's decrees and his saving desire equally prove everyone and anyone who hears the gospel can truly be saved by faith.
   ii. Calvinists say No.
   iii. Extensivists say Yes.
8. Do you believe anyone and everyone who hears the gospel is, by the grace of God, able to freely respond by faith unto salvation or to freely reject the gospel, and whichever choice the person makes, he was equally able to have made the other choice?
   i. Meaning God graciously provides in order to make both options accessible to every person.
   ii. Calvinists say No.

6. "Efficacious" means that it is absolutely successful in securing salvation for those who receive it—the unconditionally elect. Oftentimes this is used interchangeably or cooperatively with the belief in "irresistible grace."

7. Some Calvinists may not say yes, but this is a common statement of Calvinists against Extensivists.

8. Sometimes Calvinists say they believe God has a universal desire to save everyone, while simultaneously believing God's decrees override that desire. This question is designed to help avoid such an inconsistent and confusing answer.

      iii. Extensivists say Yes.

9. Do you believe Christ's death atoned for the sins of every person in the world *in the same way* so that anyone and everyone can believe and be saved?[9]

      i. Meaning Christ's death actually paid for every sin of every person thereby removing the obstacle of a person's sin so that every person has the same opportunity to believe the gospel and be saved.

      ii. Calvinists say No.

      iii. Extensivists say Yes.

---

9. An Extensivist and a four-point Calvinist can say yes, but a five-point Calvinist will say no.

Appendix 4

A Response to Calvinists' Attempt to Moderate the Sequential Order of Regeneration and Faith

REGARDING CALVINISTS WHO BELIEVE regeneration precedes faith, Jeremy A. Evans says, "This relationship is intended to be understood logically, not temporally. Temporally, the cause and effect relationship occurs simultaneously; logically, regeneration occurs before faith."[1] David Allen similarly notes, "A majority of Calvinists argue that temporally, regeneration and conversion are simultaneous events. But they often see a necessary logical order."[2] R.C. Sproul says, "When Reformed theology says regeneration precedes faith, it is speaking in terms of logical priority, not temporal priority. We cannot exercise saving faith until we have been regenerated, so we say faith is dependent on regeneration, not regeneration on faith."[3] Elsewhere Sproul seems to make regeneration more than a merely a necessary condition; he says, "We do not believe in order to be born again; we are born again in order to believe."[4]

I contend that regeneration is both logically and temporally prior to faith for Calvinists who believe in the prerequisite of regeneration for faith. Important to keep in mind, the claim that something is logically prior and not temporally prior does not make it so.[5] We may think of logical priority as meaning one thing serves to explain another thing; it provides a basis for

---

1. Evans, "Reflections on Determinism," 259.
2. Allen, "Does Regeneration Precede Faith?" 35.
3. Sproul, *What is Reformed Theology?*, 228.
4. Sproul, *Chosen by God*, 72–73.
5. Calvinists will often contend that if there is not a temporal simultaneousness with regeneration and faith, a person would be regenerate without being a believer. First, this is a problem generated not from the Scripture, but from Calvinism, a problem which does not exist in Extensivism. Second, the Scripture regularly portrays aspects of salvation sequentially (John 3:16). When someone is saved, he is not glorified until a future time (Rom 8:17, 30).

the other thing. At times, I find it helpful to think of logical priority as being informationally prior. For example, one may say printed words on a page are logically prior to a book, but it is equally true that words on a page do not cause a book; they are just a necessary condition if one is going to have a book. Also, they both logically and temporally precede a book.

Similarly, that something is logically prior does not necessitate a certain effect or even a certain cause and effect relationship; for example, oxygen is essential to fire (logically prior), but it does not necessarily cause a fire; it merely explains one of the necessary factors for the fire to exist. If a match is lit or starts a house fire, it may be the match was struck in the presence of oxygen and then dropped that caused the house to burn. One could logically have oxygen forever (or a match, something to strike it on and one who could strike it for that matter) without a fire, but one cannot have fire without oxygen; it is logically prior, and there is no essential cause and effect relationship between oxygen and fire. Therefore, we see that a logical priority can exist without a necessary effect, which is not true of the relationship between regeneration and faith.

Additionally, something may be both logically and temporally prior because these are not mutually exclusive categories (this clarification is usually lacking in most Calvinists' distinctions between logical and temporal priority). For example, John C. Lennox points out that verses like John 1:12 and 5:40 "involve a temporal priority that is simultaneously logical."[6] This seems particularly true in relationships in which there is an intrinsic cause and effect relationship. That is to say; a relationship exists in which the cause necessarily precedes the result (effect), and the result unalterably takes place because of the presence of the cause, logically and temporally speaking. To wit, the presence of one always includes the presence of the other in the same sequence; the relationship is absolute.

The very nature of a cause and effect relationship is that the cause is necessarily prior to the effect. To say a cause and effect are temporally simultaneous is nonsense. David Allen says, "How can an effect be logically prior to its cause? How can an effect be temporally simultaneous with its cause? . . . What sense does it make to say that something is 'logically' prior but not 'temporally' prior?"[7] Regarding regeneration and faith, there is an intrinsic and unalterable temporal cause and effect relationship when Calvinists maintain faith cannot be prior to regeneration and faith always results from

---

6. Lennox, *Determined to Believe*, 191.

7. He is commenting specifically on R.C. Sproul's statement, "Dead men do not cooperate with grace . . . Unless regeneration takes place first, there is no possibility of faith." Sproul, Mystery of the Holy Spirit, 105.

regeneration. Those who believe this commonly speak of regeneration being first, causing or resulting in faith.[8] Wayne Grudem gives an example:

> We have defined regeneration to be the act of God awakening spiritual life within us, bringing us from spiritual *death* to spiritual *life*. On this definition, it is natural to understand that regeneration comes before saving faith. . . . However, when we say that it comes 'before' saving faith . . . they usually come so close together that it will ordinarily seem to us that they are happening at the same time. As God addresses the effective call of the gospel to us, he regenerates us and we respond in faith and repentance to this call. There are several passages that tell us that this secret, hidden work of God in our spirits does in fact come before we respond to God in saving faith (though often it may be only seconds before we respond).[9]

Calvinist Matt Slick gives an illustration intended to demonstrate regeneration is logically prior but not temporally prior to faith. He illustrates it this way, "In a light bulb, electricity must be in place in order for light to occur. . . . Therefore, the electricity is logically first, but not temporally first because when the electricity is present, light is the necessary and simultaneous result. . . .When regeneration is in place, faith is the necessary and simultaneous result. . . . As with the light bulb and electricity, one is logically prior to the other even though they are simultaneous."[10]

I believe the illustration requires one clarification and one correction. The clarification, unlike regeneration and faith which are always found together (the cause, effect sequence is absolute), electricity and a lit bulb are not; not even electricity and light. One could have electricity without the bulb lighting or anything else giving off light; this is because while electricity does cause the bulb to light when properly channeled, there is not an absolute cause and effect relationship between the two; there is only an absolute relationship requiring the necessary priority of electricity. Therefore, the presence of electricity could exist forever without producing light, which is not true of regeneration and faith as designed by God according to Calvinism. This means the relationship between electricity and light is technically disanalogous to regeneration and faith.

---

8. See chapters 11 and 12 for quotes by Calvinists that place regeneration temporally before faith. See also David's Allen's article "Does Regeneration Precede Faith?" for others, http://baptistcenter.net/journals/JBTM_11-2_Fall_2014.pdf.

9. Wayne Grudem, *Systematic Theology*, 702.

10. Slick, "Does Regeneration Precede Faith," par. 4 & 5.

APPENDIX 4: MODERATING THE ORDER OF REGENERATION AND FAITH

The correction, regarding the specific presence of electricity "in a light bulb"; the light does not seem to be precisely "simultaneous" to the presence of electricity since light is a "result" (effect) of the cause—received electricity. The bulb lights up when an electric current is run through a filament of wire; when the electricity heats up the wire to a certain point, it begins to emit photons; photons are small packages of visible light.

Even if the time between the presence of electricity and the bulb lighting is a nanosecond (one billionth of a second), which makes the sequence undetectable by a human, it is still present because it is essential to a cause and effect relationship. Thus, it seems to me; this illustration demonstrates my point that regeneration is both logically and temporally prior to faith. One more consideration that demonstrates both a logical and temporal priority of regeneration and faith is they are not only essentially related (always found together in the same sequence), but, according to compatibilism and God's predetermined design, they are deterministically related. That is to say, faith is the determined result, effect, of regeneration. This means every time faith is present, it is, in fact, the absolute and determined purpose that results from the presence of regeneration. There are no misfires in regeneration, and there is never a time when regeneration takes place in a person's life that does not result in faith; their relationship is inviolable, according to Calvinism.

Therefore, based upon the terminology used by Calvinists, the fact that a logical priority can exist without a necessary effect, that something can be both logically and temporally prior, and that there is an immediate and unalterably determined cause and effect relationship between regeneration and faith, it seems best to recognize regeneration is both a logical and temporally prior causal condition for faith (for Calvinists who believe faith cannot happen without regeneration and regeneration always results in faith). Simply put, since the mere presence of regeneration always results in faith, and faith never precedes or results in regeneration in time and space, we are safe to say regeneration is not only logically prior but temporally and causally prior as well.

The fact is Calvinists (who believe in the prerequisite of regeneration for faith) affirm faith cannot happen without a person being regenerated, and faith will always result from regeneration, which means regeneration happens first both logically and temporally; regeneration is the cause and faith is the effect. The cause and effect are not simultaneous since the very nature of an effect is that there exists a preceding sufficient cause.

The point of their insistence upon logical priority without temporal priority only has biblical meaning if the Calvinist can answer yes to the following questions. First, can a lost sinner exercise saving faith in Christ without having been regenerated—quickened, restored? Second, can regeneration be present without resulting in faith? If they cannot answer yes to these two questions, the distinction simply obscures the reality of the prerequisite of regeneration in time and space because there exists an inextricable sequential cause and effect relationship. To state it a little differently, Extensivism believes man's faith is the prerequisite for regeneration both logically and temporally. This is something with which the Calvinist does not agree. Since the cause and effect cannot happen simultaneously in time, this distinction of logically prior but not temporally prior simply beclouds the dialogue.

Authorial Glossary

Agent Causation

"The idea that agents [people] can start new causal chains that are not *pre-determined* by the events of the immediate or distant past and the physical laws of nature."[1] I use interchangeably with *efficient cause*.

Certainty

Certainty refers to indefinite events that happen in time (contingencies); they are the result of otherwise choice of morally free beings. Because they are not the result of determinism, they happen certainly but not necessarily. God knows these events with certainty because he is essentially omniscient. Certain events do not require the absence of influences upon the person, but only that he is the libertarian efficient cause of the event.

Compatibilism

Compatibilism says determinism and moral freedom (responsibility) are compatible. A person is considered to make a free choice so long as he chooses according to his greatest desire. However, determinative antecedents establish his desires. So he makes a free choice (chooses based upon his greatest desire), but his desires were determined by his nature, past events, or God. Therefore, the person makes a pre-determined free choice. See chapter 7 for a full explanation.

Consequently, while he made a free *choice to* act or believe a certain way, he could not have chosen to do otherwise in the moral moment of decision given the same past.[2] Compatibilism includes voluntariness (person freely

---

1. Information Philosopher website, "Agent-Causality," par. 1.
2. At times I use the word choose instead of choice to emphasize the fact that compatibly-endowed people do not technically make a choice (implying the existence

choosing), but it does not include origination (ability to originate a new sequence of events) or what is known as agent causation.[3]

Constitutionally and Organically Related

Constitutionally related

Constitutionally related speaks to the nature of God's salvation plan wherein grace enablements are essentially, sequentially, and operationally incorporated into the structure of God's plan.

Organically related

Something being organically related speaks to the complex relationship between libertarian freedom and God's pre-conversion grace enablements working according to his salvific plan of grace so that the choices of a libertarian free being really do matter in a person's salvation. They have a systemic arrangement and interaction with other parts of God's plan (see also substantially related and insubstantially related below). See chapter 8 for a full explanation of these terms.

Definite Events

Definite events caused by God apart from the influence of man's otherwise choice. These events are predetermined by God; therefore, they happen *necessarily* (see *indefinite events* below).

Double Talk

This refers to the rhetorical practice of *many* Calvinists' practice of speaking, writing, and praying in such a way that actually obscures the determinism and disquieting realities of the beliefs and entailments of Calvinism and

---

of accessible options or creating new possibilities) but only freely choose the path determined by one's greatest desire. We can even say, the point of choosing is equally a point of awareness of the choosing that will be made according to the determined greatest desire.

3. Unfortunately, some compatibilists refer to agent causation without noting their meaning incorporates the idea that while the agent is the proximate cause of an event, his causing the event was indeed ultimately and unalterably caused; he freely chooses for an event to happen, but his free choice is the result of a desire that exists because of determinative antecedents. This is actually not what is meant by agent causation.

the inconsistencies between Scripture and Calvinism. The term does not include intentionality or ill motive.

Extensivism

Specifically, Extensivism believes man was created in the image of God with *otherwise choice* and God's salvation plan is comprehensive, involving an all-inclusive unconditional offer of salvation and eternal security of the believer; reception of which is conditioned upon *grace-enabled* faith rather than an exclusive plan involving a limited *actual* offer of salvation to *only* the unconditionally elected, or any plan that, in any way, conditions salvation upon merely a humanly-generated faith.

Extensivism may have some things in common with Calvinism, Arminianism, or Molinism, but does not rely upon any of them. Similarities do not equal sameness. Extensivism seeks only to present a comprehensive, consistent system of soteriology that is reflective of the warp and woof of Scripture, which may have shared beliefs with other systems of soteriology, but *Extensivism* neither relies upon nor seeks to be consistent with them.

Generally, I use Extensivism as a positive term in place of non-Calvinism.

Efficient Cause

"An agent that brings a thing into being or indicates a change."[4] Moves something from potentiality to actuality. Involves the idea that one need look no further than the individual for the cause of the action. I use interchangeably with *agent causation*.

Essentially Dissimilar Things

Two things can have dissimilarities and be the same, whereas essential dissimilarities between them means they can only be similar; they cannot be the same. For example, you and I can both be humans (same beings), even though we may be dissimilar in various ways; we still have humanness, created in the image of God. In contrast, a chimpanzee can be similar to a human (some abilities and physical characteristics), but a chimpanzee cannot be a human being because we are essentially dissimilar; they are not created in the image of God.

---

4. *Oxford English Dictionary*, s.v. "Efficient Cause."

Essential Omniscience (see Omniscience)

Faith

Spiritual faith refers specifically to the act of trusting what God has said—revealed to man (Gen 2:17; Matt 8:8-10; John 3:1-3; Rom 3:22). Spiritual faith is a gift given by God in creation as are all the endowments of man. It is also a gift in the sense that God restores the ability to exercise spiritually-restorative faith as a sinner through the provision of grace enablements (John 12:35-36; Eph 2:8). It is not a gift in the Calvinist sense of being resultant of God's irresistible grace upon the unconditionally elect; understood to be so in part by a misreading of Eph 2:8.

Grace (contrasted)

Calvinism's work of grace

Limited to the unconditionally elected, determinative in outcome, and provided so the elect will believe. This work of grace changes the elect's past or gives them a new nature that emanates new desires—compatibilism.

Extensivism's work of grace

Available to every person, non-determinative in outcome, and provides so that everyone may choose to believe or reject God's salvation while still in their sins. This work of grace enables man to make spiritually restorative decisions, which ability was lost in the fall.

Grace Enablements

Includes but are not limited to: God's salvific love for all (John 3:16), God's manifestation of his power so that all may know he is the Sovereign (Isa 45:21-22) and Creator (Rom 1:18-20), which assures that everyone has opportunity to know about him. Christ paying for all sins (John 1:29), conviction of the Holy Spirit (John 16:7-11), working of the Holy Spirit (Heb 6:1-6), enlightening of the Son (John 1:9), God's teaching (John 6:45), God opening minds and hearts (Luke 24:45; Acts 16:14; 26:17-18;), and the power of the gospel (Rom 1:16), without such redemptive grace, no one seeks or comes to God (Rom 3:11).[5]

---

5. Christ opened their minds in Luke by teaching and illumining the real meaning of Scripture (Luke 24:27), and we find the same with Lydia, who was a "worshiper of

Because of these gracious provisions and workings of God, man can choose to seek and find God (Jer 29:13; Acts 17:11–12). Moreover, no one can come to God without God calling (Acts 2:39), drawing (John 6:44), and that God is drawing all individuals (John 12:32). The same Greek word for draw, *helkuō*, is used in both verses. "About 115 passages condition salvation on believing alone, and about 35 simply on faith."[6] Other grace enablements may include providential workings in and through other people, situations, and timing or circumstances that are a part of grace to provide an opportunity for every individual to choose to follow Christ.[7]

These are grace enablements in at least three ways; first, they are provided by God's grace rather than deserved by mankind; second, the necessary components for *each and every* individual to have a genuine opportunity to believe unto salvation are provided or restored by God; third, they are provided by God without respect to whether the individual will believe or reject, which response God knew in eternity past.

The offer of the gospel is *unconditional*, but God sovereignly determined to condition the reception of the offer upon grace-enabled faith; therefore, faith is not reflective of a work or virtue of man, but of God's sovereign plan of salvation by grace through faith (Eph 2:8). This indicates faith is the means to being regenerated and saved, not the reason for being saved. This truth of Scripture does not imply God is held captive to the choice of man, but rather it demonstrates God in eternity coextensively determined to create man with otherwise choice and provide a genuine offer of salvation, which can be accepted by grace-enabled faith or rejected. Additionally,

---

God" (Acts 13:43; 18:7). She had faith as a proselyte, and God responded to that genuine faith by opening her heart to the gospel. God is always the initiator.

6. Chafer, *Systematic Theology*, vol. 7, 273–74.

7. In Matthew 13:18–23, Jesus explains the parable of the sower. He compares the four types of soils to the four kinds of responses to the gospel. In the parable, the seed is the word of God (gospel). Also, in the explanation of the true meaning of the parable, it is important to note the sower and the seed are always the same (there is no indication that he gives one hearer seed that will not germinate and another the real thing), and the only thing that changes is the response to the seed. There is nothing deficient in the sowing or the seed sown, but rather always the problem is in the recipient. Also notice the response of the good soil precedes regeneration. There is no indication in the passage that some men are predetermined by God to reject the message. Rather, it seems all four had different responses to the message, and the soil is descriptive of the heart; neither the ones that accept nor the ones that reject the seed give any indication of being predetermined. The soil indicates different responses and outcomes to the same seed, which is the word about the kingdom. Just as God created Adam with good soil, so he must grace enable everyone to be able to respond. Therefore, salvation is not a human work, nor is the good soil something innate to some, but rather it is characteristic of everyone who receives the word of God and by faith is born again.

to fulfill this plan, God is not obligated to disseminate the gospel to people he knows have rejected the light he has given them (Rom 1:18–23) and will also reject the gospel; although he may still send the gospel to them.

Indefinite Events

Indefinite events are influenced in some measure by man's otherwise choice. These events are not predetermined by God. They are known by God and happen *certainly* because he is essentially omniscient, but they could have been different had the person chosen to act differently. They are contingencies.

Libertarianism

Libertarian freedom says determinism and moral responsibility are *not* compatible. One is considered to make a free choice so long as he could have chosen differently in the moral moment of decision, given the same past. He can choose to act or refrain. His past can influence his choice, but it is not determinative or causal. The person actually deliberates, decides between various available options, and his decision can change the course of his future depending on what he chooses. The future would be different if he chose to do otherwise, which choice was in his power at the moment of decision.

Libertarianism includes both voluntariness (person freely choosing) and origination (ability to originate a new sequence of events). It is the idea of the person being the *efficient cause* of his actions, also known as agent causation. Libertarian freedom does not entail that a person be able to do anything. It does not entail that every choice must be undetermined, but only that some are. It is a force, but it is, as are all created forces, subject to God's sovereignty. He can override a person's actions whenever he so chooses. Having one's libertarian choice overridden does not eliminate a person's libertarian freedom, it only means he is not responsible for that particular decision. A difference in the range of options available to a person does not change the fact of libertarian freedom, only what options are available. See chapter 7 for a full explanation.

Major-Calvinist

Those whose beliefs have the designation of four or five-point Calvinist. The major distinction between the two is four-point Calvinists reject limited atonement. I sometimes include both under the general term Calvinist when I am not speaking specifically about the atonement. They are both categorized as Major-Calvinists because both believe in unconditional election, irresistible grace, and that God predetermined the eternal destiny of everyone.

Minor-Calvinist

Those whose personalization of Major-Calvinism results in a claim to be a one, two, or three-point Calvinist. Usually rejecting or modifying one or all of the following: total depravity, unconditional election, limited atonement, or irresistible grace.

Necessity

Necessity refers to definite events that happen in time and are the result of determinative antecedents. God knows these events because he predetermined them to happen without the influence of the otherwise choice of morally free beings. Necessary events do not require the absence of secondary causes, but only that the event is not the result of otherwise choice—a contingency.

Organically Related (see Constitutionally and Organically Related)

Omniscience

God is essentially omniscient, which means his knowledge of everything is an essential attribute of his being in the same way other essential properties of Deity like omnipotence, omnipresence, and omnibenevolence are. This is what it means to be Jehovah. He eternally knows everything; this includes actualities, potentialities, and what potentialities he would actualize.

He knows definite events because he predetermined for them to exist apart from human influence. He knows indefinite events (contingencies) because he determined to create man with libertarian freedom; as an essential property of his being, he has always known these indefinite events because he knows himself exhaustively, including his intentions, and he has always intended to create a state of affairs that included indefinite events (contingencies). He does not acquire knowledge of contingencies by looking outside of himself, down the halls of history; he does not know about contingencies, perceptively. He knows about them as an essential property of his being because he is essentially omniscient.

Repentance

Repentance and faith are inseparable. Repentance focuses upon turning *from* sin, whereas faith focuses upon turning in trust *to* the Savior. Repentance is neither a predetermined irresistible work of God upon the unconditionally elect only nor merely a humanly-generated act or work. Rather, the ability to repent is given to all by God through grace enablements and required by God for salvation (Matt 3:8, 4:17, 11:20; Mark 6:11; Luke 11:5; Acts 5:31, 11:18; Rom 2:4; 2 Cor 7:9–10).

Substantially (Substantively) and Insubstantially Related

Substantially and insubstantially related speaks to the relationship between things, people, personal experiences and other events as part of the process and the process's final product. Something substantially related indicates if it were not present in the process, the product would be different, or at least would likely be different. In contrast, components that are insubstantially related would not change the product by their absence. See chapter 8 for full description.

Total Depravity (TD)

The fall affected every aspect of man; therefore man is totally depraved, extensively speaking. TD rejects that man is partially depraved. Man is incapable of coming to God without God's redemptive grace (grace enablements), which God provides for all. This does not mean man lost all sensibilities regarding God (Gen 3:8–13; Rom 1:18–23).

TULIP

An acronym for the five points of Calvinism. 1. Total depravity 2. Unconditional election 3. Limited atonement 4. Irresistible grace 5. Perseverance of the saints. Four-point Calvinism differs in that it rejects point three, limited atonement.

Bibliography

Allen, David. "The Atonement, Limited or Universal?" In *Whosoever Will: A Biblical-Theological Critique of Five-Point Calvinism*, edited by David L. Allen and Steve W. Lemke, 61–107. Nashville: B&H Academic, 2010.

———. "Does Regeneration Precede Faith?" Journal for Baptist Theology & Ministry 11 (2014) 34–52. http://baptistcenter.net/journals/JBTM_11-2_Fall_2014.pdf, accessed 7/22/18.

———. *The Extent of the Atonement: A Historical and Critical Review*. Nashville: B&H Academic, 2016.

Allen, David L., Eric Hankins, and Adam Harwood, eds. *Anyone Can Be Saved: A Defense of "Traditional" Southern Baptist Soteriology*. Eugene, OR: Wipf & Stock, 2016.

Allen, David L., and Steve W. Lemke, eds. *Whosoever Will: A Biblical-Theological Critique of Five-Point Calvinism*. Nashville: B&H Academic, 2010.

Balz, Horst, and Gerhard Schneider, eds. *Exegetical Dictionary of the New Testament*. 3 vols. Grand Rapids, MI: Eerdmans, 1990.

Bergen, Robert D. *1, 2 Samuel*. The New American Commentary 7. Nashville: Broadman & Holman, 1996, Logos edition.

Berkouwer, G.C. *Divine Election*. Translated by Hugo Bekker. Grand Rapids: Eerdmans, 1960.

Berofsky, Bernard. "Ifs, Cans, and Free Will: The Issues." In *The Oxford Handbook of Free Will*, edited by Robert Kane. New York: Oxford University Press, 2002.

Blum, Edwin A. "John." In *The Bible Knowledge Commentary: An Exposition of the Scriptures* 2, edited by J. F. Walvoord, and R. B. Zuck. Wheaton, IL: Victor, 1985, Logos edition.

Boa, Kenneth, and William Kruidenier. *Romans*. Holman New Testament Commentary, 6. Nashville, TN: Broadman & Holman, 2000, Logos edition.

Boice, James Montgomery, and Phillip Graham Ryken. *The Doctrines of Grace: Rediscovering the Evangelical Gospel*. Wheaton, IL: Crossway, 2002, trade paper 2009, https://www.wtsbooks.com/common/pdf_links/9781433511288.pdf, accessed 7/26/2014.

Borchert, Gerald L. *John 1–11*. The New American Commentary, 25A. Nashville: Broadman & Holman, 1996, Logos edition.

Boyce, James P. *Abstract of Systematic Theology*. 1887. Reprint, Escondido, CA: den Dulk Christian Foundation, n.d.

Bryson, George L. *The Five Points of Calvinism: Weighed and Found Wanting*. Costa Mesa, CA: The Word for Today, 2002.

Calvin, John. "Commentaries on the Second Epistle of Peter." *Commentaries on the Catholic Epistles*, 22 vols. Edited by John Owen. Reprint, Grand Rapids, MI: Baker, 1979, Logos edition.

———. *Institutes of the Christian Religion* 2. Translated by Henry Beveridge. Grand Rapids: Wm. B. Eerdmans, 1997.

———. *Institutes of the Christian Religion*. Bellingham, WA: Logos Bible Software, 2010.

Campbell, Donald K. "Joshua." In *The Bible Knowledge Commentary: An Exposition of the Scriptures* 1, edited J. F. Walvoord, and R. B. Zuck. Wheaton, IL: Victor, 1985, Logos edition.

Carson, D.A. *The Difficult Doctrine of the Love of God*. Wheaton, IL: Crossway, 2000.

———. *Divine Sovereignty and Human Responsibility: Biblical Perspectives in Tension*. Eugene, OR: Wipf & Stock, 1994.

———. *How Long O Lord? Reflections on Suffering and Evil*, 2nd ed. Grand Rapids, MI: Baker Academic, 1990, 2006.

———. "Matthew." In *The Expositor's Bible Commentary* 8, edited by Frank E. Gaebelein, 3–599. Grand Rapids, MI: Zondervan, 1984.

Carson, D. A., et al., eds. *New Bible Commentary: 21st Century Edition*, 4th ed. Downers Grove, IL: Inter-Varsity, 1994, Logos edition.

Chafer, Lewis Sperry. *Systematic Theology*, 8 vols. Dallas: Dallas Seminary Press, 1947–48.

Clark, Gordon H. *God and Evil: The Problem Solved*. Unicoi, TN: The Trinity Foundation, 2004.

———. *Thales to Dewey*. Grand Rapids, MI: Baker, 1980 reprint.

Craig, William Lane. *Divine Foreknowledge and Human Freedom, The Coherence of Theism: Omniscience*. Leiden, The Netherlands: E.J. Brill, 1991.

———. *The Only Wise God: The Compatibility of Divine Foreknowledge and Human Freedom*. Eugene, OR: Wipf & Stock, 1999.

Cranfield, C. E. B. *A Critical and Exegetical Commentary on the Epistle to the Romans*. 2 vols. Edinburgh: T. & T. Clark, 1975.

Crisp, Oliver D. *Deviant Calvinism: Broadening Reformed Theology*. Minneapolis, Fortress, 2014.

Cunningham, William. *Historical Theology*, 2 vols. 1882. Reprint, n.p., 1991. http://www.puritandownloads.com/content/Historical-Theology-Vol2-William-Cunningham.pdf.

Deere, Jack S. "Deuteronomy." In *The Bible Knowledge Commentary: An Exposition of the Scriptures* 1, edited by J. F. Walvoord, and R. B. Zuck. Wheaton, IL: Victor, 1985, Logos edition.

Edwards, Jonathan. *Freedom of the Will*. New Haven: Yale University Press, 1957.

———. *God's End in Creation, in Ethical Writings*. Edited by Paul Ramsey. In *The Works of Jonathan Edwards* 8, edited by Perry Miller. New Haven, CT: Yale University Press, 1989.

Elwell, Walter A., and Barry J. Beitzel. *Baker Encyclopedia of the Bible*. Grand Rapids, MI: Baker, 1988.

Engelsma, David J. "Is Denial of the 'Well-Meant Offer' Hyper-Calvinism?" Protestant Reformed Churches in America, http://www.prca.org/pamphlets/pamphlet_35.html, accessed 11/15/2000.

Erickson, Millard J. *Christian Theology*, 3rd ed., 3 vols. Grand Rapids: Baker Academic, 2013.
Evans, Jeremy A. "Reflections on Determinism and Human Freedom." In *Whosoever Will: A Biblical-Theological Critique of Five-Point Calvinism*, edited by David L. Allen, and Steve W. Lemke, 253–74. Nashville: B&H Academic, 2010.
Friberg, Timothy, Barbara Friberg, and Neva F. Miller. *Analytical Lexicon of the Greek New Testament*. Grand Rapids, MI: Baker, 2000.
Flowers, Leighton. *The Potter's Promise: A Biblical Defense of Traditional Soteriology*. Trinity Academic, 2017.
Gangel, Kenneth O. "2 Peter." In *The Bible Knowledge Commentary: An Exposition of the Scriptures* 2, edited by J. F. Walvoord, and R. B. Zuck. Wheaton, IL: Victor, 1985, Logos edition.
Garrigou-Lagrange, Reginald. *The One God*. Translated by Dom. Bede Rose. St. Louis: B. Herder, 1944.
Geisler, Norman L. *Baker Encyclopedia of Christian Apologetics*. Grand Rapids, MI: Baker, 1999.
———. *Chosen But Free*. Minneapolis: Bethany House, 1999.
Gould, Paul. "Why Theology Needs Philosophy: A Case Study." http://www.paul-gould.com/2016/04/20/why-theology-needs-philosophy-a-case-study/.
Grudem, Wayne. *Bible Doctrine*. Leicester: Intervarsity, 1999.
———. *Systematic Theology: An Introduction to Biblical Doctrine*. Grand Rapids: Zondervan, 1994.
Hannah, John D. "Jonah." In *The Bible Knowledge Commentary: An Exposition of the Scriptures* 1, edited by J. F. Walvoord, and R. B. Zuck. Wheaton, IL: Victor, 1985, Logos edition.
Harwood, Adam. *The Spiritual Condition of Infants: A Biblical-Historical Survey and Systematic Proposal*. Eugene, OR: Wipf & Stock, 2011.
Hendriksen, William, and Simon J. Kistemaker. *Exposition of the Gospel According to John*. New Testament Commentary 4. Grand Rapids: Baker, 1953–2001.
———. *Exposition of Paul's Epistle to the Romans*. New Testament Commentary 12–13. Grand Rapids: Baker, 1953–2001.
Hodge, Charles. *Systematic Theology*, 3 vols. Grand Rapids, MI: Wm. B. Eerdmans, 1986.
Hodges, Zane C. *Absolutely Free! A Biblical Reply to Lordship Salvation*. Grand Rapids, MI.: Academie, 1989.
House, Paul R. *1, 2 Kings*. The New American Commentary 8. Nashville: Broadman & Holman, 1995.
Howard, David M. Jr. *Joshua*. The New American Commentary 5. Nashville: Broadman & Holman, 1998.
Huey, F. B. *Jeremiah, Lamentations*. The New American Commentary 16. Nashville: Broadman & Holman, 1993.
The Information Philosopher website, http://www.informationphilosopher.com, accessed 7/11/2015.
Keathley, Kenneth. "The Work of God: Salvation." In *A Theology for the Church*, edited by Daniel L. Akin. Nashville: B&H Academic, 2007.
Kistemaker, Simon J, and William Hendriksen. *Exposition of the Book of Revelation*. New Testament Commentary, vol. 20. Grand Rapids: Baker, 1953–2001.

Kittel, Gerhard, and Gerhard Friedrich, eds. *Theological Dictionary of the New Testament*. 10 vols. Translated by Geoffrey William Bromiley. Grand Rapids, MI: W.B. Eerdmans, 1985, Logos edition.
Kreeft, Peter, and Ronald K. Tacelli. *Handbook of Christian Apologetics: Hundreds of Answers to Crucial Questions*. Downers Grove, IL: InterVarsity, 1994. Logos Bible Software.
Lea, Thomas D., and Hayne P. Griffin. *1, 2 Timothy, Titus*. The New American Commentary, 34. Nashville: Broadman & Holman, 1992.
Lennox, John C. *Determined to Believe? The Sovereignty of God, Freedom, Faith, and Human Responsibility*. Grand Rapids: Zondervan, 2017.
———. *God and Stephen Hawking: Whose Design Is It Anyway?* Oxford: Lion, 2011.
Lenski, R. C. H. *The Interpretation of St. John's Revelation*. Columbus, OH: Lutheran Book Concern, 1935.
Louw, Johannes P., and Eugene Albert Nida. *Greek-English Lexicon of the New Testament: Based on Semantic Domains*. New York: United Bible Societies, 1996. Logos Bible Software.
MacArthur, John F. Jr. *Revelation 12–22*. The MacArthur New Testament Commentary. Chicago: Moody, 2000.
———. *Romans 1–8*. The MacArthur New Testament Commentary. Chicago: Moody, 1991.
Maier, Gerhard. *The End of the Historical-Critical Method*. Translated by Edwin W. Leverenz, and Rudolph F. Norden. St. Louis: Concordia, 1974.
Mounce, Robert H. *Romans*. The New American Commentary, 27. Nashville: Broadman & Holman, 1995.
Murray, John, and Ned Stonehouse. *The Free Offer of the Gospel*. Phillipsburg, NJ: Lewis Grotenhuis, n.d
Nicole, Roger. Preface to *The Five Points of Calvinism: Defined, Defended, Documented* by David N. Steele, and Curtis C. Thomas. Phillipsburg, NJ: Presbyterian & Reformed, 1963.
Oxford English Dictionary online, https://en.oxforddictionaries.com.
Packer, J.I. *Evangelism and the Sovereignty of God*. Downers Grove, IL: InterVarsity, 1961.
Packer, J.I., and O.R. Johnston. Introduction to *Bondage of the Will* by Martin Luther. Grand Rapids, MI: Fleming H. Revell, 1957.
Patterson, Paige. *Revelation*. The New American Commentary, 39. Nashville, TN: B&H, 2012.
Piper, John. "Are There Two Wills in God? Divine Election and God's Desire for All to Be Saved." desiringGod.org. January 1, 1995. http://www.desiringgod.org/articles/are-there-two-wills-in-god.
———. *Desiring God: Meditations of a Christian Hedonist*. Sisters, OR: Multnomah, 1996.
———. "Irresistible Grace." In *What We Believe About the Five Points of Calvinism*. desiringGod.org. March 1, 1985. http://www.desiringgod.org/articles/what-we-believe-about-the-five-points-of-calvinism.
———. *Let the Nations Be Glad: The Supremacy of God in Missions*. Grand Rapids: Baker, 2001.
Plantinga, Alvin C. *God, Freedom, and Evil*. Grand Rapids: William B. Eerdmans, 1974.

Rookmaaker, H.R. *Modern Art and the Death of a Culture*. Downers Grove, IL: InterVarsity, 1970.
Ryrie, Charles. *Dispensationalism Today*. Chicago: Moody, 1995.
Schaeffer, Francis A. *The Complete Works of Francis A. Schaeffer: a Christian Worldview*, 5 vols. Westchester, IL: Crossway, 1982. Logos Bible software.
Second Helvetic Confession, The. In *The Constitution of the Presbyterian Church* (U.S.A.), Part I, Book of Confessions. Louisville, KY: Geneva, 1996. http://www.creeds.net/helvetic/.
Shedd, William G.T. *Calvinism: Pure and Mixed—A Defence of the Westminster Standards*. New York: Charles Scribner's Sons, 1893. http://www.archive.org/stream/calvinismpuremixooshed#page/n5/mode/2up.
———. *Dogmatic Theology*, 2nd ed., 3 vols. Nashville: Thomas Nelson, 1980.
Slick, Matt. "Does Regeneration Precede Faith or Does Faith Precede Regeneration?" Christian Apologetics & Research Ministry website, December 4, 2016. https://carm.org/does-regeneration-precede-faith. Accessed 7/12/2018.
Smith, Billy K., and Franklin S. Page. *Amos, Obadiah, Jonah*. The New American Commentary, 19B. Nashville: Broadman & Holman, 1995.
Smith, Gary V. *An Introduction to the Hebrew Prophets: The Prophets as Preachers*. Nashville: Broadman & Holman, 1994.
———. *Isaiah 1–39*. The New American Commentary, 15A. Nashville: B & H Group, 2007.
Sproul, R. C. *Chosen by God*. Wheaton, IL: Tyndale House, Kindle edition
———. *The Mystery of the Holy Spirit*. Wheaton: Tyndale House, 1990.
———. *What is Reformed Theology? Understanding the Basics*. Baker, Kindle edition.
Sproul, R.C., Jr. *Almighty Over All: Understanding the Sovereignty of God*. Grand Rapids: Baker 1999.
Stein, Robert H. *Luke*. The New American Commentary, 24. Nashville: Broadman & Holman, 1992.
Strong, Augustus Hopkins. *Systematic Theology*. Philadelphia: American Baptist, 1907. Logos Bible software.
Thomas, Robert L. *New American Standard Hebrew-Aramaic and Greek Dictionaries: Updated Edition*. Anaheim: Foundation, 1998.
Thomas, Taylor. *A Solemn Caution Against the Ten Horns of Calvinism*. n.p., 1780. Project Gutenberg EBook, http://archive.org/stream/asolemncautionag28172gut/28172.txt.
Vicens, Leigh. "Theological Determinism." In Internet Encyclopedia of Philosophy. n.d. http://www.iep.utm.edu/theo-det/. Accessed 7/8/17.
Walvoord, John F. "Revelation" In *The Bible Knowledge Commentary: An Exposition of the Scriptures* 2, edited by J. F. Walvoord, and R. B. Zuck. Wheaton, IL: Victor, 1985, Logos edition.
The Westminster Confession of Faith (1646). Found online at The Center for Reformed Theology and Apologetics, http://reformed.org/documents/wcf_with_proofs/index.html, accessed 7/24/2014.
Witmer, John A. "Romans." In *The Bible Knowledge Commentary: An Exposition of the Scriptures* 2, edited by J. F. Walvoord, and R. B. Zuck. Wheaton, IL: Victor, 1985, Logos edition.
Zodhiates, Spiros. *The Complete Word Study Dictionary: New Testament*. Chattanooga, TN: AMG, 2000.

Author Index

Berkouwer, G.C., 211
Berofsky, Bernard, 86n9
Blum, Edwin A., 195
Boyce, J. P., 37, 207

Calvin, John, 57, 91, 94, 102, 243
Carson, D.A., 10, 40–41, 59, 184, 230
Chafer, Lewis Sperry, 15n2, 49n23, 113, 188, 191, 253n1, 254, 255n5
Clark, Gordon H., 31n2, 56, 110
Craig, William Lane, 127, 173, 188, 189n19, 191n20
Crisp, Oliver D., 89, 96

Edwards, Jonathan, 54, 90
Erickson, Millard J., 15, 92, 97n1, 107, 205,

Garrigou-Lagrange, Reginald, 167–71
Geisler, Norman L., 45n17, 63, 168n8, 178
Gould, Paul, 40
Grudem, Wayne, 166, 264,

Hendriksen, William, 72, 75n13, 212
Hodge, Charles, 179n12, 182, 184, 186–87, 205
Hodges, Zane C., 80

Huey, F. B., 214

Kreeft, Peter, 65

Lennox, John C., 27n3, 251, 263,

MacArthur, John F. Jr., 83n3, 220–21, 225–27, 234, 249–50,
Maier, Gerhard, 101

Owen, John, 133

Packer, J.I., 139, 166
Patterson, Paige, 249
Piper, John, 67, 121–34, 203n3
Plantinga, Alvin C., 65, 88

Rookmaaker, H.R., 151
Ryrie, Charles, 209

Shedd, William G.T., 56, 58-59, 65, 82–86, 89–90, 92, 103, 181–83
Smith, Billy K., 215
Smith, Gary V., 214–15
Sproul, R. C., 57–58, 67, 104, 134, 262, 263n7
Sproul, R.C., Jr., 56
Strong, A. H., 228

Subject Index

Adam, 25, 31–32, 41–42, 46–48, 58, 61, 64, 68, 73, 81–83, 87, 91, 125, 144–47, 160–62, 164, 172–73, 177–80, 225–26, 230, 237, 248, 250, 271n7,
agent, 31n2, 41, 44–46, 59, 61, 63–64, 96, 109, 187–88, 190, 267, 268n3, 269, 272
antecedents, 42–43, 46, 55, 63, 87, 93–94, 107, 109, 111, 115, 147, 161, 164, 268n3, 273
anyone, 11, 13–14, 16, 29, 34, 37, 49, 78, 98, 103–05, 110, 125, 129n8, 132, 137, 140, 142–43, 150, 159, 172, 190, 193–94, 203, 209, 220–21, 226, 234, 236, 247, 260–61
Aristotle, 31n2, 99
Arminianism, ix, xv, 14, 26, 167n3, 253, 255
asymmetrically, 41, 59–60

basis, xvn1, 54, 96, 102, 122n3, 130, 142, 176, 180, 189n19, 209, 212, 230, 244, 262
benevolence, 205, 225
Biblicist, 20n1, 22, 28

Calvinistically-generated, 2, 20, 22, 58, 83, 86, 91, 127
Canons of Dort, 49n2, 90, 102, 134n7, 207, 244
certain, 83, 93, 107–09, 127–28, 169–70, 176, 181–82, 185–91, 201, 208, 216, 236–37, 267
children, 57, 100, 142, 197, 207–08, 246

coextensive, 44–45, 61, 82, 88, 125, 128, 144, 152, 162, 173, 177
compatibilism, xiii–xiv, 2, 4–5, 8–9, 12, 17–18, 21, 31, 36, 38–44, 46–48, 50, 53–55, 59–63, 65–66, 81–88, 91–93, 100, 104–5, 108–12, 115–19, 123–25, 127, 130, 145, 147, 151–52, 161–64, 167, 171, 175, 181, 184, 187, 204, 228, 238, 267, 270
condemnation, 98, 226, 229, 231, 254–55
constitutionally, 51, 98, 268
contingencies, 45, 62, 81–83, 87, 108, 119, 124, 127–28, 152, 176, 183–85, 190, 236, 238, 240, 257, 267, 272–74
creation, xiii, 14, 25, 47–48, 57, 61, 71, 73, 81–83, 86–87, 90, 92, 125–26, 145, 151, 162, 168, 172–73, 175–76, 178, 180, 201, 215, 217–18, 220–22, 224–233, 235, 239, 243, 245–47, 249, 251, 270
cryptic, 110, 179
Cunningham, 114–16, 118–19

Darwinists, 141, 161, 245n1
decretal, 4n1, 9, 17, 25, 60, 81, 83, 85, 93, 104–55, 123–24, 127, 154–55, 163, 170, 175, 184, 238, 253n1
definite event, 50, 175–76, 236, 239, 257, 273
depraved, 21, 31, 33, 36, 66, 178, 221n3, 274

depravity, 88, 97, 100, 117, 160–61, 163–65, 178, 273–74
desiring, xiv, 55–56, 61, 63, 82, 84–85, 122, 124, 128, 174, 217
determined, 9, 39, 44–45, 52, 54, 60, 62–63, 78, 84, 87, 93–94, 103, 105, 108–12, 119, 123, 127, 147, 154, 163, 171–72, 174–76, 184, 186, 189, 204, 236–37, 239–40, 243, 246, 255, 257, 265, 267, 271, 273
determinism, 4, 16–17, 38–40, 42–44, 50, 82, 84, 87, 92–93, 103, 107–12, 114, 118–19, 124–25, 129, 161, 163–64, 168–71, 186–87, 228, 240, 267, 272
disquieting realities, 7–9, 11–12, 15, 18–19, 25–26, 28, 55, 85, 147, 161, 244, 268
doctrines of grace, 139,
double talk, 2–4, 7– 9, 11, 15, 22, 26, 29, 90, 100, 131, 206, 226, 244, 268

efficient cause, 31n2, 44, 45n17, 60–61, 63, 68, 94, 108n3, 123, 168, 170, 173, 176, 267, 269, 272
Egypt, 210–12, 216
election, 5, 11, 14, 53, 56–57, 84, 89–90, 98, 102, 113, 134, 166, 179, 207, 253–55
encryptions, 118
entail, xiv, 4, 25, 42, 44, 55, 83, 88, 104, 123, 146–47, 155, 170, 173, 185, 187, 240, 272
entailments, xiv, xvi, 1–2, 5, 7–9, 12, 15–16, 18–21, 23, 30, 33, 38, 41, 83, 88, 110, 113, 130, 157, 171, 257, 268
epistemologically, 208–09
essential dissimilarity, 64, 124, 241–42, 244, 269
essentially dissimilar, 32, 204–05, 241n4, 242
essentially omniscient, 45, 94–96, 125, 127–28, 162, 176, 183, 189, 239–40, 257, 267, 272–74
eternal torment, 25, 57, 91, 102, 170

evangelism, ix, 8, 98, 136, 139–41, 174, 210, 214
evangelistic, 132, 139, 210, 217
experience, 4–5, 27, 33, 52, 62, 64, 72–73, 89, 110–11, 133, 144–46, 171, 184, 199, 241, 251, 259
Extensivism, ix, xiii, xiv– xvi, 3, 6–7, 12–15, 17–18, 26, 31n2, 32, 38, 44, 48, 50–53, 61, 66, 82, 91, 93–94, 96, 100, 107–08, 121–24, 147, 162, 164–65, 167–69, 171, 175, 178–80, 189–90, 200–6, 226, 228, 232, 235–44, 255, 257, 266, 269,
Extensivists, 7, 10–11, 13, 16–18, 30, 38–39, 50, 53, 61, 64, 75, 77, 81, 83, 92, 106, 114, 120, 125, 132–33, 136, 142, 148, 152, 183–84, 186, 188, 200–06, 208, 227, 234–37, 239, 244, 255,
extra-biblical, 2–4, 34, 131, 136, 141, 179, 259–61

fallen man, 19, 31, 33, 44, 46, 48, 54, 61, 64, 115, 117, 147, 160, 172, 176, 180, 219, 224–26
foreknowledge, xiii–xiv, 5, 9, 11, 16–17, 56, 62, 81, 83, 92–94, 108, 119, 123–25, 127, 146, 182–83, 188–90, 235, 242
foreordain, 81, 89, 236–39
four-point, 6, 10, 16, 20, 29, 34, 273–74

general revelation, 226, 230, 232–33
glory, 2, 19, 26, 59, 89–90, 94, 96, 101, 103, 125, 151, 166, 169, 178, 186, 192, 212, 218, 221, 224, 229, 231, 241, 246–51, 260
good faith offer, xiii, 2, 34, 78, 134–37, 139–43, 153–59, 180, 196–97
gospel, ix–x, 3–4, 9–10, 12, 14, 25–26, 29, 31, 33–37, 47–79, 51–52, 66, 72–73, 96–100, 106, 121, 130–43, 150, 152–60, 162, 166, 171–72, 175–76, 178–80, 192–202, 205–10, 212, 215, 220–21, 225–34, 241–52, 259–61, 264, 270–72

SUBJECT INDEX

grace, ix–x, 3, 13–14, 16, 21, 24–25, 33, 35–37, 41, 44, 47–49, 51, 53, 67, 73, 76, 78, 83, 85, 94, 96–98, 100, 102, 113–16, 118, 126, 133, 136, 139, 142–43, 149, 154–55, 158–64, 166–73, 176–79, 182, 185, 195–96, 198–99, 205–06, 208, 214–16, 219–20, 223–24, 226, 228, 230–31, 233, 239, 241, 243–44, 251–52, 260, 268, 270–71, 273–74
grace enablements, 48, 51, 66, 178, 243, 268, 270–71, 274
greatest desire, 39, 41–42, 54–55, 83, 86–87, 93–94, 109, 115, 161, 267

hate, 41, 58, 61, 90, 104, 117, 124, 136, 163
holiness, 32–33, 37, 47, 49, 59, 61–64, 78, 81–82, 84–85, 89, 95, 103, 109, 123–124, 129, 146, 163, 165, 174, 178, 186, 214, 217, 225, 233, 240
holy, ix, 32–33, 47, 61, 63–64, 82–83, 85, 90, 95, 112, 117, 122, 124, 126–27, 129, 145–46, 150, 207, 219, 227
hopeless, 106, 247
human birth, 68–69, 71
Hyper-Calvinism, xv, 15
hypothetical, 41, 86–87

indefinite events, 50–52, 175, 236, 238–40, 257, 267–68, 272–74
instinct, 62–64
insubstantially, 52, 228, 268, 274
intentions, 185, 190, 239, 257, 274

Judas, 3, 96, 123–24, 167–68, 170–73
judgment, 48, 56, 74, 76–79, 81, 95, 102, 149–50, 175, 184–85, 195–98, 210, 212, 214–24, 227, 229, 231, 233, 237, 246–50

Lewis, Ard, 251
libertarian, xiii–xiv, 9, 14, 17–18, 21, 26, 32, 38, 40, 42, 44–46, 48, 50–53, 60–63, 81–83, 85–87, 91–92, 94–95, 105, 109, 112, 119, 123, 125–29, 144–46, 152, 162–63, 167–72, 174, 181–83, 185, 187–190, 204, 211, 228, 236–40, 242, 244, 267–68, 272–73
logical impossibility, 65

Major-Calvinist, 6, 15, 20–21, 273
meaningful, 2, 8, 34, 38, 53, 98, 104–05, 157, 233
missions, ix, 242
Molinism, ix, xv, 13, 27, 167, 269
monergistic, 35, 49, 56, 99–101, 112, 114, 255
morally free, 38, 127, 239, 267, 273
mystery, xiv, 2, 18, 22–23, 25, 55–57, 59, 78, 81, 83, 86, 95, 103, 109, 122, 131, 147

necessary, 9, 11–12, 25, 31, 73–74, 86, 89, 92–95, 108–09, 119, 131, 133, 144–45, 157, 160, 164, 168, 172–73, 175–76, 186, 188, 196–97, 208–09, 214, 224, 237, 247, 258, 260, 262–65, 271, 273
necessity, 62–63, 71, 146, 175, 178, 184, 191
new birth, 47, 67–69, 71–74, 76–78, 134, 196

omnibenovolence, 94, 146, 160, 176, 273
omnipotent, 88, 115, 117–18, 146, 174, 223
omniscience, 182–84, 187–88, 257, 270
ontologically, 208–09
organically, 34, 51, 53, 98, 268, 273
otherwise, xiv, 4, 10, 13–14, 32–33, 39, 41, 43–45, 47–48, 54, 59, 61–66, 81, 83, 85–88, 92, 94–95, 100–1, 105, 109, 111, 115, 119, 122, 124–25, 127–28, 144–46, 152, 155, 161, 163–64, 169–78, 181, 183, 185–89, 196, 205, 216, 230, 236, 238–39, 241, 257–58, 267–69, 271–73

SUBJECT INDEX

passive, 36, 49, 97–100, 103, 114–18, 145, 151–52, 259
pastor, 28, 62, 156, 174, 258
permissive, 56, 59–60, 83–85, 211, 219, 222, 237
permit, 8, 42, 58–59, 63, 82, 88, 91–92, 108, 123, 125, 127, 153, 174–75, 186–87, 208, 226–27, 237, 240, 253–55
perseverance, 36n5, 37, 274
Peter, 167–72, 185–86, 212, 232
Pharaoh, 45, 104n7, 210–13, 216
Pharisees, 70, 111, 223, 248
pleased, 3, 31, 33–34, 47, 57–58, 60, 82, 86–88, 90, 92, 102–4, 106, 122, 135, 139, 156, 239, 242–43, 255
pre-conversion, 21, 51, 98, 164, 173, 206, 268
predestination, xv, 27, 57, 94, 103, 124, 131, 256
predetermined, 36, 41–43, 46–47, 50, 58, 64, 82–84, 89, 93, 98, 105–7, 111, 116, 119, 123–25, 127–28, 140, 162, 169, 175, 178, 181–82, 184–86, 197–98, 221, 226, 228, 236–40, 253, 255, 265, 268, 272–74
predilection, 167
proximate cause, 31, 60, 124, 268n3

quickening, 21, 31, 47, 116, 227

Rahab, 210–11, 217, 227
raison d'être, 132, 169
Reformed, 12, 96, 207, 262
regeneration, 10, 13–14, 21, 31, 35–36, 47–49, 54, 56–57, 67, 72–73, 76, 80, 98–101, 103, 112, 116–17, 137, 139–40, 151–52, 157, 161–62, 166, 168, 196, 207–08, 228, 259–60, 262–66
repentance, 78–79, 119, 133n4, 134, 137, 159, 208, 212, 214–15, 233, 246–47, 249–50, 252, 264, 274
reprobates, 57, 90, 105–06, 239
reprobation, 56–57, 84, 89–90, 92, 96, 103, 107, 151
restoration, 31, 164, 180, 248

salvation, ix–x, xiii, 1–2, 4, 13–14, 25, 29, 31–36, 39, 48–53, 56–58, 64, 66, 72–77, 89–92, 96–101, 103–04, 106–08, 111–14, 116–17, 121–22, 125–26, 128–35, 139–42, 146, 148–49, 152, 154, 157, 159–60, 162–64, 166–76, 178–81, 185, 193, 195–96, 200–9, 211–12, 215, 217, 219–24, 226, 228–36, 239, 242–44, 247–48, 250, 252–55, 259–60, 268–71, 274
salvific choice, 31
same problem, 202, 232, 235, 243
secondary causes, 41, 59, 81, 92, 124, 175, 184
selectively, 47n20, 75, 137, 241, 259
sequentiality, 240
simple, 1–3, 11, 22, 28, 30, 33–34, 37, 74, 86, 92, 121, 134, 140–42, 146–47, 150, 153–54, 157–59, 178–80, 203, 206–7, 232, 249, 258
soteriology, ix, 1, 8–9, 13, 27, 104, 112, 129, 140–41, 179, 240, 269
sovereign, xiii, 3, 17, 33, 38, 45, 73, 78, 82, 100, 106, 113, 128, 144, 152, 159–60, 164, 170, 172–73, 175, 177, 186, 199, 214, 217, 230, 255, 270
speculative, 5, 8, 140–41, 180, 189
spiritual, 59, 68, 80, 97, 100, 113, 117, 119, 145, 197, 221, 223, 264, 270
spiritual birth, 67–69, 71
substantially, 51–53, 82, 206, 228, 243–44, 268, 274
sufficient, 11, 14, 22, 24, 29, 36, 45, 98, 145, 152, 157, 166, 172, 176–77, 193, 196, 204, 208, 220–24, 226, 231–33, 243, 248, 250, 258, 265

temporal, 35, 75, 127, 194, 205, 227, 262–63, 265
temporally prior, 262–66
theological fatalism, 112
torment, 33, 57, 91, 102, 170, 235
Traditional, xiv, 28n4
TULIP, xii, xv, 15, 18, 30, 37, 116, 274
two wills, 103, 122, 128–29, 131

ultimate cause, 55, 66, 84, 124, 220
ultimate responsibility, 43n14, 44, 86
unconditional election, xv, 2–4, 10, 13, 16–17, 21–23, 29, 30n1, 33–34, 50–53, 57, 73, 78, 99–100, 103, 114, 120–21, 126, 129–30, 137, 139–40, 147, 149, 151, 153–54, 156–58, 162, 179, 184n11, 194, 196, 198, 200–4, 206, 226–28, 232, 235, 242–44, 253–55, 259–60, 273–74

unequal, 169, 171
unholy, 33
universal, 14, 71, 76, 84, 96, 135, 137, 148, 173, 193, 228, 260n8

wrath, 89, 94–96, 103, 135, 139, 197, 212, 217–20, 222–24, 226–27, 230–31, 246–50
Westminster, 36n5, 84, 89, 97, 116

Scripture Index

Genesis

1:26–27	168
1:26–31	147
1:28	214
1:31	55, 63, 247
1–2	177
2:9, 21–25	247
2:15–18, 20–24	147
2:16	46
2:16–17	185
2:17	25, 33, 64, 73, 81, 177, 247, 270
2:17–18	177, 180
2:18–24	174
3	220
3:1–6	63, 177, 190, 248
3:5	64, 144
3:6	46
3:7	248
3:7–10	248
3:8–13	177, 274
3:8–19, 22–24	147
3:11–13	46
3:14–19, 22–24	248
3:14–24	81
3:15	177, 248
3:15, 21	250
3:16–19	46
3:21	177
3:22–24	46
7:1	81
9:1	214
12:3	214
15:6	81
18:19	81

Exodus

6:6–7	210
7:3	212
7:5	210
9:14	210
9:15	212
9:16	210
10:1–2	210
13:14–16	210
14:4, 18	210

Leviticus

11:44	81
19:2	33, 81
20:7	81

Numbers

20:4	77
21:1–3	77
21:4–5	77
21:4–9	67, 77
21:6	77
21:7	77
21:8–9	77

Deuteronomy

4:6–8	213
10:14	108
11:26–28	185
29:29	130

Joshua

2:8–14	210
2:9	210
4:24	213
9:9	210
24:15	180

1 Samuel

17:46	213
10:6	73

2 Samuel

12:20–23	208

1 Kings

8:58–60	213

1 Chronicles

16:23–24, 31	216

Psalms

10:16	108
19:1	251
19:1–6	225
22:28	108
85:10	212
86:5	203
94:9	183
102:27	146
103:19	108
139:1–18	183
145:5	183
145:8	212

Proverbs

2:1–12	185
4:5–7	185
6:16	185
15:3	183

15:11	183

Isaiah

12:4–6	214
32:15	73
31:1	137
45:1–5	216
45:4, 8	217
45:6–7	216
45:21–22	217, 270
45:22	216
45:23	217
46:13	217
49:3	216
49:6	214
52:10–15	214
55:3–5	214
55:6	232
56:1–8	210
66:18–19	214

Jeremiah

1:5, 10	214
3:17	214
29:13	221, 232, 252, 271
31:10	214
31:31–34	251
31:33	73

Ezekiel

6:5	183
18:23, 32	106, 121, 152, 203, 205
33:11	106, 121, 152, 203, 252
36:25–27	73, 251

Daniel

4:30–37	187

Joel

2:28–29	73

Jonah

1:1–2	215
1:2	215
3:4	215
3:5	215
3:5–10	215
3:6	215
3:7–10	215
4:2	215
4:11	215

Habakkuk

1:13	63
2:4	149

Zachariah

8:20–23	216

Malachi

1:11	210
2:10	71
2:16	174

Matthew

3:2	81, 248
3:7	248
3:8	274
3:11–12	214
4:17	136, 147, 274
5:3, 6	73
5:6, 20, 48	81
5:29	210
5:31–21	174
6:1	111
6:13	147
6:33	81, 233
7:13–14	57, 74
7:15	111
7:23, 25, 41	111
8:8–10	270
9:37	244
10:29–30	184–85
10:30	183
11:20	81, 274
11:20–21	94, 136
11:20–24	10, 49, 53, 147, 184, 248
11:21	99
12:18	137
12:30–32	195
12:31–32	172
12:32	223
12:38–42	248
15:3, 6	99
16:11	111
17:7–8	174
17:22	126
19:8	174
19:16–26	203
19:22–23	99
21:33–46	195
23	111, 223
23:6	99
23:13	219
23:37	49
23–24	214
24:14	250
24:36	136
24:38–39	249
24–25	137
25:21	111
25:41	95
26:24	3, 96, 126
26:34–35	185
26:75	185
28:18–20	35, 153, 203

Mark

1:14–15	147
1:38	203
6:11	274
10:17–22	101
10:17–30	147
10:21	139, 141

Luke

3:22	137
4:1, 14	137
5:32	136
7:9	111
11:5	274
11:9–10	233
11:43	99
12:42	111
13:1–5	223, 248
13:3	66, 210
13:3, 5	159, 179
13:3–5	94
13:5	244
13:24	233
15:7	136
18:10	140
19:10	233
22:3	123
22:22	239
23:34	49
24:7	126
24:45	270
24:47	133, 136

John

1:4–5	195
1:5	195, 198, 251
1:7–9	147
1:9	193, 252, 270
1:9, 29	48, 203
1:12	263
1:12–13	80
1:29	95, 140, 173, 207–09, 270
2:24–25	183
3:1–2	71
3:1–3	270
3:1–13	71
3:1–15	70
3:1–16	67
3:1–21	67–68
3:3	80
3:3, 5	72
3:7	72
3:8	69, 78
3:11, 34	137
3:14–15	67–69, 71
3:15	36, 68, 75, 139
3:15–16	80
3:16	10, 11, 35, 49, 66, 69, 71, 73, 95, 126, 130, 132, 139–40, 160, 180, 203, 207–8, 217, 220, 244, 248, 270
3:16–17	121, 205
3:16–21	71, 75, 80, 163
3:18	219, 247
3:20–21	196
3:34	137
3:36	80
4:14	36, 139
4:23	233
4:24	225
4:27–30, 39–42	98
4:27–42	99
4:34	137
4:39–42	52
5:19	137
5:24	80, 140
5:30	137
5:40	263
5:40–47	49
6:28–29	141, 147
6:29	140
6:38	137
6:40	80
6:44	152, 203, 271
6:45	270
7:16	137
7:17	101
7:37–39	80
8:12	193, 198–99
8:24	49
8:26, 28, 38	137
8:39	71
10:11, 15, 17–18	126
10:18	126–27
10:29	145
11:25–26	145
11:42	49
11:42, 45	52

12:9, 17–22	192	8:22	136
12:12–19	192	8:26–39	232
12:13–15	192	9:35, 42	133
12:23	192	10:2	232
12:27	192	10:2, 22	210
12:31	198	10:34–35, 43	133
12:32	152, 194, 203, 271	10:38	137
12:34	192, 196	10:44, 48	232
12:34–37, 42	158	11:18	133, 274
12:35	197	11:21	133
12:35–36	48, 96, 162, 192, 203, 252, 270	13:8–13, 38–41, 46–47	133
12:36	80	13:16, 26, 43	210
12:37	197, 199	14:1	133
12:42	197, 199	14:15–17	233, 245
12:46	195	15:11	126
12:49–50	137, 196	15:18	183
14:10, 24, 31	137	15:19	133
14:13	126	16:14	233, 270
16:7–14	80	16:30–34	133
16:7–11	270	16:31	141, 180
16:8–11	152, 196, 203, 252	17:2–4, 11–12, 17, 30–31	133
17:4	137		
17:8	137	17:4, 17	210
17:20–21	52, 252	17:11–12	271
19:10–11	127	17:24–31	246
19:39	80	17:27	233
20:30–31	12, 99	17:30	136, 159
20:31	49, 80, 140	18:4–8, 19, 27–28	133
21:30–31	139	19:8–9, 18	133
	Acts	20:21	133, 136
2:10, 11	210	20:24	126
2:21	26	22:18	133
2:23	123, 127, 239	26:17–18	270
2:37–41	133	26:17–20	133
2:38	133, 136	26:18	193
2:39	271	26:19	173
2:41	249	26:20	136
3:19	136	28:23–24	133
3:19–26	133		
4:10–12	247	**Romans**	
4:12	212		
5:31	125, 133, 274	1:5	126
6:5	210	1:9	222
7:51	133	1:16	35, 232, 270
8:6–14, 22–23, 36–37	133	1:16–17	152
8:16–40	232	1:18	111, 218, 219

Romans (continued)

1:18–19	251
1:18–20	270
1:18–23	218, 272, 274
1:18–24	245
1:18–25	246, 251
1:18–32	177
1:19–20	225
1:19–21, 28, 32	228
1:20	151, 224–25, 251
1:21–23	230
1:26–27	231
2:4	52, 212, 223, 274
2:8	101
2:11–15	148
2:15	228
3:1–2	148
3:1–10	204
3:4	225
3:9	148, 150, 204
3:9–20	150
3:10–18	148, 160, 164
3:11	233, 270
3:19	148
3:20	149
3:21–22	149
3:21–26	150
3:21–31	177
3:22	73, 148, 150, 270
3:23	149, 203, 227
3:24	126, 149
3:24–26	150
3:25	212
3:27–31	150
3:28	51
4:1–5	51
4:1–16	177
4:3	177
4:16	126, 179
5:1	133
5:8	126
5:15, 17	126
7:15–16	62
8:2	75
8:30	144
8:39	126
9:7–18	210
9:15	167
9:18	102
9:18–26	89
10:8–11	185
10:9	66
10:9–11	207
11:22	89
11:30, 32	126
11:32	203

1 Corinthians

3:1–3	174
4:4	99
4:7	167
4:16	111
4:21	111
7:10–16	174
10:13	111
11:1	111
15:1–4	207
15:2–3	73

2 Corinthians

3:11	205
4:4	198
5:14–15	203
5:19	143
5:19–20	135
5:21	75
7:9–10	274

Galatians

2:21	126
3:11	149
3:26	133

Ephesians

1:1	111
1:7	126
1:11	56, 186, 243
2:1–3	198
2:4	126
2:5, 7–8	126

2:8	270, 271
2:8–9	52, 133
2:8–10	179
4:15	174
4:24	73
4:30	145
5:1	111
5:2	126
5:3–9	81
6:4	111
6:12	198
6:18	111
6:20	111
6:21	111

Philippians

2:10	217
2:14	167
3:9	73

Colossians

2:8	99

2 Thessalonians

1:8	101
2:16	126

1 Timothy

1:12	111
1:13, 16	126
1:19	111
1:50	111
2:3–4	121
2:4	35, 106, 122, 129–30, 152, 203, 205, 208
2:6	203
3:11	111
4:1	111
4:10	121, 152, 203, 205
4:17	111
6:12	111

2 Timothy

1:9	126
2:2	111
2:13	65
2:22	111

Titus

1:9	111
1:13	111
2:1–11	52
2:10–11	203
2:11	11, 35, 48, 106, 121, 126, 152, 203, 205, 252
3:1–8	52
3:5	126

Hebrews

2:9	126, 203
3:13	64
4:2–3a	194
4:13	183
4:15	75
4:16	126
6:1–6	270
10	212
10:1, 4	149
10:38	149
11	111, 247
11:1–40	207
11:6	133, 180, 233
11:25	64
13:16	47
6:18	63, 65

James

1:3	55, 65
1:5	185
1:13	63, 146
1:26	99

1 Peter

1:3	126
1:10	126
1:15	33, 47
1:15–16	63, 81
1:23	80
2:2	174
2:9	193
2:10	126
2:22–24	75
3:8	152
3:9	106
5:5	185

2 Peter

3:9	95, 121, 128–30, 137, 203, 205, 208, 212, 220, 223, 233, 252

1 John

2:2	52, 130, 139, 152, 203, 209
3:1	224
3:1, 16	126
3:5	203
3:18	231
4:8, 16	205, 231
4:9–10, 16, 19	126
4:14	139
5:1, 4	80

3 John

1:11	47

Jude

20	111

Revelation

7:4–8	247
11:1–12	247
12:17	247
14:1–5	247
14:6–7	246
20:11–15	218, 227
21:8	111
22:17	36, 95, 139, 147, 152
2:21	205

www.ingramcontent.com/pod-product-compliance
Lightning Source LLC
Chambersburg PA
CBHW061429300426
44114CB00014B/1605